Dearest Bee

As you journey
through there speck
durations may be
heart & speech
truly blessed.

with lots love
Wendy
Burrell

Growing in Your Spiritual Journey

by
Wendy Bussell

authorHOUSE™

1663 LIBERTY DRIVE, SUITE 200
BLOOMINGTON, INDIANA 47403
(800) 839-8640
WWW.AUTHORHOUSE.COM

First published by AuthorHouse 06/10/05

ISBN: 1-4208-5104-7 (sc)

Printed in the United States of America
Bloomington, Indiana

This book is printed on acid-free paper.

Introduction

You are about to embark on a spiritual journey that will last approximately nine mouths. The intention of this devotional is to help you grow in your spiritual self and journey. To help you see life through a clearer set of spiritual eyes. There is no rhyme or set pattern to this journey. Each day is a day unto its own, with the spiritual truths and teaching it provides. Each day will bring you, hopefully, to a newer and deeper understanding of what it means to live as a spiritual person, teaching you how to face life and life's struggles from the truth God has revealed to us through His Word, laws, and commandments. May these next nine mouths truly be not only a growing time for your spiritual self, but also a growing time in who and what you are as a person, and as the beloved child of God you were created to be. I pray as you read through these devotionals, you will gain a greater understanding of who you are as the chosen beloved child. My prayer for you is that as you journey these next nine months you will go through a similar growing experience as a child growing in the womb. Over these next few mouths, I pray you will experience a type of birthing or even rebirthing as you experience the spiritual truths and the presence of God in these pages. I am excited about this devotional and how God will use it to help transform, heal and bring to a deeper wholeness, those individuals who venture down this growing journey. Enjoy the adventure, my friend, keeping your mind, heart and eyes open to all that God has in store for you as you journey down this new and exciting road. May our great God and Father bless you beyond measure as you venture forth into this season of growing and maturing in your spiritual journey and self. May you get to know yourself better, and may your relationship with God grow deeper and be challenged in new and exciting ways as each day unfolds. All I can say my friend is enjoy the journey. Enjoy as you watch God touch your life, heart and total self. Watch as God reveals who you are as His chosen beloved child with great value and worth. Watch what happens in your inner self as God tells you how much you matter to Him, as God reveals where your true value and worth come from. Let yourself know and feel the love that God wants to pour out into your heart, spirit and life. My friend, you are so loved by God. You are so valuable and worthwhile in God's eyes. Hopefully over these nine months you will realize this truth in a much deeper and more real way(s). Hopefully at the end of these next nine months, you will know that knowing about who you really are in God, the one who created you in the first place. We were all created with a plan and a purpose. None of us were created not good enough or less than. We are all here for a reason for such a time as this. The challenge is to embrace who we are as God's beloved child(ren), taking our places in the plan God set out for us. I believe it is time for the truth to be told about who you are and why you were created. Then to learn how to live your life in healthy way, instead of the often destructive ways we have become accustomed to. Let us waste no more time-----let the journey begin.

Acknowledgments

I would like to thank Laverne Fehr, Louise Rempel and Teresa Murray for helping with the editing of this devotional. Their gift of grammar and patience is so valued and appreciated. Thank you to all who have loved and supported me over the years, encouraging me onward to greater heights. To my family who are always there loving me, valuing me and putting up with me. Thank you to Heather Collins who was first to see the value in this devotional. To Gerrit and Susan Blok who have loved and supported me throughout my journey as a prison Chaplain. To God who has entrusted me with all the gifts, talents and abilities I have. Thank you to God who has guided my journey, my voice and my spirit to where I am today

Devotional

Day One

Romans 6:23 "The wages of sin is death, but the gift of God is eternal life".

No matter how we look at life and try to make excuses for life and our life choices, The penalty for living life on our terms and conditions is called sin. Sin being our need to be like God and have life as we see fit; to be the masters of our own universe, having the final word. The result of wanting life our way is death. Not necessarily death from a physical perspective but certainly death from a spiritual perspective. The penalty for living life our way and in the way we want it to go leads us down the path of spiritual death. Let us look at Adam and Eve, when the Serpent was in the Garden of Eden talking to them about what God said and didn't say. "The serpent said to the woman 'did God really say, you must not eat from any tree in the garden?' (Gen 3:2) Adam and Eve both knew what God said. Adam had heard it directly from God and Eve from Adam. If they ate from the tree in the middle of the garden, the tree of good and evil, the penalty for eating its fruit death. They were going to die. This death is a separation from God, and of absence of God in their spirit. The consequence was that they were no longer going to live forever in the company of God. If they ate the forbidden fruit, life as they understood life was going to change forever. They were now going to die a physical death! The challenge to all of us is to look to God and His ways for going through life so that in our everyday living we really do have life within us and not death. When we choose to live life our way as the song goes, "I Did It My Way", the result is a life lived outside of the blessings of God. I am not saying that we cannot enjoy our lives and live our lives to the fullest. I am not saying we are not to live life with gusto or zest, enjoying every aspect of life. What I am saying is, there is a consequence to every choice we make. When we choose to ignore the truth of God's law, when we choose to ignore the reality of the law, we suffer, as Adam and Eve did, a separation from God and God's presence in our lives. The challenge is to choose in every situation and all of our life choices to live in such a way that we are pleasing to God. Then we get to reap the blessing God has for us His children. There is no getting around it, the wages of sin is death. The gift of living life God's way and according to God's plan and purpose is eternal life. Living God's way of living brings the blessings of God. The other brings a separation from God. Free will says we get to choose which one we want for ourselves.

Prayer: Holy Spirit, teach me how to truly live my life with your blessings. Teach me with every passing day how I might know more and more what it means to live, truly live. Teach me how to stop causing death from happening in my life and my life choices. I want to live life according to your plan for my life. I want to live in the blessings you have stored up for me. Thank you, Holy Spirit, amen.

Day Two

> *2 Corinthians 11: 1-15 "I am afraid that just as Eve was deceived by the serpent's cunning, your minds may somehow be led astray from your sincere and pure devotion to Christ". 2 Cor. 11:3*

We continue on today with the penalty of sin. Think for a moment of all the times you have lied or bent the truth in some way, shape or form; the times you did not tell the truth of what was really happening. Instead you told the parts the other person wanted to hear or you thought they wanted to hear. You lied to protect yourself. You told yourself you were lying to protect the other person.

Now think about how those times and the outcomes have affected you and your life. Think about what happened because of your choice to live in a lie. Think about the harm you caused others not to mention the harm you caused yourself. We think little white lies or not telling the whole truth protects the other person or ourselves. We think the lie will white wash what we have been doing. Only when we get honest with ourselves, we realize it does just the opposite. We think we can get away with bending the truth or eliminating parts of the truth and everything will be okay. That is what we think, only we find out differently when the truth does come out and the lie is exposed. Now think of what happened when the truth came out and the disappointment it caused in the other person's heart and life. In the end that is the struggle we all face when we live in the lie of the Serpent. "You will not surely die". Gen 3:4. The bottom line is we always die in some fashion or form when we live outside of God's ways (which is the truth) and in the ways of Satan (which are the lies). Think about how you feel when you face the person you have lied to. How you feel even though they still have no clue about what you have done. If you are anything like me you feel guilty and not very good on the inside. You do not want to be around the person because what if you say the wrong thing. What if your guilt gives you away and they sense something is wrong. What if. Life cannot come into others or us when we choose to live in half-truths or lies. Life cannot come in for there is no life in death. There is no life coming into to us when we lie, only death. The lies were death to Adam and Eve and they are still death to us today. Only the truth sets us free and gives freedom to us. Only the truth gives life to those around us! Only the truth gives us the peace and life we are all looking for within ourselves. Only the truth can give our heart and spirit rest and peace. After the lie is exposed and out in the open. Then the hurt caused by the lie can heal. Something to think about! The relationship may never the same for the trust we have breached. The relationship may not be restored. If it is restored it is may not the same. The innocence is lost.

3

Prayer: Heavenly, Father, help me to see the areas in my life where I am not living in truth and light. Help me to choose to be honest and to live in integrity. Help me to not tell lies even little white ones for all lies I am learning bring death and I want to live. Thank you, Father, in Jesus' name, amen.

Day Three

> *John 8: 12 " I am the light of the world, Who ever follows me will never walk in darkness, but will have the light of life".*

There are times in most of our lives when we have been in the darkness and know what it is like to have the darkness all around us. How black it is and how hard it is to function. How the darkness engulfs us and prevents life from welling up within us or living in us. It steals the good things that are happening in and around us. We also now know what it is to live in the light and to be surrounded by the light. The light lightens the load. It helps us to see clearly. We do not stumble over obstacles we may encounter along the way. When we are facing hardships or struggles in our lives or are in times of great need or facing an illness, it is easy to find ourselves lost in the darkness. It is easy to lose our way, as it is so dark all around us. "But thanks be to God who always leads us in triumphal procession". 2 Cor. 2:14 Thanks be to God who always gives us a way out when we set our eyes, face and hearts towards Him. Jesus the light of the world shines in our hearts and the darkness is released. We can see! Jesus is the way out of the darkness and into the light of the world. Jesus is the light that shines through our darkness and fills us so that we can truly see and live again. As I reflected on this passage it occurred to me that if Jesus really is the light of the world, then all light comes from Jesus. If Jesus is the source of all light, then all light is from Him. If this is truth, we discover all light comes from the light of the world. For if Jesus is the light of the world and light comes from Him, then the light from the stars reflects Jesus' light. The light from electricity is available to us because Jesus shines His light. All light no matter where it comes from is there because Jesus shines His light into His creation. I know this concept is a bit hard to grasp and believe. But the more I think about Jesus being the light of the world, the more I can begin to see how all light would then have to exist because of the light shining from the Creator of all things. We get to walk in the light and not stumble and fall in the darkness because Jesus gives His creation light. Question: if Jesus were to hold back His light, would there still be light? Jesus gives us the option of opening our lives and spirits to the eternal light shining from the Creator of all things, which not only gives us light on the outside but light on the inside as well. I find peace in that statement and my heart finds rest. I can have light shining both within and without when I have the light of life living in me. Are you smiling? I am.

Prayer: I pray, Lord, that you will shine your light upon and in me so that I might see and know all that you have in store for me. Shine your light so that I do not get lost in the world of darkness. Let me rest secure in your light. Help me to know the peace and rest that comes from being in your light and having that light pierce my darkness. Thank you, Lord, for your light, amen.

Day Four

Isaiah 54:8 "In a surge of anger I hid my face from you for a moment, but with everlasting kindness I will have compassion on you. Says the Lord your redeemer."

Have you ever been so angry with someone that you hid your face from them and would not engage them on any level? Your anger caused you to turn your back on them and it was as if they were no longer there. You let your anger get the better of you so that all you could see was the anger? Remember how that felt? How much energy it took from you to be that angry with the person? How hard it was on your being and inner self? How your insides ached? Today we are being reminded that even the Lord in the Old Testament was that angry with His children, the people God had chosen to be His chosen people. The difference between God's anger and our anger is, in God's anger is everlasting kindness and compassion. In God's anger, love still rules and reigns. We too are to have compassion and kindness on others even though we are angry. We all make mistakes. We all mess up and make wrong choices at the expense of ourselves and others. One of the keys of God's Kingdom is freedom. The key of freedom is giving ourselves permission to let go and have compassion on them and us. To let go of our anger and our need to be right, when we let go God, the Redeemer may work in us restoring our balance, our freedom. To allow the restoration in our relationships and lives so that harmony and love can occur. We let go of our anger so that we can be safe and secure once again upon the solid rock of freedom and truth. A second key is, to not hang onto the anger, rather process it and then let it go. To yes feel the anger and why the anger is there. To maybe even find a new path of life that does not have reasons for the anger. To give yourself permission to not hold on to it, so that it does not fester and grow within you. To let love and mercy and all that love and mercy gives to us take the place of our anger. Holding on to the anger does nothing to the other person we are angry with. In the end it only destroys us and steals everything that is good about whom we are as people. That is why we are to let it go and let God deal with the other person. When we let our anger go we are allowing ourselves the freedom to live in peace and harmony once again without the burden of anger holding us back. Anger kills---love sets free. Anger destroys---forgiveness brings life and true freedom within our hearts and spirits. Anger brings destruction and death--- letting go of our anger brings life and true peace. The choice is always ours to make. Let us choose freedom and not bondage to our anger. Let us healthy life giving ways of dealing with our anger, instead of the life stealing ways of the past. The truth is no one can make you angry. In fact no one can make you anything. No one can get inside of you unless you let him or her in. If you are angry it is because you are choosing to be angry. Something to think about.

Prayer: Heavenly, Father, Dad, I am sorry for the times I held in my anger and did not have mercy for myself or for others. I am learning that I give my power away to my anger and let it control me, instead of me controlling it. Please forgive me. Set me free to love not only others and you, but myself as well. Dad, I need your help and love so I can make different choices. I need to feel safe and secure in you. Fill my cup Dad with more of you, so I can be more of me, amen.

Day Five

> Isaiah 55:1 "Come, all you who are thirsty, come to the waters; and you who have no money come, buy and eat! Come, buy wine and milk without money and without cost."

Are you thirsty and hungry? Are you feeling empty and hungry on the inside? Do you long to have your insides filled so that you do not feel empty any longer? To have that hollow feeling filled? Today we hear Jesus calling us to come to Him. To come to His life giving water, His fountain of life, to let His water fill our being and restore our spirit to new freshness and life. To allow His life giving water to heal our brokenness and the pain we carry. To allow Jesus to mend, fix and fashion our spirits so that we can be made whole once again. A place where our brokenness can be restored and our spirits and souls put back into a place of balance. Jesus says He is the only answer to our thirst. Jesus has the only water that truly satisfies our longings so that we long no more. Jesus is the life giving water that goes deep into our very being wetting our thirst. Wetting our thirsty so we thirst no more. Put your hand in Jesus' hand, trusting His love and provision in and for your life. Let your spirit drink deep of the life Jesus wants to pour into you. Trust Jesus' love and desire to make you whole, new and refreshed. Say yes to the life giving water Jesus is holding out to you. Say 'yes' to the water, the living water. No matter where you are coming from or what you have or do not have, there is no cost----just come and Jesus will fill you up. There is no cost to come; it is yours for the taking. Open your heart and let the waters flow. Let the waters flow into all that is thirsty and needing refreshing. The water is ready, the cup is full, open your heart and self to its flowing and refreshing. Come and you will have the refreshing you are looking for. The void inside of you will be filled to over flowing. The water will meet your every need. The water is the water of life. Life welling up and filling our very beings with life, true life. Come to the true source of life for your longing soul. Let the waters flow. Watch the life as it wells up within you. Let your heart will be glad and your spirit filled with the peace you have been so desperate for. Come to the waters with open hands and a heart ready to be filled. Come expecting the water to flow and flow it will. For that is the promise of God who is the given of true life and the living water. Then watch the living waters flow as they fill you up. As they touch your very being with life, healing and refreshing.

Prayer: Lord Jesus, I am so thirsty! I am longing for your life giving water in my spirit and life. Come Lord Jesus and fill me up. Make me whole. Refresh my being. I am desperate for you. I put my hand in yours trusting and waiting for your touch and provision. I am open, ready and receptive, come. In Jesus' Holy life giving name, amen

Day Six

Ephesians 1:3 "Praise be to the God and Father of our Lord Jesus Christ, who has blessed us in the heavenly realms with every spiritual blessing in Christ."

You are blessed! Can you hear this truth? You are blessed. God has, is and continues to bless you with every spiritual blessed that is ours through Jesus Christ. You are not only blessed but you are blessed with every spiritual blessing in Christ by God, our heavenly Father. Now if that does not warm your spirit and excite your soul I don't know what will. God has, is and continues to bless us, yes us. One thing I have learned in my time as a prison Chaplain is, we all hunger for a blessing. We all have a deep, deep need within us to be blessed and to receive a blessing. It does not matter how old we are or how much we have it together. We all have a place within us that needs to be blessed and have a blessing bestowed upon us. We all on some level, need to hear our parents say how proud and pleased they are of us. Or hear the words 'I love you, you are mine and I am glad you are mine.' Not all of us were given parents who were able to tell us the words we needed and still so desperately to hear. My friend, you can hear the words today. Let God our Heavenly Father bless you. Let God our Father and Dad fill your spirit with the blessing you need to receive. For you are blessed by God your Father. Our Heavenly Dad right now this very moment, is blessing you with every spiritual blessing. The blessings have already been given to you. They are a done deal. Your Father in heaven, our Heavenly Dad, not only chooses to bless you. He chooses to love you just the way you are without having to prove anything. Yes, my friend you, yes you, are loved and blessed already by our Father/Dad in heaven! You do not have to go chasing after it, or beg for it to happen, it has already been done. All you need do is receive it and believe it and it is yours. Another truth to grab hold of is: you are so very pleasing to God. You bring our Dad, your Heavenly Dad much joy and delight. Our Heavenly Father/Dad takes great delight in you and you bring such great joy to his heart. You do not have to prove anything to our Heavenly Father/Dad you already have the stamp of approval stamped into your spirit. Before the creation of the world you were chosen to be loved by God our Father and to be blessed in Him. No matter who you are or what you have done, you are loved and in the blessing of God. You are the blessed, chosen, beloved child of God the Father. You are His workmanship and greatly loved by God. The one who formed you and created you also blesses you.

Prayer: Father, Dad, thanks for loving me. Thanks, for blessing me. Thanks, for making me your own. I needed to be reminded of this truth today and to once again receive it as mine. Thank you, for loving me and blessing me and for making me your own. I am so grateful and I find rest and peace in this truth. I need your blessings Dad and am open to them. Amen.

Day Seven

Ephesians 1: 4 'For He (God) chose us in Him before the creation of the world to be holy and blameless in His sight."

We are so very good at beating ourselves up at times for all the things we have done or not done! We get out our big stick and beat ourselves up until there is almost nothing left of us. How we put ourselves down for not being perfect and for making so many mistakes. For not always knowing exactly what to do and what to say. Like we can be perfect! Do you know anyone who is perfect? I don't. Let us say no more---no longer! I will no longer beat myself up and tear myself down because I am not perfect. I will no longer think less of myself because I make mistakes and wrong choices. I am allowed to be imperfect. I am allowed to make mistakes. Today I am going to start living in the truth that I was chosen in God before the foundation of the world to be holy and blameless in His sight and to be valuable and worthwhile. I am a valuable human being who happens to make mistakes. I am not a mistake! I am precious and special in my Heavenly Father's eyes. I am good enough! I am precious and chosen, God's beloved child I am. I am here for a reason and I am not a mistake. Hear yourself say the words: I am not a mistake just because I make a mistake. I am not less than others nor am I defective. Repeat the words as many times as you need to so that they can begin to take root and the truth of how you are may be permanently stamped into your heart and spirit. I am a chosen, beloved child of The Most High God and He loves me just the way I am but loves me too much to leave me here. Therefore today I will start seeing myself as my Heavenly Father/Dad does—BLAMELESS and HOLY and FORGIVEN, PRECIOUS and SPECIAL. I AM CHOSEN BY GOD, MY HEAVENLY FATHER TO BE HOLY AND BLAMELESS. I REALLY AM GOOD ENOUGH! I REALLY AM HERE FOR A REASON FOR SUCH A TIME AS THIS. I CAN LET GO OF THE LIE AND START SEEING MYSELF FOR WHO AND WHAT I WAS CREATED TO BE WITH ALL MY GIFTS TALENTS AND ABILITIES. I AM A CHILD OF THE MOST HIGH GOD AND HE LOVES ME JUST THE WAY I AM. These words are the truth, it is my opinion that it is high time you started living in them and having them for your own. God does not know how to lie therefore these words have to be the truth. God cannot lie to you and me. Let us take hold of these words today. I am the chosen, beloved, precious child of the Most High God and He loves me.

Prayer: Thank you, Father, that you chose even me to be holy and blameless in your sight. You choose me even though you knew that I would make all the mistakes I have made and the wrong choices that have been so prevalent in my life. I receive your gift of truth and grace today. Help me, to be the child you created me to be in the first place. Help me, to see myself as you see me. Again, thank you, Jesus for making me your valuable, beloved child. I receive your love and truth in my heart today, amen.

Day Eight

Deuteronomy 30:19 "This day I call heaven and earth as witness against you that I have set before you life and death, blessings and curses. Now choose life, so that you and your children may live..."

There are some things in life that just don't change, no matter how hard we try to make them look, feel or act differently. They just do not change. Things like putting ourselves down because we make a mistake or wrong choice or beating ourselves up because we are not where we thought we would be at this point in our lives or should be. The disappointment we feel because life doesn't look like what we thought it would when we reached this stage in our life journey. The question posed by Moses today is one of those timeless questions. The choice we all have to make, whether live or die, to choose life or death, blessings or curses. At points in our lives it seems easier to choose death and curses just because of all that is happening in, around or to us. Life is crashing in on us and the only option seems to be to die. Death seems the best way out. What other option do I have, life is so hard right now and there seems to be no light at the end of my tunnel. That may be the way it seems. The way things seem and the way things are, are very often two very different things. They are often nowhere close to the truth or even reality. Yes times are tough, and maybe even unbearable, but death is never the right option no matter how right it may seem at the time. God knows and understands and is right here with us giving us the help we need if we will but ask for it. As Moses talked to the Israelites, so is he talking to us. What are we going to choose today? Life or death, blessings or curses, God's way or our way! As we look at life and all that life is or is not, what are we going to choose? We are to choose either God's way, which is life or death's way, which is death. God's way is life. In fact it is not only life: it is life abundant, life to the full. God wants each and every one of us to choose life and the blessings He has stored up for us. When we choose life our way with many earthy things and possessions we are so very often empty in our spirits. We are not whole or complete. When we choose life God's way we live both on the outside and the inside. We live in the blessings. Having the blessings in our inner life as God desires for us, gives us the very things we thought were missing in our lives. Let us repent for the times we chose death and curses. When we chose to die by living outside of God's ways and laws. Let us choose life and blessings, so that we may live and have true abundant life within us. Let us even now say no to the death and curses we have been creating within ourselves. Yes, life may be hard just now but that is no reason to give up on life. After every valley is a mountaintop, your mountaintop is just around the corner. Choose the blessings and life God has for you and the way will be made clear. The abundant life God has planned for our lives is right here waiting for us if we will but trust in Him and put our hope in His plan for our lives.

Prayer: Father God, I am sorry for the times I turned my back on you, on myself and the ones who love me. I am sorry for turning my face towards curses, death and dying. Forgive me and help me to choose life and all the blessings you have for me. Thank you, Lord, for helping me to see what I have been doing, amen.

Day Nine

Deuteronomy 31:6 "Be strong and courageous. Do not be afraid or terrified because of them, for the Lord your God goes with you: He will never leave you nor forsake you.'

Do not be afraid or terrified. How that is so much easier said, than done at times! It is amazing how quickly fear creeps in and grabs a hold of us and who we are. How fear defines us and tells us who we are, and what we will do or not do. Paul reminds us in 2 Timothy 1:7 "For God did not give us a spirit of (fear) timidity, but a spirit of power, love and of self-discipline (sound mind)". Fear does not come from God! Power, love and a sound mind come from God. God is with us even in our fears. I will never leave you nor forsake you. I will never abandon or leave you orphaned and without a way out. God tells us this promise over and over again in His Word. God in one way or another is constantly reminding us of the truth that He can never leave us alone. God is always with us whether or not we know it in our faith or feelings. Let us today choose to not live in fear (*False Evidence Appearing Real*) but rather in the power, love and sound mind God gives us. To be strong and courageous even when our insides are screaming at us to run and let the fear win. We all know the feelings that fear causes to well up within us. We all know how paralyzing our fears can be and the hold they can have over us. The part we may be falling a little short on is the other side of fear. It is amazing, absolutely and totally amazing how fear loses its power when we stand up to it and see it for what it really is---- False Evidence Appearing Real; fear is not real at all. At least the fear that keeps us locked in and bogged down. We at times live in fear, when there is nothing there to fear. We let fear tell us what we will do and not do, when we had the power within all the time to make a choice to drive the fear away, and out of our hearts and lives. This side of fear is (*Face Everything And Recover*). We at times let fear rule and define our lives when it has no right or true power to do it. We let fear have the upper hand guiding us down bad roads and leading us down paths of more fear and greater darkness, when fear has no real power to do so. No more anyway! Let us choose to take our power back from our fear. Let us decide today to face our fear and reclaim our lives. Today let us choose to be strong and courageous and not give into fear. Instead say, I choose to trust God and His power and love within me. Today I choose to take back my power from the fear and see it for what it really is----False Evidence Appearing Real. I am going to stand up to my fears and get my life back for it is my life and not my fear's. Be strong and courageous for your God is with you to save and uphold through all of life's struggles and stresses.

Prayer: Father, thank you, that you have given me a spirit of power, love and a sound mind. I accept your provision today. Help me, to embrace the truth and begin to live it in and for my life. Help me, to be strong and courageous in all I think, say and do. I am sorry, for letting fear rule and reign in my life please forgive me. I know Father, with your help I can take my life back from all I fear. I choose to be strong and courageous and not let my fears rule and reign. I claim my sound mind and all I am in you. Thank you, Father, amen.

Day Ten

Psalm 31: 14-16 ' I trust in you, O Lord; I say, "You are my God." My times are in your hands; deliver me from my enemies and from those who pursue me. Let your face shine on your servant; save me in your unfailing love.'

Have you ever felt like you were drowning in doubt or fear? Like your whole world was crashing down upon you, like you were (are) all alone in the world? David was kind of feeling the same way and was feeling like his enemies were winning and he was at the end of his rope. We all have those days and times in our lives! We all have times in our lives when we feel all alone, like God is nowhere to be found. Our prayers go nowhere and our enemies seem to be winning. The battle is lost and we are on the loosing team. Let me remind you, it is only a feeling and nowhere close to the truth. It is just a feeling because we have a God who promises His unfailing mercy and grace to all who choose it. It is only a feeling, not the truth. The truth is God is right there/here with us. All we need do is cry out as David did, to see the Glory of God manifested in our lives. Throwing our hands up and surrendering to the power and presence of God and His truth, provision and love in our lives. Trusting that even if we can't feel God and His presence. God is still there/here with us leading us through. The reason we can trust God and His promised Holy presence is, God cannot lie to us. Therefore God is here even when our feelings and fears say otherwise. God is faithful and always answers when we cry out to Him, always. The answer may not come in the shape or way we want it or are expecting it to come, but it will be here. The answer to what we are praying will be ours for that is the promise of our Heavenly Father, the Most High God. Trust God's grace and faithfulness, instead of allowing feelings or life situations to direct us down life-stealing roads. God loves us no matter how we are feeling; no matter how weak our faith is. No matter what is going on in our lives. God always loves us no matter what. God loves us always and forever. God's love for us never changes. We are always His children; His chosen, beloved child/children no matter what is happening around us or within us. Our lives and times are in His hands. God will shine His light upon us. God will save us. That is the promise of God. God is a faithful, trustworthy God. Call upon Him and see for yourselves how faithful and trustworthy He really is. Look up, God is looking down. Reach out for God. God is already reaching down to you. Step out and see how God is right here waiting for you. What have you got to lose?

Prayer: Father God, help me to trust your unfailing love. Help me, to turn to you no matter how I am feeling and no matter what is happening in my life. Help me, to rely on your promises and faithfulness and not on my feelings. I am learning that faith has nothing to do with feelings. That your love for me is there no matter what I am feeling! Thank you, Father for always being the truthful, compassionate God you are. Help me, to trust you more. Holy Spirit, guide my heart into all truth and the freedom your truth brings. I choose to trust you and your love for me, amen.

Day Eleven

Job 42: 2 'I know that you can do all things; no plan of yours can be thwarted.'

What an amazing statement that Job proclaims to God even after all that he has been through! Job had been through the most destroying times of his life. He lost everything. There was nothing left except his faith and trust in God. With an open heart and a new revelation of God bursting forth he proclaims: 'I know that you can do all things; no plan of yours can be thwarted.' I know no matter what happens you are still and always will be God. As we go through our times of trial and hardship may we, like Job, hold fast to our awesome God and the promises that say, "I am your God and you are my people. I will always be here with you and for you. I will always be your God and meet your every need. I will never; no never let you go. I am always here for you, for you are my chosen, beloved child and I love you". Life says there will be times in our lives, which will be hard. Maybe even the biggest challenge we will ever face. Our God says He will always be there with us and for us as we face those days and times. There is no time when God will not be present and available for us as we face all of life challenges and struggles. We are never alone when we have God on our side. No matter how bad life gets we are never alone. The storm may rage and the winds blow strong. No matter how strong they get our God is still stronger. The promises of God say we can trust God in everything and every situation. We can put our hope, trust and faith in God and we will never be disappointed. It may not look like we want it to look like, but we will never be abandoned or dropped by God. God cannot ever take us anywhere to drop us. Therefore what God says, God does. We can trust that in everything. There is no struggle, time or situation that is bigger than our God. There is nothing in all of life that our God cannot handle or get us through. God promises no matter what occurs He is God and will always be God. Job lost everything he had from a worldly perspective; even his friends had turned their backs on him. From the world's perspective Job was reduced to a nothing with nothing. To God Job was His most precious child. To God Job was His chosen, beloved. You my friend are God's chosen Beloved. That is how God looks at you. That is how God looks at each and every one of us. We are His chosen, beloved children with great value and worth regardless of what the world says. We matter to God and always will matter to God. We are the most precious child/children God has. We are all precious in His sight. We are the BELOVED!

Prayer: Father, help me to know the knowing that comes only from you, the knowing that your promises are always 'yes' and amen; no matter what is or is not happening in my life. Help me, to never take my hand out of yours. Help me, to keep my eyes focused on who and what you are and all I am because of you. For in you I am truly safe and secure no matter what is happening or not happening in my life. Thank you, Lord Jesus, amen.

Day Twelve

Zephaniah 3:16-17 'On that day they will say to Jerusalem, do not fear, O Zion; do not let your hands hang down. The Lord your God is with you, He is mighty to save. He will take great delight in you, He will quiet you with His love, He will rejoice over you with singing.'

Does not that make your heart just want to leap out of your chest and jump all over the place with joy? It does mine! Just imagine The God of the universe is with you! He is mighty and He will rejoice over you with singing! God rejoices over us with singing! God sings over us! We so easily fall into fear at times. We let our hands go limp and our being is hanging down. We seem void of energy and our spirits lack any kind of luster. On those days especially, we need to hear these words; our God IS MIGHTY and can save us. He does take great delight in you and me. No matter what is happening in our lives or spirits God is rejoicing over us with singing and taking great delight in us. If we will let him, He wants to quiet us with His love. He wants to bring peace and joy into our being and spirit. Picture God rejoicing over you with singing and telling all the heavenly beings how delighted He is in you. He is proclaiming the truth that God, The Most High God, is our Dad. We have the Most High God as our Father and He truly is mighty to save us in all and every situation. Let that sink in for a moment. Then reread verse 17 and put your name in there, hearing the words as they penetrate your heart and spirit. God loves us! He loves even you and me. Let my heart rejoice and the angels sing. God loves me and rejoices in who I am and whose I am. Quiet my spirit so that I may know this truth to the very fibers of my being. I am, loved by God! He rejoices over me with singing. God delights in me---even me. YEA! I am safe and secure in my God. I am safe and secure in my Father's love. My Dad's arms are always open to me receiving me no matter what. I have a Heavenly Father who wants me to hang around with Him and tells the heavenly hosts all about me. I am a delight to Him. My Heavenly Father loves me and takes great delight in who and what I am. My Heavenly Father is interested in me and what I am and all I do. I have a Heavenly Dad and He loves me. He wants me to crawl up on His knee and tell Him all about what is happening in me and to me. I am safe and secure in my Heavenly Father and Dad; let the angels rejoice! Let the heavens declare this truth, as I own it for myself. I am a chosen, beloved child of the one and only true, living God and that living God loves me. God loves me, even me.

Prayer: Thank you, Father, that you do love me and are mighty to save. Thank you, Father that you delight in me and rejoice over me with singing. Thank you, for loving me just the way I am no matter what is happening in and around me. Thank you, for being my Father and Dad. Thank you, for dying on the cross for me and making all of this possible. Thank you, in Jesus' name, for I am truly grateful and my heart rejoices, amen.

Day Thirteen

Isaiah 41: 10 'Do not fear, for I am with you; do not be dismayed, for I am your God. I will strengthen you and help you; I will uphold you with my righteous right hand.'

One day of resting on our God's promises and learning to trust Him is just not enough. We get to spend today and again tomorrow hearing the truth of God's love for us. Resting in God's arms of love. As we move deeper into the wonder of God and His love for us His children. "Do not fear; do not be dismayed, for I am your God". The Host High God, the Creator of all things. The one and only true God, is our God, and we His children. We are the adopted children of God. As the adopted children, we have all the perks and benefits that come through our relationship with God and living as His chosen children. If this is true, and it is, then what do I have to be afraid of? What could be greater or bigger than our God? What could be more powerful than the one who created everything in the first place? The answer is nothing! Nothing is bigger or more powerful than our God, nothing. Therefore we do not have to fear? Can we trust in God and really rest in His arms of love? WE CAN. We can trust God and His faithfulness. We can trust God and who and what God says He is. This is true, a true saying, and a trustworthy saying. We can give God our trust. We can give God the trust He asks us to give. What do we have to lose? Therefore, today let us move forward in God's love for us and embrace all that He has for us His children. Today, I will take my place as God's child and choose to not live in fear but in His love for me. Today I give myself permission to trust my Heavenly Father and God on a deeper level, trusting in His love for me. I will rest in His love and presence in my life. I choose to let the truth my Father is speaking into my spirit and rest there. I am a beloved child of God and God loves me. I choose to put my hand in God's hand so that He can uphold me and walk this journey with me. Remember when you were a child and you put your hand in your father's hand, how safe you felt? How you felt that no matter what came your way your dad was well able to solve 'the whatever'? No matter what happened your dad had your hand therefore all was well with the world. That is how it is when we choose to put our hand in God's hand. We have that same feeling, that all is or will be well with the world, no matter what.

Prayer: Dad, today, I am choosing to rest in your arms of love and be your child. Today, I am going to choose to trust you more and more in the love you have for me. I repent of the fear I have been carrying and ask you to forgive me. I am truly sorry for taking my hand out of your hand. I now put it back where it belongs. Help me to move forward in your love more and more. In Jesus' safe and secure name, amen.

Day Fourteen

Jeremiah 29:11-12 ' For know the plans I have for you. Declares the Lord, plans to prosper you and not to harm you, plans to give you hope and a future. Then you will call upon me and come and pray to me, and I will listen to you.'

Such words of comfort! The Most High God has plans, individual plans, for you and for me. Before we were created and brought into being, God had a plan for our lives. Plans that will prosper us and not harm us, plans that will give us hope and a future. God has plans that are for our good. We are not a come by chance people; as hard as that may be to hear at times, it is true. We are not a come by chance individual who happened to be conceived at the time we were given life. God knew us and held us in the palm of His hand, choosing to give us life at that moment. Our parents did not know what they were getting as a child when we were conceived. But God knew us and His plan for our life was already put into motion. We have a great and awesome

God who loves us and has a plan of hope and prosperity for each and every one of us, no matter who we are or where we came from. We are not a people who believe in coincidences, we are a people who can believe the finger of God is guiding our lives. The coincidences are really "god incidences". God allowed! Yes even the bad incidences, they too serve their purpose in helping to mould us and teach us through them. God is right here with us at every bend of the road and every step of the way guiding and helping our lives. God is especially guiding our lives, if we call upon Him and pray for direction and guidance. God called us and gave us life and then set a plan in place for our lives, a plan that is to prosper us and not harm us. A plan that has a future with hope, direction and purpose already built into it. Our God truly does love us. God only wants what is best for us at all times in our lives. That is hard to understand at times when our lives seem to be falling down all around us on every side. How can this be a part of God's plan? Just know that even in the midst of total chaos God is still in control. Our God is listening to our prayers and hearing our cries even if the only cries we can utter are groans and moans. Our God is a good God who only has our best interest at heart. God has unconditional love for you and me. I know at times it is hard to trust God when everything seems to be so wrong in our lives, but trust him we must, so that we can see how God works everything for our good and benefit.

Prayer: My heart today, Father, is filled with such joy and peace knowing that your hand is upon my life and guiding me along life's path. That you are interested in me and my life and all that happens in it and around it. You are influencing my life in ways I do not know. You are helping me and guiding me. You truly are my God and Father. Thank you, from a heart filled with gratitude and gratefulness. Thank you; even when my life seems all up side down. Thank you, Father, for being my Father and Dad, amen.

Day Fifteen

1 Samuel 12:20 ' Do not be afraid, Samuel replied. You have done all this evil; yet do not turn away from the Lord, but serve the Lord with all your heart.'

The amazing thing about being human is we make all kinds of wonderful and not so wonderful mistakes, wrong choices and blunders. As human beings, we want to run and hide from our mistakes, wrong choices and blunders. It seems to be the natural thing to do. Adam and Eve both hid in the bushes after they ate the forbidden fruit. They had an intimate and personal relationship with God. They talked with God face to face. Yet when they sinned, when they blew it royally, they ran away and hid. A little child runs and hides when he/she knows he/she has been caught doing something wrong. They hide so they will not have to face the music. We run and hide when we have done what is not true and right. Running and hiding becomes our defense when we have done what is not right and the music is coming. What Samuel is reminding us of here is we do not have to fear or be afraid when these things happen in us and to us. God knows and understands. Just as God knew and understood Adam and Eve God knows our very being and understands when our human side is stronger than our hearts and our desire to follow after God. Therefore instead of turning away from the Lord our God, let us run into Him. That way we can know His love and forgiveness in new and real ways, instead of hiding in the darkness. Let us run into God so that we can know God's infinite love and mercy. Let us run into God so that we do not have to sit in our fears and need to hide away. Yes it is the natural thing to do, but it does not have to rule and reign over our lives. Let us run into God so that we can be restored from whatever it is that is separating us from ourselves, others and God. Let us return to God so that we can once again rest in the joy and peace of God in our hearts and not live in fear. It is in God and in God alone that we move and breath and have our being. It is in God that we find true life and the way of living our lives within the abundance of God and His provision for us. It is in trusting God that we find our place as human beings and our joy. Guilt and shame want to drive us away from God. They want to set us apart from God. God's plan is to forgive and restore us to our rightful place. God's plan is love and comfort. God wants us to be restored and well able to live our lives once again to the fullest and not be burdened by our pasts and past mistakes and wrong choices. Let us embrace God's love, mercy and grace, running into those great big arms of love and forgiveness.

Prayer: Father, I am truly sorry for all the times I have made a royal mess of my life. I am sorry that I am not perfect and make wrong choices and mistakes. Forgive me. I need you in my life. I need your love to make me whole. I need the safety and security of being your child---your BELOVED. Help me, to accept and receive your forgiveness and then help me to forgive myself. For I am realizing Lord I need you more and more with each passing day. Help me, to realize my fears are not from you. My fears are there to drive a wedge between us. God of truth and peace, fill my life and heart today I pray, amen.

Day Sixteen

Psalm 119:11 I have hidden your word in my heart that I might not sin against you.'

I am learning how much I need to have God's Word hidden in my heart. Hidden deep within the very depths of my heart, so that when I need the presence of God and His word is in me. They are available and ready for my use because they are already in my heart waiting to come to my rescue. When I need God's presence all I need do is call upon His name. When I need a fresh touch, it is right there for the asking. When I am hurting and feeling all alone, God is there, showing me His love and presence. When life is hard and I am feeling insecure, God is only a pray away. I am never alone when I have the truth of God's Word in my heart and spirit. I am never alone when God is present and active within me. God is always there no matter what, especially when I am fostering my relationship with God. God is so much more present in and for me when I foster the relationship, than when I am trying to live my life my way, doing my own thing. Yet, having said all that, how easy it is to fall away from God's Word, laws, decrees and commandments. How so very easy to take our eyes off the most important lifeline we could ever have, and set our faces towards what the world says is important and necessary. How so easy to trust what the world is saying and not trust God. When we set our heart, face and spirit towards our loving Father and seek only Him, life moves along so much smoother. There is peace and joy. There is a sense of purpose and belonging. There is fullness inside our spirit, and a deep sense of satisfaction in our heart and being. Let us be reminded today of how necessary it is for us to stay in God's Word for inspiration within our lives. Knowing the importance of having God's Word written upon our hearts and spending time with God through His Word and quiet times. Studying God's Word so that it is written on our hearts and deep within our spirits. Then when the temptation comes we will not be tempted to fall away from God and His presence and truth in our lives. My friends the temptation(s) will come, they always do. We will have the courage and strength we need to stay away from whatever is befalling us. Temptations will always try their best to get us to follow them. That is how life works. The darkness wants us back playing and working in the darkness. Thanks be to the presence of the Holy Spirit within us. We do not have to give in to them just because they are knocking on our door. With our focus on God and His Word of life, we can choose to walk in such a way that we really do have life within us. No matter what is knocking at our door.

Prayer: I am sorry, Father, for the times I neglect your Word and the importance of that Word in my life and heart. Help me today, and every day, to seek you first. To always have you in my heart and to be connected to you always through your Word and presence in my heart and life. When I have you I really do have everything I truly need. Thank you, Holy Spirit, for being my ever-present help in times of temptation, amen.

Day Seventeen

Psalm 1:1 'Blessed is the one who does not walk in the counsel of the wicked or stand in way of sinners or sit in the way of sinners.'

I am reminded today of the times we stand at crossroads in our lives. The times when we are faced with either choosing sin or choosing grace. When we are angry or sad or disappointed, instead of facing the feelings and moving on with life, we run into sin (life on our terms and conditions). We let our anger or hurt get the better of us. Instead of looking for ways to restore what is happening we seek ways to destroy it. Instead of being honest with the people in our lives or honest with ourselves, we choose silence or some kind of negative force or influence to keep a distance. Instead of relying on God's grace to see us through, we let the pain or anger or disappointment tell us what we will, think, do or say. We give our power away to whatever is demanding it. We forget about calling on the name of the Lord, our God and Saviour. We let the darkness point the way, instead of the light. We run away from God instead of running into His tender loving arms. We chase after what the world says is right and good, forgetting all about what God has been telling us and continues to tell us even as we run the other way. If you are in such a place today then I suggest that you turn back and run into the arms of our great Redeemer and Friend; that you run back into the cleansing of Christ's healing blood so you can be cleansed anew. Tell Jesus all about what is happening. Tell Him how sorry you are for turning your back on His grace and turning your face towards the sin that so easily entraps us. Tell Jesus how much you need Him right now, how you want Him to show you the way back to life and away from the chaos you have created. The old saying goes if you sit in the barber's chair long enough you will get a haircut. If you sit in the council of sinners long enough, you will eventually get your haircut (sin). If you have a struggle with chocolate and spend your days at the candy store, you will sooner or later end up buying a chocolate bar. The temptation will too strong for any of us. If you sit in the casino and watch everyone having a good time playing the machines, you too will drop a few coins in. If you hang around what is not good for you, know sooner or later you will fall into the trap that is before you. If you spend enough time in the barber's chair, you too will have your haircut.

Prayer: Father God, I am so sorry for the times when I ran away from you and your grace and into the hands of the Evil one and his schemes to destroy me. Forgive me, for letting my feelings and emotions tell me who I am instead of trusting your love that sustains me in my time of need. Forgive me, Lord, and set me firmly on your foundation of life once again. I need you Lord more than ever. Help me. In Your name I pray, amen.

Day Eighteen

Psalm 73: 25-26 " Whom have I in heaven but you? And earth has nothing I desire besides you. My flesh and my heart may fail, but God is the strength of my heart and my portion forever.'

With all that we have and with all that this world has to offer us there are times when we forget that our only true possession is found in God, in everything God is. Our true possession is found in all that God has for us His children. When we truly look around at all that is available to us: all that we have and all that life has given us; we need to remind ourselves, "What do I really have without God's mercy and grace"? In truth without God, there is truly nothing in heaven or on earth that has any true value or worth if God is not in it. Everything that really matters in life matters because of God and everything God is. Real value is found in all that God has done and continues to do. Jesus gave His all so that we could have life and freedom from what holds us in bondage. The death of Jesus Christ on the cross and His resurrection gave us a way out of what was and into God's forgiveness. Without God there is nothing that truly has any great value or really matters. Everything that has real value comes from the hand of God. Everything that is worth having is worth having because God blesses it and gives it life. Without God in the midst of life and possessions, there is no lasting value and no real satisfaction. I can have a big house and a fancy car but without love, with whom do I share it? Without peace in my heart all the money in world will not get me peace. If I am living in guilt and shame because of past mistakes and wrong choices, then where is freedom and where is my hope for today or tomorrow? Without God in my heart do I really know where I will spend my eternity? Without love what does life hold? `Whom have I in heaven but you? And earth has nothing I desire besides you.' How so very true that is when we really think about it. Without God filling the empty void inside of us is impossible. There is nothing that can truly hold our attention. If God were to withhold His love, mercy and grace what real value would life give us? I hear people say, I have everything the world says is important and yet feel so very alone and lost. I can have every toy ever made but if there is no one to share my toys with, what good are the toys? If I end up with a full hand yet have an empty heart and life on the inside, what good is the full hand? God gives everything the zest it needs to really be fulfilling and give us the satisfaction we are all longing for. When all is said and done who have I in heaven but God. The earth holds nothing of great value if God is not part of it.

Prayer: Father, help me to stay humble in my views of the world and to not forget where my real joy comes from, for real joy and fulfillment comes from being in a relationship with you and you alone. Help me, to not get complacent or take advantage of the things, people or possession I have been given or worked for in my life. Help me, to always remember that without you at the center of my life, my life, no matter how much is in it, is still empty. I need you Lord in all I have and all that I am. Without you, Lord, what am I? What do I really have if you are not in it? Thank you, for being my all in all, Jesus! Amen

Day Nineteen

Proverbs 3: 5-6 'Trust in the Lord with all your heart and lean not on your own understanding. In all your ways acknowledge him, and he will make your paths straight.'

Trust in the Lord with all our heart. Trusting in all that the Lord is and all that we are in Him. Trusting that God is who God says He is. I know that is asking a lot from our hearts as most of us have trust issues. Most of us have given our trust to someone or something and been disappointed. Or our trust has been betrayed or broken in some way, shape or form. With the loss of our trust comes, we think, the loss of our ability to trust. Not true, trust is a choice even when you have been betrayed and hurt in your trusting. The problem with being hurt and betrayed is we fall back into our safety zones and live our lives protecting ourselves from the hurt that may or may not come our way. That protection causes the very hurt we were trying to avoid. We find ourselves trusting the wrong people or situations to prove people are not trustworthy. We pick people we know will breach our trust. Just to keep proving, we really can't trust anyone and everyone is untrustworthy. Every time we do trust and risk, we are disappointed and hurt again and again. We build up walls and more reasons to not trust, even to not trust God. We let our pasts tell us how we will live our lives in the present. We let our fears and pain prevent us from truly living our lives in today. God is asking us to trust Him and to not lean on our understanding of life but His; to stop the cycles we have built up in our lives that are causing us more harm than good. To start trusting God even when everything inside of us tells us not to trust but to self protect. God's ways are not our ways, therefore trying to figure God out and why God does what He does is just not possible. Just know that God always has our best interest at heart. God will never do anything to harm us in any way shape or form. If we let God, He can make our paths straight and restore our lives. If we let God! When we choose to trust God and acknowledge His ways, He will come and make our paths straight. Yes, trusting is hard if you have had your trust broken or been betrayed in the past. I know and understand that. So does God. I also know that our God is trustworthy and the only way we can find that truth out for ourselves is to risk and choose to trust God. Lean not on your own understanding, for your understanding is flawed. Lean on God and God will show you the way and bring the understanding. God will heal whatever needs healing. God will make your paths straight if you let Him.

Prayer: Father, I am sorry for letting the disappointments in my life shut me off from trusting you. I am sorry for shutting myself off from love and being loved at times. I am sorry for all the people I have pushed away for fear that they may or may not hurt me. Father, please forgive me, and help me to trust. Help me to trust you, to trust myself, and to trust the people who are trustworthy. I need your help so that I can learn to live in trust and trusting. Thank you, Father, for your help and understanding, amen.

Day Twenty

Hebrews 1:3a 'The Son is the radiance of God's glory and the exact representation of his being, sustaining all things by His powerful word.'

God's Word sustains all things. Jesus sustains all things. All things, yes, all things are sustained by Jesus who is the Word of God. Jesus is the sustainer of all things. That is a hard concept to get our minds around at times. If this statement is true, then I am not the master of my own universe. God is! If God is the one who sustains all things, then logically speaking, I am not the one in control. I do not have the power to be all things to all people or the master of my own universe and destiny. In other words it is all about God and not about you and me. It is all about who and what God is and not about who we are (I am). This is a hard one for our egos. We at times want to be God. We want to be able to do whatever we want to do, when we want to do it. We in our sinful nature want to believe that we are the masters of our own universe; yes, even god. We believe at times, we can control what happens to us. We can control what affects or does not affect our lives. We believe we can control outcomes, when in reality we cannot control very much. The reality is if God were to take away His hand of mercy and grace our world, as we know it, would fall apart. Without God holding all things together by His great Word life, as we know it, would not exist. How can that be you ask? Whether we like it or not the reality and truth is God is the author and perfector of all things, which happened at creation. Which means God is also the author and perfector of our lives and our world as He is the one who created them in the first place. Even when life seems to be going to hell in a hand basket and everything seems to be falling apart around us, God is still in control, and asks us to trust Him and His love for us. God's great love for us and His creation are found in His sustaining powerful Word. God's mercy and grace abound in our world, I believe, keeping life moving and holding evil back. Can you imagine what our world would be like if God

31

took away His mercy and grace? Can you imagine what our world would look like? Look at all the evil that happens with God's mercy and grace. Think about what would happen without it? Thanks but no thanks. It is humbling to think that God would care about us so much that His interest would be to give us life and sustain the life He has given us. God wants us to have abundant life therefore does all He can to give that abundant life. That is how much God loves you and me. We are truly loved by God. No matter what! God shows us that love by sustaining all things by His Word of Life.

Prayer: Father, I need to stay in your Word everyday! I need to be reminded constantly that your Word is the beginning and end. You Jesus are the beginning and the end. Your Word is the reason for all life! Remind me Jesus everyday to be in your Word whether I feel like it or not. To follow your ways and to always put you first in my life and the lives of those I love. Help me, to lean on you and not my understanding. Forgive me, for not putting you first or your Word front and center in my life. In Jesus' precious and holy name, amen.

Day Twenty-one

Revelation 3:20 " Here I am! I stand at the door and knock. If anyone hears my voice and opens the door, I will come in and eat with him, and he with me.'

To continue on yesterday's thought of being in God's Word and having God's Word safe within our hearts-----Our need to lean on God and not on our understanding brings us to the next level in our relationship with God. The next step after putting God's Word safely in our hearts is to then know God's presence. The inner presence of God is ours through the Holy Spirit. The Holy Spirit helps guide us and fills our spirit with the presence of God. Jesus stands at the door of our hearts and lives wanting to share His life with us, wanting to be apart of every part of our lives and being. Jesus stands there waiting patiently for us to decide what we will do. Will we open the door and let Him in or will we leave Him standing there? Either way Jesus is not going anywhere. Jesus will stand there patiently waiting until we decide and choose. When The Holy Spirit of God is invited in, He fills us. We feel complete and full on the inside. Sin demands we do life alone and as the Frank Sonatra song says 'I did it my way'; to do life my way as I see fit. The problem is when we demand life to be lived on our terms and conditions we end up lonely and outside of what life really is meant to be. It is only when we accept life on life's terms that we find the lasting joy and contentment we were searching for by doing life our way. The lie of the world say `he who has the most toys wins'. The one who has everything his heart desires is the one who has it all. In lots of ways we believe the lie and chase after everything we can. We chase after all our heart desires thinking it will make us happy and content when all is said and done. When in truth the only thing that can fill us and give the contentment and happiness we are all searching for is God. Lasting peace and contentment can be found in God and God alone. God wants us to have His joy and peace. God wants us to feel whole and complete. God's desire is to live inside of us, filling us with what we need in order to have everything that will make us whole. God wants to be a part of us and we a part of Him. The problem at times is God is a gentleman and will not go where He is not invited. God will stand forever at your heart's door knocking and asking to be invited in, but He will never come in without our invitation. The bottom line is God loves each and every one of us. God wants to be a part of us and all we are as human beings. God wants to fill our internal cups with all the blessings He has stored up for us. God wants to inhabit us being a part of all we are. The question is do I want God to be a part of me? Will I open my heart's door to Him today and invite Him in? The Holy Spirit is waiting for your invitation. Free will says you choose.

Prayer: Father, today, I open my heart to your Son Jesus and let you in a new. I open my heart afresh and receive you as my Lord and Saviour. Thank you, Jesus for loving me and for restoring me. I do receive you into my life and every part of me. For I know that I can't make it without you. Without you, I do not have the resources to get through each day. With you Jesus in my life I have everything I need, to live my life and face whatever comes my way. Thank you, Jesus for filling me up and coming into my life and heart, amen

Day Twenty-two

Luke 5:20 'When Jesus saw their faith, Jesus said, friend your sins are forgiven.'

When Jesus saw their faith and the fact that their faith was willing to risk and reach out, Jesus responded to them with the fulfillment of their heart's cry. The Epistle to James says in 4:2 'you want something but don't get it. You kill and covet, but you cannot have what you want. You quarrel and fight. You do not have, because you do not ask God.' The message we are being given today is we need to move out in our faith and trust God in our asking. To risk and ask God to supply our needs and grant us our heart's desire, which is an intimate and close relationship with God and all that God is. When we have that intimacy we can trust and risk in our asking God for our needs and heart's cry. Then when we ask, we can ask in faith and trust believing that God wants to give good gifts to His children; that God wants to meet us in our need and our heart's cry; that God's desire for us is abundant life and prosperity. To believe in something means we hold true to a set of facts or a knowing that what we believe is true. Faith is taking our belief and putting it into action. I believe that if I hit the light switch, the light will come on. Faith is taking my belief and hitting the switch. I believe that if I put my car keys into the ignition and turn the key, the car will start. Faith is turning the key. We know or believe that forgiveness of sin in our lives is available to us when we humble ourselves and reach out to God in trust and faith. We know that God wants good things for His children. We know that God hears our prayers and answers them. We know that God is passionately in love with us and desires to be a part of our lives. We know we are important and valuable to God. We know when we humble ourselves and ask God for what we need, God wants to fulfill our requests. When we get down and honest with God and our need for Him and His forgiveness in our lives, God's forgiveness will happen. When we trust and put our faith into the action mode and believe, we can and will be given those things we are asking for in faith. We now have because we took our belief and put it into action and asked God for what we needed and what our hearts desired. Praying in faith makes all the difference in the world. Praying in faith brings our prayers into reality.

Prayer: Father, I am reaching out to you today to meet me in my need. I am putting my hope, faith and trust in you and your promises to us your children. I am asking Father (now ask for whatever it is you are seeking God, trusting in God's love for you His chosen, precious, special beloved child). Thank you, Father, for hearing my prayer and listening to my cry to you. Thank you, for being such a faithful God and Father, amen.

Day Twenty-three

Matthew 28: 20b 'And surely I am with you always, to the very end of the age.'

What a comforting thought and truth to have as one of our pillars we stand on. That God is with us to the very end of the age. That no matter what is happening or not happening in our lives God is with us. There is no time or event that can happen in our lives when God is not present with us. Think about that for a moment. God has made a promise to you and me and all of His creation. God has put himself on the line that says no matter what, for all of time, I will be with you. I will never, not be here with you. I give my promise and word that as long as time exists I will travel your life journey right by your side. The promise is He will never, no never, leave us, forsake us or leave us orphaned. He will never pull His presence from our lives. God has promised that no matter what, He will be by our side through thick or thin to the very end of time. Our great God and Father is always present in and for our lives, no matter what. God is always with us doing whatever needs doing to the very end of the age. We are safe and secure in God, for God is always with us. I may feel alone and all by myself, but it is just a feeling, for the reality is I am not alone God is with me. Personally, I take such relief in this promise. I take comfort and reassurance in these words. I give myself permission to trust God to an even greater degree because of this very promise. No matter what God is right here with me/with you. God is never going to be busy when I am in need or just wanting to be with Him. He will never put me on hold while He takes care of other things or someone else. God does not get bored with my talking and sharing with Him. God does not turn me away even when all I have to say is my woes and complaints. God's knee is always open and waiting for me to crawl up onto it. God will not take us anywhere to drop us. His plan and purpose is always active and alive. Every single time I am looking up, God is looking down. Every time I am reaching out He is reaching back. God is always there waiting and wanting us to come into His presence and be there with Him in His tender loving care and arms. Remember that feeling of being absolutely safe and secure so long as your hand was tucked safely into your dad's? That is how we are to be when we are with our Heavenly Father and Dad---only more so. Our God is here both now and always and will always be here both now and always. Hallelujah! We are safe and secure in our God and Heavenly Father. We are safe and secure in His love and the value He places on us just because we are His and He is ours. For all time we are God's and God is ours. Let us celebrate the wonder of God's love for you and me.

Prayer: Thank you, Father God, that you are always with me and I am never alone. I may feel alone and all by myself, but they are just feelings. The truth is you are right here with me and I am not alone. I rest safe and secure in you and your promises. I choose to allow myself to feel safe in your tender loving arms and care. I choose to trust you and your promises to me. I take my place as your chosen, beloved child for that is what I am. Your chosen, beloved, precious, special child. I belong in you and you belong in me. We are one in Christ and all that Christ is. Thank you, Father God, amen.

Day Twenty-four

> *Zechariah 2: 4-5 'Run, tell that young man, Jerusalem will be a city without walls because of the great number of men and livestock in it. And, I myself will be a wall of fire around it, declares the Lord, and I will be its glory within.'*

As we look back throughout history and the story of the Jewish people we can begin to see how God has kept this promise to them. Israel is one of the smallest nations in world. It has lived its long relationship with God in an "on again, off again" one. At times Israel is so far away from God doing their own things, worshipping other gods; they lose sight of their true God. No wonder life gets all messed up for them. Then they see the error of their ways and turn back to God. They cry out to God to help and rescue them from the mess they find themselves in once again. They realize the error of their ways and seek after God. The struggle the Jewish nation continually faces is, it is not very long before they turn away again, only to find themselves in a place of needing to come back to the one and only living God, in repentance and humility. Yet throughout their journey God has always been there for them and even to this day God protects them. As I said, Israel is a small nation, few in number yet they survive no matter how hard or bad life gets. No matter how many other nations want to destroy them, they always survive. Given the odds and struggles they have faced, the Jewish nation probably should not exist. It should have been eliminated a long time ago, yet it is still here as strong as ever. The wall God promised to build around them still stands even today. No matter what you are going through today, do not ever let your situation, doubt or fear separate you from the truth and reality of God and our great God's Faithfulness! You belong to God therefore God has built a wall/hedge around you as well. Nothing will destroy you unless God wills it. Nothing can take your life unless God lets down the wall/hedge. Our body can be destroyed but our spirit and true self is safe in God. No one can destroy your spirit! No one. I know you are probably thinking about the faithful followers of God who have lost their lives when in active service. I know that happens, I cannot give you an answer except that God's ways are not our ways and our ways are not God's ways. All I know is God promises to put a hedge around us to protect and keep us safe; to somehow, I do not know how, but somehow turn everything into something good for those who are called according to His purposes. God can and will turn whatever you are going through into something good if you let God do it. (Romans 8:28)

Prayer: Thank you, Father, that your promises are always yes and amen. Thank you, that I can trust you no matter what is happening in my life or the lives of others. You are the hedge that keeps me safe and provides for all my every need. I am sorry for the times I let life get in between us, please forgive me. Teach me, Jesus, how to trust you more. In Jesus' name, amen.

Day Twenty-five

Luke 1:38 'For nothing is impossible with God.'

Have you had days when you wondered if God was really able to make a way out of whatever situation you were in? Wondered if God was really who He said He was and is? Wondered if your faith was put in the wrong place? Wondered if you were barking up the wrong tree? I surely have. Then just when I feel and think that God can't, our great and awesome God makes a way where there just wasn't a way to be made. All of a sudden life is once again back on track. God opened a path and made a way we could travel through. A door was opened where only a wall stood before. We are human and as humans we have our doubts, fears and times when life pushes down so hard upon us we feel like we are not going to make it. There does not seem to be enough within us to carry us through. We think "Not this time God! Not this time Lord! This one is too big even for you". Then God once again proves His love for us and His power and authority. God makes Himself known in new and real ways, pushing through all that is going on inside of us and around us. God once again shows Himself to be real and just who and what He says He is. We serve such an awesome and faithful God. Nothing is impossible for our God. And nothing is impossible with God on our side. God can do all things. He is a great and mighty God, awesome and majestic, now and always. Never changing, always the same. We can trust God to stay that way. We can trust God to do the impossible for that is who and what our God is. The God of impossibilities! Nothing is impossible for our God. NOTHING! The challenge to each and every one of us is to trust this promise and keep ourselves open and receptive to whatever God is doing, even when it does not look anything like we thought it would look like. Open and receptive to whatever God is doing in us. Open to whatever God is doing and how He is doing it. Bottom line, God loves you and me and will always love you and me no matter what. God can do thing less. Remember, we cannot do anything that will cause God to love us more and never do anything that will cause God to love us less. Therefore God's love for us is constant and His promises never change or alter. When God says He can do all things, then guaranteed God can do all things. We just need to watch and see what He will do next. There is a need for us to be patient, waiting upon God. The waiting part is often the hardest part. Nevertheless, wait we must.

Prayer. Today, I am going to trust you God no matter what is happening in my life. I am not going to give into my doubts and fears. I am going to live by my faith and not by my feelings or the events happening in and around me. I am going to resolve that you are bigger and stronger and more faithful than everything that is happening. Thank you, Father God, for being who you say you are and for being the one and only true God for whom nothing is impossible. The God of impossibilities, amen.

Day Twenty-six

Psalm 38:4 'My guilt has overwhelmed me like a burden too heavy to bear.'

Guilt—a very necessary part of life, but oh what a burden it can be to our lives, and us if we let it. Let me start off with the difference between guilt and shame. Guilt is what I feel when I break the rule or standard. When I have crossed the line and done something that is not right or even very wrong in my own eyes. Shame is what someone else puts on us when we break their rule or standard. Shame is the finger pointing that someone does when we break their rule or violate their standard. I have to process my guilt and decide what I am going to do with it. Shame I cannot process for it is not mine to process, therefore I need to give back the shame to the person who gave it to me in the first place. To give back the shame (you know what it looks like and feels like) put it in your hands, see the person standing in front of you who gave you the shame. Then in your minds eye and with your mouth you say, "here this is your shame not mine and I put the shame back on you where it belongs. Here is the shame and unhealthy guilt you have put upon me. I am giving it back to you, it is not mine it is yours". Now let it go. Then take back your right to peace. Take your right back to live in peace, without the shame pulling you down and locking you into their stuff and standards. None of us have the ability to be perfect or super human. None of us can successfully live in shame and unhealthy guilt or whatever else the person has put upon us. After we give back the shame and unhealthy guilt. We take back from the person whatever they stole from us when they gave us the shame and unhealthy guilt. Your guilt is something you need to come to terms with. You need to find a way of processing the guilt and then forgiving yourself for the mistake you made, so that you can get on with life and living. We all make mistakes; we all make wrong choices. We all have to come to terms with them, forgiving ourselves, so that we do not stay stuck in the mud puddle we have built up around ourselves. God built in forgiveness so that we could have a way out of whatever it is we have done or someone else has done to us. God knew these times would happen, that these life-changing events would occur, that is why God chose in His infinite love and mercy to give us a way out. God chose to offer us grace instead of the justice we deserve. Our only choice is whether we accept the gift of mercy and grace or reject it. The gift remains no matter what we decide. Free will says we can either stay in our guilt and shame or we can accept the gift of life and freedom God offers us. The choice always remains with us. Which one are you going to choose?

Prayer: Father God, I have made some really bad choices in and with my life. I have walked down paths that I am not proud of. Today I am choosing to let go of the guilt and shame I have been feeling for such a long time. I choose to start forgiving myself so that I can get on with living my life. Thank you, for showing me the way out of my past wrong choices. I repent for the mistakes I have made and ask you to forgive me and to help me forgive myself. I want to live in freedom. I want to be free. I want my life back Father God, amen.

Day Twenty-seven

Matthew 18:21-22 'Then Peter came to Jesus and asked, Lord how many times shall I forgive my brother when he sins against me? Up to seven times? Jesus answered, I tell you not seven times, but seventy-seven times.'

Forgiveness is such an important part of life and freedom. There is nothing more important to living a fulfilled life then being willing to forgive. There is nothing more important than letting go of the resentments, bitterness, anger and hatred that comes from not forgiving. Some of us think that if we choose to forgive the person, situation or event, we are letting the person, situation or event off the hook. We are saying they are no longer responsible for what happened or what they have done. That is so not true! You are not letting them off the hook you are letting yourself off the hook. Forgiveness has nothing to do with the person, situation or event we are choosing to forgive. Hear that NOTHING. The person is still responsible and accountable for what they have done or not done. Forgiving has nothing to do with them. It has everything to do with us. It is not setting them free; it is setting us free! It is not saying what they have done is right. It is saying they are no longer going to live rent free inside of me and drive my inner bus into the ditch. Choosing to forgive is allowing us to be set free from the bondage and hurt the person, situation or event has caused. To not forgive is, drinking poison and then expecting, wanting, desiring the other person to die. Can you hear what I am saying? When we choose to hold on to the past and all the past is and has done to us, it is like us taking poison and expecting the past to die, the event to die. When we choose to forgive, we are saying is the person or event is no longer going to tell me who I am. It is no longer going to define me! It will no longer tell me what I will or will not do. It is not going to hijack my feelings and sabotage thoughts and life. When we choose to forgive we are taking back control of our own lives and not letting someone or something drive our bus (our inner self) any longer. Forgiveness is the most selfish thing we will ever do. There is nothing more selfish then choosing to forgive. When we forgive we are allowing ourselves the freedom to decide for ourselves what we will feel, think, say and do or not do. Forgiveness is taking back our legal right to be free on the inside from past events. Forgiveness is truly setting us free to live again. Forgiveness is saying enough! This is my life and I am not going to let the past tell me who I am any longer. I am going to be me, without the anger, bitterness, hatred or resentments defining me.

Prayer: Today, Father, I am going to choose to start forgiving those who have hurt me and caused me pain. I am learning that when I forgive it has nothing to do with the person, situation or event I am forgiving. Forgiveness has everything to do with me. I am choosing to be free from the anger, bitterness, resentment and hatred that has locked me in and held me down for so long. Thank you, for teaching me about forgiveness and granting me the ability to forgive. Help me, to choose forgiveness in all areas and aspects of my life. Thank you, Jesus, for forgiving me and helping me to forgive others, amen.

Day Twenty-eight

1 Peter 5:5 'Young people, in the same way be submissive to those who are older. All of you, cloth yourselves with humility toward one another, because God opposes the proud but gives grace to the humble.'

Submission is such a difficult thing to do for most of us. We have a belief that says if I am submissive then I lose part of myself to the other person. If I give in to the other person they will have control over me and I will not be able to be my own self. That is not so. It is not true. Just because I submit to another person it does not mean that they own me or I am less than they are. What it means is that I choose to respect the person and the authority that is rightfully theirs. I choose to allow myself to be under another's authority at this point in time. It does not have anything to do with my position in life. It does not diminish me at all or in any way. It has no negative affect upon me or my personhood whatsoever. What it means is that I am willing to listen to another person and to allow them to have the final word at this time and place, under these conditions. We so very often allow our pride to get in the way of living in truth and freedom. Pride can prevent us from submitting to another person because we have to look good or be the image we have created, when in fact, submitting to another person usually does not have anything to with us. It usually has to do with a person's position or an event that is happening. Submission is an act of obedience to the one who is in authority due to their current position or place. As children we submit to our parent for several reasons; 1) they have more life experience and know more about what it means to live in healthy growing ways; 2) we need to be protected from parts of life until we are well able to handle them in a successful way; 3) we need to grow in a safe environment under the protection and authority of those God has put in place to guide us along our life journey. Submitting under the right conditions actually keeps us safe and healthy and helps us to avoid unnecessary conflict. Being willing to submit means we are confident and secure in who and what we are as a person. It says I can be a leader and I can let other people lead. It takes more strength to be submissive in good and healthy way than to be rebellious and demanding that everyone and everything submit to us. Unhealthy pride says I cannot submit. Healthy pride says I am confident and secure in myself to let you be strong in this situation.

Prayer: Father/Dad, help me to have a healthy attitude and outlook forwards being submissive. Help me, to respect people who have authority over me in given situations or events. Help me, to know when I am living in healthy submissiveness and when I am being self destructive in my unhealthy pride. Jesus, even you were submissive to the authorities of your day even though you did not always agree with them. That is the way I need to be. Show me, when it is necessary and appropriate to submit to the ones in authority over me. I am sorry for my wrong attitudes and beliefs about being submissive and ask that you would forgive me and help me to be the person you created me to be, amen

Day Twenty-nine

1 Corinthians 9:24 'Do you not know that in a race all the runners run, but only one gets the prize? Run in such a way as to get the prize.'

Going for the gold. That means not settling for the silver or bronze or nothing when a little more effort would have gotten us the gold. How many times do we settle for less than what is really ours? How many times do we stop the race just before the finish line? How many times do we settle for what may or may not come our way? My guess is more times than we want to admit. We get used to settling for less than what we deserve; in fact, at times it becomes a way of life. We settle just because we have learned to settle. We stop trying to reach for the gold or the top rung of the ladder of life. We stop trying when we could have reached the top rung. What happens is we get used to not having the gold, we get used to settling for whatever may or may not come our way. That is not God's plan for us and our lives. God's plan is success and abundance in our lives. God's plan is being all that He created us to be. God's plan is reaching for the HIGHER GROUND and not staying in the plains. To reach the HIGHER GROUND we have to believe that we deserve the HGHER GROUND and that it is okay for us to be successes. We need to let go of the stumbling blocks in our hearts and lives that say "No you don't deserve to be a success. No, you do not deserve all that God has in store for you. You were made to be second or third place, not first. You were created to be less than". Those beliefs are not true and nowhere close to the truth. God created each and every one of us to be already enough with all the gifts, talents and abilities we need to be the people He created us to be. God created each and every one of us to be unique and special in our own right; to be the person God wanted us to be; to live the life we are to live. Therefore we need to stop looking at what other people have and where they are in life and start looking at where we are supposed to be. Look at what gifts, talents and abilities you have and belong to you and you alone. How are you to use those gifts, talents and abilities to be a success? Or are you throwing them away or pretending they do not exist or are not yours? Today let us start choosing to be the people who reach for the gold and get it. Today let us stop settling for what may or may not come to us. Today let us chase after the gold. Chasing after the gold, the top rung in God's plan for ours lives is what we are meant to do. Remember who created you and whose you are. You are a chosen, child of the Most High God with a plan and purpose in and for your life.

Prayer: Father, I am so sorry for settling for second or third place. I am sorry for believing that I did not deserve to have success and abundance. Forgive me, for not being the person you created me be. Forgive me, for believing the lies about not being good enough. Forgive me, for settling for whatever came my way instead of reaching for the HIGHER GROUND. Thank you, Father, for loving me the way you do and for creating me to already be enough and absolutely good enough. Thank you, Father, for creating me to achieve success and to reach for the gold. In Jesus' name, amen.

Day Thirty

2 Timothy 1:7 'For God did not give you a spirit of timidity (fear), but a spirit of power, of love and of self-discipline (a sound mind).'

As you know the acrostic for fear is: F-false E-evidence A-appearing R- real or F-face E-everything A-and R-recover. The reality is most fears are false evidence appearing real. Most of our fears never come true. They are false evidence appearing real to us. Most of our fears or the things we are afraid of usually never materialize or come to pass. That is why God says He does not give a spirit of fear. For the false evidence fears are lies and as God cannot tell a lie (only the Evil One can lie) they cannot not come from God. False fears have to come from the Evil One. God lives in the truth. The truth is God is love. Love is doing the higher good for the ones we love. Giving us false fear is not for our higher good therefore they do not come out of a spirit of love. God gives us power, love and a sound mind or self–discipline that are to our higher good and well being. Let me say this again. When we live in fear, we are living in what is false. When we get down and get honest with ourselves those things we fear from a false fear perspective are illusions, not real. Therefore what use to they have in our lives? What good do they bring us? Now I am not talking about real fear, the fears that are true and harmful to us like touching a hot burner on the stove, or playing with fire and getting burnt. I am talking about the false fears that keep us locked in and bogged down afraid to move forward. The original fear is no longer a threat or controlling us, yet we let them live in our lives today. What God is reminding us of today is if we choose to trust God, and His love and provision in and for our lives, we don't have to live in the false fears that steal our joy, peace, mercy and grace. We can live in joy and peace with God's mercy and grace helping us at every bend of the road and every situation that comes our way. We can live by faith and trust that no matter what is happening. God is in control ------ well able to provide for our needs and situations. Fear is not from God; therefore when we choose to live in fear we are stepping outside of God. When we live in fear we are stepping outside of God and God's power, love and authority. God is love and His love gives us life. False fear is a lie therefore gives us death. Love, true love casts out all fear. Let us choose today to live in trust and love. Letting go of the fears that keep us from having true life within us. There is no life or freedom in false fear, there is only more fear and no life.

Prayer: Father, I repent of my false fears and ask Father that you would forgive me. Help me, to live in truth and faith in you and who and what you are as the one and only true living God. Help me, to let go of my false fears and trust you more. Help me, to rest in your love and peace using your mercy and grace as my sustaining power and resource. Thank you, Jesus, for being my very help in time of struggle, stress and every other situation I may face in my daily life. Amen.

Day Thirty-one

Philippians 4:4 'Rejoice in the Lord always. I will say it again: Rejoice.'

Rejoice in the Lord always. Reminder, again I say rejoice. If you are anything like me, you do not truly realize the power of this statement! We don't want to rejoice when life is not going our way. We don't want to rejoice when life is hurting or falling apart. We don't want to rejoice when our feelings are telling us to stay in our mud puddle (whatever our mud puddle is). We don't want to rejoice when life is not doing what we think life should be doing. The truth is, rejoicing has the power to move us out of our humdrums and back into joy. The reality is if we rejoice, then we move out of our slump, which in turn gives back our joy. You might be thinking but how can I rejoice when......? Well we can, and it is a choice to do so. It is a choice to let go of the whatevers. It is our choice to choose the presence of God and His provision in and for our lives in the midst of whatever we are going through. When we turn our eyes and hearts towards God then God has the opportunity to enter into the situation and help us through it. If we stay stuck in the situation then God cannot go there. For God (as we have learned) cannot go where He is not invited. When we choose to rejoice, what we are really saying is God can help me through this. I am going to trust God and not stay in the feelings that are happening at this moment. I am going to let my heart rejoice even though it is breaking or hurting and living in such pain. I am not going to let my feelings define me; rather I am going to let my faith lead me forward. I am going to be honest with myself. Honest with what is happening inside of me and around me. I am also going to let God in to help me through this by rejoicing and claiming His provision for me in this and through it. The amazing thing is once we start rejoicing we find our feelings beginning to shift. As we shift the rejoicing increases. As the rejoicing increases we begin to even enjoy the rejoicing and all that it is. To our amazement it is not very long before we let go of whatever it is we are going through and the presence of God begins to fill our entire being. Is it easy to rejoice when we are going through a down time in our lives? The answer is no. It is not easy at all. In fact it is often the hardest thing we will ever do. Once we start rejoicing, trusting God's call upon us to rejoice in all things--- that is all things--- we find ourselves reaping the blessing of obedience and trusting. We see the loving mercy and compassion of God welling up within us. We see the promises of God revealed in our hearts and lives.

We begin to see through a new set of eyes. `Rejoice in the Lord always and again I say rejoice.'

Prayer: Holy Spirit, remind me to rejoice. Remind me of my need to rejoice even when I do not feel like rejoicing. Help me, to trust you and your love and provision for me no matter what is happening in and about my life. I am sorry, for not turning to you sooner and for not trusting you more. Please, forgive me and restore me to my rightful place in you, amen

Day Thirty-two

1 Thessalonians 5: 16-18 'Be joyful always. Pray continually; give thanks in all circumstances, for this is God's will for you in Christ Jesus.'

Be joyful always! Again what a statement! Who can be joyful all the time? Who can have a happy face and heart everyday? The truth is we can't. But what we can do is pray continually. What we can do in all circumstances is allow the presence of God to visit us, giving us the help we need to be joyful and be filled with the Holy Spirit. This in turn brings God in and helps us to see beyond the situation into God's presence and love. Feelings are a choice. We choose what we are feeling. That is hard to believe at times when our feelings seem to have so much power and control over us. But the truth is we can decide what we will do with what we are feeling. Yes the feelings come and are very real and present to us, but we can decide what we will do with whatever the feeling is. Believe it or not we can decide what we do with them. The choice is ours not the feelings. We can either let our feelings define us or we can feel our feelings and then decide where we are going to go from here. For example: I may be angry with someone who has cut me off while driving. Yes I am angry but now I can choose to really get angry and chase the car and honk my horn or yell and scream or any number of negative things. Or I can take a step back and say a prayer for them and myself, thus letting the anger go. I can be feeling tired and run down but still have a smile on my face and a happy disposition. I can be going through the worst time of my life feeling like the world is crashing down around me. The situation is real. What I do with the situation determines the outcome. We decide what we are going to do with a feeling, not the feeling deciding what it is going to do with us. Have you ever wanted to really laugh only to find yourself in a place where you could not laugh or the timing was all wrong? What did you do? You probably stuffed the laughter instead and just smiled to yourself? That is another example of us controlling our feelings and not our feelings controlling us. We do have the power and ability to decide for ourselves what we will and will not do with a feeling when it comes our way. We are in control of our feelings and not our feelings in control of us. Yes we have to feel whatever it is that is happening inside of us and not ignore it, but after that we decide where we go from here. We choose how the feeling affects us. We choose the power that feeling is going to have over us. If I do not want to laugh or be angry, there is nothing you can do to make me laugh or be angry. Think about that for a bit.

Prayer: Thank you, Heavenly Father, that I can choose what I will do with my feelings and that you have built into me the ability to choose. Help me to be real and honest with my feelings and with myself so that I can be joyful all the time deciding for myself how the feelings I am feeling will be lived out. Teach me, to pray continually and in all circumstances trusting you in and through all things. Thank you, for making my feelings and for making me. Thank you, for teaching me and helping me. Thank you, Holy Spirit, for living in my heart, being my constant and ever present help in times of trouble and joy, amen.

Day Thirty-three

Philippians 1:6 'Being confident of this, that he who began work in you will carry it on to completion until the day of Christ Jesus.'

What an amazing thought and truth! God never gives up on us. God never takes on a renovation project within our lives and then stops half way through. What God starts, He finishes. God never stops in mid sentence and says "well, I think I have taken this one far enough. I think I will just leave this one this way and move onto the next person in line". God never says "okay I think you have enough joy, so I will stop giving you joy now or healing or prosperity or any other blessings". Our God is a faithful God, who when we let Him into our lives, He begins a good work and does not stop until the good work is completed. God is faithful and just to complete whatever He starts. The work He starts in us He will be faithful to continue until the end. We can be confident that God will not stop until we have reached our place of wholeness and completeness in Him. God will keep working out our salvation and bringing us into our place of wholeness, with our help, until we are everything God created us to be in the first place. We have the most amazing God! We have a God who cares about us. God cares about even the smallest detail in our lives and what happens to us today, tomorrow and forever. God wants us to be whole. God wants us to be totally alive and living in abundance. God wants us to live in the fullness of His mercy, grace, love and compassion. God wants us to be forgiven and to live in forgiveness both for ourselves and for others. All we need do is let Him carry on the work in us until we reach our full potential and are the person we were designed to be. Our God loves us. He loves us just the way we are but loves us too much to leave us here. What does that means? God loves us for who and what He created us to be. God knows we have taken on baggage along the way and have stored up lots of things in our hearts that do not belong there. Those things we store up do not get in the way of God's love for us. God's desire for us is to be whole and complete in Him. Therefore God wants to help us clean up our hearts so that we can be free and live in freedom. That is why God begins a good work and does not stop until the project is finished. We may leave projects undone or left until another time, but God never does that. When God starts something He carries on until the day it is finished and complete. I rejoice in you Father, God for starting a good work in me, for being the faithful God you are to complete what you have started.

Prayer: Thank you, Father, for first off starting the good work in me, and thank you for completing it. Thank you for seeing beyond my rough edges and for helping me to become whole. I am learning that in you I am already enough. I am already what you created me to me. All I need do is let you help me to let go of those things that prevent me from being your child and living in your fullness. Today, I am going to choose to be your child and to live in the fullness of your love, mercy, grace and compassion. Today, I choose to let you move forward in the work that needs to be done in me. I choose to surrender to you, amen.

Day Thirty-four

Romans 8: 28 'And we know that in all things God works for the good of those who love him, who have been called according to his purpose.'

All things. Can we hear that? All things works together for the good of those who love God and have been called according to His purposes! Not some things, but all things. Somehow I don't know how but somehow God can turn everything that happens in our lives into something good if we let Him. Do you hear that friends---if we let God. This is the key to having God turn whatever it is we are going through into something good. We have to let God turn it into something good. We have to trust God and His presence in our lives, and His workings in our lives to turn the situation we are going through into something that is good and life giving. We have to be willing to trust God and His provision in our lives even when everything looks like a royal mess. Our God can do all things, for nothing is impossible for our God. Our God can take whatever it is we are going through and can turn our life situation into something good if we are willing to let Him in and help us. Have you ever thought the situation you are in or were going through is the worst thing that could ever happen; for example we break our leg and miss the special event. The disappointment is great maybe even overwhelming. Then get our draft letter in the mail. The broken leg is not so bad anymore. We miss our plane only to have the plane crash. A relationship breaks up and our heart is broken; then we discover that the person was all wrong for us and if we had married him/her we would have ended in divorce. God really knows best. Nothing is impossible for our great and awesome God. Therefore when we trust God, God uses that trust to work good things out in our lives. When we trust God, He can and will turn everything that is happening in our lives into something that is good, even beautiful. That is the key to having this verse a reality in and for your life. You have to let God into your mistakes, wrong choices and events. You have to let God be God in whatever is happening or not happening in your life. That is the trust God is asking from us. "Will you trust my love and provision in and for your life no matter what?" For those of you who have the belief that you need to be perfect, this promise can never be yours. For God can only turn things around when there is something to be turned around. If you need to be perfect all the time then you do not need God's help.

Prayer: Father God, I take my hands off and give you permission to turn my life around and turn this situation into something good. I give you permission to take my past and turn it into something good as well. Today I choose to trust you in all aspects of my life. Yes, Father, I am willing to trust you with everything I am and everything I have. Thank you, for being the one and only true God for whom nothing is impossible. You are a totally awesome and trustworthy God. I love you, Lord, thank you, for loving me, amen.

Day Thirty-five

Genesis 8: 21-22 'The Lord smelled the pleasing aroma and said in his heart: Never again will I curse the ground because of people, even though every inclination of their heart is evil from childhood. And never again will I destroy all living creatures as I have done.'

One of the amazing promises of God is we can trust Him. We can trust who and what God is and all that God says and promises. That is the truth—the whole truth--- and nothing but the truth. One of God's promises is He will never again curse the ground and never again will He destroy His creation. We can trust these promises. We can believe in our hearts that God will not curse us or destroy us. God will not cause is to die because of the evil in our hearts! We can trust the promise of God that says He will love us no matter what and no matter where. No more curses! What we get as God's beloved, precious, special, chosen children are His blessings and love. His amazing mercy and grace! His prosperity and provision for all His creation. What we get is the freedom to be who and what He created us to be with the freedom to be human and make mistakes. What we get is an amazing God and Father who is honest, true and loves us beyond all measure. We are God's kids, His chosen children with the inheritance of all He has promised. We are truly without a shadow of a doubt God's chosen Beloved, loved and chosen before the foundation of the world to be His and He ours. Rest in His love and promises for us His Beloved. We ourselves cause the curses and death to happen in our lives, not God. We make the choices we make with the outcomes that come with the choices. We choose either to die and be cursed or to live in the blessings and provision of God. We choose---not God. God just lets us suffer the consequences of our choices. That is God's gift of free will to His creation. We turn away from God; God does not turn away from us. He cannot! God has decided to love us to the very end regardless of what we do or how we react to the love God has for us. We turn our backs towards God. God never turns His back towards us. Let us today take a good, honest look at our selves and our hearts. Which way have we turned? Have we turned towards God or away from God? Have we set our faces and hearts towards the one who loves us unconditionally or have we turned our faces and hearts towards the world and all the promises the world holds out to us? After you have been honest with yourself, is that the direction you want to be facing? If yes great! If no then where do you go from here? Back towards God or onward towards the world?

Prayer: Thank you, Father, for loving me and blessing me and making me your own. Thank you, for being the same yesterday, today and always. That promise means that I can trust you and your promises to me. Thank you for making me your own. I turn my face and heart towards you Father for that is where my true and real life lies. Thank you, for loving me both now and always. I do love you Lord for loving me and being my God, Father and Dad, amen

Day Thirty-six

Genesis 18:14 'Is anything too hard for the Lord? I will return to you at the appointed time next year and Sarah will have a son.'

Have you ever had a day, week, month, year or event happen in your life when you looked up to God and thought: "This is too hard even for you God. I know all things are possible for you God. But this one is so big and well God I don't know if you can work through this one"? Know you are not alone in your thoughts and the feeling. Most of us go through really hard times and wonder in the depths of our pain and heart if this will ever pass and if I am stuck here in this without a way out. This is bigger than God. Well I have good news for you today! Whatever it is you are going through will pass. Whatever is happening to you today will one day be a memory of your past and you will think back and say, "I am so glad this over and I am also glad for the life lesson it taught me". Know Our God is Bigger Then Anything You Are Going Through and He is Right Here With You, as you go through it. Know God is Well Able to see you through to the Other Side. Our God is bigger then everything and anything we might be going through. Our God is well able to not only carry us but to also make a way where there seems to be no way. We have a loving Father and Saviour who knows and understand and who can and will see us through. We can trust God even when we can't see, hear or even have that knowing He is there/here. We can still trust God to see us through even when it seems that it is an impossible situation or event. Our God is able to do the impossible. God brought life into Sarah's womb when she was beyond childbearing age. God gave the promised male child to Sarah and Abraham when they were beyond their earthly ability to reproduce. If God can do this for Abraham and Sarah, He can bring whatever it is you need and are being promised, into being for you too! Is anything too hard for our God? The answer is no, nothing is too hard for our God. Nothing is beyond what our God can do. Nothing is beyond the power and ability of our God and everything our God is. You may have to hang on to your thought that this too shall pass for now. Know whatever it is you are going through God will take you through to the other side. He has to; it is His promise to us. This too shall pass and you will come up the other side having grown into a better person for the experience. There have been so many times in my own life when all I had to hang on to were the promises of God. There was nothing else left. Know without a shadow of a doubt, God will bring you through and do what He has promised you. Keep your eyes and heart on God. Do not take your hand out of His hand and simply trust God and His faithfulness. It works.

Prayer: Thank you, Father, that you are exactly who you say you are. Thank you, that I can trust you. That I can put my trust, hope and faith in you, trusting that you have never brought me anywhere to drop me or let me go. Help me, to trust my faith in your promises and not my feelings. I know my feelings lie to me. You never do. I know my feelings don't always tell me the truth. Only you, Father, are the truth. I can trust you even through the way is hard and there are rough times in my life. Praise you loving Father, amen

Day Thirty-seven

> *Genesis 12:2-3 I will make you into a great nation and I will bless you; I will make your name great, and you will be a blessing. I will bless those who bless you, and whoever curses you I will curse; and all peoples on earth will be blessed through you'.*

The Abraham blessing: I will bless you so that you can be a blessing to others. I will bless you so that you can take the blessing I am giving you and share it with others. We get God's blessing so that we can take God's blessing and share it with others. Others get to be blessed because we are blessed. The more we share the blessing the more the blessing gets shared. Yes, my blessings start with Abraham but ends up blessing outward to others. That same blessing belongs to us. God wants to bless us so that we can be a blessing to others. God wants to shower down His blessings upon us so that we can show others the truth about God and how God wants us to be whole, prosper and blessed. God does not withhold blessings from us. The blessings are there. The blessings are always there. God does not put blocks between His blessings and us. I believe we block our blessings by the choices we make. We block our blessings by the things we let into our spirits. We block our blessings by turning our faces away from God. If I am living in a lifestyle that is pleasing to God and following God's laws and decrees, I will be blessed. If I am doing my own thing and living as I want to live or desire life, which is on my terms and conditions, then chances are I am not in a right relationship with God. Therefore God's blessings are not able to reach through to my spirit and life because of all the other things crowding in on me. Abraham was blessed when he was obedient and faithful to God and God's plan for his life. When Abraham did life his way, life was not the way he thought it would be. For example, when he had a son with Hagar, the servant girl of Sarah it is my opinion that Abraham and Sarah made the decision to take matters into their own hands and it delayed the fulfilling of God's promise to them. Had they waited upon God and God's timing Isaac probably would have been born to them sooner rather than later. This is just a guess on my part, so take it with a grain of salt. Are we living our lives according to us? Or are we living our lives according to God? This freedom of choice that God has given to each one of us is a determining factor for receiving the blessings God has for us His children or not receiving them. If we choose to live life according to God's ways chances are we will be blessed for that is a promise of God. Abraham's blessing is Abraham would be blessed so that he could pass that blessing on to others-----No blessings on us, no blessings to give to others. Choosing life our way or God's way. The wonder of free will, is we get to choose. God gets to bless.

Prayer: Father God, I need to tell you how sorry I am that I have been living my life according to me and not according to you. I am truly sorry. Help me, to live my life your way, being a faithful and obedient child. Help me, to let go of my need to have life my way and on my terms and conditions. I am learning that when I live life my way I do not usually get what I think I should get. Thank you, for loving me and forgiving me. Thank you, for being the gracious Father and God you are. I am so very grateful, amen.

Day Thirty-eight

Romans 7:8 'But sin, seizing the opportunity afforded by the commandment, produced in me every kind of covetous desire. For apart from law, sin is dead.'

Have you ever found yourself in a place where your body is screaming at you because you said no to it? You say, "No body, I am not giving you that chocolate cake, or the cigarette you are craving. I will not just sit around all day; I will get up off this couch and exercise". Do these bring back examples from your own life experience? Here are a couple of examples from my life. I decided to change the way I ate to help my body be healthier. Instead of just drinking fruit juice in the morning, I starting drinking a protein drink. My body got so hungry and ached for more food even though everything it was craving was being supplied in the protein drink. My body was getting more then it ever had before. It wanted the sugar in the orange juice, not the healthy stuff in the protein drink. For two weeks it acted as if I was not feeding it at all. It yelled at me for days complaining and wanting its own way. I decided I was going to exercise more regularly. I started playing badminton at lunchtime with another staff member. At around 11:30 my body said "food". Badminton started at noon. I had to fight off the hunger in order to stay committed to playing badminton. My body was using every excuse it could find to get its own way. How about dieting? We start a diet and all we want is sugar. We are told no chocolate because we have to cut down on the caffeine intake, and all we want is chocolate; nothing else will satisfy. This is the power of the sin principle Paul is teaching us today. When we say no to our bodies they rebel, get defiant and throw temper tantrums. When we say no to our bodies they do everything in their power to get our attention, so that we will give into whatever it is our body wants. We say "no" to our bodies; they say "oh yea!" they proceed to give us a hard time. But thanks be to God who is greater than our sin and can save us from this demanding body of ours and bring us into triumphant living. How do we get the triumphant living? By putting our focus on God and His provision of mercy and grace in our lives. We can get past the screams of our bodies into the place where we have control once again. By trusting God and His desire for us to be whole and complete, we can say no to our bodies and find the life we are searching for. Is it always easy? No! Is it worth it? Yes! Reclaiming our ability to control our bodies is one of the most liberating things we can do. It truly does set us free. Just remember your body has a really long memory and does not give up easily. There will be days when it will take every once of strength you have just to keep walking down the right path, and saying the whole time "this too shall pass". This too shall pass. What an awesome God we love and have as our Father and friend. Our bodies do not have to have the final say, our spirit can.

Prayer: Thank you, Father, Holy Spirit, that you are in me helping me to overcome the power of sin in my body. Thank you, that in Christ I have the resources to overcome my body's desire to live life, life's way. Thank you that I am a victor and not a victim to my body. When I have Christ in me, I have all I need to do all I need to do. I am blessed beyond measure! In Jesus' name, amen.

Day Thirty-nine

John 14: 15-17 'If you love me, you will obey what I command. And I will ask the father, and He will give you another Councilor to be with you forever-the Spirit of truth.'

We are not alone! There may not be other people around us but we are not alone. We may be by ourselves, but we are not alone. When we have the Spirit of God within us, we are never alone! That is right, we are never, no never, alone when the Holy Spirit resides in our spirit. God is with us even when we cannot feel God or sense Him. God is always with us. He is there/here walking the road of life with us. If you are anything like me there are times when I feel like God has moved on. God has decided to move on to do something else. I feel God is not here keeping His promises and being my constant source of life and living. Then I remember that it is just a feeling and not the truth. Once again my feelings are not telling me what is true. For the truth is God, the great I Am, is with you/us. "I am always with you" God promises. "I will never abandon you. I will not forsake you. I will not leave you orphaned. I will never take you anywhere to drop you. I will never, not be there with you and for you. I will never take you anywhere to drop you off and just walk away." I will never leave you alone even when you turn your back on me. Then the feelings of being alone drop off and the reality of God once again takes hold. We are once again safe and secure in my Father's loving, tender arms right where we belong. The truth starts to well up once again even if I cannot feel God. Even if God seems far away, I can still trust the promise and faithfulness of God in my life. We are once again in our Father's arms allowing His love to be our constant source of all life. Our spirit gives us the ability to trust and live as the precious, beloved children we are. There is such a comfort knowing that we are not alone and that God is always with us no matter what is happening or not happening in our lives. We serve a truly faithful God and Father. God our Heavenly Father loves us beyond everything and anything, with a pure and never ending love both now and always! With a love we can trust. With a love that is constant, pure and unconditional. Can we be more blessed? I do not think so. We are God's children and we belong in His tender loving arms and care no matter what our feelings are telling us. No matter what the world says. No matter what our body says. No matter what life says. Our Heavenly Father/Dad loves us and nothing and no one can change that love or alter it in any way shape or form.

Prayer: Father, forgive me for the times when I get so caught up in my feelings that I forget the truth of your word and promises. Forgive me for letting my feeling define me, for letting my feelings tell me who I am and how I should believe and act. Thank you, that I am more then my feelings. Thank you, that I can trust your love. I am safe and secure in your love no matter what. I choose to believe in your love for me, amen.

Day Forty

Judges 6:11-12 'The angel of the Lord came and sat down under the oak in Ophrah that belonged to Joash the Abiezrite, where his son Gideon was threshing wheat in a winepress to keep it from the Midianites. When the angel of the Lord appeared to Gideon, he said, The Lord is with you, mighty warrior.'

Gideon had a different opinion of himself than God had of Gideon. Gideon would say he was the last person to be called a mighty warrior. The way Gideon saw himself was nowhere close to the way God saw him. The two views just didn't match! Some of us feel like Gideon. Gideon saw himself as the weakest, smallest member of the clan. God saw Gideon with the potential of God's power and presence in his life to be the mighty warrior God created him to be. Gideon saw himself as a nothing. God saw him as a mighty warrior, the one who would save God's people. When we are weak, God is strong. When we are strong it is because God is working in us and we become like Gideon, a mighty warrior! God uses everything that God put in us to be all that God needs us to be. God did not create us to be "less than". He did not create us with a half measure. Gideon saw himself as "less than". God saw Gideon as so very much more. God did not create us to be not good enough! God created us to be exactly what He created us to be. He did not create us to be what He created another person to be. We are all already enough. We are all filled with the gifts, talents and abilities that God has set aside for us and us alone. Therefore we do have to believe anyone or anything that says otherwise. We are what God created us to be.

63

We are the precious, chosen, beloved children of God with value and worth. We matter more than we will ever know or truly begin to understand. It is time to be what God created us to be, for such a time as this. In order to take our places as the person God created us to be, we have to choose to trust God and allow God to start working in our lives and hearts to bring out the best in us, just as Gideon did. To be what God created us to be we need to begin to see ourselves as God sees us. Gideon saw himself as a less than valuable person. God saw him as a mighty warrior. Gideon saw himself as not good enough. God saw him as the gifted man who would rescue his People. Ask God to show you how He sees you and how He created you to be. You may be surprised at the answer you get.

Prayer: Father God, forgive me for believing the lies that others have filled my life and spirit with. Forgive me, for not believing your word and the truth in your word about who I am and whose I am. I am sorry, for letting other people and events define me. I choose to take my place as your child. To be the child you created me to be. Thank you, for already making me enough. I chose to believe you and not the lies any longer. In Jesus' name, amen.

Day Forty-one

Judges 6:16 'The Lord answered, I will be with you, and you will strike down all the Midianites together.'

Yesterday we committed ourselves to God to take our places and to be all that God created us to be. We committed to stop listening to the lies or half-truths about our personhood, to accept our value and worth in God, to accept ourselves as the gifted, talented individual God made us to be. Now hear God's reply to our commitment; 'I will be with you, and you will strike down all the Midianites together.' God has made a commitment to us to be here with us. To help us achieve His goal and purpose in and for our lives. God will help us and be with us every step of the way. Was Gideon afraid at times? I believe so. Did he doubt? Yes. Did Gideon wonder if he had heard God right and this was really happening to him? I believe so. Did Gideon take his place and become the mighty warrior God called him to be? YES! Why? Because he put his trust, hope and faith in God and went forth believing that if God said he would be there helping and leading him then God would do it. Walking in faith and living by the promises of God is not always easy, our feelings get in the way and try to derail us. Our old patterns, behaviours and beliefs try to pull us back into the lies and bondage from before. But we are not called to live by our feelings! We are called to live by faith and what God is putting into our hearts and lives. By faith Gideon conquered the Midianites. It was by trusting in God's power, presence and purpose in and for Gideon and the Israelites that Gideon had the courage and strength to do what God was asking him to do. Gideon chose to trust God and in trusting became the mighty warrior God called and equipped him to be. When God calls He also equips us with all that we need in order to do all that God is asking us to do. When God calls He also supplies. What is God calling you to today? What answer are you giving God? Are you saying "yes, I will go even though I do not see myself in this role" or are you saying as Moses did, "send Aaron he's so start; come on send Aaron; he is so good; every one loves him Lord. Send Aaron. Only Lord, just do not send me"? Every person God called in Scripture had everything they needed to do all they were being asked to do, it will be the very same with you. Moses told God he did not speak well enough. Jeremiah told God he was too young. Isaiah told God he was a man of unclean lips. God's response to all of them was the same. Trust me, your God and Father. Trust my call upon your life and all the way I will provide for you. Each went forth in their call. Each saw the mighty hand of God at work in their lives and the ministry God had called them to.

Prayer: Heavenly Father, I choose to be a person of faith. I choose to walk holding on to your hand and trusting your power, presence and purpose in my life. Help my unbelief. Help me, to trust you more and walk in your plan and purpose in and for my life. I choose to trust you, Lord, my God, amen.

Day Forty-two

Judges 6 17: ' Gideon replied, "If now I have found favor in your eyes, give me a sign that it is really you talking to me.'

When all was said and done Gideon still needed a sign from God to help him grow and let go of his fears and doubts. Gideon still needed to know the knowing that comes only from God and that it is God's plan. Gideon put out his fleece asking God to make the fleece wet and the ground dry the following morning. God did just as Gideon asked. That was not quite enough for Gideon his faith was still weak. He asked God to make the ground wet and the fleece dry. God did that as well. Then Gideon had the courage to move forward in God and God's request for his life. Know it is okay to venture forth even if everything inside of us is screaming NO. Our God is a really big God for whom nothing is impossible or beyond His reach. If we are living according to God's laws and decrees, if we are living as faithful, obedient children. God knows. Know God is pleased with you and like Gideon will give you the sign you need. I am not saying that we are to put God to the test. What I am saying is that it is okay to ask God for a sign to help your unbelief. Putting your fleece out is not testing God. It is building confidence in yourself and your relationship with God to do what is being asked of you. Here is a truth I feel you need to hear right about now. All we need do to please God is to just stand, sit, knee or lie down and breathe. It really is that easy to please God. God's love for us and His presence in our lives, happens because God chooses to love us and be present in our lives. All we need do is ask and God is right there doing what God does best and that is love us and help us. We have found favor in God's eyes. We are God's joy and delight. Maybe it is time to start living that way and to claim the blessings God has for us as His children and chosen Beloved. Instead of choosing unbelief— maybe it is time to choose belief and faith even if you need to put out a fleece or two. God knows and understands. Besides putting out a fleece helps us to really know which plans are from God and which are not. Faith grows as we stretch our faith. As we determine within ourselves to walk in faith and allow faith to grow in us, the more faith we will have. The more we trust God, the more trust you will have in God.

Prayer: Father, I have let the world define me and tell me who I am for so long that I am having a hard time seeing myself through your eyes. I need a sign that says I am valuable in your sight and that I am your precious, chosen, beloved child. I need you to help me see me as you see me, not as I have been taught or come to believe. I want to be all that you created me to be. Help me, as you helped Gideon so I too may be a faithful, obedient child of the Most High God. Help me, Jesus, amen.

Day Forty-three

1 Peter 5:10 'And the God of all grace, who called you to his eternal glory in Christ, after you have suffered a little while, will himself restore you and make you strong, firm and steadfast.'

Being human we do not like to have to suffer. Most of us want to go through life without any hardships and suffering. We want a smooth ride with no bumps twists or turns along the way. Life should be easy! The question I hear asked all the time is "Why Me"? Why do I have to go through this? Why do I have to suffer this way? The answer of course is why not you? Who or what says any of us is exempt from life sufferings? In reality none of us are. We all get our share of suffering and some get more than others. The problem with the belief that says, I should be exempt from suffering, is it is not realistic or even possible. Life is not easy and life is certainly not fair. Life is filled with all kinds of struggles, challenges and pit falls. We will all have points in our lives where we suffer and have hard times we need to struggle through. Again life is not fair, it never will be fair! If we are being honest with ourselves, it is only through the times of suffering that we gain our strength, trust and growth. It is only through the hard times that we get to truly realize the faithfulness of God and His love for us. The true potential of who and what we are as people is refined in our times of suffering. Our trust in and for God increases every time we face the hard times in our lives. An example of what a struggle can give us is compassion. When we have really struggled through something, we know what it is like. When we see someone else going through the same experience, we share compassion with him or her. We help bring them hope to make it through themselves. We can tell them with all honesty that this too shall pass and you will make it through. Life has taught us that lesson. Therefore, we pass the lesson on. As much as we do not like the valleys and all the valleys bring, it is in the valley that we learn our life lessons and grow. It is in the valley that we experience God in ways the mountaintop can never show us. The mountaintops are great and wonderful times. They fill us and remind us of God's love, presence and peace. But it is in the valley that we experience God's mercy, grace and compassion. The valley times in our lives truly do make us strong and much more able to have compassion for others as they go through their valley times. The valleys, if we let them, help to teach us about life on life's terms and the mercy of God as we face whatever it is life is giving us. It is not easy but it is worth it. If life were always easy how could we know our limits and the extent of our skills, gifts and abilities? Without the valleys where would we learn the extent of our humanness and the value of who and what we are as people? Without our valleys how would we grow?

Prayer: Father, thank you for the valley times in my life and thank you for the mountaintops. I am learning that both are important and necessary. Help me, to not get bitter or resentful because I am going through a valley time. Help me to see what I am to learn and how I am to grow. Then help me to get through to the other side. Thank you, for your love and faithfulness. In Jesus' most precious and compassionate name, amen

Day Forty-four

Psalm 81: 11 'I am the Lord your God, who brought you up out of Egypt. Open wide your mouth and I will fill it.'

Picture a nest of baby birds with their mouths all open waiting for mom to fill them. Not only are they waiting but they are also doing everything in their power to get mom's attention, so that they are not left out of the feeding that is taking place. They are truly making themselves know a to mom and their need for her food supply. They make as much noise as they can so mom puts food into their mouths. That is how I feel we are to be with God. We are to have our mouths open wide waiting for God to fill us. Waiting for God to pour into our lives all that He has stored up for us. Waiting on God with expectant hearts and our mouths wide open so God can just pour into us. Telling God in our own way that we too need His provision and food for our spirits. Showing God we are open and receptive to all God wants to pour into our lives and spirits. God has brought us out of our Egypt, whatever that may be for you. Or God may still is bringing you out of your desert experience. Either way, God has made provision to set us free from whatever holds us in bondage and slavery. God has called us up out of our bondage and slavery into the Promised Land, a land flowing with milk and honey. Now God wants to fill our mouths, our whole being to overflowing with all that He has for us. God wants to bless us and keep us. God wants to give us good gifts. God wants us to be all that He created us to be in the first place. We are to live freely in the land with all His blessings and provisions pouring down upon us. There will be times when we have to face our giants. There will be a reclaiming of the land that needs to take place. There may even be hard times ahead. That is called life. Let us today decide that we are going to open wide our mouths and hearts so that God can pour into us from His bounty of love, mercy, healing, grace, compassion and so on. Let us be open vessels for God to fill with not only His presence and Spirit but also with everything else He has stored up for us His children. We are part of the family of God. We are, part of God's family with all the wonder it brings. We are part of all that God is because we choose to be His children. Let us rejoice and be glad for all that we are and all that we are becoming because God chooses to love us as we choose to love God in return. We have been set free. Let us begin today to live in that freedom. Life is short. So very short when we look at the infinite limits of time as space. Let us not waste our short time grumbling and complaining. Instead let us live our lives with gusto and to the fullest. For today is all we really have.

Prayer: Yes Father, I want you to fill my mouth. I want to be filled with you and your presence and Spirit and everything else you have for me as your beloved, chosen child. I open wide my mouth and ask you to begin today to fill me up. To fill me up to overflowing! Thank you, Father, for being so patient with me and for accepting my prayer. I love you, Lord with all I am and all I have, amen.

Day Forty-five

Psalm 81:12-14 But my people would not listen to me; Israel would not submit to me. So I gave them over to their stubborn hearts to follow their own devices. If my people would but listen to me, if Israel would follow my ways, how quickly would I subdue their enemies their foes.'

Most of us at times in our lives have felt this way. We look up to God and wonder why life is going as bad as it is and why so many unblessed things are happening in our lives? We wonder why life is heading down the path it is? We wonder way God has gone silent? When we move away from God and do not listen to God when God is speaking to your hearts and lives, God gives us lots of chances and then God gives in to our stubborn hearts and allows us to follow our own devices. God lets us take our own paths knowing what the destination looks like. What happens is we move out of God's grace and into going through life on our own. There is a saying that goes like this; if you want to make God laugh tell Him what your plans are. I think the saying says it all. What boggles my mind is when we live life our way and under our terms and conditions, why would we expect God to bless us and show His unmerited grace to us? Why would we ever think that God would bless us in our stubbornness, temper tantrums and demanding life our way? The truth of God's love for us is whether we are living life our way or God's way, God never gives up on us. God never totally leaves us to our own devices. Does God ever really totally give up on us? NO! Does God let us suffer the consequences of our choices and own devices? YES! The way we get back into God's good graces is by repenting of our need to have life our way and according to our desires and devices. Getting down and honest with God, humbling our selves and asking God for His forgiveness and mercy. Asking God to release us from wanting life our way and asking God to help restore us to living life God's way. The door is once again open for God to work actively in our lives and the events and situations we find ourselves in. God wants to be a part of our lives. God wants to bless us and guide us through all of our lives and our life situations and events. God wants to give good gifts to us. We hinder the blessings, gifts and good things by turning away from God, by doing our own thing and living life our way. We get back into God's good blessings and grace when we humble ourselves and repent for being so selfish and self-centered. Then the mercy and forgiveness comes and it actually showers down upon us. We are once again restored to a right relationship with God and the healing begins in our hearts and lives. Thank you, Father God, for showing us the way back to you and out of our often so damning selves.

Prayer: Father, I am truly sorry for turning my back on you and for walking my own path. I see now that I have moved away from your grace and blessings and wondered why my life has become so chaotic and messed up. Forgive me Lord! Forgive me and restore me to a right relationship with you. I am learning that I can't make it without you. I can't have your blessings and my way as well. Thank you, for loving me the way you do and for restoring me to a right relationship with you. I am grateful, amen.

Day Forty-six

James 1:12 'Blessed is the man who perseveres under trial, because when he has stood the test, he will receive the crown of life that God has promised to those who love him.'

Blessed is the person who perseveres under trial, because they have stood the test. There are many areas of our lives that are tested. For example our willingness to hang in no matter what we are facing and having to deal with, to persevere when the going gets hard or tough, to be willing to stand up when it would be easier to lie down or throw in the towel and say I cannot do this anymore. The challenge is to just be willing to see the trial through to the end even though it might be costing you everything you have or thought you had. Why would we want to press on and persevere instead of simply give up? For a couple of reasons: 1) It pleases God's heart when we trust Him and go through the trial and come up the other end a better and stronger person and more able to face the challenges of life and living the Christian lifestyle. 2) There is a crown of life waiting for us. God has promised the crown of life to all who choose to love God and live according to His ways. 3) Life's lessons and character building are learned in the hard times not in the easy periods of life. I do not know about you. As for me, it is when life is hard and I have to really rely on God that I grow in my trust and relationship with God. When my resources are at an end and there is nothing left in me to fall back on, when I throw my hands and heart up in the air, choosing to let God work in and through me, then the presence of God is strong and His grace ever flowing. It is when I have absolutely nothing left of myself that God can move in and truly begins His good work in me and through me. When life is easy I don't need God as much. It is in the easy times of my life when I am strong in myself that I think I do not need God and am much more apt to rely on myself and on my abilities to see me through the trail, instead of trusting in God and His faithfulness. I know what trusting my abilities gets me----not very much. It is very humbling to realize our need for God. It is even harder to realize the truth of our need for God when we thought we could do it all alone and bear up under almost anything. Yet somehow when we look up and put our hand in God's. His mercy and grace are there. God's strength is always sufficient and has the endurance to see us through. God never disappoints us when we trust in His promises and provisions for our life, especially in the hard and rough times that we all have to face and endure. What a comfort knowing that our God truly is able to do all things no matter what. It is comforting to know that God's love does not hold grudges. God's love is unconditional and not based upon us. God's love is there for us because God chooses to love us no matter what. What amazing love God has for us!

Prayer: Father, I repent for not seeing my need for you at all times in my life. My need in both the easy times as well as the hard ones. I repent also for the whining I do when life is hard, when I feel and think it should be easy all the time. I am sorry, help me to trust you more. To trust you no matter is happening in my life and the lives around me. Help me to be the faithful, trusting child you created me to me. Thank you, Jesus, amen

Day Forty-seven

John 14 1-2 'Do not let your hearts be troubled. Trust in God trust also in me. In my Father's house are many rooms, if it were not so, I would have told you. I am going there to prepare a place for you.'

Do not let your heart be troubled. Trust in God trust also in me. This is such a difficult thing to do at times. How do I not have a troubled heart when someone I love is dying? Or when I have just lost my job and there isn't another one to go to? How do I trust when my world seems to be falling apart and there is no light at the end of this huge and vast tunnel I find myself in? How do I trust when everything around me is all up side down? How? The answer lies in our choosing to believe God and His promises even when everything is showing evidence to the contrary. When we can give ourselves permission to trust God and to take our hands off whatever it is we are going through, it is amazing how God can move in and give us what we need to make it through. Yes, the person may still die but you have the grace and peace to walk through it. Yes, you might not have a job but you now have the resource to reclaim your confidence and get out there looking for another one without giving up even before you got started. Yes your world may still be falling apart, but wisdom and knowledge are now resources available to you. You find yourself having them and using them, finding solutions where you thought there were none. You have the peace and calm of God within you that gives you what we need in order to face what you need to face. That is what Jesus is saying when He says, 'do not let your heart be troubled trust in God trust also in me'-----Trust in who we are (God) and who you are in us. Remember just because we trust God does not mean life is going to be easy all the time. What it means is we choose to put our hope, trust and faith in God, no matter what is happening or not happening in our lives. It means we allow God's peace to be ours instead of worry, stress, confusion and every other emotion that tries to hold us captive and locking us in. It means we can tap into who and what God is and come out the other end with those resources at our disposal. We choose to let God's light shine in our hearts and lives no matter what happens especially trusting in God when life is hard and our resources are just not enough to carry us through causes the darkness to lift and therefore we see better and do not stumble and fall as much. Our limited supply of resources has just grown ten fold. We can look at life and the situation with much different eyes knowing we are not alone. We can see our way through because the light is now shining brightly in our once dark tunnel. What an awesome God we serve! Life is hard at times; as I have said, that is called life. God says do not let your hearts get caught up in all the trouble life will bring your way. Instead trust in God's love, mercy and grace.

Prayer: Help me Heavenly Father/Dad, to trust you no matter what is happening in my life. Help me, trust your love for me even when I can't see it or feel it or know it is there. Father, I want to have your peace in all areas of my life. I want to live with your peace, joy and resources in my life. Help me, to trust you more. Help me to be a faithful and trust-filled child. Help me, to trust and not get caught in the darkness I may be going through. Thank you, Lord Jesus, amen.

Day Forty-eight

Matthew 5:14a 'You are the salt of the earth, But if the salt loses its saltiness, how can it be made salty again?

You are the salt of the earth. We are the ones who make a difference in this world. We are the ones who choose to bring light and life to those we are in relationship with and who cross our daily paths. We are the ones who walk as light therefore we cause the darkness to be exposed and the truth to be revealed. We add salt to a meal to enhance the flavour and bring out a better taste in the food we are eating and cooking. As children of God we have the ability and right to bring life back into situations that are causing death to happen. We have the right to speak the truth and bring the freedom truth brings. We are to share the love that heals the past and brings the present back into a place where life can grow. Examples: 1-standing up for the under dog and helping that person get the things they need. 2-Telling the truth when a lie may get you out of trouble, but the truth brings freedom. 3-Using your wisdom and sharing your knowledge about a situation when that word or knowledge would help bring light to the situation. Even though it may be easier to keep silent and not say anything. 4-Building others up instead of tearing them down. 5-Speaking a kind word instead of a harsh one or nothing at all. 6-Not hiding your relationship with God because you fear what others may think. 7-Standing up for what is right even if it costs you more than you want to pay at the time. 8-Being willing to make a difference in our world, instead of always just going with the flow. We are to make a difference in our world and communities. The challenge is, if salt loses its saltiness what good is it? Can it be made salty again? There was a quote shortly after WWII that went something like this: "They came for the communists but I wasn't a communist so I did nothing, they came for the Catholics but I wasn't a Catholic so I did nothing, they came for the Jews but I wasn't a Jew, so I did nothing. Now, they are coming for me, and there is no one left". Let this motto not be our motto! Let us be the ones who stand up and are counted for what is right. Let us be the ones who are willing to stand up even when standing up is hard and we might get shot at. It is so much easier to look at ourselves in the mirror each day when we have made a difference instead of sitting back and letting someone else do it. When we belong to God and are His children we are salt and light. We have the light of the world shining and living within us. Let us therefore shine our lights so others can see and know that a light is shining.

Prayer: It is so easy to sit back and not get involved. It is even easier to stand back and not say anything. Yet Father you ask us to be salt and light, which means not getting involved and not standing up is not part of your plan for us your children. You are asking us to be people who are willing to make a difference in this world. Help me, have the courage and strength to stand and be counted, even if being counted causes me to come face to face with those who hate you or me. I want to be a history maker. I want to be one who is willing to fight the good fight. With your help I can do all that and more, amen.

Day Forty-nine

Matthew 18:1 'At that time the disciples came to Jesus and asked. Who is the greatest in the kingdom of heaven?'

It is so easy to get caught up in this kind of thinking. Who is the greatest? Who has the most? Who has made it in the world's eyes? Who is on the top of the heap? Who has the top rung on the ladder? Who is the best and most powerful of all? We spend so much time and energy on trying to figure out who the biggest and the best are. Then we strive to be like them. When we listen to the TV advertisements, we are bombarded with ads that tell us this is the best, no this new and improved product is now the best. Use this product and you will be the best and have the most.

Ours is better, no ours is. It is a never-ending story of bigger and better. Our heads spin at times trying to even think it all through. Our head knows better! But we listen anyway and get all caught up in the competition. We know within our hearts that what we are being told is not true. Yet how many times do we rush around trying to make ourselves or our families and friends better than the rest? If we are being honest with ourselves, lots of times! The only struggle with this thinking is God says the least of you is the greatest in the Kingdom. The one who is last will be the first in the end. The rich have a really hard time getting into the Kingdom of God because their riches are here on earth. The poor shall inherit the kingdom. To be truly rich, we need to give it all away. We get by giving. More is less. In God's eyes we are all perfect, whole and complete. In God's eyes we are all already enough and just the way He made us. In God's eyes, we are His precious, chosen, beloved, child whom He loves, cherishes and values. In God's eyes it is not the world's standards that count. What counts is our place in Him. Our place in God holds the true value. In God's eyes we are the most important person alive. In God's eyes we truly matter for no other reason than because God says we matter. I don't know about you but this truth brings peace and joy to my heart knowing no matter what, I am now and will always be loved by God and we always be His chosen, beloved child. It is not what I have or where I have gotten myself to that really matters. What really matters is ----- Am I loved by God and others? It is not what I have that truly counts in life. What counts in life is what I do with what I have and who I share it with. In the end all that truly matters is, what have I done with my life that matters in God's eyes? Have I lived my life to the fullest, being all that I could be? Have I shared my life with others and God? Do I have people who love me and do I love others? If the answer is yes then I have become great in the Kingdom of God. If the answer is no, then maybe it is time to reevaluate my life and life choices. It is not what we have that ultimately matters. What matters is who we are in God's eyes.

Prayer: Thank you, Father, that I matter and am valued, loved and accepted by you. Not for what I do or have, but because I am valued and loved, for just being me the child you created me to be. Help me, to see myself as you see me and to love myself as you love me. Holy Spirit, reveal the truth in me, amen.

Day Fifty

Psalm 139:13-14 'For you created my inmost being; you knit me together in my mother's womb I praise you because I am fearfully and wonderfully made; your works are wonderful, I know that full well.'

Before you were born God knew you. God, knew you before you were given life on this earth. Before breath was in your lungs, you were with God. God gave you life. Before anyone on this earth had a chance to meet you. You were a member of God's family. You existed in God before you existed as a human being. You have value and worth because God says you have value and worth and for no other reason. Your value and worth is based upon who God created you to be and not by life's circumstances. God determines your value and worth; God, nothing else, has a vote in the matter. God held you in the palm of His hand and said you are going to be born as a human being. Why? So you can have the human experience? You were not a mistake! God knew exactly what He was doing when He created you. You were born at just the right time and in the right place. It is so amazing and mind blowing, to know that our being, our spiritual self, was with God, before it was here on earth. Which means we are not mistakes, junk or any other belief that says we are less than valuable and worthwhile. God knew us and we are fearfully and wonderfully made. We, that is you and I and everyone else, is fearfully and wonderfully made. We are here on earth for such a time as this because God decided that this was our time to live. God decided that we have a purpose and reason for being born during this time frame. This is our time for our lives to exist. We are now and have always been known by God and God decided to give us birth and life. Take that in my friends, deep within. We, you and I, are valuable and worthwhile. We, you and I are precious and special. We, you and I, are chosen and have a reason for existing in the here and now. We are not mistakes no matter what circumstances caused our lives to be born, no matter how we came into this world, how or why we were conceived. We were given life because this is our time to live. The circumstances of our birth do not matter. What matters is God knew and formed us in our mother's womb guiding our every breath of life. Let us rejoice and celebrate! Let us tell the world that we matter and we are here because God says it is time and our time. What an amazing and awesome God were serve and love! We are VALUABLE! We MATTER! Hallelujah. We are here because God said we should be here and for no other reason. Our lives are the direct design of God and His plan for us. Let us rejoice and be glad.

Prayer: Thank you, Father God, that I am not a mistake. I may have been a surprise---but I am not a mistake. This is my time and I am here for a reason. Help me, to find out what that reason is and then to live it out to the best of my ability. Holy Spirit, help me to love me, the person I was created to be. Help me, to let go of the lies and live my life in the truth that I am good enough and made by God for a reason and purpose. Thank you, God, for giving me life and helping me to live it. I am truly grateful, amen.

Day Fifty-one

Daniel 3:15-18 'Now when you hear the sound of the horn, flute, zither, lyre, harp, pipes and all kinds of music, if you are ready to fall down and worship the image I made, very good. But if you do not worship it, you will be thrown immediately into a blazing furnace. Then what god will be able to rescue you from my hand? Shadrach, Meshach and Abednego replied to the king, O Nebuchadnezzar, we do not need to defend ourselves before you in this matter. If we are thrown into the blazing furnace, the God we serve is able to save us from it, and he will rescue us from your hand, O king.'

Most of us will never know what it is like to have to choose between God and State. To have to choose between our God and our country! We have the freedom here to be able to have our faith and the ability to practice it without the fear of being thrown into the furnace. We live without the fear of someone pointing the finger and having us arrested because of our faith and relationship with God. For the most part we are free to practice our faith without fear and intimidation. We are so blessed. We do not have to hide our faith or make excuses for the faith relationship we have with God. But what if one day you had to stand before the authorities and choose? What if one day you were arrested and thrown into prison for what you believe or say you believe? What would you do? Would you stand for your faith or would you fall? Is there enough evidence in your life, actions and choices to convict you of being a Christian? Is there enough evidence to convict you of being a person who chooses to live by faith? Could you be charged for having your faith within the lifestyle you live and the choices you make? Am I, you, willing to trust God to be here with you/me no matter what befalls you/me? Will I trust God even if it means standing in front of a blazing furnace or firing squad? Does my faith hold enough value for me that I will not renounce it when it is being put to the test and challenged by the state? In a time of persecution of my faith will I hold fast to what I say I believe? The answer for me is, I pray so? Ultimately, I hope so, but who really knows until the test comes. I don't know what real persecution is. I have never had to face real persecution, especially persecution on a life or death plane. I live in a first world where acceptance of other people's faith is the norm and for that I am truly grateful and thankful. I pray if that day comes I will be like Shadrach, Meshach and Abednedgo and trust my God will save me even if I have to be thrown into a burning hot furnace. I pray if that day comes I will hold fast to what I say I believe and stand firm in my trust relationship with God. I pray I do. I also pray I never have to find out if I will or will not. This lesson has challenged me to ask myself if my relationship with God is in such a place that it is the most important possession I have?

Prayer: Thank you, Heavenly Father, that no matter what befalls us you are there. No matter what we have to face, you face it with us. You are truly a faithful God for whom nothing is impossible. A faithful God who promises to never abandon us, forsake us or leave us orphaned. Father, I choose this day to walk with you. I choose to trust you and to the best of my ability live according to your ways and laws with your help. Help me, Holy Spirit, to be faithful and trust no matter what befalls me, amen

Day Fifty-two

Proverb 18:21 'The tongue has the power of life and death, and those who love it will eat its fruit.'

How true this proverb is. How so very true. Our mouths speak both words that bring both life to the person we are speaking to or brings death. Our words have the ability to heal or hurt. They can bring out the best in others and us or the worst. Our tongues are both healing salve and burning fire. Our tongues can build up or tear down. They can calm a raging storm or cause one to happen. They are so very small yet wield such force. How many times have we said something only to want to take them it back, and change what has just come out of our mouth? When we have allowed our emotions to get the better of us and caused harm and hurt because we were harmed or hurt, we let our tongues be the instrument of pain and more hurt towards other. Not to mention the times we use our tongues to hurt ourselves and to let our human side rule and reign instead of trusting God and God's presence in our life and being. How many times have our tongues been used for evil and not for good? Too many times I feel. The second half of the proverb today teaches us that when we love it we eat its fruit. That fruit can be either positive or negative. There are some who use their tongues to bring life to everyone they meet, greet and have a relationship with, who never say a bad word about any one; if they have nothing good to say, they do not say anything at all. Their tongues are used only for good and not for any thing else. These tongues are instruments of life and bring life to others. There are people who use their tongues for harm even though they do not know the person they are using their words against. There are some of us who use our tongues to cause harm and disharmony to everyone who crosses our paths. They throw out words regardless of where they land or the harm they may cause. The power of our tongue is truly a life or death matter. Either we are bringing life and getting life from the words we are putting out or we are getting death. Our tongues are either being used for the furtherance of God and His Kingdom or it is being used for the furtherance of Evil's kingdom of hurt, death and darkness. The choice as always is our to do as we see fit. To use our tongues to help build others up or to tears them down. To bring either life or death! Which one are we? How are we using the gift of free will that God has given us in the power of our minds, emotions and our tongues? Our tongues really do have incredible power. Let us today use them for bringing life and healing to others and us. Let us commit today to use our tongues in ways that have a positive affect upon those we meet, greet and love.

Prayer: Father, help me to use my mouth, tongue and words to bring life and not death. Put a guard around my mouth so that only words of life flow from me. I am sorry for the times I have used my mouth and words to harm others or cause others harm. Please forgive and restore me for your name's sake. That is not the way I want to live any longer for Jesus' sake and my own, amen.

Day Fifty-three

Proverbs 15:4 'The tongue that brings healing is a tree of life, but a deceitful tongue crushes the spirit.'

A healing tongue is like a tree of life. Our tongues can speaks truth and love and can build up; when they do they are a tongue that bring light and life to the person we are speaking to or with. Kind words and words spoken in season are truly and absolutely life giving. Words that act as a soothing salve cause wars to stop and anger to be stilled. We all know of times in our lives when we were spoken to with words that touched our spirit, our core, right down to the very fibers of our being. We know how we felt afterwards and how those words encouraged us and helped us to gain value in and for our lives. Words we remember as life giving. Life changing words that might have even changed our life's direction and purpose just because someone took the time to speak them. Words that brought value to our lives and who and what we are as people. We know and remember words spoken that were words of truth and life to our very beings even though we did not want to hear them at the time. We all know about deep hurting words. How the deep hurting words go deep into our being, touching the subterranean depths of who we are as a person. We know the affect those hurting words have on our spirits and the fiber of our very selves. A deceitful tongue crushes the spirit. I see it all the time. Someone in a position of power or authority tells a child that they are "not good enough" or will never amount to anything. The child believes the words spoken. They take them to heart. Therefore those damning words cut deep within the child, possibly changing the way the see themselves forever. Even if they were said in jest, the words can cause a child to start down a road proving the not good enough words (lie) they have been told. They spend their whole lives making choices and doing things that prove they are less than. Proving they are the words spoken into their lives. They believe the words and start causing them to be true in their actions and life choices. Words have a very powerful effect on us whether we believe it or not. The expression "sticks and stones may break my bones but words will never hurt me", is so far from the truth. Our bones can heal from the stick and stones but our heart stays broken. Today is a reminder to choose our words carefully and wisely, especially when speaking with children. They believe what we say even if we did not mean it! If we are saying hurting, damaging words they stick to the child like glue. If the words are life giving words they bring life into the child. If they are hurting words, the words can bring an unknowing death to the child we are saying them to. Let us use words that are healing, life giving and positive. Words like a tree of life growing out of us to others we are talking to. Let our words be words of life and truth. Let not harsh or damning words be found in our mouths or on our tongues.

Prayer: I need your help Father. I need it really badly. I know there are times when I let my anger or the upset side of me, rule my tongue and words. I let my feelings get in the way of my words. I am sorry. Help me to think about the words I am saying and to use them to bring life to myself and to others. Let my words bring life and light to all who hear them. Please put a guard around my mouth stopping all words that would cause hurt or harm. In Jesus' name, amen.

Day Fifty-four

Proverbs 25:20 'Like one who takes away a garment on a cold day, or like vinegar poured on soda, is one who sings songs to a heavy heart.'

Picture if you will, you are feeling down and your heart is heavy. You decide to go to the mall just to get out and have a change of scenery. You pass by someone who has a smile on his or her face; then you realize that you yourself have a smile on. Then another person passes you by, they are singing or humming a song to themselves. Before you know it you find yourself humming that same song. You hear people laughing and you smile or chuckle to yourself. You meet someone who takes time to say hi and it lifts your heart. Your trip to the mall has had a positive effect on your mood and your outlook on life. The trip to the mall has shifted your mood. The power of being positive and sharing that positive attitude and posture with others, whether intentionally or unintentionally, has a ripple effect in its ability to shed some light into a dark place. How many times has a simple kind word changed a person's whole day and the way their heart was feeling? I can think of times when my heart has been so heavy and loaded down feeling sorry for myself and I meet someone who has a cheery disposition. I feel better having spent time with their cheerfulness, even if the effect lasted for only a short while. Out of the blue a call comes and the person on the other end says 'not to worry, this too shall pass'. The burden is not as heavy as it was. The heart is not feeling so all alone. The burden is shared and not so burdensome. How about when someone puts their hand on your shoulder and says 'not to worry it will be okay'. Or maybe they do not say anything at all they just put their hand on your shoulder. Kind, words sing to our hearts and spirits. words remind us that God really is in control and we can let go and let God. We are not alone in this big world with no one caring even if it feels that way. Words of life that sing to the heart and help the heart feel lighter and less burdened are more powerful than life itself at times. Simple words or actions have a positive effect on someone, allowing the Holy Spirit in us to ooze out and touch another life. We can be a blessing to others and not even know it. We can be the presence of God to someone just by giving him or her a simple hello or smile. We do not know how our words or actions affect others. Therefore let us be people who are willing to step out with our hellos, smiles and kind words. We may be changing a life and not knowing it.

Prayer: Father, may I use my words, body language, the joy in my spirit and every other good gift you have given me to help bring life back into another person's heart and spirit. Remind me when I forget. Thank you, a simple smile, kind word or the singing of a song can help brighten someone's day. Even mine! Thank you, Jesus, for putting a song in my heart that I can share. I am grateful, amen.

Day Fifty-five

I John 1:9 'If we confess our sins, He is faithful and just and will forgive us our sins and purify us from all unrighteousness.'

As a person who works in the correctional environment I have discovered that being humble and allowing ourselves to live in humility is one of the hardest requests we ask of ourselves. Our pride, arrogance and need to be right get in the way all the time. To walk the path of humility is one of the hardest things we do. So many of us have such a need to be right and on the top rung no matter what it costs others or us. We think by being humble it will make us less than. WRONG! Being humble, in fact shows a greater ability to be who we really are as people. Humility is the path of healing and life for ourselves and our spirits. Confessing our sins is truly cleansing! In fact confession can be the most cleansing thing we ever do. It removes such a load off our spirits and lives. Confession gives us the chance to be real and let go of the secrets and shame that has held us captive for many years. An expression I have heard is. "All may confess, none must confess, some should confess." None of us have to confess. None of us are told that we must sit down and confess all our sins, even the deep dark secret ones. Some of us because of our pasts and the choices we made or others made for us really need to get it out in the open. We need to let go of the darkness and secrets that keep us locked in and bogged down. Confession is the only path that leads to true freedom. No other path has the ability to set us free as the path of confession. That is why confession can be so healing and releasing for us. It truly is the only way we can get our freedom back. It is the only way to get the monkey off our backs. Telling our story and sharing our lives helps release us from the guilt, shame, secrets and prison they hold us in. When we confess before God, ourselves and another human being, we give ourselves permission to enter into the mystery of Christ and His healing presence and power. The act of confession is like a filter, filtering out the toxic memories and beliefs that surround our past and the impact they have upon us. Confessing is the cleansing for our spirits and souls, setting us free from all that is holding us hostage to our past. Telling our story truly does release us from what was and helps to bring us into all that could be. When we risk our story in all truthfulness, God is faithful and just and does purify us from all unrighteousness. Unfortunately the only way to find out if this is true is by risking the truth and telling our story. The only way to enter into the freedom that confessing our past sins and mistakes brings is to step out in trust and telling it just the way it was. We holding nothing back. We putting everything out on the table, then walking away from it, and leave it behind.

Prayer: Father, I need to confess that I am afraid of telling my story and all that I have done or has been done to me. I am afraid of the rejection I may feel and having to go through the pain again. Help me, to trust and risk so that I might be released from the hold my past still has over me and from all unrighteousness. Help me, to trust you and the people you send to help me. Show me, how to pick the right person so that I may release these memories and pain, I do want to be free and to live in freedom. In Jesus' name, amen.

Day Fifty-six

Psalm 150:1-2 'Praise the Lord. Praise God in His sanctuary; praise Him in His mighty heavens. Praise Him for His acts of power; praise Him for his surpassing greatness.'

We hear this message to all the time! Praise God. Give praise to the Lord. Let us praise the name of the Lord. Today we are being told and reminded to take that praise to the highest level. In everything we do, everywhere we go, in all of our thoughts, in every activity during the day, evening or night. No matter what, where, when or why we are to praise the Lord! This is not saying that we are to praise the Lord only when our feelings say "Praise the Lord" or when we think we should praise the Lord. This is saying we are to praise the Lord in everything, in all things, no matter what is happening or how we feel. Why is it so important to praise the Lord? Why do we have to let go of what we are feeling in order to praise the Lord? It is quite simple actually. When we praise the Lord not only does it bless God but it also blesses us. I know personally when I take the focus off of me and put the focus on God, being obedient to the call of praising God, regardless, I feel better. If I am praising God with joy in my heart the joy increases. When I am praising God, even if it's out of an act of obedience and not because I want to, my spirit seems to transform. The heaviness or downtrodden feeling is lifted and I find myself wanting to praise more, and even sometimes getting lost in the praise. Yes we are to praise the Lord, for praising the Lord brings joy to God's heart and ours as well. Another reason for praising the Lord is it makes us feel happy on the inside. Praising the Lord really does bring joy to our heart. This is the wonder and mystery of following God and living in obedience to God; the wonder of living in the blessings that flow from that obedience and the willingness to live according to God's standards and commands. Our God knows all things and gives that knowing to us so that we can reap the blessings and benefits. This is a great mystery yet not so mysterious. When we praise the Lord whether we feel like it or not, the praise opens a channel between God and ourselves, which in turn allows God to move in our spirits and hearts. When we praise God, God chooses to inhabit our praises, which brings the presence of God close and powerful. When we praise, our spirits and hearts forget they are downcast and begin entering into the gift and the power that praising brings. Let us today, remember to praise the name of the Lord our God. Then watch how your day goes.

Prayer: Thank you, Father, for showing us how to be truly human and to live our lives fully with all the blessings of your mercy, grace and love. When we live life according to your plan and purposes we truly do get life abundant. Thank you for loving us so much and for showing us the way even through a simple thing like praise. I will choose to praise your name, Lord, even when I do not feel like it, amen

Day Fifty-seven

2 Timothy 3:13 'What you heard from me, keep as the pattern of sound teaching, with faith and love in Christ Jesus.'

Growing up I heard so many wonderful sayings; at least I thought they were sayings until I grew older and realized that the words were in fact, great words of advice. Sayings like: do unto others, as you would have them do unto you. Always be prepared for you never knew what life might throw your way. Walk with your head up, then you will not bump into too many things along life's path. Look before you leap. A penny saved is a penny earned. I could go on with all the sayings that were given to me as a child. Some of them have changed my life without me even realizing the changes that were taking place. Paul is teaching us the same lesson. What we learn from Scripture and from Jesus Christ in his Word, if applied to our lives as a pattern of sound teaching will give us the resources and abilities we need to live life God's Way with all the benefits and blessings. We will also live life in such a way that it is pleasing to God and beneficial to our lives, and the lives of others whom we meet, greet or know as long time relationships. Sounds teachings that are kept front and center of our life and our life choices will also have a positive effect on us and on the people with whom we have relationships. One of the teachings is God's sound advice to always love first. No matter what is happening or not happening in your life, no matter how we are feeling, no matter what is going on in or around us, God's good advice is to always have love in your heart. That means always doing the higher good for the person we love or have to deal with. It means treating others with honour, dignity and respect at all times, no matter what is happening or not happening. If we do no more than that, our lives will be very different in that we will not be allowing anger, bitterness, resentments or unforgiveness to build up within our hearts and spirits. We will be living according to the greatest commandment to love one another as God has loved us. This in turn brings life, joy and peace to our lives and relationships. Love truly is the answer to all of life! Love covers over more than we can even begin to know or even understand. When we love first, we are allowing life to enter in. We are allowing the light that heals, restores and truly brings more life to be part of us and, everything we do in life. Let us love first, then watch and see how life begins to change around us. Let us choose to honour, respect and guard everyone's dignity, especially our own, for that will in itself change so much around us. Then if we add love; doing the higher good for the people in our lives. Can you imagine the ways life would be different?

91

Prayer: Father, I open my heart and my spirit to living life according to your patterns of sound teaching. Teach me how to live my life in such a way that it is not only pleasing to you, but also to me and to those with whom I have a relationship. I am sorry for all of my wrong choices and decisions I have made and for being so selfish at times. Forgive me and help me to be more like you. Thank you, Holy Spirit, for teaching and helping me as only you can, amen.

Day Fifty-eight

Colossians 4:10 'My fellow prisoner Aristarchus sends you his greetings, as does Mark the cousin of Barnabas. (You have received instructions about him; if he comes to you, welcome him.)'

Today we are being reminded of our need to have hospitality, to be open and receptive to the whole family of God. It is so easy to get caught up in our own little worlds. We are all so busy and have so many demands upon our lives and time. Many of us feel like we are being pulled in every direction. We do not have enough time for what we need to do let alone add more to our already full plates. I do not feel that God is asking us to get even busier. What I feel God is saying is that we need to be more welcoming and receptive to the people in our lives today and then to others. Not busier but more hospitable. Here is an example of how we are to be more hospitable with those already in our lives. How many Sundays do we go to church and only talk to the same people? We do not expand the circle of people we meet and greet on Sunday morning. When new people come to the church do we make them feel welcomed or do we just leave that task for somebody else? If we leave the task to whoever might do it, newcomers may not be made to feel welcomed. Do we share a smile with others or do we just keep our heads down so that our eyes do not have to see what is really going on? Am I open to listening really listening to what people are saying to me, or am I just putting in my time. I have often wondered if I am doing my part to make the family of God a true family? Am I building up the family God has given me or tearing the family down? One way I am living this principle out in my life is to intentionally greet people at church when I am standing at the door or the coat rack. I say hi to every person who crosses my path at church. I lend a helping hand when one is needed. For example, we have someone in a wheel chair that cannot go down stairs for a coffee, so I bring one up for her. She may end up with several coffees, but several coffees are better than none. Another gentleman has eye problems and has a hard time pouring the milk into his coffee. When I see him there I pour the milk for him. Can he pour the milk himself? Yes. Is it easier when I pour it for him? Yes. These are simple things that help make a positive difference within the church family I enjoy Sunday mornings. I pray that we are all those who build up and make the family better and who welcome not only the new member or visitor but also those we see each week. There are always little things we can do to help make our world a better place to live. It honestly only takes a little effort on the part of each member of the family to make a happy loving family. Let us commit to doing our part.

Prayer: Father, I confess my need to stay safe in my little circle of comfortable people. There are so many times when I could be more welcoming and open to new people but choose to stay with those I already know. Forgive me. Help me to reach out to others and to help them feel like they belong to the family of God that we truly are. Thank you, Jesus, for helping me I this area of my life, amen.

Day Fifty-nine

Colossians 4:13 'I vouch for him that he is hard working for you and for those at Laodicea and Hierapolis.'

I have asked this question before. Now after two months of these devotions I will ask the question again. Is there enough evidence to convict you of being a Christian? Is there enough evidence from your life and lifestyle choices for the world to prove to the courts that you are Christian and live as a Christian? Are you living according to God or according to the world? Are we really living our everyday lives according to God's laws and God's call upon our lives as His children? Or are we living according to what the world says is important and what is expected of us? Am I the same on Monday to Saturday, as I am on Sunday morning? Does my choice of language differ on Monday from what it is on Sunday at church? Do I need to hide certain reading materials and bring out others because a Church friend is coming over, or the pastor is on his/her way? Are my house and possessions ready for those visitors anytime, any day? Would a surprise visit catch you off guard and in a place of embarrassment? Paul here was vouching for a brother, who is hard working and will continue to be hard working, no matter where he lives or works. If Paul were here today, could he say the same thing about us? Do we act one way, because people are watching or do we consistently act the same because we know God is watching? Are we living our lives to please the world or to please God? It is so easy to choose to please the world and forget about how we are grieving God's heart. Today is a test for how we are growing and changing in our journey of spiritual growth and healing. A good question we can use to test ourselves is if Jesus were here would I do this? Would I say this, would I act this way? Would I be the same if Jesus were standing here beside me? If Jesus were here beside me right now would He be pleased with my actions and life choices? If the answer is "yes" then keep on, for you are on the right path. If the answer is "no" then maybe you need to do some adjusting in your life choices and actions. If Jesus were here would I still be the same person I am right now or would I have to make some adjustments because Jesus is visible to my eyes? How are you doing? How well are you living your life as a witness to your faith and relationship with God? Can Paul say of you, "I can vouch for him/her that she/he is a hard worker and a good witness for God and her/his relationship with God"? A true challenge to our faith and lifestyle choices!

Prayer: Jesus, I want to be pleasing to you all the time. My heart's desire is to be the same, no matter where I am, whom I am with or what I am doing. I want to live my life in such a way that there is enough evidence to convict me in the court of law for being your child. Help me, Holy Spirit, to be the same in every situation, always pleasing to your heart. Help me, to see those areas of my life that need adjusting. In Jesus' most powerful and mighty name, amen.

Day Sixty

Jeremiah 33:3 'Call to me and I will answer you and tell you great and unsearchable things you do not know.'

I remember when I was in my late teens or early twenties, I was ten feet tall and invincible. I knew all the answers; so don't even bother asking the questions. Today as I have reached the half-century point in my life I realize that knowledge and wisdom and those unsearchable things only come through our relationship with God. True knowledge and wisdom is a gift God grants His children and those who ask God for it. God is so generous in granting and bestowing wisdom upon His children that He gives it to all who are willing to ask for it and then receive it as the gift it is. God takes great delight in helping us learn and grow and be those children He created us to be in the first place. Therefore, if you lack wisdom ask God. If you want to know great and unsearchable things, go to the one knows all things. If you want to have true knowledge and wisdom in you life go to the source. The source will fulfill your request and you will find just what you are looking for. God created us to be already enough! God created us with everything we need in order to be the children He created us to be. If your heart is wanting more, then ask for the more you are searching for. Go to the one who can fulfill your heart's cry and desire. If you feel you are lacking in any area of your life, go to the one who is well able to meet our every need. Call out to God and God will answer you and give even more than what heart feels is lacking. Friends, we have a God who truly loves us in every sense of the word and longs to give good gifts to His children. All we need do is to reach out to God, and ask. The Epistle of James says 'you have not because you ask not' (James 4:2). Let us today start asking for the things we feel we are lacking in our lives, and for the things God desires to place within us. Let us not be in a place of lacking any longer. We have the Most High Living God as our God and He is well able to fill us up to overflowing and so very much more. Let us be like King Solomon, he asked God for wisdom and knowledge so that he could be a good king. Solomon wanted to be a good king who would rule God's people fairly and justly. God gave to Solomon all he asked for and so very much more. God can also give to us. All we need do is ask with a trusting and open heart. God wants to fill us with all the good gifts He has stored up for our asking. Let us risk and ask God for what our heart desires.

Prayer: Father God, I am reaching out to you and I am asking. I am calling out to you to fill me, teach me and tell me great and unsearchable things. I am opening myself up to you, asking you to fill me up so that there is nothing lacking in my life. I want and choose to be the child you created me to be. Help me to take my place, my rightful place as your chosen beloved child. Fill my cup Lord and make me whole, amen.

Day Sixty-one

Colossians 4:2 'Devote yourselves to prayer, being watchful and thankful.'

We as Christians, I feel, do not truly comprehend the power of prayer. We have no idea of how powerful prayer really is and the power God places in our prayers. Prayer is the most powerful tool we could ever have. Prayer truly does change things when we pray in faith. In the Gospels, how many times do we see Jesus going to be alone and spending time alone with God? Jesus knew how important it was to be alone with His Father, how important it was to spend time with His Father to be filled and refilled by His Father. We too need to be alone with our heavenly Father to be filled more and more with the Holy Spirit. We too need to learn from God, and to allow God the opportunity for touching our lives. Prayer is the most powerful tool God has given us. There is nothing more powerful than prayer. Prayer invites the Most High God into our lives. Prayer invites God into the lives of others and every possible situation that we invite God into. Through prayer God is given permission to bring His mercy, grace, love, peace and power into us and into everything we are praying. When we pray our lives are transformed in so many ways. Prayer not only works for the things we are praying for. It works within us as we pray. We do become more watchful of the things that need prayer and in return we get a heart that is filled with thankfulness and gratitude. Our heart becomes more thankful because we see the truth and reality of God in our own lives and in the lives of those we are praying for. My prayer for us all today is that we would pray first then do whatever else needs doing; that our first reaction to all of life would be one of prayer and the inviting of God into all of life and all that life gives us. May we first and foremost turn to God asking for His help and provision rather than to turn to whatever comes next. May we be people of prayer and willing to pray at all times and in all situations. May we invite God into every aspect of our lives and the lives of others we have the privilege of praying for. Prayer really does help change the lives of those we are praying for. It is not hard to see the evidence of prayer in the offenders I work with. I can usually tell those offenders who have someone praying for them; they are more open and receptive to hearing spiritual things. They are more open to making spiritual things their own. I see in offenders who pray a change in attitudes and even beliefs at times. The ones who pray are calmer and have more peace in their lives and hearts. They have joy and amazement when they witness the answer to a prayer, when they see first hand that God does answer prayer. They are often like little children excited by a gift they have been given or the coming of a special occasion. Prayer does work! Therefore let us be people of prayer inviting God into everything and all things.

Prayer: Holy Spirit, remind me to pray. Remind me to take time and invite you into all of life's situations, expecting and knowing you will be there every time I ask and have invited you in. Help me to stay as close as possible to you our heavenly Father, never moving away from you. Never venturing out alone and on my own, but always having you beside me in everything I do, and everything I am. Thank you, Jesus, for teaching us about prayer and the power it has in our lives and the things we are praying for, amen.

Day Sixty-two

Isaiah 59:1 'Surely the arm of the Lord is not too short to save, nor His ear too dull to hear.'

We have the most amazing and awesome God! For there is nothing that is impossible for our God! There is nothing that is beyond the power of our God. There is nothing that is out of the reach of our God. God's arm can reach everywhere. No pit is too deep, no grief too overwhelming, no loss to hard, nothing is beyond the reach of our great God. We have the Most High God on our side who is well able to reach down in every, and all situations to help us and to even save us when we need saving. God's ear is always attentive to our cry. God is never too busy that He cannot hear us when we are calling out to Him. The music is never too loud or the vacuum too noisy. Our God is always there waiting, willing and wanting to help. There is no hole too deep or situation so bad that our God cannot see us through. God can make a way where there seems to be no way. I have seen God do the impossible! I have seen God make a way, where from all human perspectives there was no way. I have watched God open a door or window where there seemed to be a brick wall. I have watched God transform and even remake broken lives so that people could come out of their darkness and into God's light. I have watched God take a hopeless life and turn it into a valued treasure. I have seen God bring life back into a dying spirit and have that spirit begin to truly live again. There is now so much life in their spirit they want to share that life with others, helping them to get out of their darkness. I have seen God expose the lies of a person's life, exposing the hurt and damage those lies have caused. Then God brings revelation and healing, truth and life. I have seen God set the captives free in more ways than I could ever even begin to share with you. I know first hand that our God is real and available to us. All we need do is call upon His name. The name that is above all names and He is there every single time. There is not a single time I can even remotely say God did not answer when called upon. There is no situation or event or individual person for whom God did not appear. Jesus said to Jairus when he was told that his only daughter has died, to just believe (Mark 5:22-43). I say the same to us all. We are just to believe in the power and promises of God and they will be seen in our lives and the lives of others. Just believe! That is the answer. Just believe in who and what God is and who and what He says He is. Then we too will see and believe. We too will have the evidence in our own lives that God is who He says He is. When we call upon His name great and incredible things will happen in our lives as well. Reach out today my friends putting your whatever into the hands of the one who can help you through. Put your problem, struggle or pain into the hands of the one who can help you deal with them. Just believe and watch and see our Great God at work.

Prayer: Here I am, Father. I come to you in my brokenness and need. I am crying out to you. Help me. I am asking you to reach down and touch my life and my spirit so that I too, can become whole. I need your touch, in my life, so I can come out and live. Thank you, Father, for sending your Son Jesus, making all of this possible. Thank you, Holy Spirit, for touching my life, for making me whole, and for coming when I called upon you. Thank you for telling us the truth and being who you said you were and still are. In gratitude and awe I say thank you and amen.

Day Sixty-three

Isaiah 60:1 'Arise, shine, for your light has come and the glory of the Lord rises upon you.'

No matter how you are feeling this is a true statement. One that we can trust no matter what our feelings are saying to us. Arise, shine for your light has come and the glory of the Lord does rise upon you. The glory of the Lord is present, in all of God's creation. You are a part of God's creation; therefore the glory of the Lord arises upon you. The glory of the Lord is here. The light is shining. We give into our feelings at times and forget that God's light is shining within us. That we are safe and secure in that love and light. Rest assured, my friends, that God is in you and His light is shining brightly in your heart and spirit. Sometimes all we need do is believe it on our faces and that very light in us shines through us in new and very real ways. Have you told your face lately that God is in you and you are in Him and He in you, that God loves you and is in love with you? It is true; therefore you are the child of the Host High God with all the perks, benefits and blessings. Maybe it is time to tell yourself or reinforce the truth within your heart, spirit and face. God's light is shining in your heart, life and spirit. The glory of the Lord is all around; trust God's presence and you will see His glory. Trust God's truth and promises, and you will see God. Trust God's Word, it will be manifested in your life. Arise, arise from whatever it is that is holding you back and let the light of God shine upon you, through you and in you. The light has come into the world therefore it is in you and me. Rejoice and be glad your light has come and the glory of the Lord rises upon you. Rejoice and be glad for you are safe and secure in the light of God's love and presence in your life. We are so blessed. Blessed beyond measure. Blessed beyond our wildest hopes and dreams. Let us begin to live as those who are loved and blessed of the Lord of all light and true life. 'Arise, shine, for your light has come and the Glory of the Lord rises upon you', both now and always. We have so much to be glad about and so much to rejoice in and over. Our Lord has come and His Glory shines within and upon us. Amen and amen. We are alive in Him who gives life. We are alive in the Glory and Light of Jesus the true light of the world. Rest assured my friends, rest in the power and promises of our Lord and God. Rest in trust and faith and you will see the light and glory of our great God rest upon you shining in your life and heart.

Prayer: Hallelujah and thank you. My heart sings for joy. I have the glory of the Lord within me, and within my life and spirit. I am no longer alone or on my own. I have the glory of the Lord with me now and always. Hallelujah! I am an adopted child of the Most High God who is my Father and Dad, my Saviour and King. My all in all! Thank you, Jesus, for shining your great light in me and releasing your glory in my life and heart, amen.

Day Sixty-four

Genesis 27:34 'When Esau heard his father's words, he burst out with a loud and bitter cry and said to his father, Bless me---me too, my father.'

The cry of every child's (person's) heart! We all need the blessing of our father. We all need to know the blessing of being blessed by our fathers. When we are not blessed we too cry out with that same agonizing and deep felt cry of Esau. Father bless me—me too, my father bless me too! We are designed, created to have the blessing of our earthly fathers. When our earthly fathers do not bless us, there is a void within and our cry is as Esau's. Bless me father—me too. What does it mean to be blessed? What does a blessing look like? To be blessed is to be validated, loved, told you have value and worth. Told that you matter. A blessing is the words of love and truth every child needs to hear. The words of love that help make us whole and valued by our father/parent. The blessing of a father helps the child know who they are. When we are not blessed, our sense of self is not fostered and developed. Without the father's blessings there is a void, a hole, in our lives. A hole that says we are not really truly valuable and worthwhile. That is why, when Jacob got Esau's blessings, Esau burst out with a loud and bitter cry, BLESS ME----ME TOO, MY FATHER, BLESS ME TOO. If you are lacking your earthly father's blessing, then reach up to your heavenly Father because He longs to bless you. He longs to tell you who you are and how valuable and worthwhile you really are. He longs to tell you how precious and special you are and how you matter, that you matter more than anything else. Your Heavenly Father wants you to know that you are His chosen Beloved created to be loved by Him. Your heavenly Father, created you to be valuable and worthwhile, to truly matter. You are already enough! You are good enough! You have everything you need to be the child God created you to be. All you need to do is start receiving the blessings God has for you and living this truth out in your life. Receive your blessing. Receive the blessing that is yours and fill that emptiness that sits in your heart and spirit. Receive the truth and allow your spirit to live and have life. Then pass your blessing on to your children and tell them that they are valuable and worthwhile and that they matter. Tell them how much they matter to you and how much they mean to you. How important they are to you. Tell them you are glad they came into your family and life. Tell them they belong and have a place all their own. Tell them that you love them and how glad you are to have them. Bless your kids; it is the best gift you will ever give them. Give your child the hug they are longing to have with the words of love attached to the hug. The truth is if we do not bless our children others will bless them for us. The others may not be the ones you want blessing your children! The drug dealer, pimp, gang, wrong boyfriend or girlfriend----the list is long of those who are very willing to bless our children telling them how important they are to them.

Prayer: Thank you, Father, for making me already enough! It is beginning to sink in---yes Me---I, am enough, good enough. Thank you, for creating me to be a valuable and worthwhile human being. For filling me with what ever I needed to be the child you created me to be. Thank you for creating me to be a lovable and worthwhile person. Today I am choosing to believe this truth. Help me, Holy Spirit, to move it deep into the very fiber of my being, amen

Day Sixty-five

Matthew 17:20-21 'Jesus replied, because you have so little faith. I tell you the truth, if you have faith as small as a mustard seed you can say to this mountain, Move from here to there, and it will move.'

It does not take much faith in order for God to move in our lives or the lives of others. In fact it takes very little faith! If we have the smallest amount of faith, the same amount of faith found in the capacity of a mustard seed, (which is one of the smallest seeds) we could say "move" to the mountains in our lives, and they would move. We could say to the roadblocks in our lives "out of the way" and out of the way they would go. I know first hand the small amount of faith it takes for God to move in our lives. I have witnessed God move mountains through the smallest amount of faith. I have witnessed God move very large mountains in people's lives. Mountains of fear, mountains of shame, regret, pain, guilt, hurt, darkness, lies and so on. If we just choose to believe that God can move the mountain, the mountain will be removed! God wants us free! God wants us living as free children. In His freedom! Free from our pasts that haunt us in our present. Free from all the things that keep us locked in our self made prisons. All we need do is ask God to open the prison door and it shall be opened. Release us from the shame and the shame is released. God can and will set us free from the darkness and lies holding us back. God will move mountains if we but ask Him to. That is God's heart's desire for us His children. Yes, faith is a gift given to us by God in His great mercy and grace. It is also a choice to believe in what God is saying in His Word and the moving of that Word spoken to our hearts. Ask for the gift of faith and faith will be given to you. Just believe and it will come to pass. We don't know how, but it will. `And we know that in all things God works for the good of those who love him, who have been called according to His purpose'. (Romans 8:28) Just have faith and watch and see all that will happen in and to your life. Just chose to believe and God will do the rest. Step out in faith and God will make sure you do not step out in vain. Let yourself trust in God and God will prove Himself trustworthy. We do our part, which is to step out in faith and God does the rest. No matter how small your faith is, it is big enough to see God's handiwork manifest in our lives. All it takes is enough faith to fill a mustard seed and we will see God in all His Glory. All is takes is for us to let down our defenses, hand to God our fears and whatever else is holding us back. Place them in God's care then watch God move in your life. Watch God start removing your mountains. Step out, my friend,

Growing in Your Spiritual Journey

in trust and the small amount of faith you have. What do you have to lose?

Prayer: Holy Spirit, help my unbelief. Help me to have faith, faith that God is who He says He is and that if I ask God, God will and can move the mountains in my life. I am asking for my faith and trust in you, God, to be strengthened so that I can just believe. Thank you, Holy Spirit, for filling my heart and spirit with faith. Thank you, for filling me with faith that can move mountains. Thank you for never lying to me and for always being the faithful, awesome God you say you are. I choose to believe and have faith in you. In Jesus' name Amen.

Day Sixty-six

Matthew 15:18 'But the things that come out of the mouth come from the heart and these make a person unclean.'

We spend a lot of time, energy and effort to ensure that our outer bodies, our outer beings are clean and neat and tidy. Our outsides look great, but what about our insides? We often spend so little time ensuing our inner selves are clean, neat and tidy. The Scripture before us today is telling us that it is not so much the outside of our beings that we need to be spending our time, energy and attention on. It is our insides, which needs our focus and attention. For what flows out of the mouth comes from our hearts. It is what comes out of our mouth that truly shows where our heart is. It shows what condition our heart is in. If what is coming out of the mouth is clean and pure then the heart is clean and pure. But if what is coming out of our mouths is hurtful and angry and filled with lots of painful energy then we know our hearts are not in the right place. What is clean, neat, and tidy is filled with love, joy and peace, which comes from our focus on God. If out of our mouths is flowing the unclean, then we need to do some house cleaning in order to make our insides as clean as we make our outsides. If we have a heart that is angry, we may be using a lot of angry words or heated force in our choice of words. If our heart has been betrayed, we may keep people away and use words that push them away. If there is fear in our heart, we may use silence or scared words, anxious words to voice our heart. The reality is where our heart is, is usually where our mouth is as well. I have noticed that with the offenders with whom I work. When they first come into the institution their language is usually very colourful and filled with words that are not very wholesome. After they have been in the treatment mode for awhile they start to want to clean up their use of colourful words and even ask for ways to help them change. Their outsides want to reflect the changes that are beginning to happen in their insides, their heart. Another example is most of our offenders come in with large anger problems. They have used anger in a variety of ways to help meet their needs. We start working on why they are angry and what the root cause of their anger is. Together we identify where their anger started and why it is there in their life. Once the root point is found, we then pull out the root and allow healing to fill the hole. The reason for the anger is uprooted; therefore, the need for the anger is removed. The offender discovers him/herself on a much deeper level seeing who they are without their anger. They discover they do not need to be angry any longer and can have patience with life and others. Their use of anger starts to drop off. When we look at how we react on the outside of us and the ways we act or react we begin to see what our heart really does look like. What condition is your heart in?

Prayer: Father, it is true, I spend a lot of time and energy on how I look and what my outside looks like. I need to spend time cleaning up my insides as well. Show me the areas of my heart that are unclean and need work. Show me how I can clean up my heart so that it is clean and whole as well. Thank you, Jesus, and Holy Spirit, for helping me, amen.

Day Sixty-seven

Joshua 23:14 'Now I am about to go the way of all the earth. You know with all your heart and soul that not one of all the good promises the Lord your God gave you has failed. Every promise has been fulfilled; not one has failed.'

Joshua is pointing out to us and to the Israelites that God is a faithful God who does not break promises and does not go back on His Word. No matter what is happening in God's creation He will never go back on a promise He has made. It is the one thing we can trust with everything we are and everything we have. If God says He will do something it will be done! It not be the way we want it to be done or in our timing, but it will be done. When we look at all the promises in Scripture we see that everyone has been fulfilled, except the last promise of the coming of Jesus for the second time. Our God has faithfully kept every other promise. Now let us bring those promises down to a personal level. God promised that He would never leave us nor forsake us. We may at times not feel God's presence but that does not mean He is not there; whenever we call out to God, God answers. Whenever we reach up He is reaching down. Whatever is happening in our lives God is right there with us. In Joel 2:25 'God promised to give back the years that were stolen'. Take a look at your life and see how God is repaying you for what was stolen from your life and rejoice. If you cannot see the ways, ask God to point them out to you for they are there. How about the promise to Noah to never flood the earth again? We have had terrible rains and flood times but none that would cover the entire earth. Our God is a trustworthy God who does keep His promises. All we need do is trust God, and keep asking for those promises to be fulfilled in our lives. How about the promise to Israel that it would never be completely destroyed, that there would always be a remnant that would survive. With all that Israel has gone through over the centuries and being such a small nation, odds are that they would have gone the way of the obsolete like many other nations and peoples. But no! They are still here. Why? Because God promised that they would not be wiped from the earth. They would always have a voice and a people. Many conquering nations have tried to wipe them out so as to erase them from the pages of history. Many have tried, but no one can because of God's promise to them, that said no one would. There would always be a remnant upon the earth. We have a faithful God for whom nothing is impossible. We have a God who is worthy of our trust and who is trustworthy. We can put our hand in God's as His child knowing in our heart of hearts we are safe and secure. That is a promise and a promise we can take to the bank! God is faithful. Look around you asking God to open your eyes to His faithfulness. You might be surprised!

Prayer: Father, my trust has been betrayed so many times in the past. I find it hard to trust! I want to trust you and your promises but I am afraid to trust at times, help me. Help me to trust at all times and show me what it means to trust you. Show me again and again that you are who you say you are, so that I can build up my faith and trust in you. With you, Heavenly Father, this will be accomplished in my life, amen.

Day Sixty-eight

1 Peter 1:13 'Therefore, prepare your minds for action; be self-controlled; set your hope fully on the grace to be given you when Jesus Christ is revealed.'

Get yourself ready for action. Get yourself ready for the grace that is given to you when Jesus the Christ is revealed to you. Each day is a new day in our relationship with God. Each day has its struggles and joys. Each day brings new beginnings and new endings. As we grow in our relationship with Jesus, each day brings new revelation of who Jesus is and who we are in His love and grace. Everyday has something new; therefore, we ought to be in a place of openness and action in order to receive and grow in it. What I have learned during my years as a Christian is, I have to be in a place of being receptive to God and God's blessings and revelations in order to receive them. The more open I am, the more I can receive the blessing that comes from being a child of God through His Son Jesus Christ. I have to have my heart open and ready to allow God in deeper. My mouth has to be open in order for God to fill it. Honestly, there are times when I do not want to do my quiet time every morning and every night. There are times when I would rather be lazy and do something else—like watch TV or sleep. There are times when I do not want to have to preach another sermon or offer another service. There are times when I have to force myself to sit down and focus my attention towards God and our relationship. That is my human, lazy, self-centered side. There is no self-control in that side of me. My self-control needs to come from my spiritual side that sets its hope fully on the grace given to us through Jesus Christ. Whether I feel like doing my quiet time or not, I still do it. I still open my life and heart to the presence of God through being quiet before Him. Then and only then do I receive the blessing that comes from being obedient and in the action mode of my faith. The grace of God flows for a couple of reasons; 1) I am being faithful to our relationship and spending time with the one I say I love and 2) I am being blessed for that faithfulness and willingness to set myself aside and spend time with my God. The reality is Jesus is very often revealed to me in new and more real ways because I choose to stay open to God and His revelatory presence. There truly is a blessing in the faithfulness and willingness to follow the hope and glory of God in an active, self-controlled manner. I can choose to give into my laziness or I can choose to be faithful in my relationship with the one I say I love. When we love someone, we want to be close to him/her. We want to spend time together and enjoy each other's company. It is the same with our relationship with God; in order for it to grow and strengthen we need to spend quality time with Him. We need to grow the relationship.

Prayer: Father, I repent for the times when I would rather do something else and not be with you. I repent for wanting life my way and on my terms and conditions. Forgive and help me to have a greater and deeper desire to spend time with you and be faithful to our relationship. Help me, to be more self-controlled so that your grace may be revealed to me in new and more real ways. Thank you, Jesus, for loving me the way you do and for wanting to spend time with me. Remind me when I am slacking off, amen.

Day Sixty-nine

1 Peter 2:24 'He himself bore our sins in his body on the tree, so that we might die to sin and live for righteousness; by his wounds you have been healed.'

Jesus bore our sins! Jesus paid the price for our sins. The debt caused by our sins has been hung on the tree of sacrifice, which Jesus bore when He chose to hang on the cross. Jesus stood in our place paying what we owed, therefore releasing us from the debt. We get to become dead to sin so that we can live new lives. We are free to take on a new life, the new life of righteousness and freedom in Christ. It would be like someone coming to you and offering to pay your mortgage off just because they want to. Or like someone announcing in court that they are willing to do your jail time. They are willing to pay the price for you; you are free to go on with your life because another person is paying your debt. You are not responsible for it any longer. That person stands in your place paying for your choices and mistakes. When Jesus chose to hang on the tree and be crucified in our place, He paid the price for our debt to God. Jesus paid the debt of sin and the consequences our sins have caused. The choice Jesus made to stand in our place offers us the choice of how we will live our lives both here on earth and hereafter. We can be free to live as debtless people before God, to have a clean slate, and to be completely free and washed of everything we have ever done or not done. When Jesus hung on the cross He paid the sin debt of every human being. Every person on this planet earth who ever lived or will ever live has been given the same gift. It is called the grace of God, God's unmerited loving favor. God's grace is extended to everyone, bar none. The challenge is will we take the gift of grace and the payment of our debt? Will we accept that Jesus paid our debt for sin? Will we say yes to God through His Son Jesus Christ in order to receive the payment? The mortgage money is there to pay off the mortgage. You still need to take the money and pay the bill. The sentence has been handed down, yes, someone else is willing to do your time, but you have to agree to the gift, you have to agree to that person doing your time for you. The gift of being made right with God is being offered, we still need to humble ourselves and take the gift. We need to receive the gift as ours and allow the payment to take place. The choice is ours, either we take the gift or reject it. If we take the gift, the next step is righteousness before God and the healing of our spiritual selves. God restores us as His children and heirs. The other choice is turning our backs on the gift and rejecting the gift and staying in your sin, your wrong choices and mistakes. The gift is redemption, being brought back into a place of balance and rightness. We decide what we do with the gift God is offering us. The choice is always ours to make. That is the love God extends to us. God's love, that allows us to choose for ourselves what we will do and accept into our lives and spiritual selves.

Prayer: Jesus, I accept your gift of payment for my sin (my selfishness and self-centeredness). I accept the price you paid for me. So that I can be free from what was and brought into all that you have for me as a child of yours. I am sorry for all that I have done and open my heart and life to you. Forgive and set me upon the path of righteousness for your name's sake, I receive your payment for me and all I have done and will ever do, amen.

Day Seventy

1 Peter 3:9 'Do not repay evil with evil or insult with insult, but with blessing, because to this you were called so that you may inherit a blessing.'

Some of us were taught "don't get mad get even". As we go through life there are times when we find ourselves being hurt by someone we trust or love. We find ourselves in a place of wanting to give back an evil with another evil or an insult for an insult. We want ours back; we want the scales brought back to a place of even. Only there can never be a place of even because even means, I get a little bit more. Now what do we do? We try to get even; you hurt me so I will hurt you just a little bit more. Then we are even. John Paul Getty was once asked "When is enough, enough?" John Paul Getty was a famous economist and financier. The question that was asked was regarding money. When do we have enough money? It also applies to revenge, getting back from the one who has hurt us. The answer John Paul gave was "when you have a little bit more". In others words we never have enough money. We will always want to have a little bit more than what is now ours. That is also true with causing hurt for hurt and insult for insult. We can never have enough when getting even. We always want just a little bit more. We always want that little bit more to right the scales in our favor. You hurt me; I hurt you a little bit more. Then you need to hurt me a little bit more and I hurt you a little bit more and so on and so on. It never stops. The only way it stops is when we stop it and say enough. I am going to bless you instead of trying to get even. I am going to let this go for it is costing me too much to keep this pace up. I am moving away from this trap. I am choosing to move into the blessings and inheritance God has for me. I am going to live life according to God's ways and not the way of the world. Enough! Yes, you have hurt me or insulted me or caused me pain in some way, but I am not going to take it to the next step. I am going to bless you and let it go. Not only is it the right thing to do. More importantly it is God's command for healthier living and a longer life of living in freedom and blessings. When we choose to bless, not only are we walking away from the one-up-manship, we are moving in God's mercy, grace and love, which is far better. We get forgiven by God and set free from the one-up-manship, because we choose not to harbor the need to get even. We lose ourselves from the continuum of never being enough. Being free to love the other person even though they have hurt us. I am not saying you have to trust them, but you can love them and set them free from your spirit. The releasing opens a door for the blessings of God to pour down upon us. The blessings pour down because we are not blocking ourselves with anger, bitterness, resentments, hurts, etc. The pathway is free and clear for incoming blessings plus everything else God wants to pour into us and our spirits and lives. The challenge is to not get caught up in the need to get even and have just a little bit more but to let go of whatever has hurt us and to move away from the bondage and pain it causes in our hearts and spirits.

Prayer: Father, thank you, for this valuable lesson today. Thank you, for teaching me the freedom of choosing to bless someone who has hurt me. Choosing to bless so that I can be free to get on with my life and not get caught up in the little bit more syndrome. I am blessed. Thank you, Father. Thank you for this wonderfully freeing lesson today. I am truly blessed. You are so wonderful to me! Amen.

Day Seventy-one

1 Peter 4:8 'Above all, love each other deeply, because love covers over a multitude of sins.'

Love does cover over a multitude of sins in ways that go beyond belief and reason at times. In my work with offenders I have seen, the power of love at work and how it does change lives. One of my volunteers lost her father.

Yes, he was 91 years old. Yes, it was his time to go home to be with God; yes, yes, yes. I asked the offenders if they wanted to write cards to the volunteer and gave them no real direction except the suggestion to write the cards. The love that was expressed in those notes was amazing! There was deep-heart felt compassion and caring. Why would they even take the time to think about the notes, let alone write them? The answer is not hard or complicated. It is because the volunteer loves them and they know it. The volunteer shares herself with them from a love perspective, with purity of heart and a deep sense of caring and they know it. They know they are loved and not judged. They know that this is a way to give back to the volunteer when she needed some giving back. Love is the answer to all of life and life's hurts and pains. Love allows the other person the courage to risk and to trust. It helps bring out the true side of them and see how much better it is to live as free people who are able to love and be loved without strings attached. Love changes the darkness into light and the despair into joy. Love really does allow the person we love the courage to risk life and live. When we have been hurt a lot or been betrayed or rejected, when we have tried to love and be loved, it is hard to put our love out there for fear it will be stomped on or abused or misused again. When we love from a pure attitude and without strings attached there is a calling in our hearts to respond to the love that is being poured out to us. Our hearts will want to respond and risk being loved again, for love is the true calling of each of our hearts. Pure love allows us to see beyond what the person has done or not done. Pure love takes the person at face value which in turn gives them permission to venture forth to receive the gift of love we are offering. I see it all the time. The offenders say things to me like, "I know you talk to us from your heart and you care about us and about who we are. I know I can risk and trust with you because you are not out to get us or use the textbook stuff on us". That is the power of love and the truth of what love is. Love does cover over a multitude of sins and all that the sins have done to us. The call is to love with a pure heart with no strings attached. Yes, that is a major risk but the blessings out weigh the possibility of getting hurt. We need to be wise in the ways we love others but we also need to be free to love and be loved. Love truly is the answer. When we love first and foremost we can change the world around us. Love can change us.

Prayer: I wonder if I have ever known what true love is? With your help, Father, I can know true love and all that true love means. Help me to love and be loved with a pure and simple heart. Help me to trust and love as a child with the simplicity of a child. Thank you, Holy Spirit, for teaching me about love and the ability to love. Thank you for first loving me just the way I am. Help me to love others with the same kind of love, amen.

Day Seventy-two

1 Peter 5:7 'Cast all your anxiety on him because he cares for you.'

Cast, throw, heave, pitch, chuck, toss all (not some) all your cares, anxiety onto God who cares for you and loves you. That is, give all, every care and anxiety to God and allow God to care for you. Our God is well able to take care of us and supply our every need. Are you anxious about your finances? Give them to God and ask Him to help you. Are you worried about your life or your children? God loves you both more then you can imagine and I know He can well take care of you and them. Are you anxious about an illness in your life or the life of someone you love? Give God an open door to work in and through your illness or the illness of another. Do you need people in your life to love you and help you? Are you asking God to supply your need for a family or friends who will love you and be there for you? Or are you sitting in your mud puddle feeling sorry for yourself? God can only work in our lives in those areas of our lives we give Him permission to work in. If we are holding on to our worries or anxieties, God has to let us stay there. It is the free will gift God has given us. Are you hanging onto your cares and worries? Are you holding on to them real tight? If you are then you are on your own. God is not helping you. If you are inviting God into your cares, worries and anxieties, God is right there He wants and willing to help you get through whatever it is you are worried or anxious about; He is always there. There is a proverb that says, "if you worry, why pray and if you pray, why worry?" What good advice! If you are praying about something and offering it up to God and asking God for His help, why are you taking it back and holding it tight once again? If you are hanging on to whatever it is you are praying about, then why are you wasting your time and energy praying? Let God be God in the situation. Worrying or being anxious about something or someone is not going to change the person or situation. Active prayer will, however, change it. Being anxious is not going to help whatever you are anxious about. That will stay the same. What will change the anxiety is inviting God into whatever it is you are anxious about. Prayer is the most powerful tool we have; we have learned that lesson. Let us use it fully and watch and see how God works out the answers to our prayer and helps as only God can. Is it time to get off our rocking chairs of worry and start living again? Is it time to take our lives back from worry so that we can truly live again? If the answer is yes, let us cast, throw, heave, pitch, chuck or toss all our cares, worries, or anxieties upon the one who can truly do something about them. Let us cast our worries onto God asking for His help, courage and strength to see us through.

Prayer: Jesus, I cast all my cares, worries, anxiety and whatever else is holding me back onto you and accept your help. I accept your ability to fill me with what I need in order to be the child you created me to be. Today, I am choosing to trust you with all of my life and the lives of those I love. With your help I can do all things; even cast my anxieties, worries and cares upon you. I am sorry for worrying and being anxious. Forgive me, and fill me with your peace and the ability to live in your peace. I really do want to be free from my need to worry or be anxious. Help me, Father, to accomplish this, amen.

Day Seventy-three

2 Peter 3:9 'The Lord is not slow in keeping his promise, as some understand slowness. He is patient with you, not wanting anyone to perish, but everyone to come to repentance.'

This passage before us today is a hard one to bring into our spirits and lives at times. We can be so impatient! We want what we want when we want it and that was yesterday. When God asks us to be patient with ourselves, and others, and with Him, it is because God is not finished with them or us. This in turn makes us upset and even more impatient. Sometimes God cannot heal us because we are holding onto unforgiveness or bitterness. God cannot move in our lives because we are filled up with resentments or anger. God says we have to let go of the unforgiveness, the resentments and bitterness and then He can move in our lives and heal our diseases. God is not being slow in answering our prayers He is being patient. Waiting for us to get down and honest with ourselves and those things we are still hanging onto that block God's ability to work in our lives and spirits. God is slowly and patiently waiting for us to humble ourselves and let go of those things that hold us back or in bondage. God is waiting for us to repent. Repentance is being honest with God regarding the things we have done or not done in our lives. Repentance is giving our selves permission to be humble, regretting our choices and actions, and telling it as it is. Repentance is turning the opposite direction and walking differently and making different choices with our lives and our reaction to life. Repentance is making a conscious choice to handle ourselves differently and to be honest in our dealing with ourselves, others and God. To choose honesty and truth causes life to be and not life-stealing. God wants all of us to come to the honesty of repentance and truth in all of our dealings. Why do we need to humble ourselves and repent? So that God can keep His promises in our lives and give us all the blessings, mercy and grace He has stored up for us as His children. God cannot bless that which is against who and what He is. God's grace is there for us only if we are willing to take it and make it our own. Example: If you are choosing to give your life away to drugs or alcohol and let the drugs and the alcohol cover up your hurts, pains and past, then God's grace and mercy are held back because God cannot go where He is not invited. If you repent of your use of drugs and alcohol and ask God to help you overcome them, then God can release His promise of healing and restoration into your life and spirit. God needs us to partner with Him in our lives and life journey. When we do God, is right there fulfilling His promises. The gift of free will says, we choose whether God's promises are released within us or held back. Free will says God is invited or held back. Free will determines God's presence and promises in our lives. In other words we choose either life or death in our life choices and dealings. We choose, no one else.

Prayer: Heavenly Father, I am sorry that I have been holding on to unforgiveness and bitterness in my life. I have allowed it to separate me from you in those areas. Forgive me and help me to forgive others. Help me to receive all that you have for me today. Set me free from my anger and resentments and help me to love even those people who have greatly harmed me. With your help, Jesus, I can accomplish this. Thank you, for loving me and forgiving me. Help me, to do the same, amen.

Day Seventy-four

1 John 3:1 'How great is the love the Father has lavished on us, that we should be called children of God! And that is what we are! The reason the world does not know us is that it did not know him.'

What does it mean to lavish? Picture yourself in a swimming pool or large body of water, the water is all around you, there is no part of you that is not touched by the water. The water is touching every part of your being. That is what it means to have the love of the Heavenly Father lavished on you in its great abundance and truth. His love is poured out on us in such great abundance that it is like being in a swimming pool or lake surrounded by all the love He has already, in the past, lavished upon us. All that love is open and available to us each and every day. God at the creation of the world chose to love us His creation/children. God chose to love us with such a great measure of love that it not only fills us but surrounds us as well. There is such an abundance of God's love that it never runs dry. God's love is constant and it never stops overflowing towards us, thus filling us and keeping us safe in His love. God's love is like the `never ending story---it keeps coming and flowing no matter what. There is no end to the love God has for us and there never will be an end. If that was all God did was love in the lavishing way He does, it would be enough, but God does not stop there. God takes it one step further and calls us His children. We are the children of God. We are part of God's family! We are not orphans or lost children. We are the children/child of the Most High God who chooses to be our Father and lavish His love upon us. We are a part of the family of God with a place all our own, a place that has our name on it, a place where we can rest, be loved and feel at peace and ease. A place in God where we can feel totally safe and secure! A place where we are never alone (we might be by ourselves, but never alone) for the Father is always with us no matter what is happening or not happening in our lives! The promise of God is to never leave us, forsake us or depart from us in any way regardless of what we are doing or feeling.....GOD IS ALWAYS HERE WITH US LAVISHING HIS LOVE DOWN UPON EACH AND EVERY ONE OF US AT ALL TIMES AND IN EVERY WAY. What more can we ask for? Have you ever seen the Kraft Dinner commercial where the four boys are standing in the kitchen waiting for the cement truck to back up to the window? Mom is in the living room and shouts to the boys to not make a mess. The boys are standing holding their bowls and spoon waiting. All of a sudden the cement truck starts pouring the Kraft Dinner into the kitchen right on top of the boys. You see the boys with their bowls and spoons surrounded by all this Kraft Dinner. Got to love that commercial for it is just the way our God is! We are in the middle of His love just like the boys are standing in the middle of all that Kraft Dinner. What a wonderful God we have! We are truly loved by the Father, our Dad. We are loved, amen.

Prayer: How can I ever say thank you for loving me the way you do, Father? I am sorry for pushing you away at times and not letting you love as your heart longs to. I never knew you loved me-----you loved me that much. I choose today to receive the love you have for me, help me to open my heart and let your love fill me. I want to be a part of your family. I want to be apart of you and you of me. Thank you, for loving me with your lavishing love. I am truly and totally grateful, amen

Day Seventy-five

1 John 3:11 'This is the message you have heard form the beginning: We should love one another.'

There is no other life message more important than the message to love one another. The most important act we can do in life is to love each other and love each other well. When we love first, we do not have to let our mistakes bring destruction upon our relationships, because everything we do in life is from the perspective of doing what is best for ourselves, and the other person or people in our lives. When I do my best for you even if the end result is not as I intended it to be, at least I gave it my best shot. My motives were clean, pure and innocent. Therefore, even if it falls apart or misses the mark, it was not intentional; no harm was intended, even if harm happened. We can accept each other much more readily when the motives of the other person were not intended to harm or cause hurt/harm. It just means we are human and as humans we make wrong choices and mistakes. The wrong choice or mistake was not to harm or hurt but because we are not perfect. We know that sometimes bad things happen even when we did not intend them to. That is the amazing joy of being human. We can be in error. We are not perfect. We can make mistakes and still live in love and loving relationships. The relationship stays strong because no harm or hurt was intended. The harm or hurt comes from the reality that we will at times makes very wrong choices and mistakes that may hurt ourselves or others. Therefore living in imperfection is acceptable and forgivable. Mistakes are just part of all that life is and holds. We love and are loved even though we make terrible wrong choices and really bad mistakes, because love is the key to living life, to truly living life. Love is living life freely, without holding to what was, but moving on to all that comes with a new day. With pure, clean, innocent love we can trust the other person, knowing that their intention is to love us and not harm us. That is true freedom. Then we able to love each other, knowing that the ones we love will make mistakes and wrong choices for that is what happens in life. The security comes from the knowing that it was just that a mistake or wrong choice, and not an intentional harming or hurting. Our humanity actually gives us permission to not be perfect and to allow others the same freedom. Our love is still freely given for we know that in the end the love we share is stronger than the mistakes we make. We know true love is there for the higher good of the one we are choosing to love and be loved by. The love is not going to be used or abused.

Prayer: Thank you, Lord, that we love you and you love us love us freely and without reservation. Thank you that our first love is in you. Therefore we have the security and ability to love others because no matter what happens you, Father, always love us. No matter what life brings we are always loved by you and are safe in your arms of love. Father, that gives us the freedom and safety we need in order to truly risk our love, knowing that there will be times when the risk brings hurt and harm. Yet we are always safe and secure in you and in your love for us. I am grateful for the love you have given to me, yes even me, amen.

Day Seventy-six

1 John 4:19 'We love because God first loved us.'

Such a simple yet such a profound statement! We love because God chose to first love us. We know what true love is because God in His infinite love and mercy chose to love us and be a part of our lives, even the tiniest details of our lives. We get to know what true love is because God our Heavenly Father teaches us to love and what it really means to love and be loved. Because of the Fathers love for us we get to know how to love others. We can allow ourselves to be open to the love that is being given to us without fear or worry. The fear of being loved or of loving others is greatly diminished because of the unconditional love we know and feel from God, our Heavenly Father. As you know the definition I really like for love is love is doing the higher good for the other person, doing what is best for the other person, putting the other person's higher good before ourselves. That does not mean just doing the easy loving, it means doing the hard loving as well. Like saying no when it would be easier to say yes. You put limits on what you will accept or not accept. Loving another person may mean that we say no and draw a line that we will not cross, nor can they cross it. To truly love someone may mean that we say yes when it would be easier to say no. For example going out for supper when you really want to watch the ball game on the T.V., or watching the ball game on the T.V. when you would really like to go out for supper. If you allow your teenager to go out to a dance or party instead saying no, the no is best or easiest for you, but not for them. You are putting the higher good of the other person before yourself. If we were all to do that, what a wonderful place this world would be to live in. If we would but choose to love the other person first instead of loving ourselves first, this world would be a much better and safer world to live in. If we all chose to walk in love, we would choose to do what is best for the ones we love and for ourselves. There would be less hate and fighting going on. I would be out of a job if people chose to live loving others first. If we chose to love first, no one would choose crime or jail. We choose to love others with an unconditional love because God loves us that way. When we have God's love within us, we are truly able to freely give our love away without self-protecting. No matter what happens in our lives, God's love will see us through. And if need be, God will kiss our bow bows better. When we are loved with a pure, clean love, we feel safe and secure to love others and allow others to truly love us. The amazing power of true love!

Prayer: Father, thank you, for loving me and teaching me what it really means to love and be loved. Help me, to love even when it would be easier to just walk away. I am sorry for the times I was selfish and did not put the higher good of the person I said I loved first. Instead I put me first and what I wanted. Please forgive me and help me to love better. In Jesus' holy and loving name, amen.

Day Seventy-seven

3 John 11 'Dear friend, do not imitate what is evil but what is good. Anyone who does what is good is from God. Anyone who does what is evil has not seen God.'

Our first reaction to this statement is I don't imitate what is evil! I do not do things that are evil! Now think about how we do at times imitate what is evil and not what is good. Have you ever been cut off by another driver and wanted to chase them and cut them off? You might have even sped up at first then thought twice about what you were thinking and doing. Have you ever given into the urge to give back what you have been given? An eye for an eye, a tooth for a tooth! They hurt me, therefore, I have the right to hurt them back. How about taking a parking space when you know the other car was there before you? But you have the advantage and move in first, then walk away with them yelling at you. Have you ever found a wallet and did not give it back with all of its contents? Or maybe did not give the wallet back at all? How about being in a tired place, your body is played out but you have made a commitment? There is no energy left and putting one step in front of the other is all you can manage. You just need to go to bed and spend some time alone. Yes, that would really help bring you back into a place of balance, so you go to bed and immediately fall asleep. Instead of telling the truth about how you were feeling, you make up some excuse to make you look good or to get you off the hook. How about telling lies instead of telling the truth, or bending the truth to make us look better? Anything we do that puts us into the darkness is not from God, therefore, it is imitating evil. Anything we do that keeps us in the light is of God and therefore keeps us on the path of doing what pleases God. When we choose to do what pleases God, we are functioning from a God perspective and therefore are pleasing to God. Anything we do that is not from a God perspective is, if we are being completely honest with ourselves, not and not from a place of life within ourselves. If we are not living in life and light, we are not following God. Anything we do that is not is not

God's plans and desire for our lives. What we are doing is choosing the darkness instead of choosing the light. Doing good and doing what is right is living in the light of God. Anything that is not from the place of light and life is not of God. It is quite simple really. Today we are being asked to check ourselves, our behaviours and choices to see if there is anything in us that is either bordering on the darkness or definitely not of God. If there is anything in the darkness in our lives, then maybe this would be a good time to make some necessary adjustments or alterations. If there are areas or places in our lives that do not reflect the light of God, then maybe it is in need of tune up. We either choose to live our lives in the light or in the darkness. The gray areas are not of God either.

Prayer: Father, I am sorry for the times when I chose to walk and live in the darkness. When I choose to let the darkness tell me who I am, when I choose to let the darkness tell me what I should or should not do, I am not living your way. Please forgive me, and help me, to live my life in such a way that it is and not life-stealing. Help me, to choose to do what is right and good. I want to live my life in such a way that is good and pleasing to you Father God. This will be good and pleasing to others and you. Thank you for loving me and being my constant source of life. Thank you, God, that you are light. In you is only light, no gray areas or darkness, amen.

Day Seventy-eight

Jude 20 'But you, dear friends, build yourselves up in your most holy faith and pray in the Holy Spirit.'

Dear friends build yourselves up. That would be enough said, but it does not stop there, it goes on to say in your most holy faith and praying in the Holy Spirit. First off we need to build ourselves up. We are so good at times at putting ourselves down. We take away from who and what we are as people. Some of us have been taught to not build ourselves up, to not build on what we have as gifts, talents and abilities. We are taught to take away and even put ourselves down. Then we wonder why we have low self-esteem and low value and worth placed on who and what we are as people. We need to change the way we think about ourselves! We need to change the way we see ourselves. Why? So we can begin to see the person God created us to be; to see ourselves as God sees us, and not as we have been taught to see or not see who we are and all that we were created to be. When was the last time you gave yourself a compliment? When was the last time you said thank you to yourself with a kind word of love, honour and respect? When was the last time you looked at yourself in the mirror and told yourself how beautiful you are both inside and out? I would venture to say it was not yesterday. The reality is we are beautiful. We are all gifted, talented and have great abilities. The problem is we often make excuses for them or pretend they are not as good as they really are. Here is the truth: God says you are beautiful, valuable, special, precious, worthwhile, chosen, His beloved. You have been set aside with a plan just for you. You were born in this time frame for such a time as this and are here for a reason. If all of this is true; and it is: then maybe it is time to start believing it and living it in your daily lives. God knows exactly who you are and the truth is He has given all you need to be the person He created you to be. You are not a mistake; you were not short changed at all. Now the challenge to each and every one of us is to start believing it and living this truth out in our daily lives. We need seeing ourselves as God see us. Start slowly, if need be, with a statement of faith. I am God's child and I am here for such a time as this. I am here for a reason and have my own unique gifts, talents and abilities. God knew exactly what He was doing when He created me and gave me birth. I am precious and the chosen, beloved child of the Most High God. I am valuable and worthwhile. God loves me. I am His child. Pray in faith asking the Holy Spirit to help you believe this truth and receive it deep within your spirit. Pray believing your value and worth is in God and not in what others say or believe about you. You are the child of the Most High God, the King of kings and Lord of lords. What more can we possibly need?

Prayer: I am your chosen, beloved child, Father. I am your precious, special, gifted child. Today, I am going to believe your truth of who and what I am as your child and who you created me to be. I am going to stop receiving what others have said I am. I choose to receive your truth into my spirit. Help me to make it real and alive within me. Thank you, Father and Holy Spirit, for making it real for me. Help me to be patient with myself. Help me to be kind and generous to myself, amen.

Day Seventy-nine

> *Esther 4:14 'For if you remain silent at this time, relief and deliverance for the Jews will arise from another place, but you and your father's family will perish. And who knows but that you have come to royal position for such a time as this?*

Today is another reminder that there are no accidents in God's kingdom and plans. Esther is faced with the challenge of risking her life for the potential saving of her Jewish people. Esther is being asked to go to the king to ask for her people be saved from the coming disaster. Of course Esther is afraid and worried that she herself may perish if she goes to the king. In her fear and anxiety Esther's uncle Mordecai says, 'and who knows but that you have come to royal position for such a time as this'. For such a time as this! You, my friends are here on earth for such a time as this. You are here in this time frame because you were to be born in this time frame. Not in the past or in the future time frames, but for such a time as this. We all have insecurities at times, that is called being human. We all have times when we feel less than, or not good enough, times when we wonder why we were born and why we take up space. Here is the answer to those times of questioning and uncertainty. You are here because God needs you here in this here and now. God's plans include you being here with all your gifts, talents and abilities. God knew exactly what He was doing when He held you in the palm of His hand and gave you life. God knew what He was doing when He decided on which gifts, talents and abilities He was putting into your spirit and life. God knew what He was doing when He trusted you with all He has trusted you with. God knew what He was doing! We are given what we need in order to be the people we are supposed to be. Yes, we are all replaceable---but no one can take our place. Did you hear that? Yes, you are replaceable, but no one can take your place! Yes there is another person who can do whatever it is you are doing. Yes, some other person will take your place when you leave, but they are not you. They will not do as you do, for you are unique. Only you can do whatever it is you do in the way you do it. Yes at some point someone will replace your body, but they can never replace you. When I leave the treatment center, there will be another to take my place and do my job that is a given. But the new person will not be me and will not do the job as I do. They will fulfill the position, but they will not be me! The person cannot replace the impact I have upon the institution. There is not another 'you' anywhere, and you are here to be you with all your bumps and bruises, goods and not so goods. Only you can be you. No one can take your place. Therefore enjoy who God created you to be and be the best person you can. For in reality when we stand before God, God is not going to ask us why we weren't so and so, God is going to ask us why we were not ourselves? The question is not why was I someone else? The question is why am I not me? Why am I not the person I was created to be? Doing what I was created to do?

Prayer: Heavenly Father, I am sorry for all the times I put myself down and did not stand up and be the person you created me to be. I am sorry for believing that I was less than others. I now see that I am here for a reason, for such a time as this. Please forgive me, and help me, to take my place and be the person you gifted me to be. In Jesus' holy name, amen.

Day Eighty

Philippians 4:13 'I can do everything through Christ who gives me strength.'

We can do everything through Christ who is our strength and gives of that strength freely and with abundance. This is an absolute truth! The problem is we have to choose to trust God and the promise of God's strength in everything we do or are called to do. The problem is we are sooooo human, and as humans we allow ourselves to get caught up in our feelings and what we think about ourselves or in what the world has told us about our frailties or inadequacies. We forget to trust and believe our heavenly Father who can supply all our needs and equip us to do all things. There are so many times when we think we are alone and have to do everything on our own. We think we have to face everything alone and there is no help for us anywhere, when in fact, we are not alone. Can you begin to hear that? You are not alone. We have the Holy Spirit in us, working through us at all times. We do not have to believe what the world is telling us is true. We have the Most High God in us. Revealing all truth to us. Filling us with what we need in order to be the children God created us to be in the first place. Besides, God does not take us anywhere to drop us or let us go. We have Christ in us, our Hope of Glory. We have the Holy Spirit in us, which is our salvation; our source of strength and everything else we need to do and act. We have Christ in us; what more could we need? What possibly could we be lacking in our spirit and ability to carry out God's call upon our lives? We have God on our side and if God is for us, who can be against us? Let us choose today to trust the presence of God within us, through the gift of His Holy Spirit, trusting and believing that we can do all things through Christ, who gives us strength and everything else we need. Embrace the light within you and let your light shine. Then watch and see all that will unfold in your life and the way you live your life. You are a chosen child of the Most High God. Celebrate and be glad. Rejoice my friends, rejoice! You are lacking nothing if you put your hope, trust and faith in God. You lack nothing. God promises to supply all our needs, and we know God cannot tell a lie. Therefore we have everything we need to be the person we were created to be, and to do all that is being asked of us. We can do all things through Christ who gives us strength. And that is the truth! All things! You are already enough. You have everything inside of you already. All you need do is give it permission to come out. All you need do is help let it grow and develop. All you need do is open yourself up to all the possibilities that God is asking of you and your life. In my opinion what do we have to lose?

Prayer: Today, Father, I am going to turn a new page in my life. Today, I am going to start choosing to believe that when I have you in me, I have the strength to do all things and I am lacking in nothing. I can do all things through Christ who gives me strength. Thank you, Jesus and Holy Spirit, for living in me and giving me everything I need to be me. Today, I am choosing to trust you Jesus and Holy Spirit, amen.

Day Eight-one

Colossians 3:2 'Set your minds on things above, not on earthly things.'

That can be a real challenge in today's day and age. There are so many things vying for our time and energy, not to mention our attention. It is so easy to get caught up in the things of the world and lose track and sight of spiritual things. The struggle with life is the earthly things are in our face and get our attention on a regular basis while with spiritual things we have to be intentional. It is this very reason that causes us to forget about our need to feed our spiritual selves, and be intentional about our spiritual journey and its place within our lives. Our spirit is like everything else in life: if you don't use it, you lose it. It you don't take time to grow and be spiritual on your spiritual journey, your spirit withers away just like muscles that are not used. Today is the reminder of how important it is for our spiritual well being to be front and center in your daily lives. We need to be willing to set aside time each and every day to help our spirits grow and stay growing. We need to make spending time with God a regular time slot, a priority in our daily routine. There is a need to set aside time every morning before life starts getting hectic to spend time alone with God. If spending time alone is not possible, then how about including the family in our daily quiet time with God. Before we drop off to sleep take some time with God, even if it is just for a few moments. While we are alone in the car or standing in a line up, sitting on the toilet, or whatever moments we have during the day that are just 'hanging-around' moments, how about spending those moments with God? When we spend time with God we build up our spirits and spiritual selves. During our day we can take time to be still, if even for a few moments, to regroup and be with God. It is not as hard as you think. If you start you will be amazed at how everything falls into place. If you drive to work or take public transit, you can still pray and be still before God. We all need to use the toilet during the day; how about taking an extra couple of minutes to be still and quiet with God as you sit on the bathroom throne. When preparing a meal, add a prayer or thought of God and His importance in your life. Say a thank you to God for always being with you, and being your source of strength and true life. Let your light shine in the moments and it will shine in the minutes and hours. Remember God loves spending time with you and misses you when you are not around. Take time to be with the one who loves you the most. Take time everyday to grow your relationship with God and thus enhancing your spiritual self and journey as well. There are usually spare moments in our lives that God would love to share with us. The challenge is will we share them with God?

Prayer. Heavenly Father and Holy Spirit, help me to be more intentional in my time spent with you. I repent for putting you so very often last on my list of things to do. Help me put you first. Remind me when I am forgetting to take some time with you during the day, even if it is just a moment or two. Forgive me Lord, and thank you, amen

Day Eight-two

Colossians 1:27b 'To them God has chosen to make known among the Gentiles the glorious riches of this mystery, which is Christ in you, the hope of glory.'

This never ceases to amaze me. That God would choose to make Himself known to His creation. That God would choose to reveal Himself in real and evident ways. That God would reach out to us so that we would have the choice to either choose Him or turn away. Regardless of our reaction to God, the Creator of all things wants to have a personal and alive relationship with you and me. Whether we choose the offer love or reject it, it is still God's desires to love us and be in a relationship with us. This is truly the mystery of God's grace and love! God has chosen to make known to everyone, all peoples, all of His creation, the glorious riches of this mystery. The great mystery of whom and what is available to all people (even us) through the gift of Jesus the Christ and His death and resurrection. The great mystery of the hope we all have and which is ours if we want it. The mystery that Jesus the Christ would choose to live in us. The choice of God to bring us the hope that lives in His gift of mercy and grace, which is His Glory and presence in His creation and in us. Without hope or a vision we truly do perish. Without hope or a vision, we do not have what it takes to put one foot in front of the others and face all that life throws our way. Hope is the sustaining force that keeps us going. Hope gives us the courage and strength we need to face all that life is giving us and throwing our way. Hope is the light at the end of the tunnel. The light of hope is shining in the darkness, showing us the way through. It is giving us the ability and desire to keep going and seeking after the light. Hope is a gift of life and light when all else has failed us. The hope is the enduring force during the hard times and the light shining in our lives during the good times. This truly is a mystery. Why would the Creator of all things even want to be in a relationship with us, knowing how selfish and self-centered we can be as humans? The answer lies in the love God has for each and every one of us. The love that God bestows upon us no matter what! No matter what we have done or not done. No matter how good or bad we have been. No matter how selfish or kind. God wants to be in a love relationship with us and gives us the mystery of that love through His mercy and grace, the mystery of His never-ending desire to love us, His desire to be in love with us. We have the hope of Glory available. All we have to do is open our hearts and it will come in.

Prayer: Father, how can I ever say thank you enough for the way you love me and the way you never cease to love me. I am truly grateful for all the love you shower down upon me. Help me to receive it more and more. Help me to walk in your love and then to help others walk in it as well. I am truly grateful for the hope and glory that is mine today and everyday, amen.

Day Eight-three

Colossians 4:5 'Be wise in the way you act toward outsiders; make the most of every opportunity.'

Be wise. What great advice! We can all gain in this area of our lives. There are so many times in our lives when we are not wise; we are anything but. Think about the times when you take one foot out of your mouth, just in time to put the other one in. How about the times when you knew if you went down that road you would have to suffer later, but you went down the road anyway, and yes you suffered. Or the time you promised you would do something or be somewhere and you failed to follow through to the completion of the promise, only to have it come back and haunt you no end. All the times in your life when you could have chosen to be wise, but chose instead to anything but wise. The attitude of wisdom is to be the same regardless with whom we are dealing, whether someone of like mind or an outsider. When we deal with outsides (those who do not see life as we do) we need to be wise and do what is wise. There is a need to be consistent and have integrity in our dealings with others. Doing what you say you will do, and not doing what you say you would not do. Speaking and living in honesty, so that there is no misunderstanding because you said one thing and did another or you spoke from both sides of your mouth. Living in truth, which is a hard to do at times, is a responsibility we all share. We have a tendency to lie and cover over what we do not what to be revealed. The problem is we are the temple of the Holy Spirit and a reflection of God to others. When they see us, they either see God shining through us, or He is nowhere to be seen in our choices and behaviours. If we are not living according to the ways of God, then we are not very good ambassadors for God. There is an expression and I can't remember the whole expression but it starts with "we are our neighbours Bible, they read us everyday". When your neighbour reads you, what are they reading? Are they reading a God reflection or are they reading a reflection of the world and what the world holds true and right? I was once told to write a little card to put in my pocket, which reads, "If Jesus were here would I do this?" Just thinking about that helps me to do and say things that are pleasing to God, and therefore to everyone I meet and greet. The reminder truly helps me to think about what I am saying and what I am doing. If Jesus were here would I do what I am about to do or say what I am about to say? If the answer is yes keep going. If the answer is no take a step back and evaluate what you are about to say or do. What are you reflecting in your actions, words and lifestyle choices?

Prayer: I am learning that my head and body truly do want to be wise at times. My heart wants to do what is right and Holy Spirit, remind me or show me the times when I am not living according to my heart and when I am following my head or body. Show me when I am not being faithful to myself and to you. I want everyone I meet and greet to see in me a reflection of my God. What I say is important in and for my life. Thank you, Holy Spirit, for helping and teaching me how to live in the light, amen.

Day Eight-four

Colossians 4:6 'Let your conversation be always full of grace, seasoned with salt, so that you may know how to answer everyone.'

What is grace? Grace is God's unmerited, loving, favour; the unmerited presence of God within God's creation. Grace is the free gift of God's love, mercy and compassion, which God chooses to give all of His creation. It is free and available to everyone. However, not everyone takes the free gift nor does everyone want it. Picture this gift like someone standing in front of you with a big bowl of candy (or your most favourite thing). The bowl is there, it is being offered to you, all you need do is reach out and grab/take the contents for yourself. The only way to get whatever is in the bowl is to reach out and make it yours. The only way to get the contents of the bowls is to reach out, put your hand in the bowl taking as much as you want or desire. It is the same with God's free gift of grace. It is there for everyone to have and to hold. It is available for all, for everyone who desires it. All we need do is reach out and grab/take it. It is the same with our use of language and the language we use in our conversations. We all have the ability to use loving favour (grace) in our language choices. We can all be kind and generous in our choice and use of words, but not all of us use grace in what we say or how we say it. There are times when we use harsh words when soft words would have had a much better result; or when we use negative or hurting words, which cause strife and pain instead of toning down our language and using words that would heal or bring about restoration in the person's life. What the lesson is teaching us today is we have a choice of how we deal with each other and the language we use when doing so. God gives each and everyone the ability to use grace in our conversations, or to use words that are not . The choice is ours to be either light in this world of darkness, or to be darkness. There are times when we need to add salt to our conversations as well. What is salt? Salt is something we add to food to enhance the flavour. We add salt to enrich the taste. Salt can add a sparkle to what we are salting; it can also cure or season the food. In our conversations there are times when we need to season our choice of language so that it enhances the one we are talking with. There are times when sharing on a deeper level challenges the person and helps them to see through different eyes. The words help to bring out deep truth that is necessary for the person to know. The words help the person understand what is really going on within them or with their actions, or why they are feeling or doing what they are feeling or doing. There are times when we need to be absolutely honest and speak the hard words that only we can speak. There are so many different ways in which we can use grace and salt in our daily lives and conversations. May the salt we add help make a positive difference in the world around us. Let us use our words wisely and with salt when necessary.

Prayer: Father, I am sorry for not using my words and interactions with others as a way of showing grace and putting salt into other people's lives. Please forgive and help me, to learn when to use grace in my choice of words and when to use salt. Thank you for your unconditional love to me; help me to love others the same way. In Jesus' name, amen.

Day Eight-five

2 Thessalonians 3:3 'But the Lord is faithful, and he will strengthen and protect you from the evil one.'

It is so very true we have a faithful God! Our God is so faithful. He is truly faithful in everyway. Every single time we put God to the test He shows Himself faithful. Every time we lose faith, God is still faithful. When we do not have the ability to hold on to our faith, God holds on for us. We have the most awesome and incredibly faithful God and we only know a glimpse of this truth. As you know one of the many promises of God is that He will never abandon us, forsake us or leave us orphaned. One of my favourite promises! Can you tell? (I use this promise a lot to remind us of how safe and secure we really are in God, our Heavenly Father. I believe this with everything I am and everything I hold true.) God cannot ever leave us alone to fend for ourselves without His help. He just can't do it. If this promise is true, and it is, then when we need strength to stand up against whatever it is we need standing up for, God is there. When we need God to protect us and fight our battles for us, He is there giving it His all on our behalf. If the darkness is closing in on us, God promises to shine His light. If evil seems to be winning the war, it is not true because we have read the end of the book. We know evil is defeated. Evil looses. There is no time, place or situation where God is not present and available to our needs and us. There is nothing that can separate us from the love God has for us His children and our place in His love. We can truly put our hope, trust and faith in God for He will never disappoint us or set us up to fail. God does not take us anywhere to drop us! Our God is a faithful God who is exactly who He promises to be. God will never change or move from where He is now. Jesus said "I am the Alpha and the Omega, the beginning and the end. I am the same yesterday, today and forever. I have always been and will always be the one and only true God who chooses to love you unconditionally, who chooses to be here with you no matter what you are doing or not doing or whatever befalls you." God is well able to protect us from whatever the darkness throws our way and from whatever happens to come into our path. We may have to stand up against it, but when we stand we are not standing alone. We are standing with the Most High God for whom nothing is impossible. Reminder: you can never do anything that will cause God to love you more and you can never do anything that will cause God to love you less. My friends, God is faithful because He chooses to be faithful. God loves us no matter what because He chooses to love us no matter what. God loves us not for what we do or don't do, but because He chooses to love us. No matter what is happening in life. Can you hear that friends? No matter what happens in our lives! God will always be faithful and God will always love us. The bottom line is, that is the way it is and the way it will always be. And as Lilly Tomlin would say: "And that's the truth!"

Prayer: Thank you, God, for always being the same and never changing. Everything around me changes, I change and the world changes, but you stay the same. Therefore I can put my hope, trust and faith in you for you will never do anything to harm me, shame me or disappoint me. I choose today to trust you and to let you be my Most High God. I receive your love and your faithfulness into my heart and life. Thank you, for loving just the way I am. I love you in return, amen.

Day Eight-six

2 Thessalonians 3:13 'And as for you, brothers and sisters, never tire of doing what is right.'

I do not know about you, but there are times in my life when I tire of doing what is right. I tire of having to do the right thing all the time. There are times when I would just like to throw in the towel and say the heck with it. I am going to do what is wrong today and the heck with the consequences. Then I come to my senses, give my head a good shake, and take up the cross again of doing what is right. It is tiring at times to always do the right thing! There are times when I would just love to yell and scream at the offenders I work with for they push and push and push. Yes, I would love to yell at the staff who are not much better than the offenders at times, but where would it get me? Yes, I would feel better for the instant or the moment but then what? Yes, I would release the tension in me but what ripple effect would the release cause? There are times when I would love to say. "Go away and leave me alone. There is nothing left, you have taken everything I have and now you want the one last ounce of me that is still hanging on." But to do that would cause a backwash that would be harder to clean up than the action and release. No, doing the right thing is not always the easiest thing to do, but it is the right thing to do. Are you in a place in your journey where you just want to throw in the towel and run and hide? Or just want to scream and tell the world to stop, so that you can get off? Are you struggling with an injustice and the injustice seems to be winning? Do you want to play by their rules and their game even though it would cost you your very soul? Do you feel like you are drowning and going down for the third time? Know you are not alone in what you are feeling or in how you are feeling. Most of us will find ourselves at one time, or another in a place of just not wanting to do what is right. We want to do anything but what is the right; to have a moment in time to let the pressure out and help stop the chaos that is going on inside of us. We think and feel the heck with the consequences. We are human and as humans we at times run out of resources, our toolbox is empty. But thanks be to God who always leads us in triumphal procession and gives us what we need in order to take the higher path and do what is right, good and faithful, to do what is right no matter what is happening or not happening. Our God is just so amazing that way. God does not want us doing what is not right so gives us every opportunity to do what is right. We truly do have a faithful God who is worthy of our trust and faith. We have a Heavenly God and Father who truly does know and understand. Therefore is always waiting in the wings to fill us with what we need in order to do what we need to do. It is not always the easy path, but it is the right one.

Prayer: Thank you, God, for being such a faithful God who does not change and who is always here for us. We are so weak at times it is reassuring to know that when I am weak you are strong, when my faith isn't enough yours always is. I put myself in your tender loving care for I know in you I am safe and secure and have all I will ever need. I choose to be your child both now and always, amen.

Day Eight-seven

> *1 Timothy 1: 5-6 'The goal of this command is love, which comes from a pure heart and a good conscience and a sincere faith. Some have wandered away from these and turned to meaningless talk.'*

The goal of love or loving others, God and us is to love from a pure heart, a good conscience and with a sincere faith. Living and loving from a pure heart means, no matter what we do or say, it is done with a sense of purity, with no ulterior motives attached. Therefore no negatives attached in any way, shape or form. It loves someone for the pure and simple reason that God asks us to love first. The call upon our lives is to love first and foremost, no matter what. The goal of love or loving others, God and us is to love from a pure heart, a good conscience and with a sincere faith. As I said, it loves someone for the pure and simple reason that God asks us to love first. The call upon our lives is to love first and foremost no matter what is happening or not happening. A reminder: true love is doing the higher good for the person we love and giving our love. Treat them with honour, dignity and respect. When we love this way we are living and loving as love commands. When we have ulterior motives or intentions that are not from love, we are not allowing the call of love to light our path. What we are doing is feeding our selfishness and desire to have life our way and on our terms and conditions. When I am not functioning from a place of purity, I am not letting my love light shine forth into all I am and all I choose to do. When I love and live with a true sense of love and purity, then and only then will I have a clear conscience, a conscience that is not negatively affected by my ulterior motives and selfish desires. A good conscience is found in living our lives in such a way that no one can say anything negative about us, for there are no negatives in our actions or choices. We live our lives in a place of honour and integrity. When I am being honest and when my words and actions match, I am clear of a bad conscience! My conscience eats at me when I am living and going through life in such a way that I know it is wrong. My inner voice yells at me or tries to tell me to take another path, for this one is not life giving. To be able to live with a pure heart and a clear conscience I need to know that no matter what, God is for me and not against me. When I have the assurance that I am loved by God, my heavenly Father, then I have the courage and the strength within myself to risk honesty, truth and integrity in all that I am and all that I do. When I have a sincere faith and walk with the knowing that God is always with me I can love from a place of purity, for I am safe and secure in the love of my heavenly Father. I do not have to live my life in such a way that causes a bad conscience, for I know that when all is said and done God, my Heavenly Father, still loves me and I am okay in His love. My faith in God's promises remains my sustaining force. I know that when my love is rejected or used or abused I am still safe and secure in my heavenly Father's great arms of love. That gives me to courage to love even when my love is not being honoured or respected.

Prayer: Thank you, Father, for always loving me and never letting me down. Thank you, for always telling me the truth and for helping me when I need your help. I now ask that you would teach me how to live everyday and in everyway with a pure love. Help me, to live in a state of purity in all I do, say and am. Show me how to put love first no matter what. Holy Spirit, teach me and show me the better way, then give me to courage and strength to live in it, amen.

Day Eighty-eight

Genesis 4:7 `If you do what is right, will you not be accepted? But if you do not do what is right, sin is crouching at your door; it desires to have you, but you must master it.'

"One of the most significant books to be published in the last few years in the field of human relationships is a book entitled *Emotional Intelligence*. In it, the writer Daniel Goleman argues that although the intelligent side of life is important, so also is the emotional side. He claims that whereas the key topic in education used to be IQ---Intelligence Quotient---the hot topic today is EQ---Emotional Quotient. Goleman says his research shows that this present generation of children are more emotionally troubled than the last. On the whole, he claims, children are growing more lonely and depressed, more angry and unruly, more impulsive and aggressive. It is a fallacy, he concludes, to believe that what makes for success is intelligence alone. Our emotional life needs to be considered also. I have to agree with him. Over the years I have met many business people---among them managers and executives---who lost their jobs not because of a lack of intelligence or business acumen but because they couldn't master their emotions. They were unable to cope with feelings of frustration or they lacked compassion and empathy---and so they were forced to leave their jobs. Recently I talked to a man---a brilliant and experienced manager---who told me that he was removed from a post because his emotions got the better of him. When confronted by his board over any matter he would quickly `lose his cool', as we say, and his inability to master his emotions led eventually to his dismissal. It is vital that we learn to master our emotions before they master us." Excerpt from *Everyday With Jesus.* Jan/Feb 2004, *Thriving Spiritually.* Copyright Selwyn Hughes 2004, CWR, Waverley House, Waverley Lane, Farnham, Surrey, GU98EP, England.

What Selwyn is saying is so true. Without a good handle on our feelings and emotions we find ourselves in a place where our feelings and emotions control us and not us controlling them. We let our feelings and emotions tell us who we are and not the other way around. Our emotions and feelings dictate how we will act and react, what we will do or not do, and how we will feel in any given situation. Our emotions and feeling define us, therefore we lose sight of who we really are as a person. Without a healthy grasp on our feelings and emotions and the ability to keep them in check we do ourselves more harm than good. We will often find ourselves doing or saying things that we will regret later. Feelings and emotions are just that---feelings and emotions. They are neither right nor wrong. What we do with them is what makes them right or wrong. If we have a good handle on your feelings and emotions and can keep them in check when they need to be kept in check then we have the upper hand. Feeling them when we need to feel them and not feeling them when we do not gives us control over our feelings and emotions; when our feelings and emotions decide for us, then we have lost control of who and what we are as a human being The feelings and emotions decide for us. Having the ability to shut them down when they are overwhelming or out of control is healthy and . Allowing them full reign in our lives only causes hardship and pain. Let us today evaluate the state of our emotions to see if they are controlling us or we them.

Prayer: Father, I am beginning to see that I need a healthy handle of my feelings and emotions. I need to control them and not them me. Help me, to see my emotions for what they really are, just feelings and emotions. Help me to control them and process them in healthy and ways, so that I may enjoy all parts of who and what I am as your child. Thank you, Holy Spirit, for being my guide and constant helper, amen.

Day Eighty-nine

Jeremiah 1:5 'Before I formed you in the womb. I knew you, before you were born I set you apart; I appointed you as a prophet to the nations.'

It is so comforting to know that before we are born, before we are given life, God knew us. Before we had any life growing within us we were known by God and within God's plan and purpose for our lives. God knew exactly what He was doing when God formed us in our mother's womb. Before you had life in your beings God knew you and even had a name He called you. If you want to know the name God has for you, simply ask and God will tell you what it is. If you ask God, He will tell you the name He calls you. God knows us! Before anything happens in life, before our parents even knew that they were going to have a child. God knew and was planning our birth. God knew that we, you and me, were going to be born. Therefore, we are not mistakes! We are not come by chance. We might have been a surprise, but we are definitely not a mistake. The amazing thing about God is, God does not stop there. Giving us birth is not enough for God. We are all born with a purpose, and we have value and worth, long before we are conceived in our mother's womb. We are here for a reason. We are here for such a time as this. For some of us, we have a hard time hearing that we are here for a reason and for such a time as this. We were formed in our mother's womb and have value and worth because God says we have value and worth. We have life because God said we were to be given life. We not only have value and worth, but we matter more than we will ever know or even begin to understand. We have such great value and worth in God's eyes for we are His chosen beloveds. We are God's children. We are children of the Most High God. Which means that we are here for a reason, and all have a task, job, position, a place within God's scheme and in God's plan. I find such comfort in that knowing that I am a part of God, and God is a part of me. We are one within the purposes of God. Unique, valuable, precious, special, chosen and beloved; we belong. Not only do we belong, we also have a place in God's family. We have a place that has our name on it and can only be occupied by us. We are God's chosen beloved. We are both now and always safe and secure in God's tender loving care, because God's love for us has always been and will always be. God's love for us is the same yesterday, today and forever no matter what. We are here for such a time as this because God wants us here for such a time as this. Let us rejoice and celebrate.

Prayer: Father, I am so grateful that I am in you and you are in me. I am grateful that I was chosen before the foundation of the world to be a part of your family. I was not born to be separate from you or you separate of me. I was born to be together with you; we are one. I have value and worth and I matter more than I will ever truly know or understand. I may have been a surprise to my parents but not to you. I know now that I'm not a mistake, that I am good enough; you made me good enough. I am yours both now and always. Thank you, Father, for loving me and creating me to be loved by you, with every blessing and value you placed in me and for me, amen.

Day Ninety

2 Corinthians 12: 7 `To keep me from becoming conceited, because of the surpassingly great revelations, there was given me a thorn in my flesh, a messenger of Satan, to torment me.'

There is a part of us that wants to be perfect, which wants to have no defects, hardships, or any other shortcomings. If we are sick, we want to be well. If we have a handicap, we want it to go away. If there is any part of us that is not perfect, we want God to change it and or fix it. We do not like having imperfections or shortcomings. Deep inside of us we want to be perfect and without hardship in our lives.

145

Only that is not the way it works. We see here today, Paul complaining, because he has a thorn in his flesh. We do not know what the thorn is; what we do know is that Paul did not want it there anymore. In fact, Paul prayed three times for the thorn to be removed. Then Paul came to the conclusion that the thorn was there to keep him humble and his focus on God. Paul realized that the thorn was not a curse but rather a blessing. The thorn put Paul into a position where he had to rely on God and God's mercy and grace in and for his life. We all have a thorn of some kind, a shortcoming, a something as part of us that is there to help keep us humble as well. The reason being, we as human beings are now and never will be in a place of perfection. We all have something that reminds us of our humanity and our need for God and other relationships. These imperfections and shortcomings really do help us to stay humble and appreciate what we do have. Without thorns in our lives what would keep us humble and focused on God? I know I need my shortcomings, my imperfections. Those growing areas of my life remind me when I need reminding to stay focused on my need for God, and for God in my life. Yes, I would love to have my thorns taken away, to have a magic wand, big pill or quick fix so I would not have to process and deal with the things that are within me, the things that are a part of my make up. In all reality without them I would probably get arrogant or totally self-righteous. Without our shortcomings or imperfections, burdens, handicaps it would so be tempting to take our focus off of God. It would be so very easy to keep the focus on us. It would be so easy to focus on what we want or think we need, instead on God where our focus needs to be. Let us rejoice and celebrate our thorns. Let us celebrate those areas of our lives that keep us humble and focused upon our true source of strength and life. Life is short, far too short at times. Let us celebrate all we are and all we have. Rejoicing in the many blessings that are poured down upon us with each passing day. Let us focus on all the good that is in our lives and not the thorns.

Prayer: Thank you, Father, that I'm not perfect. Thank you that I need you in every part of my life and in every way.

Without you I really am nothing! Without you I would get so caught up in me that I would lose sight of all that is really important. Father, I repent. I repent for always wanting life easy and for wanting it to go my way. I want what I want when I want it and that is nowhere close to how you want me. Please forgive me and help me to be content in my life and what I have been given. No matter what life gives me, for I know all things come from you. Thank you, Father, amen.

Day Ninety-one

2 Corinthians 12:9 'But God said to me. "My grace is sufficient for you, for my power is made perfect in weakness." Therefore I will boast all the more gladly about my weaknesses, so that Christ's power may rest on me.'

It is so hard to say thank you! We as human beings are not very good at saying thank you. We do not give thanks for the good things that happen in our lives. We especially do not say thank you for our weaknesses or the bad things! We do not want to be weak. Somehow we have developed the belief that we are to be strong all the time. The only problem with that belief is that God never gets to be strong in our weaknesses. We do not experience the blessings we get from God when we allow ourselves the privilege of being weak. When we are strong all the time, we give the impression that we do not need help nor do we need people around us. When we are strong all the time, people think that they are of no value to us, and they are not needed in our life journeys. If it is true that God works best in our weaknesses, then how can God truly work in our lives if we are never weak? If we have it together all the time, then God's all sufficient grace can never be shown through our lives. God's power is made perfect in us, when we allow ourselves to need God and God's power working in us.

God's all sufficient grace can only be shown when there is a need for it to appear. If there is no need because we are strong all the time, how can God's all sufficient grace be manifest in our lives? Like Paul, we too, must boast in our weaknesses. We need to give ourselves permission to be weak and to be human. There is a need within each and every one of us to give ourselves permission to be human; a need to be human with all our weaknesses and needs, to be in a place of not having it all together all the time, to be real with others and ourselves. There is a need within us to say to those who love us and want to be a part of our lives. "I need you to be strong, for right now I am not. I need to lean on you for I am having a hard time with all that life is putting on my plate." Instead is seeing our weaknesses a negative in our lives, we need to begin to see them as opportunities for God to work in us, through us and with us. Our weaknesses are opportunities to embrace, not only more of God, but also more of who God created us to be. In conclusion: we do not have to run from our weaknesses. In fact, we are to do just the opposite. We are to give ourselves permission to be strong when we need to be strong and weak when we need to be weak so that God's grace and power can be manifested us. Being real and living in the moment is so . Being real in the moment is one of the greatest gifts we can ever give ourselves. It is a gift for it means that we are being honest and real, not only with ourselves but also with others and God as well. It is not a weakness to say we need help; it is actually strength, a great strength. It is giving ourselves permission to be whom and what we are as human beings.

Prayer: Again Father, I need to repent for my fear of being weak. I need to tell you that being weak and seemingly out of control often scares me. I am beginning to see that I don't have to be strong all the time. Whether I am weak or strong has no bearing on my value or worth. My value and worth come from you and not from what I am or what I do. Help me to bring this truth deep into my very being, so I can trust you more in all things and not be afraid. Bless me Father, I need your blessings and love more and more. I need to know who I am in you, amen

Day Ninety-two

Psalm 31:1 'In you, O Lord, I have taken refuge; let me never be put to shame; deliver me in your righteousness.'

I am so grateful that God is our refuge that God is that safe place, we can always run into no matter what is happening or not happening in our lives. God is the refuge. The refuge that is constant and always available to us, at all times, and in all ways. The amazing truth about God is it does not stop there. He is our strength and our source of total life. When we are open and receptive to God, God truly is our all in all. When I think of a refuge, I think of a place that is totally safe, absolutely secure and a place where there is no fear; a place where we can let our guards down and not worry about whether we will be accepted or not; a place where there is no darkness nor hazard to block our way or interfere with our journey. That is what God is to us. He is our refuge. He is our hiding place. Our safe place! The one place that is ours, totally ours. A safe place where we are always safe and secure no matter what! A safe place where we are always under the protection of our God and Father. Our safe place where we can run to at any time, under any circumstance, no matter what is happening around us or in us. Our refuge is always there for us waiting to take us in, and to be all that we need it to be. God truly is our refuge, our safe place. The other truth about God is He will never shame us. God will never ever set us up to be shamed. We can fully put our trust in that truth. God loves us far too much to ever set us up, to ever bring us anywhere to drop us or in any way cause us harm. God is now and always will totally be our refuge, our strength, our truth and our deliverer. He will deliver us in our time of need. That is one of God's promises to us His children. Why is God our refuge, strength, deliverer, source of all life and our reason for living? He is all that and so very much more to us for one simple reason. When we stand before God, we will be blameless, holy and righteous in His sight. When our time comes to stand before God we can stand there having been washed, loved and protected by God and His Son Jesus the

Christ. The amazing truth about all this is it happens not because of anything we do, but because of all that God is in us, for us and about us. God's gift of life, refuge, strength, protection, and deliverance happens because God chooses it to happen just because He loves you and me that much. We have an absolutely trustworthy God who wants to be our refuge, our strength, are righteousness and who will always be there with us and for us. What more can we ask for? What more do we need? In my opinion nothing! I have all I will ever need when I have God in my life and everything God is. God's love is truly sufficient in every sense of the word. God is love and that love is ours when we open ourselves up to it and receive it as our own.

Prayer: Father, you are my strength and my refuge. Today, I choose to run into you. Today, I choose you as my refuge and my safe place. You are my God. You are my refuge. I am choosing to trust you and to allow you to be my safe place. No matter what! Help me when I am weak so that I never lose focus or ever take my eyes off of you. Father, you are truly all that I will ever need. Thank you, amen.

Day Ninety-three

Romans 6:23 'For the wages of sin is death, but the gift of God is eternal life in Jesus Christ our Lord.'

The wages of sin is death. What kind of death are we talking about? Is it a physical death or some other kind of death? Do we die instantly or is a process? First off let us talk about what sin is. What is so powerful about sin that it causes death? Why does sin cause us to die? Sin is defined as self. Sin wants life on our terms and conditions. Sin is saying no to God, and yes to us. Sin is anything we do that separates us from God and God from us. Sin wants life as we see life and expect life to be. I want what I want when I want it. That is sin and when we live this way we are not living according to what God asks of us. God asks us to live in an attitude of loving relationships with others; to live our lives in such a way that we are honest, respectful and guarding everyone's dignity through the manner in which we choose to live. When we live life on our terms and conditions we are only thinking about ourselves, nothing else or no one else matters in our life expectations. When we are separated from God, the result of the separation is death because there cannot be life, at least not true life. True life comes from our relationship with God and others. When we live life on our terms and conditions and do not allow God to influence our lives, we are living apart from all that God is and apart from everything God has for us as part of His creation. I believe the road to hell is paved with the word no. No God, I won't, I can't, I will not do it your way. It is my way or the highway! No! I will not do anything or be anything that does not look like I want it to look like. Just like Frank Sinatra and Elvis Presley sang in their song, `I did it my way.' It is the `I did it my way' that separates us from God and leaves us locked into death and life without God. The death happens both here on earth and in the Kingdom of God or heaven. The death is a spiritual death. A dying in our spirits and who and what we are as spiritual beings. The death is that void or emptiness we feel inside of us when we do not have God in our lives. But thanks be to God, who has given us the gift of eternal life, through His Son our Saviour, Jesus Christ, our Lord. Thanks be to God, who has shown us a way out of our death and into His gift of eternal life. God has shown us through His death and resurrection the way back to God. the way back to having life, true life within us. God has once again opened the bridge back to Himself by believing in His Son, and the gift of life we have through His Son. We can be released from the power of sin and death in our life by trusting in who and what God is and His life giving Word to His creation. When we say yes to God we are saying no to our need for self and yes to God's provision of life forever more. This is a real struggle for all of us because the desire to have life our way is so strong within. We do not want to have to live our lives according to anything other than what we want. That is called sin. The problem with having life that way is there is a price to be paid and the price is a spiritual death, a separation from the promises and provision of God and His love for us His children.

Prayer: Father, I apologize for wanting life on my terms and conditions. I apologize for wanting life my way. I want life, I want eternal life with you, Therefore, Father, forgive me. I am learning that I cannot live without you. Without you I only have survival, not life. I need you; I need you in every part of me. Help me to live life your way, and not mine. Thank you for loving me just the way I am, but loving me too much to leave me the way I am. Thank you, for making me your BELOVED, amen.

Day Ninety-four

Ecclesiastes 3:1-4 `There is a time for everything, and a season for every activity under have heaven: a time to be born and a time to die, a time to plant and the time to uproot, a time to kill and the time to heal, a time to tear down and the time to build, a time to weep and to time to laugh, a time to mourn and a time to dance.......'

There is a time for everything. Everything has a time. Everything has a season. Everything has a reason. When we look at life there are times when we want life to go on just as it has been going on without changing and without stopping. We want things to stay the same, maybe even to go back to the way it was. Only that is not how life is lived, nor how life works. There are beginnings and there are endings to everything, to all of life. Everything has a starting and ending point. Nothing under heaven is without a beginning nor without an end. All of life is designed to have a starting and finishing point built in. All life starts and then at some point stops. Look at nature and how it starts and stops. The trees have a coming to life season, a growing season and then a time to go into sleep mode once again. A time to be born and a time to die! Ask the farmer, they will say, with all certainty, there is a time to plant and then a time to harvest. A time for life to start and a time when it will finish! We all face losses in our lives whether we like it or not. No matter how hard we fight it, there will be times when we will need to say good-bye. That good-bye can be to a friendship, a relationship, a job, or loved one. As we say good-bye it is okay to feel sad, to grieve, or to feel a deep sense loss. It is okay to feel the feelings and all that the feelings represent. What is not okay is to stay in the feelings. There is a time to weep and a time to laugh. There is a time to be sad and a time to rejoice and live again. And there is a time to get over our sadness so that we can get back to the business of living our lives once again. This is all part of God's plan. In God's plan there is a time for everything under the sun, and everything under the sun has its time. There is a part of us that does not want life this way. We want to be able to control what is happening to the people we love and have in our lives. We beg, plead, try to bargain with God so that whatever happens in their lives, it is according to what we want for them. It may not be what is best for the person, but it is the best for us, so we manoeuvre and do our level best to have it turn out our way. Only as I said, life just does not work that way. Life is not lived on our terms and conditions. Life is lived on life's terms and conditions. A time for everything and everything with a time schedule attached. Learning how to accept this truth makes life a whole lot easier. A tough lesson to learn! Maybe the hardest lesson to learn. Unfortunately, learn it we must. For the blueprint is set. There is a time for everything and everything has its time. Life is designed to have starting and ending points built in. This reality remains no matter how hard we try to fight against this truth; it is the way it is. Instead of fighting against the natural timetables of life, let us instead enjoy life to the fullest while it is with us. Then when the time for endings comes, we can say "I lived it to the fullest, it is now time to move on to the next phase of the journey". Let us enjoy the journey called life with gusto, living our lives to the fullest enjoying the journey and all it has to offer. Then we will have lived our lives with no regrets.

Prayer: Father, I know in my heart that everything has a time, and everything has a reason but there are times when I just do not understand. I do not understand my feelings at times and the reasons why things happen the way they do. What I do understand is that you love me and no matter what life is giving me, you are right here with me, giving me, what I need and helping me through every situation. Thank you, Father, for being such a faithful Father and loving me the way you do. Help me to accept the things I cannot change, so that I can move on with my life and all that my life is. In Jesus' name, amen.

Day Ninety-five

Proverbs 25:28 'Like a city whose walls are broken down is a man who lacks self-control.'

For the one who lacks self-control, life is hard and unmanageable. Those who lack self-control do not have the inner resources to control what their lives are telling them to do, say, think, act or react. Those who do not have a healthy control of their feelings and emotions do not have the ability to stand up, even under the simple life events, let alone the most difficult of situations. Without self-control there is no way to stop our lives from going out of control. There is nothing to stop us from jumping off the deep end with no way back. Think back for a moment when you were out of control. Now remember how powerless you felt and how unmanageable your life was. Remember the feelings empty, no resources to fall back on, alone, maybe even lost within yourself. There were no resources to tap into. There was no ability to stop the powerlessness. Nothing left! That is what powerlessness is. We have no self-control to reclaim our sense of balance and self. It is in a place where something or someone else tells us what we will do in a given situation or set of events. Being in a powerless, out of emotional control place, is lonely and difficult. That is why proverbs says, 'a city whose walls are broken down is the one who lacks self-control.' The city without walls has no protection. This city that is in a state of brokenness without walls to protect its self; it is vulnerable to its enemies. Anyone who wants to overtake the city can just come in without opposition or hindrance. That is the same with you and me when we are lacking healthy self-control; people, situations and events tell us how to feel, think, act and react. When we are out of control there is nothing to stop people, situations and events from invading our insides. There is nothing, no barriers, to stop us from being in a powerless position or place. We have no way of protecting ourselves without the ability to prevent people, situations and events from invading us. That means we need to have healthy boundaries and the ability to say no when we need to say no. A boundary is a moveable line we control that says who gets close to us and who does not. Our boundary is that space around us that protects us, and keeps us safe and in a place of healthy self-control. The truth is nothing can get inside of us unless we let it or them in. Nothing can invade our insides unless we are in a place or state of being out of control. If our lives are in a place of unmanageability, what is there to prevent people, situations and events from coming and taking over? We need to decide for ourselves what our insides look and feel like. We need to decide what we will do with our feelings and emotions and how they will impact our lives. We, as mature adults, need to have a good solid handle of our feelings and emotions and how they are being lived out within us and without. Only we can decide, only we can get a good handle on what goes on within our spirits and emotions.

Prayer: Holy Spirit, teach me how to be in control of what happens to my insides and my feelings. Show me any area of my life I need to repent of so that I can live my life as you created my life to be lived. I repent for giving my power away and allowing my life to become unmanageable and out of control. Forgive me, and help me to make better choices with my life and the feelings and emotions you have given me. Thank you, Holy Spirit, amen.

Day Ninety-six

James 3:8-9 `But no man can tame the tongue. It is a restless evil, full of deadly poison. With the tongue we praise our Lord and Father, and with it we curse of men, who have been made in God's likeness.'

Think about the power of your tongue for a moment. Think about how many times in your life you used your tongue in hurtful and harmful ways. Think about the times you said things you wish you could have taken back as soon as they left your tongue; the times you took one foot out of your mouth just in time to put the other one in. In almost the same breath you blessed someone and built him/her up, only to then turn around and curse him/her, causing harm without even batting an eye. Think about the times when you have used words of love to bring joy to the person, then in the same breath used words that hurt right to the very core of the person you were talking to. Think about how easy it is to use hurting words, when loving words would be just as easy. How easy it is to use words that bring life to the one we are speaking to, yet we choose to use words that will hurt them instead. It is just as easy to use words that bring life or a blessing to someone, as it is to use words that do just the opposite. That's the challenge before us today. The challenge is to use words that bring life and light, instead of using words that bring death or darkness to the people we are speaking to. To use words that build each other up, and not words that tear each other down. To be people who speak life in all and every situation and not people who speak death and harm. To use the gift of language and the power it contains, to be light in this world of darkness. To be people who use words of life and light. To shine God's light and life to everyone and everything we come in contact with! One of the gifts that God has given us is the gift of free will. Let us use the gift of free will in the use of our tongue so that we are seen as people who only talk from a life and positive perspective and not a death and dying one. Yes, the tongue is a powerful tool. Yes, the tongue has the ability to speak life and death. Yes, the tongue can be used to bless or hurt. Yes, the tongue can be used for either good or death. The truth is we choose which one it will be. We choose in which direction our tongues will be used. We decide! We will always have the choice of how we use the power we have been given in our tongues. We decide the direction or impact of our words when speaking with others and ourselves. We choose what our words will look like. We choose; our tongues do not choose. Our tongues voice the words, they do not choose them for us. The challenge before us today----how am I using my words and what affect do my words have upon others?

Prayer: Heavenly Father, help me to use my tongue as an instrument of life and not a weapon that causes death and harm. I am sorry for the times I have used my tongue in hurtful and harmful ways. Please forgive me, and help me to only use my tongue in ways that will bring life. Holy Spirit, remind me when I am using my words in a hurtful, wrong manner. Holy Spirit, put a guard around my mouth when I need one, amen.

Day Ninety-seven

> *1 Corinthians 9:25 'Everyone who competes in the games goes into strict training. They do it to get a crown that will not last; but we do it to get a crown that will last forever.'*

There are times in my life when I am so lazy. When I would rather do nothing than do the things I know are right, good and beneficial, not to mention, pleasing to God. There are times when I follow what my body wants and not what my spirit knows I need. At times I am not very disciplined. That is what Paul is reminding us of today. We need to be in training spiritually so as to get the crown that lasts forever, and not settle for the crown that will not last. This means training ourselves to listen to our spirit and the Spirit of God within us, instead of listening to our human self, which wants what it wants and when it wants it. It means training ourselves so that our spirit and the Spirit of God inside of us, is stronger than our desire to not do what is right and good. This is not easy but with practice all things are possible. Just like the athlete, there is a need for us to be disciplined, strong and well able to compete in the race. When we discipline ourselves we too will have the resources to draw from. We too will be strong, so that we can choose to follow our spirit and the Spirit of God within us and achieve the crown that lasts forever. As humans we often chase after things that do not last. We chase after them with great gusto and enthusiasm. The problem is when we achieve them. We find out that what we have been chasing was all wrong and not what we really wanted. I am writing this devotional during the 2004 Summer Olympics. This year it seems that there are more and more athletes who are being caught for doping. They are throwing away all the years of training, throwing away all they have worked for because they thought they could get the prize by cheating and chasing after a false dream. Even if they won the Gold metal they still would have lost on the inside of themselves. Why? Because they cannot get away from themselves and the lie they know they have lived. The prize is not really a prize! It is the same with us in our lives. What prize are we chasing after? I have seen in my life journey people who have climbed the corporate ladder only to discover they were on the wrong one. The ladder they were climbing did not give them what they were really searching for or seeking for their lives. There are those who give everything they have to reach the top rung of the ladder, only to look back to see how much they lost during their climb to the top. I have seen this happen more times than I want to remember. What ladder are we climbing? What goal are we chasing after? Is it a goal that has lasting treasure? Is it a goal that will satisfy in the end? Are we chasing after a prize that will last or are we chasing after something that can be taken away from us? Are we climbing a ladder that will satisfy us in the end, or are we climbing a ladder that leads us to emptiness or disappointment? Today we are being asked to check and see what prize we are working towards, to check our lives and goals to make sure when all is said and done we can look back and say, "Yes, I put my energy and life's work into something that has lasting value and is a treasure for me to keep and maybe even share."

Prayer: Thank you, Father and Holy Spirit, for being in me and for giving me the courage and strength to follow you and your Spirit within me. Thank you, for helping me come to terms with my human self. Thank you, for being my constant source of life and light. Help me, when I am weak to be strong and to face my need for discipline head-on. Holy Spirit, I need your help every single day of my life. Please help me as only you can, amen.

Day Ninety-eight

Hebrews 10:30-31 'For we know him who said, "It is mine to avenge; I will repay," and again, "The Lord will judge his people." It is a dreadful thing to fall into the hands of the living God.'

How many times when we are hurt or have been hurt, do we want to strike out and hurt the person or people or event that has hurt us? We want to get even. We want our pound of flesh. I would venture to say lots of times. How we want to get even! How we want to get ours back! Someone or something has harmed us and we want to get even. The only problem with the "get even" or "get back our fair share of what happened to us is" when does it end? When is enough, enough? The truth is getting even is never enough as we learned the other day. In reality I get even, then you get even. I get even again, and so on and so on and so on, it is a never ending story of getting even. For my even is just a little bit more than what you gave or took from me. That is why God says, "it is mine to avenge; I will repay." When we leave it in God's hands and allow God to work in, through and about whatever it is that has happened, then it is not us who is righting the wrong, it is God. And because it is God righting the wrong, the outcome is always far better than we could ever have expected or asked for. When we allow God to act as our avenger, we are allowing God's mercy, grace and justice to prevail. God's mercy, grace and justice are by far the better way. We may want to curse the person, situation or event, when in fact, what needs to happen is a blessing. Our natural instinct is to hurt the other person as much as they have hurt or harmed us. This turn hurts us again. When we let God be God and have the final justice, the outcomes are always to our greater good, not to mention the greater good of the person whom God is repaying. The reality is when we allow God to avenge, we do not get caught up in the cycle of getting caught in the blaming, hurting, resentments, bitterness, anger, and so on. God's Way is the better way. God's way sets us free from the cycles of having to get even and our fair share of what was done to me. The other truth is when we do something to someone and cause him/her harm in any way, we have to live with ourselves afterwards. Sometimes that is harder to live with than getting even; then the harm is done to us. When we let God be the avenger, we are releasing the person, situation or event from within us. This in turn sets us free to do other things with the energy. We are also not caught up in the hurt or pain which results from the one-up-man-ship getting even brings. Allowing God to have the final word truly does set us free to get on with our lives. Allowing God to avenge the wrong done to us means the other person does not live rent free inside of us. The person, situation or event does not drive our inner bus causing us to crash and burn all the time. God is right! When we let God have the final word and the right to avenge whatever wrong has been done to us the outcomes are always so much better. Not to mention how much better our insides are because we are living in true freedom, freedom from the need to get even and have our pound of flesh.

Prayer: Father God, help me to trust you in all things, especially those things that hurt. Help me to take my hands off and trust your right to avenge. I am learning that when

I do it your way, there is always life in the end. When I do it my way. Who knows what the end result will be. Teach me, Father, to live my life according to your laws, ways and commandments. Thank you, Father, for bringing life into my life and for showing me how to really live my life. I am truly grateful, amen.

Day Ninety-nine

John 10:2-3 'The man who enters by the gate is a shepherd of his sheep. The watchman opens the gate for him, and the sheep listen to his voice. He calls his own sheep by name, and leads them out.'

Only the shepherd uses the gate, for he/she has the authority to come and go. The shepherd can walk freely among the sheep. The sheep listen to his/her voice because they know the sound of the shepherd's voice. The shepherd's voice is familiar to them therefore the sheep will follow it. All others, who come in do not have the authority to be there. Therefore, they do not know the sheep by name and cannot lead because the sheep will not follow them. Only the shepherd can lead the sheep into what is truth and . This is a good lesson for us. There are so many different ministries out there. How do we know, which is from God and which is not? The ministry looks good. It sounds good. It even seems to do well. How do we know if it is from the true living God or counterfeit? The answer is quite simple. If the ministry does not honour and glorify Jesus the Christ and if it does not point you to Jesus the Christ it is not from the living God. If the ministry does not honour and follow Scripture, it is not from God. For the ministry to be valid it must point us through the Holy Spirit to Jesus, to God. Anything that takes away from Jesus is not from Jesus. Anything that says the Holy Spirit is not of God is not pointing us towards the one and only true, living God. Any suggestion that what Scripture teaches is wrong is something we need to stay away from. Anything that does not honour God, Jesus and the Holy Spirit is not Scriptural, and therefore something to turn away from. The ministry that ignores the Holy Spirit or keeps the Holy Spirit in the background and at a safe distance is not honouring to God. Therefore is questionable in its practices and is more than likely not from God. If the teachings glorify man or points to the Holy Spirit and neglects Jesus Christ, I would say be very wary of this ministry. For the Holy Spirit's job is to glorify Jesus Christ, and all that Jesus is. Anything short of that is not based on the tenants and truth of Jesus' teaching. Jesus is the good Shepherd, and will only lead His sheep into green pastures and all truth. If you are not being lead into the truth of Jesus Christ and are not seeing life, true life, from the ministry, then I would suggest a need to take a second look at that Ministry and what they are teaching. Anything that does not honour God, Jesus and the Holy Spirit is not pointing you in the right direction. Jesus said in `I am the way, the truth and the life.' (John 14:6) If what Jesus is saying here is true than anything short of Him being the way, the truth and the life is not from Jesus, and therefore not based on what Jesus taught and still teaches. The sheep know the shepherd's voice and follow him/her because they know they will be safe and secure in the shepherd's care. We need to have that same sense of being safe and secure when following our Good Shepherd.

Prayer: Thank you, Jesus, for only telling us the truth and for leading us into all truth. Thank you for your Holy Spirit. Thank you that the Holy Spirit glorifies you and reveals you and your plan, not only for your creation but for our lives as well. Fill me with the gift of discernment so that I will know what is from you and what is from somewhere else, or something else. Holy Spirit, fill my spirit with your truth so that I may have a discerning spirit, amen.

Day One Hundred

1 Corinthians 1:8-9 `He will keep you strong to the end, so that you will be blameless on the day of our Lord Jesus Christ. God, who has called you into fellowship with his son Jesus Christ our Lord, is faithful.'

This is one of the promises of God. God promises that He will keep us strong to the end. God promises that we will be blameless on the day of our Lord Jesus Christ. To be blameless is to be without fault. Blameless is being found innocent. Blameless is being released from all charges, set free. Blameless is not being held responsible any longer for what we have done or not done. It is being released from the full measure of the law and all that the law demands of us. God promises that if we accept His gift of salvation and eternal life, we will be blameless in His sight when we stand before God's judgement seat. That's the promise! When we stand before God, we will be found blameless, without blame! This blamelessness has a catch. In order to be found blameless when we stand before God, we must be in fellowship with God's Son, Jesus Christ, the Lord, and have accepted His promise of being blameless. Jesus is faithful; He will keep the promise of us being blameless if we accept His gift of forgiveness. Jesus does that by paying our sin debt, which in turn sets us free from the debt we owe. The freedom from the debt is wrought through the acceptance of God's gift of His forgiveness. God is committed to doing His part, if we are committed to doing our part. We become blameless because we have God paying the price of our sin and choices. It is through God's Son Jesus Christ, who takes all the blame on Himself. Jesus pays our debt for us. Remember it is like us standing before the judge in a court of law, only to have another person come forward to agree to do our time for us. It is as if another person hears our charges and the penalty we are to pay and says, "I will do their time; I will pay their debt; they are free to go". We are standing before the judge knowing we have committed the crime, knowing that we should pay the full measure of the law, knowing we have to do the time, but someone else stands in our place doing the time for us, paying the debt we owe. Their choices and action makes us debt-free and therefore blameless. We have someone else go to jail for us in our place. We get to walk out the door a free person. Jesus has done just that for us. He has stood in our place paying our debt. Jesus has agreed to pay the price so that we become blameless. The price is paid. Therefore we can stand before God having been set free from all possible charges against us. We are blameless, released from all charges. We have been forgiven of all we have done or not done. When we stand before the judge of the universe, our slate is washed clean. No charges are held against us. What an amazing gift God has given to everyone who receives the gift! I just love being reminded of how free I am in God's gift of forgiveness. It just makes my heart sing and want to dance. I am free, truly free, to not only live my life here on earth, but to live it in freedom for all eternity. Free from all that was.

Prayer: I am so sorry, Father, that because of my sin, you had to send your Son, to earth as a little baby. You sent your Son as a baby to grow up into a sinless man, in order to pay the price of the sacrifice that would set me free. In humility, Father, I repent. I repent for all of the times I committed a wrong, which separated me from you. Forgive me. Thank you for paying my sin debt. Thank you for making me blameless. Thank you, Jesus, for your willingness to take upon yourself all that I owed. I am truly grateful and I say thank you, amen.

Day One Hundred One

John 3:34-36 `For the one whom God has sent speaks the words of God, for God gives the spirit without limit. The Father loves the Son and has placed everything in his hands. Whoever believes in the Son has eternal life, but whoever rejects the Son will not see life, for God's wrath remains on him.'

All true life comes from God, through the Spirit of Jesus Christ. When we accept Jesus into our lives, He fills us to overflowing with His Spirit. Jesus does not give half measures. Jesus does not hold back the gift of His Holy Spirit to anyone who asks for it. Jesus fills up each and everyone of us with His Holy Spirit when we ask to be filled with the Holy Spirit. For those of you who have doubts and fears about not having the full blessing of God, or having only a half measure of God's Spirit, you can release that lie from your spirit and your heart. You can rest in the truth that, not only are you already enough in God, but you are complete in everything God created you to be. When we ask for the Holy Spirit to fill us, we are filled to overflowing with His Spirit. The Holy Spirit comes into everyone who asks for the Holy Spirit. God does not give half measures! We may not be able to embrace the fullness of the gift of God's Spirit, but that does not mean it is not there within our hearts and spirits. This means you have the Spirit of truth living within you. Hear that my friends----hear that deep within your spirit. You are already enough and you have the Spirit of the living God living within you, if you asked for Him in your life and heart. How do we know that this is true? How can we trust within ourselves that we have the Holy Spirit when we ask for the Holy Spirit? We can trust the promise of the Holy Spirit. Why? Because it is just that---a promise. And, as God cannot tell a lie or break a promise, the promise is true. God cannot ever do anything that goes against His character; therefore, when God makes a promise, it is a promise that last forever. That is who God is. A faithful, trustworthy God who will never lie to us nor do anything that goes against who and what

165

God is. If you have any doubts or fears that your name is not written in or has been left off the list in God's Book of Life you can release that fear. The doubt is not from God, it is from the evil one. Let go of the doubt or fear and let the peace of God fill you as you ask for the assurance of your place in Him. The gift of eternal life is given to everyone who asks for it. When you have the Holy Spirit living within you, you have the gift of eternal life and you do not need to doubt any longer. There are no, ifs, ands or buts about it! You are safe and secure in the everlasting truth of God's Word and promises. You need not fear God's wrath. You need not fear condemnation. You are safe in the truth of God's Word, love and promises. God cannot reject His own and you are His own if you have the Spirit of God living within you. God's wrath does not apply to you. God's wrath only applies to those who choose to live outside of God's gift of mercy and grace. God can only love you and receive you as His own since you are now living under the umbrella of God's grace and loving mercy. The promise is true. All you need do is choose to believe and let go of any doubts or fears, for they are not part of the promise.

Prayer: Thank you, Heavenly Father, for making me your own. I know I do not deserve the gift of eternal life. In fact, what I deserve is your wrath. But because of your love for me, I get your gift of life and your Holy Spirit living within me. I got to have my entrance paid into your Heavenly Kingdom and the gift of eternal life with you and your Son. I am so grateful. Thank you, Jesus, amen.

Day One Hundred Two

Zephaniah 3:17 'The Lord your God is with you, he is mighty to save. He will take great delight in you, he will quiet you with his love, he will rejoice over you with singing.'

The Lord your God is with you! That is a statement. The Lord your God is with you. God is with you! God is always with you even when you do not realize it. God is never not with us. God promises to be with us and as God cannot tell us anything but the truth, God is with us, end of story. I do not know about you but for me this verse brings great comfort and much joy in my heart and spirit. God is with me, with you, no matter what is happening in my life, your life, or not happening; God is with us. Not only is God with us, He is mighty so save. God has the power and might to save us and help us because He is with us. To take this one step further, God knows when we need saving; God knows when we need His help. Is this not the most comforting verse? God is here and He is mighty to save. Wow! Now let us go one-step further. God takes great delight in you. Did you hear that? God takes great delight in you. He will quiet you with His love; He will rejoice over you with singing. It is hard to believe at times that God, the Most High Ruler of all creation and the universe, would take great delight----no, not just delight----but great delight---in you. That God would even want to take delight in us blows me away at times. With everything we do at times, without a doubt, this truth amazes me. That God would take great delight in who and what I am causes my heart to sing and rejoice. I matter to God. Say that to yourself----I MATTER TO GOD. Say that again. I matter to the Most High Living God. Little old me matters to God! God cares about me! I am valuable to God. I am so valuable that God delights in me and cares about me I am important to God, so important that He takes time to be with me and delights over me. When I listen to God and am still before God, He quiets me with His love. God helps me in all of my struggles and quiets me with the love He has for me, and it does not stop there.

167

God rejoices over you with singing. God sings over your life, heart and spirit. I can see God telling all the heavenly hosts about us as He sings over us and rejoices over who we are as His children. God loves us and loves to be with us. God wants to be our all in all. He wants to be everything we need Him to be and so very much more. We have the most amazing and awesome God. We have a Father/God/Dad who is everything we need Him to be and, as I said, so very much more. We are valuable and precious to God, our Heavenly Father, and matter so very much to Him. We matter so much that He takes great delight in us and rejoices over us with singing and song. We are blessed, truly blessed! Our God loves us. Loves to be with us. Our God quiets us with His amazing love. Our God rejoices over us with singing. What more could we ever need or desire. God loves us! We are precious in His sight. We are His chosen Beloved.

Prayer: Thank you, Heavenly Father, for loving me as much as you do. Thank you, for considering me so precious and valuable. Thank you, for delighting in who and what I am, and taking the time to rejoice over me with singing. Help me receive this deep, deep within my spirit, for I have a hard time receiving this truth at times. Tell my spirit, the truth about who I am and all I am to you. Thank you, Holy Spirit, amen.

Day One Hundred Three

1 Samuel 2:1-3 `Then Hannah prayed and said; "My heart rejoices in the Lord; in the Lord my horn is lifted high. My mouth boasts over my enemies, for I delight in your deliverance. There is no one holy like the Lord; there is no one besides you; there is no Rock like our God. Do not keep talking so proudly or let your mouth speak such arrogance, for the Lord is a God who knows, and by him deeds are weighed."'

Have you ever been so high on God and God's presence in your spirit that you felt like you would jump out of your skin, or burst because you were so overflowing with the Holy Spirit? A time when the Holy Spirit is so very present that you could almost taste the presence of God within you? Your heart is rejoicing and the joy is brimming out of you. You feel like nothing you have ever felt like before. You are high on the incredible presence of God in your life and the truth within you. It is like you can take on the world and are more than you ever imaged yourself to be. You know that you know, that you know, God is with you. God is filling you and His deliverance is with you. That is how Hannah was feeling. She knew beyond all shadow of a doubt that God was real and that God had answered her prayer. She knew God has heard her cry for mercy. God had heard her cry and she got the mercy she was crying out for. Hannah was high on who and what God is. There was nothing that could or ever would compare to her God. Hannah knew deep within her spirit that no one could or would ever compare to the power and presence of God. God was her rock. Her solid rock in which she could trust at all times no matter what was happening or not happening. There was now no need for pride, arrogance, or any kind of falsehood. God brought the truth to her and she was bubbling over. Hannah was humbled and awed by God. We can give ourselves permission to be humble before God. We can allow ourselves to let go of all the things that prevent us from being who we really are. We can be like Hannah and take our places with a true sense of humility and awe in who and all that God is. A true sense of what is real and true. A true sense of what is and honest within ourselves. Hannah risked with God. Hannah really risked with God, telling God exactly what she needed and God came through for her. God wants to come through for us. When we in truth and humility come before God, God is faithful and just and will give us what we need. All we need do is ask, ask God for what our hearts are crying out for. We need to cry out to God with honesty and truth pouring out of us. We seek to seek God in our need. When we have laid it all out before our great and awesome God, we watch and see all that God does in and for our lives. God delights in seeing His children filled to abundance. God delights in seeing us filled to overflowing with all that God is. God delights in bringing us into all we are and were created to be. God wants us to sing out like Hannah did, `My heart rejoices in the Lord. The Lord is my horn lifted high.' Open your heart and let God fill you as He filled Hannah. Give yourself permission to truly get down and honest with yourself and all you need God to help you with in your life. You will be amazed at how God answers your prayer.

Prayer: Heavenly Father, I come to you on bended knee asking for your help, peace and freedom. I come in humility to set my face towards you and all you are so that I can be all you created me to be. I am discovering that I cannot live, truly live, without you and your presence in my life. Come, Lord, and fill me up and meet my every need. I need you and all you are within me. I am crying out to you. Come, Lord Jesus, come, amen.

Day One Hundred Four

Psalm 143:8 `Let the morning bring me word of your unfailing love, for I have put my trust in you. Show me the way I should go, for to you I left my soul.'

Each new day is truly a new day. Each day is a new beginning. Yesterday is gone, finished, completed. Yesterday is now part of the past and therefore we cannot go back into our past to change or alter it. In truth, we cannot go back and change it in any way, shape or form. What was done yesterday is part of yesterday's news. It cannot be altered or changed in any way. All we can do is move on with this new day and all this new day brings. With the help of God's Word and God's unfailing love for us, we can move on from yesterday and move into all that today holds for us. Today is the first day of the rest of your life, the first day of all that begins anew, afresh. Today is the day of God's unfailing love for us. Let us say yes to today. Let us receive anew the gift of God's great love, and the new beginning we have in each new day. "I choose to put my trust in you, Father. I choose to rest in your unfailing love for me no not matter what happens during this day. I rest my heart and spirit in your tender loving care knowing that no matter what happens, I am safe and secure in your unfailing love. Show me throughout this day the way I am to go. Father, to you and you alone I lift up my soul, my very self. Show me throughout this day the wonder of all you are. Show me the love you have for me as your child, your precious, special, chosen, beloved child. Show me how much I matter to you and how valuable I really am. I have been lied to so often, which makes it hard for me to let go of yesterday and to trust your love for me today. I open my heart to your truth and your unfailing love for me. I want to be free, totally free. I want to be all you created me to be. I want to know your freedom. I need your love and truth in my heart and spirit. Teach me the way of your love. Teach me all the benefits and blessing that come from being your child, your chosen beloved child. I choose to trust you and put my hand in yours, so that you can lead me safely through each obstacle I will face as I journey through life. Help me to trust you more and more and to live in your unfailing love for me. Teach my heart how to live in you and in your unfailing love for me. Show me. I am open and ready to receive all that you have for me. I am learning that life is lived in the present and not in holding on to what happened to me in my past. Help me to let go of what was, so I can have all you have for me in this new day. Without your help, I do not have the courage or the strength to let go and move forward with my life. With your help, Dad, all things are possible. I choose to live in all you are so that I can be all you created me to be."

Prayer: I am so grateful for the privilege of being your child. I am grateful for having all that I have because of your unfailing love for me, your precious, chosen, beloved child. Show me each and every day what it truly means to be your child and to have a Father like you as my Father/Dad. I choose today to be your child and to trust you with my heart, life and spirit. I choose you Father/Dad as my rock upon which I stand and put my trust, amen.

Day One Hundred Five

Matthew 11:28 'Come to me, all who are weary and burdened, and I will give you rest.'

How comforting it is. How so very comforting to know that no matter how heavy life gets, or how weary we are, we can always find our rest in God. No matter what, we can always go to God and find our much-needed rest in Him. God is always there. Yes, always there, no matter how tired we are or how burdensome life may be. Even when we find ourselves in a place of not having enough strength to reach out to God, we can still to cry out in our weariness and heavy loads. God is still there reaching out to us. No matter what life is giving us or putting on our plates, we can always find our rest of God. Always! All we need do is come. The coming can be in groans and moans. It can be through a deep sigh. It can take any form at all. There is no right or wrong way to tell God we need Him. God does not care how we reach out; all God cares about is that we do. All that God cares about is that we come to Him. God cares that we reach out to Him as He reaches back. What a faithful, so very faithful, God we serve. How truly blessed we are! We have a God who loves us no matter what. God is always waiting with open arms to hold and receive us and to give us the much-needed rest our heart is searching for. If you are weary, burdened and heavily loaded down, God is standing there in front of you with open arms ready and waiting to receive you. God is waiting, your rest is waiting, and all you need do is to reach out to God. God will be right there reaching back giving you your much-needed rest in His peace. There are some countries that punish their rule breakers by putting a yoke upon them. The size and weight of the yoke is determined by the severity of the broken rule. If the broken rule or infraction is minor the yoke is light and the time you carry it is short. If the infraction is large, the yoke is really big and heavy and the time you carry the yoke is long. Jesus is saying to us today that when we are weary and burdened by life and our choices, we do not have to carry the yoke ourselves; we can come to the one who can set us free from the burden and weariness. When we come to the one who can help us, we will find our rest and the freedom we are searching for. The challenge is to humble ourselves. Then, once we have humbled ourselves, we come into the rest and peace being offered. The challenge is to let go of our pride or need to be right and enter into the rest, joy and peace that is ours, when we come into God's presence and gift of life. The challenge is to reach out to God and put our hand in His so that God can fill us and give us His peace. The peace and rest is waiting. It is always waiting. All we need do is reach out for it and it is ours. We do the reaching; God does the giving of His rest and peace. What a deal!

Prayer: Forgive me, Father, for there are so many times when I get lost in my weariness and in the burdens I am carrying. I get lost and forget to reach out to you for the much needed help I need. Remind me, Father, that you are always there. All I need do is cry out to you and you are there. I am crying, Father; I need your rest, and I need your peace. I need your help for I cannot do it alone. Thank you, Father, for helping me, loving me and always being here for me, amen.

Day One Hundred Six

John 20:25 'So the other disciples told him, We have seen the Lord. But he said to them, Unless I see the nails in his hands and put my fingers where the nails were, and put my hands into his side, I will not believe it.'

Doubts and the power of doubts in us are so amazingly strong at times. Here Thomas is proclaiming his doubts. Thomas had heard all that Jesus had to say about the resurrection and Jesus' coming back to them. Thomas was with Jesus the whole time He ministered on earth. Yet Thomas had such a hard time believing that Jesus really had come back. In fact, Thomas has such a hard time that he said, unless he saw proof of Jesus' return and evidence that speaks louder than words he would not believe. Friends, there is nothing wrong with our doubts. Hear that! There is nothing wrong with having doubts. What makes them right or wrong is what we do with them. If we allow our doubts to drive a wedge between our relationship with God and ourselves, they are wrong and life-stealing. On the other hand, if we allow our doubts to help us grow in our faith and relationship with God our doubts become . Our doubts are because they open a door for growth and development. We may at times want to see hard-core proof that God is who God says He is. We may think we need to put our hands in Jesus' side and see the nail marks on His body. Believe it or not, it is okay to feel that way. Only do not let that feeling drive you away from all the blessings God has for you. Instead of letting the doubt pull you away from God, let it push you into God, as you to ask God for the help you need to overcome the doubts and questions. Let the doubt help you grow in the knowledge of His truth and the reality in His creation and in us. Sometimes we just honker down and get real stubborn in wanting and needing life on our terms and conditions. We get so stubborn that we fail to see beyond our stubbornness and the truth that is smacking us in the face and heart. Do not let your need to grow, know and understand be like Thomas'. Thomas came close to allowing his doubts and fear drive him away from God. Thomas could have lost his faith because of his fears and doubts. We can give our doubts and fears permission to steal our relationship and faith in God. We can allow our doubts and questions to gain a negative power over us. Or, we can use them to gain a deeper truth and understanding of who God is and who we are in God. We can know a deeper truth of all we are because of all that God did for us. Thomas saw and chose to believe. We do not have the same privilege of seeing the resurrected Jesus. What we do have is the evidence that God gives us if we allow God to show us and help us overcome our doubts, fears and questions. God knows there are times when we struggle and fight to understand. It is in our struggling and questions that we find truth and a deeper knowing and understanding that can come to us in no other way. The struggles, questions and doubts are not the issue. The issue is how are we using the struggles, questions and doubts in our living relationship with God? The other side of this coin is God has provided a way out of the struggle if we want a way out. God gives us a way out of the doubts if we want to know the truth and the real answers to the questions and doubts. The choice is caught up in the gift of free will. We can either choose to go with God even though we may not know or even understand, or to give into our doubts, questions and fears and throw in the towel. Always remember along with the gift of free will, God has given to us His gift of unfailing love. We can stay in our doubts and fears and struggles or we can trust God to show us His truth and love. The choice is, as always, ours to make. Doubts, questions and struggles are normal and natural; there is nothing wrong with having them. They are part of our human condition. The challenge is to use our doubts, fears, struggles and questions to push deeper into God and not away from Him.

Prayer: I do have doubts at times and I know how I give into my doubts and what they do to my faith relationship with you and to me. Help me to not let my doubts push me away from you, Father; rather let them draw me closer. I want my doubts to be used in life giving and growing ways. I need my doubts to draw me closer to you. In Jesus' most precious and faithful name, amen.

Day One Hundred Seven

John 21:23 `Because of this, the rumor spread among the brothers that this disciple would not die. But Jesus did not say that he would not die; he only said, If I want him to remain alive until I return, what is that to you.'

Gossip and rumors are deadly! They have the power to destroy and kill without even trying. Think for a moment what gossip and rumors have done to your life or the lives of people you know. A person is a good person, giving generously of who and what they are as a person. They are a blessing and an asset to the community and everyone who knows them. Then one day out of the blue someone says something about the person, something totally out of character and so not like the person. What happens? The gossip or rumor begins to take hold and for some strange reason you start believing it and not only believing it but agreeing with it. The gossip or rumor is false! Someone who had a wrong motive and wanted to hurt or cause harm to the person for some reason started the rumor. What have we done with the gossip or rumor? The years of experience with the person or all the ways we know them is thrown out the window and we let doubt and lies take hold. All of a sudden the person is the gossip or rumor but none of it was true. None of what we heard had any truth about it. That is the power of gossip and rumor. That is why we need to stay away from them and not get caught up in them at all. Let the facts speak for themselves and not the rumors or gossip. Let the truth be the trail we follow and not the damning gossip and rumors. I have seen it myself. A person's reputation is destroyed because of a wrong piece of information that was started by a gossiping person. The gossiping person for whatever reason started the rumor and it caught on like wildfire. So much harm can come through the spreading of gossip and harmful rumors. It takes a lifetime to build a good, solid reputation; it takes moments to destroy it. Let us not be the bearers of gossip or rumors. Let us not get caught up in the rumor mill or the gossip train. Let us be truth speakers and truth speakers alone. If we do not have anything good to say about someone, let us not say anything at all. If we do not know the facts around what we are speaking of, let us stay silent. Let us be the ones who build others up and not tear them down. Let us shine our light into the darkness, exposing the darkness for what it really is, darkness. There is no life in gossips and rumors. There is no life in the darkness. Life is found in building others up and making a positive difference in who and what they are as valuable, precious, human beings. When we speak the truth and only the truth, life is the result. When we spread gossip or rumors, we are choosing to spread death and darkness. We cannot have it both ways. Either we are light and life or death and darkness. To recap, when we choose to gossip or spread rumors we are stepping outside the greatest commandment of all which is to love first and foremost. The call of God upon each and every one of us is to love first and to be instruments of God's love to this hurting world. Let us once again commit ourselves to the call of love and be love in everything we say, do, think and are.

Prayer: Father, remind me when I am letting go of your commandment of love and being love to this hurting world. Remind me for I so easily forget. I choose this day to follow you and truly take my place as your chosen, beloved child. I choose to be light and to walk as light in this so often dark world. Thank you for your light within me and for all you are teaching me and helping me to be. Thank you for being my light within me. I am truly grateful, amen.

Day One Hundred Eight

John 20:28 `Thomas said to him, My Lord and my God.'

It is an incredible moment in our lives when we like Thomas have the revelation that God really is who He says He is the moments when we look up and say "My Lord and My God". There is no other moment like it. All the doubts seem to just fad away. It is like a whole new world has opened up for and to us. We begin to see life from a completely different perspective. It is like a huge gestalt that floods in and shakes our whole foundation. It shakes how we have looked at life until this point in time. It is the most amazing and awe-inspiring experience that can ever take place in our hearts and spirits. That is what doubting Thomas had. Doubting Thomas had been questioning what the other disciples were saying. Thomas was having a really hard time believing that Jesus (even though He had forewarned them that He would come back) was here in the flesh, that Jesus was visible to the naked eye and that He was eating and talking. How could it be? How could Jesus who was dead and buried come back from the dead? How could his mind get around what everyone was saying to him? Thomas just could not put the pieces together no matter how hard he tried. Then the moment of truth! There Jesus was standing right in front of Thomas. There was no doubting now. His eyes were seeing for themselves what he had been told. His eyes were seeing the truth. Thomas looks at Jesus and says "My Lord and My God. My Lord and My God you are really here. You are really standing right here in front of me. I can see you with my own eyes and know for a fact that you are real and you are who you say you are". Hopefully each and every one of us come to that same knowing and understanding that Thomas had. Hopefully each and every one come to the point in our faith journey, where we can say without doubt or fear that Jesus is God and He is who He says He is. That incredible point in our faith journey when we like Thomas, know that we know that we know that God is real. We know deep within our bones that we can put our hope, trust and faith in God. That is my prayer for you today. I pray you would have that assurance and trust that tells you with absolute certainty that yes, God is who God says He is and I can believe it and trust it. May you have a revelation today that truly opens your eyes and heart to the truth and reality of God and His Son Jesus the Christ. May the peace that comes with the revelation be yours in all its fullness. May you be truly blessed this day by our great God and Father and His Son Jesus the Christ.

Prayer: Holy God, I want that revelation and truth in my heart and spirit. I want the knowing that says yes, I believe. Please come into my heart and show me the truth as you showed Thomas and so very many others. Reveal yourself to me today. I come before you in trust and with a great expectation. Come Lord Jesus come, fill my heart today, amen.

Day One Hundred Nine

John 20:29 `Then Jesus told him, because you have seen me, you have believed; blessed are those who have not seen yet have believed.'

Here we are in a new day. Perhaps yesterday you prayed the prayer asking for God to give you the revelation of Himself and who He really is. You asked in faith and it did not happen. Where do you go from here? How do you go on? You asked and it did not happen. Hear what Jesus is saying to us. Blessed are you who have seen me and do believe. BUT, more blessed are those who have not seen me yet still choose to believe in me and all I am. More blessed are we who choose to walk in faith and trust even though we did not get to see Jesus in the flesh or see a revelation of Him. More blessed are we when we can say in our hearts and with our mouths that we believe. We believe not because of what we have seen and not seen. We do not believe because of what are eyes are telling us. We choose to believe because Jesus has touched our hearts and our hearts are changed. We believe even though we do not have the feelings that go along with the change and the deepened faith within our beings. We believe because we choose to have faith and trust in the words and truths of Jesus and all Jesus says He is. We believe because our hearts and spirits say we believe. What an amazing gift of faith that is. We do not have to see with our eyes to know what our hearts are telling us is true and real. We do not need to see with our eyes to let our hearts and spirits trust and receive. We do not have to have concrete proof to step out in faith and to have the blessings God wants to shower down upon us. We do not need to have outside proof. We can rest on what our hearts are telling us. We can go with what our insides are revealing to us. More blessed are they who have not seen yet still believe and choose to walk in faith. Watch and see all that God will do with your willingness to simply walk in faith and trust. Wait in anticipation of God in all you are and are becoming. Watch and see how God will shower down the blessings upon you in your everyday life because of your choice to walk in trust and faith. That is the promise of God. He blesses us more for simply trusting and believing even though we have not seen with our eyes. We are truly a blessed people and have the most amazing and awesome God. Faith is based upon the promises of God and God's faithfulness. Faith is not based on what our eyes see or do not see. If I were going on sight alone, why would I ever need faith? There is no faith in sight! Faith comes from choosing to trust even though our eyes cannot see it at the moment. Faith is trusting. Sight is seeing. More blessed are they who have not seen yet still choose to believe.

Prayer: Thank you, Lord, that I can trust you. Thank you that I can walk in faith knowing that your promises are always yes and amen. Thank you that I am your child and have a place within you and your kingdom. Thank you that I belong. Thank you Father for your love for me as your chosen, beloved child. In gratitude and trust I choose to walk in faith. I choose to just believe, amen.

Day One Hundred Ten

John 16:12-13 `I have much more to say to you, more than you can now hear.'

This statement is the wonder of our relationship with God. There is always something more Jesus wants to teach us. There is always something more to learn. There is always something more! Our relationship with God is not stagnant; it is alive and real, growing and evolving all the time. I find that so exciting and amazing! God is always teaching us and helping us to grow in our relationship with Him and others. A day does not go by if we are reading God's word and spending time with God, that God does not add to what we know, think and have within our relationship with God. God loves to reveal new and wonderful things not only about Him, but about us as well. God is alive. Therefore our relationship with God is alive and living. A living, growing and evolving relationship is what God wants to have with us. God wants us to be ever growing in who and what we are as a person and in our relationship with God. Then as we grow and as the relationship grows God reveals more of His mystery; the great mystery of God's amazing love for not only His creation, but for us as well; the absolute wonder of God's mercy and grace towards His creation and all that He has created; the incredible gift of forgiveness God has for each and everyone of us as we become more honest in ourselves and in our lives. I have heard it said many a time that it is a pretty sad day if we have not learned something new. It is exciting to think that God cares for us so much that God wants us to learn something new about Him everyday. God builds into our growing process a desire for us to gain knowledge of His word and how that Word brings life and true living. Then God adds to our knowledge wisdom. Then to our wisdom He adds joy and hope. Then to the joy and hope the ability to truly live our lives and be all that He created us to be. The wonder of God's love and plan for our lives! Have you ever wondered what God's plan is for your life? Let me tell you. God's plan is that we would have joy, peace, mercy, grace, hope, forgiveness, healing, blessing and salvation, true life, and the ability to live our lives and so very much more. Then God adds to that the individual plan for each of our lives. In God's love and wisdom His plan is revealed to us when the time is right, when we are ready to hear and know the plan and have the ability to carry forth all God is asking of us. It is also revealed to us when we start asking God what the plan is for our lives. God has so much to teach and tell us, let us open our hearts, minds and total selves to all that God has for us today and every day. For each new day is an adventure in God and everything God is. When we are hungry for God searching for new ways to experience God, He is right there showing us. Teaching us all we desire to know and learn. There is no end to all that God wants to reveal to us His children, God's chosen Beloved. Let us be people who hunger after God with a true desire to know God better and His plan and purpose for our lives. We will be amazed at all God reveals to us.

Prayer: Father God, I do open myself to your love for me. I open myself to the plan you have for my life. I want to be the person you created me to be, taking my place and walking in your ways. I am sorry for the times I knew you were calling to me and trying to speak but had shut you out. Please forgive and let us start afresh today in our love for each other and the relationship we both desire. Thank you for your great mercy and grace and the forgiveness I have been given. I am so blessed to be your child. I now take my place and truly open my life to you, amen.

Day One Hundred Eleven

Hosea 2:19 'I will betroth you to me forever; I will betroth you in righteousness and justice, in love and compassion.'

Betroth is not a word we use today. To be betrothed to someone is to give a promise to marry or to be given in marriage. It is a promise for future intentions of marriage. Here God is saying through the prophet Hosea that God promises to marry Israel. God promises to take Israel as His bride. God is choosing to be betrothed to Israel and is making His intention known. God is also prophesying His intention to marry all His children for generations to come. God has promised His creation the covenant of marriage, which means we have been given the promise of God to be His bride, His chosen beloved for all time. God is giving us the promise of taking us to Himself. Why? So that we can have a covenant relationship with God within the marriage promise. We are the bride of Christ! The chosen beloved of the Most High God! We have been given the intended betrothal. The promise has been pronounced so all the world will hear. The declaration has been signed, sealed and delivered. When we are betrothed to someone, the next question is, when is the wedding? When will this betrothal be complete? It will happen at one of two possible times. One is when we die; when we stand before the judgment seat of God. If we have accepted the betrothal, the wedding takes place. We become in that instant the bride of Christ. The other time is when the second coming comes. Those who are still alive and living on this planet earth that we call home, will be taken up in the clouds and will be joined with Jesus. This second opportunity will happen when Jesus comes back on His white horse to reclaim His creation. If you have accepted the promised betrothal, you will then become the bride as you are joined together with your betrothed. It is such a comforting thought to know that this is not the end. To know that when we die, it is not the end either. When we die it is a new beginning. When our times comes to leave this world we get to start again in the kingdom of God with all the blessings, benefits and promises. When we die or when someone we love dies, it is not good-bye, but rather "so long" until we meet again; "so long" until it is my turn to meet you in the clouds with the Heavenly Father standing by your side. Knowing that all the struggling and stresses of this world are not for naught, all the struggles are part of the journey and process. We who accept the betrothal have the promise of eternal life as the bride of Christ. What a glorious day that will be! When we join in the marriage of the Lamb at His wedding feast, we will get to live forever with the one who loves us the most. We will get to live forever with God's unconditional love for all eternity. What a day! What a glorious day that will be!

Prayer: Jesus, I do accept your betrothal. I do accept your invitation to be your bride and to live with you for all eternity. Thank you, for loving me so much and for being the awesome and amazing God you are. Thank you that this is not the end when my time comes to leave this world but rather a new beginning. I accept the promise and hold on to it with great anticipation. I await the wedding feast of the Lamb, amen.

Day One Hundred Twelve

John 12: 44-46 'Then Jesus cried out, "When a man believes in me, he does not believe in me only, but in the one who sent me. When he looks at me, he sees the one who sent me. I have come into the world as a light, so that no one who believes in me should stay in darkness".'

Think about this for a moment. Jesus says He is the light of the world. Jesus says He is light, pure light. If that is true then all light comes from Jesus and who and what Jesus is. Everything that is light is from Jesus. I have spent a good number of hours reflecting on this simple thought. If Jesus really is the light of the world, then the light that comes through electricity is a reflection of Jesus' light. The light from a flashlight or fire comes from Jesus' light in the world. The light from the sun or moon or stars is from the light that Jesus is. All light that is light comes from the light that is Jesus. I know it is hard to get our heads around this concept but if Jesus is telling us the truth, then all light is a reflection of Jesus' light regardless of where it comes from. Like I said I have spent a good number of hours thinking on this thought and what this means and I am no where close to understanding it. If Jesus is the light of the world and if all light does come from Jesus, then when we stand in Jesus' light we stand in pure light. Therefore it will pierce our darkness. Jesus' light will turn our darkness into light. When the light shines in the darkness the darkness cannot stand. The darkness has to give in to the light. The darkness has no power when the light is shining. Even the light from a small birthday candle, when lit, pierces the darkness in its light. It does not matter how small the light is, it breaks through the darkness and its light shines forth. There is no darkness that is greater than the light. The darkness has to give in to the light when the light is lit, that is a fact—a truth. Belief in Jesus is also belief in the Most High God the Creator of the universe and all life. When we believe in Jesus and the Most High God we have Jesus' light in our lives. Whatever darkness there is will be pierced by the light of Jesus and His light in our lives and in the world. The darkness in our lives and hearts can and will be made light by the presence of Jesus' light in us. The light that shines in the world shines in us. We now have light instead of darkness. Some of us have grown up with terrible darkness in our lives. We know first hand what it means to have no light shining within. When we meet Jesus and let His light shine within our darkness it truly does shine. The light pierces our darkness and there is now light shining. Some of us may still be in our darkness. We may still be living in a dark place. Let the light of God shine in your darkness and the darkness with have to give in to it. Let Jesus' light shine into your darkness and the darkness will no longer be as dark. The more we let Jesus' light shine in us the more our darkness is dispelled.

Prayer: Jesus, I want your light shining within and in me. I want my darkness pierced and your light shining in its place. I give you permission to come into my darkness and bring your light. Let your light shine brightly within my life and me. Thank you, for bringing your light and piercing my darkness. Thank you, for shining your light in me. Thank you, for piercing my darkness with your amazing light. I am so very grateful, amen

Day One Hundred Thirteen

Romans 12: 18-19`Do not boast over those branches. If you do, consider this: You do not support the root, but the root supports you. You will say then, Branches were broken off so that I could be grafted in.'

This promise goes right back to Abraham when God told Abraham that he was going to bless Abraham so that Abraham could be a blessing to others. God was going to use Abraham and his seed to bless all of God's creation, that is to bless everyone who is ever born and will ever be born. God's desire in blessing Abraham is to change the course of history. God wants to start a new page in the book, with a new beginning in our hearts and lives. From Abraham's blessing, the Jewish nation is born. From the Jewish nation, Jesus is born. From Jesus comes the greatest gift ever given---the gift of salvation. The gift gives us the right and ability to be back in a right relationship with God. This means we are no longer separated from God because of original sin. Original sin is the eating of the forbidden fruit by Adam and Eve. We, who choose to believe in the promise given to Abraham and the gift of blessing and salvation promised, have the open door to live in freedom. We have freedom from our past mistakes and wrong choices. Freedom from the bondage of what we have inherited from our families. Freedom from the consequences of original sin and the bondage original sins puts us in. This freedom is available to all who desire to receive it. This freedom is given freely to all by God's great mercy and grace. God gives it to all who enter His family. God gives the opportunity to move from what was into everything God has for our lives and us. As this verse says, we are grafted into the promise. The promise of blessing and life! We are given a second chance to be in a right relationship with God. The second chance is a different path; a path of release from the pressures and bondage the old path caused. If we choose the gift of mercy and grace God is offering us, we have a way out of our wrong choices and mistakes and the wrong choices and mistakes of others. We have a new path that leads us to life and blessing instead of curses, darkness and death. We get to join the family line that sets us free from sin and death. We get to join the family line that opens the way of life and salvation. We are grafted in so that the root now supports us with all the life force the root has. We, who were once without hope, now have hope. Why? Because of the promise given to Abraham and all who follow in his promise. We are truly blessed beyond measure. Therefore we too can now be a blessing to others for we ourselves are blessed. We have a new life force flowing through us, giving us hope for today and hope for tomorrow. We now have the inherited rights and privileges of being a part of God's promise of blessing. We can now take this promise and share it with others so they too can come into the promise and all the promise holds for today and tomorrow.

Prayer: I am so grateful that Abraham was willing to receive the promise and believe it and in his obedience it was credited to him as righteousness. I get the gift of blessing and salvation as I am grafted into the root of true life. Thank you, Father God, for opening the way for me to enter into your plan of salvation and for restoring me who was lost. Thank you, for opening the door so that I could join your family and have a place of my own. I would like the Abraham blessing. Bless me, so that I can be a blessing to others, amen.

Day One Hundred Fourteen

Romans 12: 20 'Granted, but they were broken off because of unbelief, and you stand by faith. Do not be arrogant, but be afraid.'

I hear individuals all the time who do not hold a healthy reverence towards God and the sovereignty of God. I hear people diminish God's place and authority as King of kings and Lord of lords. I hear individuals say 'the big guy upstairs' or other statements along those lines, which I feel is disrespectful and dishonouring towards God and who He is as the Most High God. Our God is sovereign and deserves to be treated with the honour and respect that is due His name and sovereignty. We need to have a healthy respect and fear of who and what God is. When calling upon God's name or engaging God in any shape, manner or form we need to reverence God. In the Jewish tradition they would not even speak the name of God and when they wrote it, they left out the vowels so as not to dishonour God. Their tradition did not want to bring God down to human form or image. There is a reverence and honouring of God and God's place in creation and all of life. I am not saying that we have to go that far. What I am saying is we need to have a more reverent view of God and who and what God is and His power, sovereignty and authority within creation and beyond. It is so easy to be arrogant and to put ourselves above God at times. It is easy to fall into the trap that says, "God is there but who cares, for He is not going to do anything anyway. Judgment day will not happen, it is just a myth started to keep humans in line". Our arrogance at times puts us in a place of wanting to bring God down to our level or to dismiss God altogether. The reality/truth is God is real, and as God cut off the Israelites for their disobedience and desire to have life on their terms and conditions, God can surely discipline us. God can certainly hold us accountable for our arrogance and need to have life our way. The Israelites chose to believe or think God would not cut them off from His presence, or discipline them for their selfish ways and behaviours. They thought it was okay to do whatever they wanted to do and that nothing bad was going to happen to them. We too need to take a second look at our attitudes towards God, to see whether or not we have a healthy fear and reverence towards God and who and what God is. Or, are we like the Israelites who thought they could do whatever they wanted to do and get away with it without any consequences or ramifications? There has always been and will always be a need for a healthy reverent fear of God. A healthy fear that puts God in His rightful place as the Sovereign God He is. Do we have that healthy fear in our hearts and in our relationship with God? Or are we one of the ones who take God for granted, bringing God down to our level and not fearing God in a healthy life giving way?

Prayer: Father, forgive me! Forgive me, for all the times I did not hold you in the place of honour and respect you deserve. Forgive me, for not having a reverent fear and respect for you and your sovereignty in me and your creation. Forgive me, for thinking that I could be God and do whatever I wanted to. I am truly sorry. Teach me, how to reverence you in my whole life. Thank you, Father, amen.

Day One Hundred Fifteen

Philippians 2: 4 `Each of you should, look not only to your own interests, but also to the interests of others.'

We are so very blessed! We are blessed beyond measure when we really sit down and think about all the blessings we do have. We are blessed in so many ways and with so much. We at times think we should have more or be blessed more. However with all of our blessings and all that God has given us, for some strange reason we are not very good at sharing our blessings. Some of us are not very good at sharing with others some of the blessings we have been given. We want and try to hang on to our blessings and hoard the blessings, so they stay ours and only ours. That way others will not get any of the good that is happening to us. I believe that steals the blessings away from us at times. I believe if we do not give it away, we lose it. I have traveled a lot in my life. There were times when I traveled alone and times when I traveled with others. The times I traveled alone, the memories are there, but other people were not with me to share the memories and experiences with me. When I traveled with others, it is not only the memory that is good, but also the reactions of the ones I was traveling with. It is always better to do something with another person or people for they add to the fun, memory and experience. Having people to share life with is so much better in my mind than walking through life alone. I believe that our greatest need is relationships and without relationships we die. If our greatest need is relationships. Then what happens to our relationships when we are selfish and do not share with those with whom we have a relationship? What happens to us when we choose to live as loners and without relationships in our lives? When I think of myself only, and what I need or want, there is no room in me for others and what they need or want. If I do not share what is happening to me or in me, others cannot journey with me; they are left out of my life and experiences. I get pulled into myself more and more. If I have to hoard my blessings, then the other person or people in my life do not get to share in what God is doing in my life. They do not get to share in all that God is blessing me with. This in turn may prevent God from working in their lives because their faith does not have the opportunity to grow or be stretched. It is so very important to share our lives with others and to have others share theirs with us. This is what makes us healthy and complete individuals and people. We are designed as people to live in community. We all have families, friends, associates or acquaintances in our lives who are there, yes, as individuals. They are also there as part of our lives with whom and through whom we share and love. We all have people in our lives from one perspective or another. Hopefully we are doing the best we can to build each other up and help each other to be all that we were created to be. Let us therefore share the blessings we are being given, so that others are encouraged to do the same. It is truly better to give than to receive. I believe the more we give away the more God pours into us. Test my theory and see if it is true.

Prayer: Heavenly God and Father, I am beginning to see that being selfish and self-centered is not good for me or for others. Help me, to be more giving of myself and to stop being so selfish with what I have and what you have given me. Teach me, how to share and be willing to share of my blessings and myself. Help me, to be more like you Father, who gives so generously to us. Thank you, Holy Spirit, amen

Day One Hundred Sixteen

Luke 10: 31 'A priest happened to be going down the same road, and when he saw the man, he passed by on the other side.'

When Jesus gave this illustration of the Priest, the Levite and the Samaritan, I believe Jesus was saying that, sometimes we get caught up in our own positions and images of power and status and we forget about the commandment to love each other. Sometimes we are afraid of the one we are passing by-like the homeless person on the street or the teenager who is dressed very differently with the body piercing, baggy clothes, spiked coloured hair, or whatever they are wearing that is different. We do not understand, therefore there is fear and we all know what we do when we are afraid. We run, walk or just get away from what is causing the fear. It is the same with people everywhere. It is called the human condition. I am not saying we are to face everyone we are afraid of; that would be wrong and dangerous. What I am saying is, there is a need for us to be real with what we fear and to allow ourselves to risk and love on a deeper level. The Priest and the Levite did not want to become unclean therefore chose to ignore the hurt man. The Priest and Levite had their own agenda and the hurt man did not fit into their agenda. The Samaritan carried no alternative motive or agenda, therefore could help him and reach out his hand of generosity. The Samaritan reached down into his pocket and heart and gave to the one who was hurting without strings attached. He saw someone in need and reached out to help him. Is that not what Jesus is asking of us? When we see someone hurting, we too are to reach out and help the person make it through the hurt. We too are to share of what we have and have been given. There are times we see someone crying and walk on the other side of the street or ignore him/her in church. We see someone without food yet cannot find it within ourselves to give him or her food. We see young children being abused or hurt and we turn a blind eye. There are so many ways we walk away from the hurting people whom we see on a very regular basis. Here is a simple test. When was the last time you put food into the food donation box? When was the last time you gave someone a hands up? When was the last time you reached down deep within yourself to be there for someone else? When was the last time you put someone else first, before your wants or desires? Today we are being challenged to be people who care and give of ourselves to help others who need our help. What can we do differently to be the kind of person who is willing to reach out when another person needs our help? How can we make a difference in this world we live in? How can we share the light that is within us? What can we do to show that we care enough to share? We all cannot do everything. But all of us can do something and that is all that matters. We can all give on some level, even if the giving is just a smile to someone who is sad.

Prayer: Father, I am sorry for all the times I walked away on the other side thinking only of myself and not the other person. I am sorry that I do not even do the simple things that would make a big difference in someone's life. Forgive me, and help me, to be more open and receptive to seeing where my help could be used and more willing to help when help is needed. Thank you for forgiving me, and helping me. Help me, to do the same for others. In Jesus' name, amen.

Day One Hundred Seventeen

Ephesians 4:26 `In your anger do not sin. Do not let the sun go down while you are still angry.'

Have you ever let your anger stay inside of you, hanging on, just sitting there and festering inside? Have you been in a place where you know you need to say something to someone about something that has angered you, only you cannot find the words? Maybe you are or were afraid of bringing up the situation or problem for fear it may not go well, and the outcome may be more than you want to deal with. How about the times you have been angry and instead of processing it, you explode and spew out your anger all over the place? I would venture to say that most of us are in one of the categories or maybe even two or three of them. A lot of us choose to deal with our anger by either the 'sitting on it' method or the 'exploding out our anger' method. When we get angry with someone or something and sit on the anger, the anger does just that. It sits inside of us gaining power and intensity. In fact, when we let the anger sit for a while, it begins to take on a life of its own. Our anger begins to control us, not us controlling it. We find ourselves being angry even when we do not want to be angry. We find ourselves having to deal with our anger even if we don't want to. Our anger at times is the only emotion left that has permission to express itself and it comes out even when we want to say loving words to someone or share in a positive way. I can hear some of you saying `I don't get angry, I never feel anger, I am not an angry person'. The truth is we all have the emotion of anger within us. We have all been given the emotion of anger. Therefore we all at some time in our lives will feel that emotion, whether we like it or not or admit it or not.

Anger is a part of the human condition. What Ephesians is saying to us today is it is okay to be angry but it is not okay to sin in your anger. It is okay to have healthy "in the moment" anger that voices the feelings and emotion without causing hurt and pain to whatever we are angry with/about. There is nothing wrong with our anger; what we do with it makes it right or wrong. What we do with it, makes it either or life-stealing. It is important to not let the sun go down on our anger. To not let the anger stay for more than a short time. To deal with whatever is causing us to feel angry before we go to sleep. That way when the morning comes, we are ready to start a new day with a fresh set of feelings. Hanging on to our anger only causes us to get stuck in our mud puddle of angry feelings. Getting down and getting real with our anger and how it is affecting our lives, brings us the freedom we need to be the person we were created to be in the first place. That is why we are being told to not let the sun go down on our anger. Letting our anger sit inside of us or explode only causes harm to others and us. Not letting the sun go down on our anger allows us to be open, honest and up front with what we are feeling and why we are feeling that way. Healthy anger is being angry in the moment. It gives us permission to deal with the situation that has caused the anger in the first place. Unhealthy anger is letting the anger fester or letting it build up until you explode causing great harm and whatever else. Unhealthy anger is when we do not forgive, when we constantly bring every little thing up from the past that has caused us to be angry, when we refuse to forget anything. Unhealthy anger is holding on to every little detail and using them to cause hurt and harm. Let us choose to be healthy people in the use of our anger, and work things out so that we do not let the sun go down on our anger and angry feelings.

Prayer: I am beginning to realize that I need new ways of dealing with my anger and the angry feelings I have at times. Holy Spirit, teach me how to process my anger in healthy growing ways. Help me, to not let my anger fester so as to hurt others or myself. Help me, to see my anger as an emotion that I can control instead of it controlling me.

Thank you, for loving me the way you do and for helping me when I need help. Holy Spirit, be my constant guide and source of all life within me, amen.

Day One Hundred Eighteen

Jeremiah 31:3 'The Lord appeared to us in the past saying: I have loved you with an everlasting love; I have drawn you with loving-kindness.'

Such words of comfort! I have loved you with an everlasting love; I have drawn you with loving-kindness. Simply put God's love never changes and never will change. God's love for us is now and will always be the same. Why? Because God cannot change the love He has for us. God's love is always the same and never changes because that is the character of God. We are now and always will be loved by God; that is a promise that can be counted on and held tight. We are safe and secure in God's love and nothing can ever change that. The love our Heavenly Father, the Most High God has for us, you and me, is everlasting. It never runs out. There is no expiry date on His love. God's love is a constant power source that can never run dry. The love God has for us is the same every single day of our lives. It does not change because of our behaviour or lack of good behaviour. It is not altered, increased or decreased, when we are doing well or not doing well. It does not increase because we find ourselves really close to God and God's presence is almost tangible. God love us with the same intensity even when we are going through the dark night of the soul. No matter what place we are in spiritually or physically. God's love for us is always the same. God's love for us is not based on our performance. In fact God's love is not about us at all. God's love for us is based upon His choice to love us and to be in love with us. God loves us because He created us to be loved by God. God's love draws us. It pulls us towards Him and His love. If we go to

1 Corinthians 13 we get a good idea of what God's love is. 'Love is patient and kind. It does not envy or boast, it is not proud. It is not self-seeking, it is not easily angered, and it keeps no record of wrongs. Love does not delight in evil but rejoices with the truth. Love always protects, it always trusts, it always hopes and always perseveres. Love never fails'. Now let us put God's name in the place of love. God is patient and kind. God does not envy or boast. God is not rude or self-seeking. God is not easily angered and God keeps no record of wrongs. God does not delight in evil but rejoices with the truth. God always protects, God always trusts, God always hopes and God always perseveres. God never fails. I believe that is the kind of love we are all looking for and want in our lives. That kind of love is surely the kind of love I want in my life. That kind of love draws us into wholeness and being whole, into being all we were created to be in the first place. That kind of love sets us free to be ourselves without any pretense or illusion. That kind of love is the love God has for us no matter what! The love that does not change or alter, the love that is the same yesterday, today and forever, the love that is based upon who God is and His choice to love us and be in love with us, always. The love God has for us is clean, pure and simple. There are no strings attached, not will it ever have strings. God's love for you and me is the kind of love we all search for in our lives. Well that love is just a prayer away. It is now and always right here with us, always the same and never changing. Let us embrace it and make it our own.

Prayer: Thank you, Father God, for loving me with a love that is pure and clean and , with a love that never fails and never ends. I want that kind of love in my life. I open my heart to receive your love and all your loves is and means to me as your chosen, beloved child. Thank you, Jesus, for bringing that kind of love into my life. Teach me, how to love you in return. I want to live in that kind of love in all relationships, especially my relationship with you, amen.

Day One Hundred Nineteen

Galatians 2: 16 'Know that a man is not justified by observing the law, but by faith in Jesus Christ that we may be justified by faith in Christ and not by observing the law.'

The Jewish book of the Law holds all of the laws within the Jewish tradition. To truly follow the Jewish tradition you must obey the law. The Jewish tradition has a foundation, which is based upon the following and observance of the law. The law is the focal point of their relationship with God and being justified before God. Atonement is found in the following and observance of the law and all that the law requires. Without the observance of the law one cannot be justified before God and the community. The struggle with this form of justification is one can never be totally justified by following the law, for none of us is perfect and without error. The only true way of receiving atonement (at one with) from God is through the sacrificial shedding of Jesus' blood, which is a once and for all time sacrifice. We are justified in God's eyes by having faith in Jesus Christ who is the fulfillment of the law. We are justified before God not because we observe and follow the law, but because we have Jesus in our lives who has paid the penalty for our sin and sin debt. We are justified through the shedding of Jesus' blood, hence the release from the power of the law upon our lives. We in ourselves can never do enough to make up for all that we have done in error or wrong choosing. We can never make the past right in our own steam or resources. The only way we can be justified before God is through the sacrificial blood of Jesus the Christ on the cross at Calvary. For atonement to happen in the Old Testament there had to be the shedding of blood, an animal's life was given for the atonement of both known sin and unknown sin. Without the sacrifice there was no forgiveness. Jesus is the atoning once and for all time sacrifice that sets us free from the past. Jesus' shed blood sets us on the new path of being restored and made right with God and God's law. It is the great gift of mercy through Jesus' death on the cross that sets us free to truly live again. It is the taking of our sin debt by Jesus that allows us to stand justified before God, having been set free and forgiven from all we have done or not done. There is no other way for us to be free and forgiven from all our wrong choices, mistakes etc., except through the mercy and grace of God's forgiveness. The release comes when we accept the gift of God's grace and mercy. The forgiveness is ours because of God's grace and incredible gift of mercy. Our sin debt is paid because when Jesus died on the cross He took them upon Himself, therefore canceling them out for us. Our sin debt is cancelled because Jesus died on the cross, conquering sin and death, thus releasing us and setting us free to have true life within us and a ticket into the kingdom of God. We get the gift of God's salvation, mercy and grace given to us because of God's great love for each and every one of us. The gift is made available to us because God wants to be in a love relationship with us. God wants us to spend eternity with Him in His heavenly home. God is madly in love with us and wants us with Him for all time, hence the gift of His love and freedom.

Prayer: Thank you, Jesus, for dying in my place, for paying a debt you did not owe, a debt I could not pay. Thank you, for releasing me from the bondage of sin and all the consequences it bring. I am truly grateful. Thank you, for loving me that much. In Jesus' name, amen.

Day One Hundred Twenty

1 Timothy 2:4 'who wants all men (people) to be saved and to come to a knowledge of the truth.'

In our world today I hear people saying in groups or as individuals that there is no absolute truth, that there is nothing that is sure and true from an across the board perspective. What is truth? How can we really know what truth is? Truth is relative to the one speaking it. What I believe to be true is what is true whether others believe it or not. If I believe that something is true for me and I believe it, then it has to be the truth. If that is true and truth, then truth is relative to the one speaking it. If truth is relative then there is no absolute truth, for real truth has to stand regardless of who is speaking it or under whatever circumstances it is spoken. Truth has to be the same no matter what the time frame is or the circumstance. Jesus said that He was/is the truth. If you want truth then you need to go to Jesus, for He is the one who is the truth. How can Jesus be the truth? A better question is what is the truth? Truth is the fundamental foundation upon which spiritual reality exists. The starting and finishing point of spiritual reality has to stem from the same place; it cannot change or fluctuate because of situations or events. Truth is truth regardless of who speaks it or when or where it is spoken. If that is truth, then there can only be one truth upon which spiritual reality is formulated and based. When we look at Scripture and the commandments, laws, decrees and precepts in Scripture, we discover as we put them together, it is the foundation upon which all spiritual reality grows and from which it flows. The reality of positive life consequences and outcomes are laid out in such a way that if stood upon, would produce a life filled with love and healthy relationships. In the New Testament we get Jesus saying that He is the one who brings the truth and all truth stems from Him and His existence. Let's take something simple to test this premise. The first commandment is love the Lord your God with all your heart, soul, mind and strength and love your neighbour as yourself. If we live by this truth, then our lives and relationships will be whole and functioning from a perspective. When we do not love God, our neighbours and ourselves, we find ourselves in a place of being lost and having hurt and pain in our lives. When we live our lives in a self-centered way, the result is harm to us and to others, not to mention confusion and upheaval in our lives. Balance and well-defined lives come from loving God, loving our neighbours and loving ourselves. If we put love first, then all the other pieces in our lives would come together in such a way that they bring life. It is when I am selfish and self-centered, demanding life on my terms and conditions, that life starts to fall apart. When we put love first in all our dealings with life, the end result is true life and wholeness within our lives and relationships. When we look at all that Jesus stood for and the lessons He taught us, we begin to see that the truth Jesus said is actually the truth upon which true life is lived and lived out. Therefore to say there is only one truth is correct, for all life is to be lived from the premise of love. When we love first and live according to the law of love, we have truth in our lives and spirits.

Prayer: Thank you, Father, for truth. I have a deep sense of gratitude in my heart knowing that there is absolute truth and I can have that truth in me and in my life. Help me, to have a solid foundation of spiritual reality, which is the basis of all truth. There are so many lies floating around. I want the truth in me and in my life, so that I can have real life within me. Thank you, for being the truth. Thank you, for being trustworthy in all you say and do. Thank you, Jesus, for only telling us what is truth and reality, amen

Day One Hundred Twenty-one

John 16: 7-8 `But I tell you the truth: It is for your good that I am going away. Unless I go away, the Counselor will not come to you; but if I go, I will send him to you. When he comes, he will convict the world of guilt in regard to sin and righteousness and judgment.'

Jesus is once again telling His disciples and us exactly who He is and what His role is in the world. Jesus knew that the only way He could be in all places at the same time was by His Spirit. As a human being He could only be in one place at a time. Jesus could not touch our lives in the way He does without leaving this world and then sending the Counselor, His Holy Spirit, to be with us. Jesus had to die on the cross not only for the forgiveness of our sin, but also for redemption, the being made right with God and ourselves. As the Holy Spirit, God can be everywhere at all times. The Hoy Spirit lives in us when we accept the gift of truth and salvation, and open our hearts to the in-filling of the Spirit of Christ, the Saviour of the world and us. When we open our lives and hearts to God and the Holy Spirit, the Holy Spirit takes up residence in our hearts and can guide and lead us from the inside out. The Holy Spirit begins the good work of changing our lives, restoring our brokenness, healing our pasts and hurts and most importantly convicting us of our guilt. The Holy Spirit convicts us of our guilt in regards to sin and righteousness and then the coming judgment. It is so easy to get caught up in sin (being selfish and demanding life on our terms and conditions) and the affects sin has upon our lives. We need the guidance, love and mercy of the Holy Spirit helping us, and pointing out areas in our lives that need adjusting, the areas in our lives, that are not right with God and hence cause an imbalance in our lives and relationships. God wants us to be in a right relationship with Him, others and ourselves. God wants us whole, vital and alive. That is why Jesus died on the cross. Jesus died on the cross so that there would be a way out of all that was, and thus opening the way back into the wonder of who we are as part of God's great gift of creation. The Counselor/Holy Spirit is now available to each and every one of us who make God a personal God; a personal God who works from the inside out, helping us change our lives, restoring us and making us new. We are new creations. We are new creations, therefore let us rejoice and be glad. Let us rejoice as we are being transformed from our sinful nature into the precious, chosen, special, worthwhile, beloved children we are and are meant to be. God loves us! We are all loved by God and everything God is. That is the truth. The amazing reality is we can have that incredible love within us making us whole, alive and real; all we need do is ask and it is ours. The Holy Spirit is within our hearts showing us how to truly live our lives. Let us follow the leading of the Spirit of God both on the outside and inside.

Prayer: Thank you, Jesus, for sending your Holy Spirit to us and making it possible to have you inside of us changing our hearts and making us whole. We are so grateful that you, God, are a personal God who loves us from the inside out. Thank you, for loving even me. Thank you, for seeing me as your BELOVED, precious and valuable. With a deep sense of gratitude I say thank you. I want more of your truth within me making me whole, amen.

Day One Hundred Twenty-two

> *Acts: 4: 10 `then know this, you and all the people of Israel; It is by the name of Jesus Christ of Nazareth, whom you crucified but whom God raised from the dead, that this man stands before you healed.*

There are a lot of people today who do not believe that Jesus has the power or ability to heal. They believe that what happened in the Acts church cannot happen to people today. That people might have been healed during the Jesus' time on earth and shortly thereafter, but healings do not happen today. We have doctors and the medical profession to bring about whole and healthy bodies. Medical science is the answer for today, not the presence of God in His creation doing the healing. Personally, I believe that God does not change and if God healed the people in the Old Testament, if God healed the people of the New Testament, then God can heal us today. In fact, I know first hand that God does heal today and does do miracles and wonders as well. I witnessed God one day heal one of my volunteers who was crippled and in a wheel chair. God asked her to forgive a resentment she had been carrying for a very long time. As she let the resentment and bitterness go. She got up out of her wheel chair and to the best of my knowledge has not gone back to it. I have seen offenders I work with receive prayer for an illness or disease in their bodies. God in His infinite mercy and grace brings healing to them. We have a God for whom nothing is impossible. That means nothing is impossible for our God. If God is the same yesterday, today and forever, then what God did in the past He can do today. Therefore God can heal today just as He healed in the past. All we need do is just believe and it will happen. Does God heal everyone who asks? No He doesn't. There are times we need to do our part before He can do His part. The example of my volunteer is a good one; if she chose not to forgive, to be obedient, God probably would not have healed her. She would have been stuck in the past pain and in her wheelchair. There are times we ask for a healing but in our hearts we want to be sick. It services us to be sick. Therefore to receive God's healing means we cannot be sick any more and that is just not an option for us. God cannot bring His healing if we do not want it. God wants us healed and living in wholeness; that is His desire for us. We need to remember the gift of free will, which might, and often does, interfere with God's desire of bringing us into wholeness. There is also the ultimate healing, which is returning home to be with God. There are times when we pray for a physical healing and the person dies. We get angry because they die, forgetting they are now completely whole and free, living with God in their eternal home. Ask God for your healing. You may be surprised by our Great and Awesome God and just get it. God loves you and wants you to be whole and totally alive. Just believe and trust God's love for you. When we ask in an attitude of faith amazing and wonderful things happen. When we ask in an attitude of unbelief and doubt we block the power and presence of God in the life of the one we are praying for. That includes us as well. If God really is the same yesterday, today and forever, then so is His power and mercy. Trust God and watch all that will happen in your life and the lives of those you are praying for. If by chance you are not healed, then take it one step further and ask God why. I do not know why some people are healed and others are not. All I know is what Scripture says, 'Go back and report to John…. The blind receive their sight, the lame walk, those with leprosy are cured, the deaf hear, the dead are raised, and the good news is preached to the poor.' (Matthew 11:4-6)

Prayer: I do believe! Jesus I need your healing touch. I need_____to happen in my life and heart. I come to you Jesus so that you can heal my body and make me whole. Show me where I need to let go and help me have the courage and strength to be the child you created me to be in the first place. Thank you, Jesus, amen.

Day One Hundred Twenty-three

1 Timothy 2:5 'For there is one God and one mediator between God and men, the man Christ Jesus,'

There is one big "G" God! There is only one God with the power to answer prayer, heal the body and creation, restore life, pierce the darkness, tell the truth, be light, love unconditionally, forgive, have mercy, grant grace, fulfill His promises and so very much more. One true God who never changes and will never change, who is the same today, tomorrow, yesterday and for always the same. No other god can say that and be speaking the truth for there can only be one. There are lots of little "g" gods, like the pagan gods and goddesses, the Greeks gods, Celtic gods, Norwegian gods, the god of power and money, the god of self and so on. These little "g" gods, at times claim they have the power but when push comes to shove and they are put to the test, they fail. In 1 Kings 18:16-46 Elijah takes on Baal. The prophets of Baal believed Baal was all-powerful until Baal was put to the test. Once tested Baal was shown to have no real power. The promises of Baal were not time tested and proven. The God of Elijah was shown to be real and well able to do as He said. There is only one big "G" God and that big "G" God is the God who has created all things. There is only one big "G" God who was in the beginning, and who will always be the same. The big "G" God is the one and only true God who holds the balance between life and death, good and evil. The beginning of the Old Testament states in Genesis 1:1 `In the beginning God created the heavens and the earth'. In the beginning God, and God created everything. Everything that exists, exists because God created it. Nothing exists without the creative hand of God at work in it. The second half of this passage then goes on to say that there is only one mediator between God and men, the mediator Jesus Christ. Jesus is the one chosen to stand in the gap between God and God's creation to mediate for us, to be the one who pleads our case, who is our advocate. Jesus Christ is the one given the power and authority to stand before God, in between God and us. The one who stands before God, defending us, pleading our case and telling the facts and truth. There is no other god in all of creation that has that authority. If this statement is true, and it is, then there is only one true God and Jesus is His mediator. What does that say about others gods? If this is true, then maybe the others gods are not telling us the truth. If we believe the others gods and they do not have to power they are telling us they have, then our eggs are in the wrong basket and we have the potential of loosing everything, just like the prophets of Baal lost everything when their god was put to the test. There are times when we need to have the bottom line in our lives. In my opinion this is one of those times. If God is really God, then all we need do is ask Him and He will tell us the truth and show us the evidence if need be.

Prayer: God, Creator of all things, I get confused at times with all the different gods proclaiming to be real and true. I get confused and run away at times because I do not know which direction is right and . Forgive me, and help me, to know the truth. Give me the knowing that allows me to stand on what is true. I do not want to follow false gods. I want the one true God to be the God of my life. I am open to the truth and receive it willingly. Thank you, Jesus, for standing in the gap for me, and being my mediator, amen.

Day One Hundred Twenty-four

John 14:6 'Jesus answered, "I am the way and the truth and the life. No one comes to the Father except through me."'

Jesus said: 'I am the way, the truth and the life. No one comes to the Father but my me.' With all the world religions, with all the different voices of religion out there, how do we really and truly know which is right? With every world religion telling us they have the answer how do we know? How do we trust? How do we pick? Which one is the real one and how do I really know for sure? Jesus tells us how we can know; Jesus gave us the answer. Jesus says with boldness that He is the answer. He is the only true way to God the Father. All the other ways do not lead us to the one and only true God. All the others ways lead to something but not to the Father. Jesus says if you want the way to God, the Father—I am the way. If you want the truth—then you need to get the truth from me. For I am the truth, the truth is found in me. If you want real life---then real life comes from being in a relationship with the Father through me. Everything else is false! Everything else leads us down the wrong path with a destination that may not be what we were searching for. This is arrogance and exclusivity you might say and you are right, it is. God is exclusive. The exclusivity comes from His statement that says to find true life and the truth; you find it through a relationship with God through His Son Jesus Christ. No other relationship will give you life, truth and the way to God. They will give you other things, but not what Jesus is offering. You want the one and only true God? Then you have to go through His Son Jesus and the gift of forgiveness and eternal life will be yours. We all have been lied to in that we have been told what the world wants us to hear. We all have had people tell us things that were not true and that lead us down wrong paths. It is hard to trust at times when we have been lied to in such a variety of ways. It is hard to put ourselves out there only to find ourselves once again being told lies. I know that and I understand. This time it is different! This time trusting is the right answer, the only real answer to life and living both here on earth and in the hereafter. This time trusting means you will be trusting the truth, and that makes all the difference. If you want the truth, the way and eternal life, then set your face and heart towards Jesus and you will find it. How do we know that? We know it is the truth because Jesus cannot tell a lie. If He is the truth, then He can only tell us the truth. For there are no lies in the truth, no half measures, nothing but the bottom line truth. For that is who and what Jesus is. Therefore when Jesus makes a statement or promise we can trust it to be true because it has to be the truth. There are no lies in Jesus and Jesus cannot tell a lie. Is this arrogant and exclusive on God's part? Yes, but the end result is life abundant here on earth and life eternal when we pass on to the next stage of our spiritual journey. The end result is life forever more. I'll take it.

Prayer: I open my heart and my mind to you, Jesus. I want the way, truth and life in me and my life. I do not want anything false in my life any longer. I want to have life in every sense of the word. I read that you are the life, the truth and the way and that is what I am looking for in my life. I am looking for true life so please come in and make me whole. Thank you, Jesus, amen.

Day One Hundred Twenty-five

1 John 4: 10 & 19 `This is love: not that we loved God, but that he loved us and sent his Son as an atoning sacrifice for our sins. We love because he first loved us.'

Do you know why you were born? Do you know why you have life? Why you are the individual person you are, with the personality you have and all the other wonders of you? The answer is God created you to be all you are and so very much more. You are here with everything you are, with the gifts, talents and abilities, because God chose for you to be here and to be the person He created you to be. God wanted you born so that He could know and love us/you as human beings. God gave you life so that you could know God's love for you. After you know God's love, hopefully you return the love that God puts in your heart back to God. This is love, not that we loved God, but that God loved us. God loves even us with all the stuff we have done or not done; with all the choices we have made both good and bad. God loves us first and foremost, regardless of everything that happens or has happened. God picked you and me first, before we even had life. We were chosen by God to be loved and valued by God for no other reason than because God wants to know us and love us. God chose us to be loved by Him regardless of what we do or whether we choose to love Him back; God still loves us. Now that has got to be the most amazing gift anyone could ever ask for or need---to be loved no matter what! God chooses to love us so that we can learn and know what love really is, then return that love God has given us back to God and to each other. If God had done only the giving of His love to us that would have been enough. It would have given us more, so much more than we deserve. If God had stopped there with His grace and mercy, we would have so much more than we deserve, but God in His infinite love and mercy did not stop there. God went one step further and sent His Son into the world to be the atoning sacrifice for our sins. We now have a way out of our sin and the wrong choices we have made regarding ourselves, plus the wrong choices of others upon our lives. Why has God done all this? Because God loves us and was willing to pay our sin debt and all that we owe. The simple reason of God's love for us is God's love for us. God loves us so much He does everything in His power to show us His love, and to be in a love relationship with us. Now that is love! And that love is waiting for each and every one of us without any strings attached. All we need do is ask for it. All we need do is reach out to God and tell God how we want that kind of love in our lives. The gift is free. The love is ours. The mercy and grace have already been extended. Let us walk as people who are truly loved for no other reason than we are loved.

Prayer: How can I ever say thank you God for loving me first when at times I am so unlovable? How can I ever express my gratitude to you for loving me, and never giving up on me especially when I have given up on myself? Thank you with a deep sense and feeling of gratitude for who you are and for loving me the way you do. Help me, to take that love and love others and love myself, amen.

Day One Hundred Twenty-six

1 John 4: 7-8 'Dear friends, let us love one another, for love comes from God. Everyone who loves has been born of God and knows God.'

Now that we know we are loved by God and will always be loved by God, no matter what happens, it is now time to carry that love to others and to us. It is time to take the love God is filling us with, to help others know more about God's love. Why? So that they too may know the truth that God loves them. God loves all of us no matter what! Love comes from God and everyone who loves has been born of God. God knows that person personally and intimately. If God's love is in you, because you accepted God's gift of love and salvation, then you are born of God. The truth is because you are born of God, God loves you intimately and personally. No ifs, ands or buts. You are loved by God. End of story! God's love is in you regardless of whether you feel it or sense it. God's love is in you and it is not based on how you feel or even on what you think. God's love is based on the promises of God. Everyone who loves has been born of God and knows God. Why? Because we can only know real love when we have the real love of God within us. When we have the real love of God within us, we have the desire and ability to know love----love for ourselves, for others and for God. True, real love comes from a loving relationship with God. Let us now move out in the love we have been filled with to fulfill the call upon our lives to love others. To show others the love of God and the blessings we can have from living in God's love. What does that look like? When someone insults you, you don't insult him/her back. If someone cuts you off on the highway instead of giving them the finger, give them a prayer asking God to bless them, for they do not know what they are doing. Another example is letting someone in a hurry have the space in front of you in line, or slowing down to let another car move in front of you. Not giving back hurt for hurt, but love for hurt. Doing the right thing when the wrong would be easier. There are so many ways we can show love to others, let us begin today. You may be totally surprised at the outcomes that come from loving first and foremost. Let us today find ways of showing God's love to others and then watching how God uses the love in their lives. When we love, we are instruments of positive change in our world. We are instruments of God's love in our world. We are bringing light into the darkness and exposing the darkness for what it really is. When we love first and foremost, we chose to live as children of light; children who bring light, which then pierces the darkness and exposes the darkness for what it really is.....darkness. The more we risk in our willingness to love, the more we are able to love. The more we put our love out there, the more love we begin to feel on the inside. The more we reach out in love the more love comes back to us. It is the law of the harvest. What you sow is what you reap. Sow love and reap the blessings that come from your willingness to sow love into our often loveless world.

Prayer: Help me, Holy Spirit, to love others. Help me, to shine your love light in me to others. I need your help to fulfill this request. Help me, to love first and foremost to all who come into my life for whatever reason. Help me, to be an instrument of love and love's light in my world. Thank you, Holy Spirit, for being my constant source of courage and strength. Thank you, for being the light that shines in my life, amen.

Day One Hundred Twenty-seven

Ecclesiastes 4: 9-11 'Two are better than one, because they have a good return for their work: if one falls down, his friend can help him up. But pity the man who falls and has no one to help him up! Also, if two lie down together, they will keep warm. But how can one keep warm alone?'

Two are better than one. Sharing an activity or event with another person makes the activity or event more enjoyable. Going for a walk on the beach with a friend or someone you really enjoy being with brings great pleasure to ourselves and our spirits. Sharing laughter makes the heart lighter. There is an old proverb that goes like this: A problem shared is a problem halved. We are designed to live and be in relationships; without some kind of relationship we die. In fact, our greatest need in life is to have relationships. When seniors living in a nursing home have a pet or animals come to visit, they are more alert, sociable, and generally healthier. Children with special needs who are given riding lessons or the opportunity to swim with the dolphins are much more responsive and more physically able. Offenders who are released with supports in place within the community or the family structure are less likely to re-offend. Teenagers who come from loving, supporting homes with parents who spend time with them are much less likely to get into trouble and stay in school longer. They will probably go on to further education of some sort. When we know people care about our welfare and us, we are less likely to get into trouble or do harm-causing events and choices. Married men generally live longer, healthier lives than non-married men. Our greatest need is relationships and without good, healthy relationships in our lives we suffer more from ill health, depression, sadness, loss of purpose and generally are not as happy or joyful. We need people in our lives, people who love us and care about us. Then, when the struggles of life come our way, we will have the resources to handle them better. Why? Because we have caring, loving, people who love us and travel the journey with us, helping us in whatever way they can. Several years ago a friend of mine lost her mother suddenly to an unexpected illness. I asked my friend what I could do to help. Her response was, just be there. Be there during the wake and be there for the funeral. I was just there, not saying anything or doing anything, just being there. Every once in a while she would look over to make sure I was still there. Knowing she was not alone was all she needed to help make it through this time of stress and struggle. Knowing I was there just in case she needed a shoulder to lean on was all she needed to give her the extra ability to do all she had to do. Did I do anything physical? No, all I was, was the light shining in her hour of darkness. Two are better than one. It is true for pieces of strings it is also true for our lives.

Prayer: I am learning that I need people in my life. I need healthy relationships to be with me as I travel this life journey I am on. I repent for pushing people away who try to love me and help me. I repent for not trusting and letting people in. I repent for keeping them at bay. Please forgive me and help me, Holy Spirit, to have healthy relationships in my life. Help me to love the people you give me to love.

Thank you, Holy Spirit, for being my constant source of true life and light, amen.

Day One Hundred Twenty-eight

Philippians 2: 4 `Each of you should, look not only to your own interests, but also to the interests of others.'

As human beings we can be so very selfish at times, so self-centered that we cannot see beyond our noses or self interests. We get stuck in our own selves and our self desires and what is happening in us or about us only. It is very safe to live this way.....no one gets in and we do not come out from behind our safety zones. The problem with living this way is it is also very lonely at times. Our greatest need as you have heard me say several times is relationships and without relationships we die. Therefore, to only look out for our own interests means we are short changing ourselves in our greatest need. We are not giving ourselves permission to have others know us or us know others. I have heard it said to have a friend we need to be a friend. To have friends we need to open ourselves up to being a friend to another person, a friend being someone who knows our song and sings it back to us when we are forgetting it. A friend is someone who asks you how you are and sticks around to find out the answer. They do not leave until you tell them how you are really doing. To have a friend means we have to be there for others and have their best interests at heart. If I am only looking out for me, I am not looking out for others. I cannot look out for others, for I am not moving beyond my needs and what I think or feel I need. If relationships are our greatest need, and I believe they are, and if we are designed to live in community, then there is a responsibility for us to look out for the interests of others. There is a responsibility for each one of us to know what is happening around us and with the people we are in relationship with. Have you ever known someone who was taking the wrong path in life and walking down a path that would lead them to destruction and/or harm? You knew they needed some help, but you, for whatever reason, just did not offer any help. Then you discover or hear that they ended up in a royal mess. You also know that if you had just taken a little time and put a little effort into them, they might not have ended up where they are. The person would have had a chance to move off the path of destruction and back onto the path of life. The God given responsibility of living as a human being within community and relationships is to love and support each other and be in relationship with others. The responsibility we all have as inhabitants of this planet earth we call home is to be there for the ones who love us and we choose to love. The need we all have is to look out for each other and to be there for each other as we journey together. This does not mean that we are to take care of everyone and become lost in others to the exclusion of ourselves. What it does mean is we live loving each other and being there for each other when the help is needed. We care for the best interests of those we share time and space with, and all we need to do to take care of ourselves. I need to love me first and as I love 'me' I can then love others. If I do not love myself I will have a really hard time loving others. The call is one of love. When we choose to live in the call of the love we are committed to loving ourselves and others as we journey through life.

Prayer: I am grateful for the people you have placed in my life and with whom I am in relationship. I know I complain about them at times. I know I do not always appreciate them, but they are important to me and who I am as a person. Help me, to be there for them when they need my helping hand or even a warm hug. Also Father, help me to let others be there for me when I need their help and loving kindness. Thank you, Father, amen.

Day One Hundred Twenty-nine

Ecclesiastes 3:11 `He has made everything beautiful in its time, he has also set eternity in the hearts of men; yet they cannot fathom what God has done from beginning to end.'

I am learning, slowly, yet learning that God does make everything beautiful in His time. When we trust God with our lives and pasts, He really does make our lives beautiful. I see it everyday with the individuals I work with. I watch as God takes broken and damaged lives and puts them back together. How He takes people out of their darkness and puts them in His light. How He restores lives by putting back the broken pieces, lost pieces or pieces eaten by the dog. We have such an amazing, awesome God for whom nothing is impossible when we give Him permission to work in our lives and in His creation. There is a song written by Bill Gaither that goes like this.

Something Beautiful, something good,
All my confusion, God understood,
All I had to offer Him was brokenness and strife.
But He made something beautiful of my life.

There are so many times in our lives when all we have to offer God is brokenness and strife. When our minds are so full of confusion we feel lost and alone. We feel like no one understands. No one could possibly know what we are going through. We are lost with no way out. Then God comes alongside of us with our permission and says, `I understand, I can help if you will let me. I can turn your brokenness into something beautiful, because I made you to be beautiful in the first place. I can restore all things.' Our hope is rekindled. We risk and trust God. Then to our total amazement God comes through for us and we do become something beautiful, valuable and worthwhile. God does take everything we offer Him and turns it into a valued treasure. God does make something beautiful of our lives in His time! "Thank you, God, for seeing beyond our confession and brokenness into the preciousness that is ours because you created us to be precious and special, valuable and worthwhile, chosen and beloved. Thank you that we can never be too broken or lost for you not to reach and help in our time of asking. We are truly blessed beyond measure. Our blessings go beyond measure when we have you in our lives to help see us through no matter is happening or not happening. Help me to let you turn my brokenness and strife into something beautiful for I am realizing it is time. Father, it is time for me to let you take my broken heart and turn it into the valued treasure you created it to be."

Prayer: Father God, I am learning that the only true way out of my brokenness and strife is through your love and in your time. I put my life in your care and ask you to restore me, restore the beauty of my life in your time. I cannot do it without you. I cannot do it alone. I need your help and healing presence. I need your restoring presence Lord, amen.

Day One Hundred Thirty

Ecclesiastes 3:1 `There is a time for everything, and a season for every activity under heaven.

A time to be born, a time to die, a time to plant and a time to uproot, a time to kill and a time to heal, a time to tear down and a time to build, a time to weep and a time to laugh, a time to mourn and a time to dance, a time to scatter stones and a time to gather them, a time to embrace and a time to refrain, a time to search and a time to give up, a time to keep and a time to throw away, a time to tear and a time to mend, a time to be silent and a time to speak, a time to love and a time to hate, a time for war and a time for peace. A time for absolutely everything in this world! A time to hang on to things and people and a time to let them go; everything has a time, a reason or a season. All things have a time frame in which they exist. There are few certainties in this life. One of those certainties is we all are born and one day will die. No one knows when that will happen or how. What we do know is that one day we will see our day to die. Even relationships. There are three types of relationships.....those relationships that are in our lives for a reason, for a season or for a time. At work here, I am in the offender's lives for a reason and a season. The reason is to help them grow in their faith and spiritual journeys. The season is the duration of their sentence. There are others that are in our lives for a time like family members, spouses, long time friends, or those special people God gives us to love. Everything thing in life has a time. Everything has a span of time in which they exist. Nothing lasts forever! Tears may last for a while but then the joy comes. The growing season is short lived and then the harvest time comes with great rejoicing, or if the harvest is lost, with sorrow. Even the pain in our lives has a time and season if we let it. The lessons will be learned and the healing will take place. I am in awe of God and His great plan for His creation and His children. When we give ourselves permission to trust God, absolutely and totally amazing things happen in our lives. They happen in ways that are so much a reflection of God's love for us as His children and members of His great family. As we go through life let us always remember that there is a time and a season for everything. A time to hang on and a time to let go! Take a few moments to think about the things in your life that you have been hanging onto that need to be let go. You need to let go just because the time has come to let go and it is the right time. Now think about the things you need to be bring into your life, but you have been holding them back. One of the goals in life is to have a balanced perspective of life, living and relationships, knowing everything has a reason, a season and a time. When I look at life from this perspective it is much easier to see the beginnings and the endings as all part of God's great plan and I do not have to get caught up in them. Rather I can enjoy and celebrate them even when the endings hurt for a while.

Prayer: Help me, Holy Spirit, to trust your timing in everything. Help me, to not get bent out of shape when my healing, or my life, or the lives of others, or events do not happen on my time schedule. Help me to trust the truth that you knows what you are is doing and it will happen in your time. I am so impatient, Father. Thank you, Lord, amen.

Day One Hundred Thirty-one

Ecclesiastes 5:15 `Naked a man comes from his mother's womb, and as he comes, so he departs. He takes nothing from his labour that he can carry in his hand.'

`Naked a man comes from his mother's womb, and as he comes, so he departs.' He takes nothing from his labor that he can carry in his hand.' As we come into the world so we will depart from this world. There is nothing we can take with us that is outside of ourselves. The only thing we take with us is what is in our hearts. If our hearts are filled with hurt and pain, then that is what we take with us into eternity. If our hearts are filled with joy and much healing, then that is what we take with us on our journey. Our spirit is what moves on to eternity, not our bodies. When we die we get a new body. We get a new heavenly body. This earthy body we are using here during our stay here gets to remain here on earth. This is just a reminder that accumulating lots of possessions is not the lasting treasure we hope it will be. In fact, when our turn comes to journey on, others spend and use our wealth and possessions. Others get to enjoy them or use them up. I remember when my adopted mother was alive. She put great value on her china, antiques and other possessions. She took great pride and joy in them. When she died, yes, we treated her things with respect and honour when dividing up the family treasures and household items. Yes, we honoured her and her treasures. But in truth, we, the children did not have the same sense of value for a lot of the items she treasured. In fact some of the items none of us wanted. Some of the items held no value at all. I remember a lady one day saying to me. "I have the responsibility for the all of the family heirlooms and antiques. They are all in my home. I am so afraid that something is going to happen to them, that there will be a fire or someone will break into the house one day and destroy them." She felt in bondage to the heirlooms and antiques. She felt trapped by them. Do not get me wrong. I am not saying there is anything wrong with having nice things or valuable items. What I am saying is there are more important treasures we need to have in our lives. The more important treasures are relationships and friendships, meaningful people in our lives who know us, really know us and value us and we them. These treasures are the ones we take with us when we depart this world. These are the treasures that last an eternity. I often tell the residents there are no saddlebags on coffins. We cannot take our earthly possessions with us. Our heart is the saddlebag we fill up and carry onto the next phase of our journey. What is in your saddlebag? What are you carrying with you when your time comes to leave this earthly home we live in? Do you have good solid relationships and memories of every kind and sort? If the answers are yes-------then celebrate and be glad. If the answers are no------then what do you need to do differently so you can fill your saddlebags? What condition is your heart in? Eternity is an awfully long time to have our hearts filled with lots of unnecessary baggage and things we really do not need.

Prayer: I am so sorry that I have looked at my possessions and wealth as more important than my relationships. I put my possessions or wealth first and foremost, forgetting at times how important my family is, my friends are, my loved ones mean to me. Help me, to be faithful in loving the people in my life and building up good relationships, so that my heart is full when I depart this world with good things I want to take with me. Forgive me and help me, get my focus in the right place and my saddlebags filled up for all eternity. In Jesus' name, amen.

Day One Hundred Thirty-two

Ecclesiastes 9:10 'Whatever your hand finds to do, do it with all your might, for in the grave, where you are going, there is neither working nor planning nor knowledge nor wisdom.'

So many of us waste our lives never venturing out. Never trying new things or experimenting with new and challenging areas of learning, growing or becoming, we are stuck in our routines. Each day is the same, holding the same things, never changing. Some of you have wanted to do something for years but have been afraid to do it. Maybe you do not have the time, or the finances, or the inner permission to venture forth in your desire. We hide it away on the back burner pretending we might get to it one day only to discover too late, that it is too late. I remember a senior lady in my church that always wanted to sing professionally. Her heart's desire was to be a professional singer but she got married and had children instead. She was now in her eighties and still hung on to the regret that she never gave it a try. She never gave herself permission to risk and see if she might have been a successful singer. She died never knowing. She died filled with regrets, anger, sadness and a sense of bitterness towards her husband and children. I know another young woman who wants to sky dive. It has been a want for several years and she is arranging for her first jump. This young woman will risk her fears and face them and jump out of the plane. This wish/want will become a reality and not a regret later on in her life. She is biting the bullet and risking her all to fulfill her dream and heart's desire. What are you putting off? What is your dream? What is sitting on your back burner that you need to bring to the forefront and risk doing? I have always wanted to try ceramics but never did because I do not have a sense of colour and colour coordination. This year I am making nativity sets for my nieces and one for myself. I am making other treasures for loved ones as well. I am risking and having a great time doing it. I am not as bad as I thought I was. In fact, I have discovered a hidden talent, that I did not know was there. A pleasant surprise! When my time comes to leave this planet earth I call home. I can honestly say I have conquered my fears and did those things I had in mind to do. When we die and are in the grave there is no time left to do those things we have always wanted to do. I have a friend who has always said, ever since I met her, that when she retires she will get all the pictures in the picture albums. If she were listening to Solomon's advice and wisdom, she would not wait, for the time may never come. Let us heed Solomon's wise words and do whatever our heart/hand finds to do, no longer wasting time or making up excuses. The day is now and this is the hour, reach out and risk, you may be totally surprised at the outcome. Carpe Diem---seize the day. Seize the hour for it will never pass this way again. Let us not be the ones who come to the end of their journey here on earth having lots of regrets and bitterness because we were not willing to seize the day. Let us live out our hopes and dreams making them a reality in our lives.

Prayer: I do not want to live in regrets any longer. I do not want to spend my life wishing I had done something or not done something. Let me be bold in the living of my life. Let me risk and do the things my heart and hand would have me do. Let it be when I reach the end of my days here on earth, I can say that I have no regrets, that I did the things I have always wanted to do and faced my fears. Help me, Holy Spirit, so I can reach my end of days having fully lived my life and enjoyed the journey, amen.

Day One Hundred Thirty-three

Matthew 16:23 'Jesus turned and said to Peter, Get behind me, Satan! You are a stumbling block to me, you do not have in mind the things of God, but the things of men.'

I love this passage of Scripture because it reminds me that I can at one moment be totally wholly living in holiness, then the very next moment have the things of this world front and center in my life and choices. How susceptible we are to both sides of our human condition, the carnal side and the spiritual side. Just before this passage, Peter revealed his knowing that Jesus is the Son of God and the Son of Man, which could only have been revealed through his intimate relationship with God. Not five minutes later Peter is called Satan and told to get behind Jesus because he was no longer in the things of God but now in the things of men. What a blow! What an ego crusher. What a reminder of how human we really are. How set we are on having and living life our way and according to how we want and see things. How vulnerable we are to the influences of this world and the darkness that so easily steals our light. Our spiritual side wants to think like Peter when he was revealing the truth of Jesus. We want to be spiritual all the time and have the things of God in our actions and thoughts constantly, front and center in our lives. We want to believe we have it all together spiritually, that we are on the side of God at every moment of my life. No side tracking for me. Full steam ahead in the right direction, no side trips for me. The truth is, our human side, our carnal side, our selfish side wants life on our terms and conditions and as we see it happening or unfolding. Our human side wants what it wants when it wants it. The struggle and challenge is knowing which side is fueling our thoughts and life choices at any given time. How do we know when we are truly connected to God and when we are following our human wants and desires? The answer for me is when I have my hand in God's hand and my eyes fixed on God, then I am usually on the God track.

When I have my hands in my pockets and looking at me, then I am doing what I want or think is best. Where is our focus? Is our focus on God and God's will for our lives and His creation, or are our eyes focused on our perspective for life and living? The first commandment of God is to love the Lord your God with all your heart, soul, mind and strength and the second is to love your neighbour as yourself. When we put love first and foremost, then usually we have the things of God front and center. When we choose to live life according to the ways of God, then usually God is first and foremost. Let us put God first and foremost in our dealings with the world and with all the decisions we have to make on a daily basis. If we are seeking after God, we will find God. If we are seeking after our human wants and desires we will find so many other things but probably not God. Yes God is in all of His creation and all He has made but God has given us free will to make our own life choices and to decide what we will seek after. Life is so much better with God leading the way. Life is so much more fulfilling when we are heading towards life in all our choices and actions.

Prayer: Holy Spirit, I need your help at all times. I need you helping me at every bend of my life's road guiding me and showing me which path I am on and which direction I am taking. Without your help I know I will at times choose the wrong way. Thank you, Holy Spirit, for being my ever-present help at all times in my life. Thank you for loving me and caring for my every need. I need your help. Thank you for helping me, amen.

Day One Hundred Thirty-four

Matthew 16:25 'For whoever wants to save his life will lose it, but whoever loses his life for me will find it.'

When I first read this verse I thought to myself, how can this be? How can I gain my life by losing it and how can I lose my life by hanging on to it? Then the truth of this verse hit home. If I hang on to the past hurts, pain, shame, guilt, secrets, hate and so on, I truly do end up losing my life. I lose my life because I will not have lived my life in the present and in all the present has to offer me. I will have lived my life in the past and all the past represents. But if I let go of the past with all of its hurts and pain, then and only then, do I get to have a life in the present, living in my today. It was like a major revelation to me. By letting go of the hate and anger I could find peace and joy. Letting go of the guilt, shame and secrets gave me the freedom to trust and not consider myself less than worthy of love. When I let go of the sadness, there was lots of room for laughter and joy. When I released the resentments and bitterness, there was room for love. It was true. If I hung on to the past, the past was all I got from life. But if I let go of the past, then I could begin to live in today with all that today has to offer. The more I hung on to the darkness of yesterday, the less the light was able to shine in my present. The more I lived in the past the less I could see the blessings and joys of what today was offering me. When I moved into the present, the darkness no longer had a hold on me, locking me in and keeping me prisoner. The light was able to shine and the more I let go, the more the light shone. It is true! In order to save my life I have to lose all those things that prevent me from having a life today. The more I hang on to them the less I am able to live and enjoy life. `For whoever wants to save his life will lose it, but whoever loses his life for me will find it'. When I come to terms with my past and all that it holds, then and only then can I begin to have a present and future. Yesterday is gone, tomorrow is a mystery, today is a gift that is why it is called the present. Living in the past will only steal the wonder and joys of all that today can and does hold. The reality is God has to be at the center of our lives. God has to be the one guiding and helping us live in freedom and truth. Without God's help we get stuck in what was, stuck in the past and all the past was for us. When we are stuck in yesterday, we forget about what today holds for us. When God is with us, life is what we get in return. "Thank you, God, for this truth and revelation today. Help me to make it so in my life. Help me to let go of those things that are preventing me from having a life today and being able to enjoy this life I have been given. Help me to really put yesterday behind me for that is where it needs to be. I want the freedom to be able to live in today without my yesterday holding me captive."

Prayer: I have been trying so hard to hang onto everything both good and bad in my life. I am beginning to realize that I can let go of them and be free. Truly free! Thank you, for opening my eyes to this truth and the freedom this truth brings into my life. Help me, to lose my life so that I can find it. Help me, to be the person you created me to be, living my life fully and fully being alive. Thank you, Holy Spirit, for revealing the truth to my spirit and setting me on the path of true life. I am so very grateful, amen.

Day One Hundred Thirty-five

Matthew 16:26 'What good will it be for a man if he gains the whole world, yet forfeits his soul? Or what can a man give in exchange for his soul?'

Here is a reminder of what was taught a couple of days ago. Have you ever noticed that there are no saddlebags on the coffins you have seen in your trips to the funeral home? No matter who you are or how much you have accumulated in your life, or not accumulated, not one of us takes anything along other than what is in our hearts. The only things we take with us are what we have stored up in our hearts. What a sobering truth! In the end all that truly matters is what is in our heart. In my time as a prison chaplain and doing on call chaplaincy at the local hospital I have discovered, when people are dying they ask, for the most part two very basic questions. 1) Was I loved? 2) Did I love well? Did I have people who loved me? Who invested their love in me? Are there people that I love and into whom I have invested my love? Have I over my lifetime allowed others to love me and have I allowed myself to love others? Have I risked with my heart and have I allowed others to risk with me? Nothing else seems to matter when we are standing at the door between life and death. All our wealth, money, possessions, toys, houses, etc have no real value. The only thing that has value is the relationships we have fostered along life's path. We spend so much time and energy amassing wealth and things at the expense of our relationships at times, only to discover when our time comes to leave this planet earth, the material things we have invested in and struggled over have no real value. They are not what are really important. They are not what hold the value for moving on to the next phase of our journey. How disappointing and hard to swallow! We spent so much of ourselves competing with the Joneses, trying to be the best or having the best we forgot about what was really important. We forgot about the people God put in our lives to love and be loved by us. We forgot about our relationships and wake up one morning alone without anything but our wealth, toys and things. Life is so very much more than our possessions! So very much more! We can be a very sorry bunch of shallow people at times. Let us, today commit to having healthier relationships and investing our love and time into the people we say are important to us. Let us, when we reach the end of our road say with confidence, I was loved and I loved well. I gave myself permission to love others and have others love me in return. Then when our day comes to move on, we can move on in peace knowing we gave life and love our best short, knowing that we have allowed ourselves to walk the path of love and of being loved. Then having no saddlebags on our coffin will not matter, for our hearts will be full. The outward things will not be holding us back, as we will have lots of good stuff in our hearts ready to move on with. Our inner saddlebags will be stuffed with all that really matters in life.

Prayer: Father, I am sorry that I have put such importance on what the world says is important and have forgotten about what you say is important. I am sorry for not giving myself permission to live my life in and life-sustaining ways. Forgive me, for not investing in the people you gave me to love, for not giving them my love or time. Instead I put things first that had no lasting value. Thank you, for this second chance. I needed the reminder. Remind me, every day about the importance of loving my family, friends, life and me first. Help me to be honest with my love and relationships. In Jesus' mighty and powerful name, amen.

Day One Hundred Thirty-six

*Revelation 3:20 `Here I am! I stand at the door and knock.
If anyone hears my voice and opens the door, I will come
in and eat with him, and he with me.'*

Let us look at this passage of Scripture once again. Have you noticed in this Scripture it says Jesus stands at the door of our hearts knocking? Why doesn't Jesus just come in? Why does He stand at the door knocking? The answer is Jesus cannot go where He is not invited. Jesus cannot go where there is no room made for Him to go. That is why He stands at our heart's door calling our names and knocking for us to let Him in. We have all the control. We decide if Jesus is welcome or not. We decided whether the door is to be opened or stay shut. Us! We have the power of choice and the freedom to choose. My friends that is true of all of our lives. We decide which places in our lives God is welcomed and which places we keep locked away. Which places God is invited to enter and which place is locked up so tight that even the dust cannot get in. We have, and will always have, the final say. God wants to be in all areas of our lives but if we are not ready or do not want Him in those areas, He cannot break down the door or force His way in. Jesus stands waiting patiently for us to decide what it is we want from Him and our lives. If we want to stay locked away in our mud puddles even though that is not what God wants of our lives, He says okay. I'm patient. I'll wait until you are ready. I will not force you to do anything. On the other hand if we are ready for a deeper relationship with God and ourselves, we can simply open the door to our hearts and the locked areas. God will come in with His healing hand, bringing life and freedom. The choice is always ours. That is called free will. God cannot go against His gift of free will to us. Whatever we decide is what God does. His love is that pure and constant. If you are ready to risk on a deeper level of intimacy with God today, then give God permission to come in deeper. If you are still at the place where you need God on the outside, then don't open the door. God will stay outside calling your name and loving you just as before. Take a moment to examine your heart asking yourself what it is you really want from God? Do you want to go deeper into all that God is? Do you still need to stay behind your closed door keeping God at arms length? If you want God to come deeper, then ask God to come deeper. Ask God to show you how you can know Him more intimately. God will surely show you. If you need to stay in your comfort zone, then simply thank God for His love for you and His patience in that love. Whatever it is you need. God is ready to fulfill that need for you; all you need do is ask. God loves us far too much to ever take away our freedom to choose for ourselves, even when that choosing is harmful to others or us. That is the unconditional love God has for you and me, God's chosen beloved children.

Prayer: I am sorry for holding you, Father God, outside of my locked room and places in my life. I am ready to go deeper with you. I open the door to my heart and the locked places in it for I am learning that every time I trust you life gets better. Every time I put my hand in yours amazing things happen in and to my life. I am choosing to trust you, Father God; come and make me whole and the child you created me to be. Thank you, for loving me just the way I am but too much to leave me here. Thank you, for being you and all you created me to be, amen

Day One Hundred Thirty-seven

Revelation 3:19 'Those whom I love I rebuke and discipline. So be earnest, and repent.'

Those whom I love I rebuke and discipline. We do not like to hear these words on one hand; yet they bring such comfort and assurance on the other hand. I find it very comforting to know that God loves us enough to take the time to rebuke us, to discipline us when we are wrong and to help bring us back onto the right track of life once again. As children we did not like having to suffer through discipline. In fact, some of us protested very loudly at times because we were being disciplined, yet all the while feeling a sense of belonging. A sense of being loved because the people we care about and who say they care about us, care enough to make sure we have what we need in order to grow up well adjusted. They love us enough to enable us to be the person we were created to be. The people who said they loved us were willing to spend time and energy disciplining us and showing us a different path. They were willing to invest in us. When children are not disciplined or when they are allowed to exhibit negative behaviour, they often feel like no one loves them or cares about them. No one cares enough to take the time and energy needed to help them grow in healthy ways. They often feel like, who cares if I do this or don't do that. Who cares what I do anyway, so I might as well do what I want to do and the heck with the rest. Without discipline and boundaries the child ends up doing things they regret later on in life. They end up making choices that are harmful to themselves and often harmful to others. Without discipline the child does not learn to respect, to love and how to live in healthy relationships. They do not learn how to have healthy control over their emotional selves. Emotional control is learned through being disciplined and taught how to live as healthy individuals. It is the same with us as adults. There is a sense of love and being loved when people, and especially God, take time to point out the error of our ways and help us to change. I see it all the time with the offenders I work with. Do they get angry with me at times for telling them the truth? Yes. Do they know I care? Yes, and that is what keeps them coming back. Residents have often told me "Wendy we know you care and that is why you do the things you do for us". Discipline causes us to feel loved and valuable. When God is rebuking us or disciplining us, instead of getting upset or angry, let us rejoice that God cares enough about us to discipline us. Rejoice that God takes the time and energy to help us walk a different path and learn the valuable life lessons we need to learn. As we begin to let go of the areas in our life that are not , life takes on a completely different perspective and truth. Let the second half of this verse be the rule of thumb you use when you sense God is rebuking or disciplining you. Repent. Tell God you are sorry for the wrongs or errors in your life and then get on with life and living. Why stay stuck in your mud puddle when God has given us all a way out? Repent, for the kingdom of God is near. Repent, for that is where the freedom we all long for is found. Repent, and tell God you are sorry for the things you do that separate you from God and others. Do not run away from being disciplined' instead run into it. You might like the ends results better!

Prayer: Father, I thank you for loving me enough to rebuke me and discipline me. Thank you that you care enough to help me change my life stealing ways into life giving ways. I am sorry, for the times I grieve your heart because of the wrong choices I make or the errors I create. Help me, to live my life so that it is pleasing to you and life giving to me. Thank you, Father, for your discipline and never changing love for me, amen.

Day One Hundred Thirty-eight

John 21:15 'When they had finished eating, Jesus said to Simon Peter, "Simon son of John, do you truly love me more than these".'

Jesus asks Peter three times. "Do you love me more than these?" By the end of the third time Peter was feeling almost heart broken. How many times is Jesus going ask about my love for him? How many times do I need to repeat the words, "yes, Lord" you know I love you?" Three times Peter had denied knowing Jesus; three times Jesus asks Peter "do you love me". Jesus knew how much Peter loved him. Jesus knew exactly where Peter stood in his love for Jesus. I feel Jesus needed to fully reinstate Peter to the position of the rock he was called to be. Peter had to know in the very depths of his being that he was truly forgiven by Jesus for his denial of Jesus. Peter after the third question of his love for Jesus was ready to take his place as the leader of the new church being formed. I feel Jesus asks us as well "do you love me?" Do you love me more than these? Working with drug and alcohol addicts I know at times their first love is the drug or the bottle. They love the drug or bottle more than anything else. They would say that the drug or the bottle is their first love. Jesus was asking Peter, am I your first love? Do you love me more than anything? Am I first in your heart and life? Peter in all honesty could say, yes Lord you are my first love. There is nothing else in my life that I love more than you. Can we say the same thing? Do I love God/Jesus more than anything else? Is God/Jesus my first love or is there something else that has first place? Take an honest moment to ask yourself these questions. You may be surprised at the answer you get. Now go deeper still. Look at the place these valuables have in your life: money, substances, sex, gambling, food, attention, resentments, self-pity, anger, bitterness, hatred, power, control or manipulation? Where are they on the scale of your love and attention? There are so many things that we can, and often do, put before our relationship with God/ Jesus. Just as Jesus challenged Peter regarding his love and willingness to put Jesus first and foremost in his life, so too Jesus is challenging us. Who or what is our first love? Who or what has the first place in our hearts and lives? Is God first? Or does something else have first place in your life? Truly food for thought and reflection! When you come to your conclusions and have been completely honest with yourself, then either rejoice that your first love is God or repent for putting God in second, third, fourth place. Maybe you want God at the bottom of your list? If that is true then at least be honest with yourself. If you want God first then be honest with that as well. The question today is what is first in my life and is that the way I want it?

Prayer: As I reflect on this challenge today, I feel there are things that I put first before you, Father. Therefore, I repent! I repent, of the areas of my life that are more important than you God. Please forgive me and help me, to put you first in all areas of my life. Help me, to put you first so that my life can be in a place of balance with my priorities in the right place. Thank you, Jesus, for loving me the way you do and for helping me to see the truth in my life, amen.

Day One Hundred Thirty-nine

Ecclesiastes 12: 12-14 `Be warned, my son, of wanting in addition to them. Of making many books there is no end, and much study wearies the body. Now all has been heard; here is the conclusion of the matter: Fear God and keep his commandments, for this is the whole duty of man. For God will bring every deed into judgment, including every hidden thing, whether it is good or evil.'

After all that Solomon had learned, had been through and had in his life, with all the knowledge and wisdom in his heart and mind, with all the wealth and possessions, with everything he had and had accumulated in his life. Solomon's final conclusion in life is `Fear God and keep his commandments, for this is the whole duty of man.' When everything is said and done, when the last whistle blows, all that matters in life, all that has anything that is lasting is the fear of God and keeping God's commandments. There is nothing more lasting or important. Relationships are important and so very valuable in our lives. Money is essential for living, especially in the first world countries. Possessions are wonderful and give us great pleasure. In the end it is the fear of God and the keeping of His commandments that make everything else truly worthwhile. For God will bring every deed into judgment. Every thing we do, will one day, be, judged by God! There is nothing in life that is not seen by God and therefore judged by Him according to His standards, laws, decrees and commandments. We hope and pray that the secret things we do will remain secret and hidden. We pray that our bad choices in life will remain locked away in our secret volts. In reality and truth when we stand before God on our day of judgment everything will be out in the open, everything will be in full view of God. Hence the reason for keeping a clean slate and repenting for everything we have done that is not pleasing to God. Hence the need to have a healthy fear of God in our lives and heart and to follow His ways in everything we do and everything we are. Then when we come face to face with God, we will have nothing to fear, for everything will have been revealed, repented for and cleansed. We will stand before God cleansed from all our unrighteousness, forgiven and free. Solomon was right, what is most important in all of life is to fear God and to keep His commandments. That is where life is truly lived and where we are the freest. Living in a healthy fear and reverence of God helps us live our lives in a way that is truly in all aspects of who and what we are. Solomon lacked nothing in his life. He had power, wealth and fame. Solomon had seven hundred wives and five hundred concubines. His wisdom and prestige went throughout the whole world. Yet, when his days were coming to an end, he could honestly says with absolute certainty that the only thing that has lasting pleasure and true value is our relationship with God and living according to God's way, laws, rules, decrees and commandments. Nothing else brings value to life for everything else was fleeting. Knowing God is the only truth that brings life to every part of our lives. In the end all that truly matters is was I loved by God and did I love God in return.

Prayer: I am so grateful, Father God, for my relationship and the love, security and safety I feel in you. There is nothing more important than your love for me and my value and worth in being your child. Thank you for loving me, and blessing me and filling my cup to overflowing. Thank you, Father, for making my life full. Thank you, Father God, for showing me, that my life has meaning. I rejoice in all I am and all I am becoming because of your love for me and your desire for me to be all you created me to be. I am so glad you found me and I am your child. With a deep sense of gratitude I say, thank you. Thank you, for loving me the way you do, amen.

Day One Hundred Forty

Philippians 2:3 `Do not nothing out of selfish ambition or vain conceit, but in humility consider others better than yourselves.'

It seems to come so naturally to us, to be selfish and self-centered, to want life on our terms and conditions. To think about ourselves more than we think about others and who and what they are as people. To not think about what others need in order to make it through the day and/or life like the rest of us. Original sin (sin being self and our need to be god over our own lives, masters of our own universe) causes us to want life on our terms and conditions and our way, regardless of whom we hurt at times and how we make it happen. It causes us to want, what we want, when we want it and that usually is yesterday and, if not yesterday, at least this very moment. It causes us to be thinking about what we want and when we want it without regard for others. When we live our lives this way, we end up hurting others whether we want to or not. The reality is we cannot focus only on our wants and desires without hurting others. Today's Scripture reading is asking us to think of others before ourselves and to be humble in our approach to life and people instead of being selfish and self-centered and self-thinking. We are being asked to live in humility. Humility is not being proud or haughty, not arrogant or aggressive; humility is not thinking less of ourselves but rather thinking of ourselves less. It is being willing to put the other person on a higher plane than ourselves, rather than on the lower plane or back burner. It is doing the higher good for the other person, and putting their needs in a place of importance and value, instead of ignoring them or expressing their lack of value or worth in your mind or actions. We are being asked to think of others and their needs, instead of ourselves all the time and what we want or think is important or valuable to us. It is showing another person how their life is of value and worthy of honour and respect. It is showing them that they have a place in your life and you in theirs, that they are more than just a nobody that hangs around you. It is showing and telling another human being that their life is just as valuable as yours and you are willing to be there for them with support, love and respect. You value them in a way that is honouring to them and who and what they are as a person. It is so easy to live our lives just for ourselves and to not think of the impact it might have on other people. Everything we do has an impact in some way, shape or form. It never ceases to amaze me when a resident comes up to me when they are about to leave the institution and says thanks. Thanks for the ways you have helped me. Thanks for all I have gained from your teaching and all you have taught me. There are times when the thanks make sense, for I have had lots of contact with the resident. There are the other times when I have had little contact with the resident and they still say thank you. We do not know how we are affecting another person, by the weight of our words and how they are used. Let us be wise in our dealing with others, recognizing their value and worth in God. Let us be humble and honest with others and with ourselves. The benefits surely out weigh the costs.

Prayer: Father, I am so very sorry for usually putting myself first and for not thinking of others. I am sorry, for not thinking of how my actions or inactions affect others. I do not think about what would be beneficial to others and their lives and relationship with you. I know I can be rather selfish and self-centered at times. I am learning, my selfishness does others no good and nor does it benefit me. Please forgive me, and help me to be the person you created me to be in the first place, without always having my focus on me. Thank you, for loving me so much and forgiving me the way you do. In Jesus' name I pray, amen.

Day One Hundred Forty-one

1 Thessalonians 5:18 `give thanks in all circumstances, for this is God's will for you in Christ Jesus.'

We look at this statement and say to ourselves; how can I give thanks in all circumstance? How can I give thanks when I am hurting beyond belief? Or when I am so tired I just want to curl up and wither away? Or when I am so busy I do not know whether I am coming or going and I seem to meet myself in the middle at times? How can I give thanks when everything around me is falling apart? I could go on with the list of How can I give thanks.....God knows our circumstances and all we are going through. God knows what is happening in our lives and hearts. God knows what we are going through and that is why God says give thanks. I know it does not always make sense to give thanks when we are in the midst of whatever we are in. The truth and reality is when we take a step back and start giving thanks our hearts and situations change. When we take our focus off whatever it is we are going through and off ourselves, and put our focus on God, it is amazing how we start feeling different inside. When we start giving thanks in all circumstances we begin to see how much we really do have to be thankful for. When we focus on our blessings and the presence of God in our lives and all we have because of God in our lives and His provision for us and in us, it is amazing how our attitudes begin to change and we do become grateful and thankful. When we look beyond ourselves and into all that God is and all God is to us, we begin to look at life differently and see life through a different set of eyes. When we give ourselves the opportunity to look beyond what is happening to and in us, we can see life from a different perspective. Giving thanks in all circumstances causes our hearts and spirits to respond differently, and therefore, we respond differently. Life may be just as hectic or hurtful or hard, but now we have God coming in and touching our hearts and spirits. Why? Because we have given ourselves permission to open up to God's presence in whatever it is we are going through. As we open up to God and God's presence and gifts in the circumstances we are going through, we now have different resources to fall back on. The peace of God is now a part of all that we are going through. Or God may calm the storm that is raging within us while the storm still goes on around us. God may calm both storms inside and outside. God may send reinforcements to help us through. A friend of mine had to have emergency surgery, which meant she had no income. Her friends came along side of her and gave her gifts of money to help see her through. Giving thanks in everything is a gift we can give ourselves, a real and precious gift. Giving thanks opens us up to seeing the hand of God working in our lives. Giving thanks affords us the opportunity and ability to move forward and not get stuck in whatever is happening in and to our lives. Giving thanks changes us from the inside out, which in turn changes our perspective in our life situations. Yes, there still may be hard and most difficult things we have to deal with, but we now have new resources to fall back on and help us through. Giving thanks puts the focus back on God where it needs to be and off the circumstance we are going through. We do our part; God does the rest.

Prayer: Heavenly Father and Most High God, I am sorry for not being grateful. I am sorry for not giving thanks even in the hard times, for getting caught up in myself, and what was happening around me. I am sorry for getting stuck and not being able to see beyond myself. I am sorry for closing my eyes and heart so I could not see your hand at work in us. I now realize I was short changing myself because I was hanging on to me and not inviting you into all and every situation. Forgive me and remind me to always give thanks no matter what is happening or not happening in others and me. In Jesus' most precious name, amen.

Day One Hundred Forty-two

Matthew 25:23 ` His master replied, "Well done, good and faithful servant! You have been faithful with a few things; I will put you in charge of many things. Come and share your master's happiness".'

Trust is such an amazing gift we give to ourselves and to each other. In fact, I feel it is the most amazing gift. For without trust in our relationships we really do not have relationships. Without trust there is no glue to hold the relationship together. Trust is the binding agent that allows the relationship to hold a solid and true structure. Think about the people in your life today or from the past who have been trustworthy. They bring a smile to your face and cause your heart to almost skip a beat, because of the memory and trust you have shared. Now think about how they made you feel. People who are trustworthy are safe to be around, because we know exactly where we stand and there are no sideswipes, backhands or surprises. They are steady and sure. We can risk and know that even if we fail in our risking it will be okay because we can trust and not fear. Therefore we are willing to put ourselves out there more and grow in new and sometimes scary ways. Always feeling supported and loved, knowing that knowing that says, yes it is okay, and I will be okay even though right now I am not. Trustworthy people are the safety nets in our lives; they are always there no matter what. They are the constants in our lives that give us the ability to keep moving forward, trusting and risking, knowing that no matter what happens they will be there for us and with us. Now think about how you felt around the people who were not worthy of your trust, the ones who have betrayed your trust. People who are not trustworthy--- hurt us, shame us, causing bad feelings to happen inside of us. They make us want to stay in our safety zones and not risk or venture forth beyond what is safe. When all is said and done there is very little that is safe about those people. Therefore we do not like to be around them. We never know what is coming next. Betrayal in some form is usually the menu of the day. We are not safe because we never know what is going to happen next, as a breach of our trust. The wonderful people in our lives who choose to be trustworthy, who choose to not betray our trust, give us a comfort and peace just being around them. It does not matter how much we give them they will always hold our trust and not betray us. They do not use or abuse our trust even in the tiniest way. They honour and respect the relationship we have together as individuals and within the relationship, no matter what! Now the ones who are not trustworthy, it does not matter how small or insignificant the trust is we are giving them. They will usually find a way of breaching our trust and betraying what we have given them. They find a way to take our trust and use it to their gain and our loss. There is no joy in the relationships that are not trustworthy for there cannot be joy within them. The reason being---we are always waiting for the hammer to fall. Whereas in trustworthy relationships there is much joy for we can be ourselves in the truth of the relationship without any worries or fears.

Prayer: Father, I repent for the times I have taken someone's trust and not hold it dear and precious to me. I am sorry for the times I let my selfishness rule and reign in my life and heart and not the value of the trust being given to me. Please forgive me, and help me to be a trustworthy person in all areas of my life both big and small. Thank you, for your forgiveness and your love. In Jesus' precious and trustworthy name, help me start again, amen.

Day One Hundred Forty-three

> *Matthew 25:40 `The king will reply, `I tell you the truth, whatever you did for one of the least of these brothers of mine, you did for me.'*

The reference in this passage is for all of us to respond to the hungry, thirsty, lost, homeless, the sick and prisoners of our society. Do we have to respond to every single one? Do we have to be all things to all people doing everything that needs to be done? The answer is no. None of us can be all things to all people, that is an impossible task. What we can be is something to some people and if we all are something to some people than the needs of the less fortunate will be met to a much higher degree. Sometimes we get so caught up in our own little world that we do not see beyond our front door. We forget that there is a big wide world out there with individuals who need a hand up or a soft loving voice. We get so comfortable in our living space; we do not see that there are others who just need a little help every once in a while. There is incredible value in such simple things as; a simple note or card for the person receiving it when they are sick or in the hospital or not feeling up to par; a kind word or a smile to a stranger we meet on the street as we pass them by. A break away from the children for a single mom or dad who is carrying the total burden of raising the family, and finding it exhausting and needing a time out for themselves. A short phone call to a shut in whom never hears from anyone and spends his or her life alone. A latch key child, who always comes home to an empty house, can find security in being invited to another's home for milk and cookies after school until the parent gets home. Spare change given to a homeless person even if we know they are going to buy booze or illegal drugs. If they have spare change then they might not have to steal to meet their needs. Better still giving them a sandwich and a cup of coffee to help them make it through the day. There are so many ways we can make a difference in our world and in the lives of those who share our world. Ways that do not cost us much but make a vast different in someone else's life. Yes, it means moving outside of ourselves at times in order for us to think of others before ourselves. The truth is, in the end it makes such a difference not only to the ones we reach out to, but in our lives as well. It is amazing how simple gifts of ourselves help touch others and then bounces back to us. They are blessed, but so are we. They feel the touch of love in their hearts and our hearts are touched as well. The only difference between the sheep and the goats of this passage is what they did and did not do! They were all people living their lives doing what came naturally to him or her. The difference comes in how we live our lives and whom we invite in. The reality is we can all do something to show another person they matter and have value and worth. We can all in some way, shape or form make a positive difference for someone even if it is small and seemingly insignificant. We are learning that the falling of a leaf or tree in one part of the world, affects the other part of the world in some way. Let us be history changers or makes.

Prayer: I so needed this reminder today, Lord. The reminder to get outside of myself and help make a difference in someone else's life, even if it is a very small thing I do. Help me, to see where I can make a difference. Help me, to be willing to reach out and touch another's life. Thank you, for giving to me and reaching out to me. I appreciate it more than I tell you and more than I know at times. Thank you, Lord for loving me and giving me what I need to make it through my day and life. Thank you, for being real to me, amen.

Day One Hundred Forty-four

Matthew 26:24-25 `The Son of Man will go just as it is written about him. But woe to that man who betrays the Son of Man! It would be better for him if he had not been born. Then Judas, the one who would betray him, said, "Surely not I Rabbi?" Jesus answered, "Yes, it is you". `

Betrayal! It has to be one of the most hurtful things we can do to another human being. It cuts deep and has a long tail attached. Betrayal hits us in the very core of our being and to the very depths of our fiber. Betrayal is the breaching of our trust, which in turn weakens our ability to let others close or near us. When a person is betrayed the foundation of trust and trusting is weakened. If the betrayal happens enough the ability to trust can be shut down or locked away. When we are betrayed a part of us is lost to the betrayer. They steal a part of our ability to reach out and risk especially if the betrayal keeps happening. The betrayer violates our confidence and is proven to be false in what they say or do. When we are betrayed we can feel powerless, helpless, hopeless, empty, lost, alone, scared and so on. But thanks be to God who always leads us into triumphful procession! God has the ability, power and authority to restore, rebuild, or refashion the lost and broken pieces and the pieces of our lives that have been eaten by the dog. When we allow God into our hearts and lives. God can and does show and prove to us that there are trustable people. More importantly God teaches us that God is trustable and that we can truly trust God in everything and everyway. The more we ask God to prove He is trustworthy, the more He does prove it. That is the amazing truth of God. God's character says He cannot tell a lie, therefore God can only tell the truth! God says that

He is here with us no matter what. He will never leave us abandon us or forsake us. God has not brought us this far to drop us and will never ever drop us. No matter what happens in our lives or to us, God is always right here with us supplying all our needs and being the faithful God He is. God's love for us, His children and creation, is so strong and sure, that He commits to always being with us regardless of what others do, say, act and so on. God is always right here with us going through this journey of life. People betray us, we betray others and ourselves, but God never, no, never even gives us a glimpse or hint of any kind of breach of trust. God cannot betray us! God cannot go against His character. God cannot be anything other than what He promises to be. For God cannot tell a lie, He has to always tell the truth. The truth of the matter, God is a faithful God. God is constant and true from the beginning of time to its end. God is always the same. Therefore God is faithful and trustworthy. If you have doubts try God out and see what God does. You might be pleasantly surprised.

Prayer: Most High God; I confess that I have been betrayed in the past and because of that betrayal I do not trust as I need to trust. I need your help to heal my heart and teach me how to trust again. I confess that my heart is afraid to trust because of the hurt it has felt. Please forgive me, and help me to grow and let go. Thank you, Holy Spirit, for always being here with me and helping me whenever I need help. I am grateful. Come deeper into me so I can continue to grow and be who you created me to be. In Jesus' healing name, amen.

Day One Hundred Forty-five

Matthew 26:41 'Watch and pray so that you will not fall into temptation. The spirit is willing, but the body is weak.'

Watch and pray---two very valuable and important words. Watch---keep our eyes open, look attentively to what is happening around about us, keeping our attention fixed on what is going on, being alert. In other words to watch is to be ready and on your guard for whatever may or may not be happening. If I am watching something then I know when it is moving or shifting. If my eyes are not on whatever I am to be watching I can look back and it is gone. Have you ever been with a young child? You turn your head for just one second and puff they are gone from sight. You panic as you search for the child who is perhaps off playing in the toys or wondering about in their own little world. We are to be watching and keeping a close eye on the things around us. For if we are not watching, we may be tripped up. There is a need to be attentive to what is happening around us, so that, we do not fall into temptation or get trapped because we were not paying attention. We all have areas in our lives that cause us to struggle with temptation. My struggle is with food---if I do not keep an eye on myself, I can so easily fall into the temptation of eating far too much, which cause me to gain weight. Prayer is the tool, the key to staying alert and being on our guard. Prayer is the channel for God to work in our lives and in every situation we find ourselves in. Praying for strength and the ability to maintain an even keel in our spiritual and physical lives is the key to being successful or falling flat on our faces. Our spirits may be so very willing but our body of flesh is so very weak at times. If we take our eyes off our flesh and the desires of the flesh, we soon find ourselves giving into temptation and all the resulting affects. What am I focusing on? Am I focusing on my spirit and relationship with God or am I focusing on my flesh, my body and all that it is demanding of me? Not many of us really like working out! We do it because it is good for us. It helps keep us strong and fit and it has many great benefits for us. Given a choice to have all the benefits without all the hard work, we would probably opt for the no exercise route. For those of you who love to exercise, bless you, I thank God for you because you encourage the rest of us who are not as enthusiastic about sweating. The reality, is we all need to put time and energy into our bodies, so that it has what it needs, in order to function the way it was created to function. It is the same principle with our spiritual selves. In order to have the spiritual strength to face off temptation, whatever it may look like, we need to strengthen our spirits. That strengthening comes from being watchful and praying. When we are watchful and pray regularly, we have the strength and courage to face life. Without giving into our weakness, the strength and courage are there for us to tap into to. When we set our faces towards God, the power is taken out of temptation, because the courage and strength we need is available and waiting to be put into action. Let us be mindful of where we are putting our focus. Let us be strong and courageous when we are tempted to following the desires of the flesh. Let us be the ones who choose to live life to the full.

Prayer: Lord, I am so grateful that I do not have to face life alone. I do not have to do everything on my own. I have you Holy Spirit, helping me and guiding me every step of the way if I ask you to help and guidance. Thank you, for being my ever-present help in all of my life situations. Thank you, Lord, amen.

Day One Hundred Forty-six

Mark 3: 27 `In fact, no one can enter a strong man's house and carry off his possessions unless he first ties up the strong man. Then he can rob his house.'

I was exiting one of our local stores the other day, when I overheard a mother say to her approximately six year old son; 'you make me so sad'. I felt guilt that mother was putting on her son is so unfair. The truth is no one can get inside of us unless we let him/her get in. No one can make us feel or think anything we do not want to feel or think. No one can get inside of us unless we let him/her inside of us. Think about that for a moment---if you are bent on not laughing, even if you watch the funniest movie or the most incredible comedian you will not laugh. Have you ever had someone try to make you angry? Only to find that they would not because you had decided you are not going get mad, no matter what. Have you ever tried to fight with someone who would not fight back? Can you remember how frustrating the experience was? It does not matter what you do they just do not react. The truth and bottom line is no one can make us anything, unless we give them permission to get inside of us. Unless we let others tell us what to feel, think, say, do, act or react, they cannot get inside to change our feelings, thought or emotions. We all have the power and authority to decide for ourselves, what happens on our inside with our feeling, thought, opinions, actions and reactions. What someone does may cause me to process my thoughts or feelings. I may have to decide what I will do with what my feelings or thoughts are, but the reality is I decide---not the other person. My thoughts are mine and no one gets to them unless I choose to let them in. That six-year-old little boy could not make his mother sad---she chose to be sad, because of what her son said or did. In my opinion, it is time we take back our feelings, thoughts, opinions, actions and reaction. We need to decide for ourselves what will happen inside of us. We need to decide and not someone else deciding for us. It is time to stop letting others define us or tell us how we will feel, think, act or react. No one else! It is time to drive our own bus and stop letting others drive it for us. It is time to take back our right and ability to decide for ourselves what we will feel, what we will think, how we will act or react in any given situation. Our decisions are ours decisions, let us take back our right to live as we are meant to live and not as others say we should. This lesson will take practice but once you see the results of keeping your power (your right to decide for yourself) you will be encouraged to keep moving forward once you see the difference this lesson learned makes in your life. You will wonder how you ever managed without it. It is your life, your feelings, thoughts, opinions, action and reactions. It is time to decide for yourself how you will live them out and how they will be lived out in your life. It is time to take back your power to decide for your own life and self.

Prayer: Lord, I am so sorry for not learning this lesson earlier in my life. The lesson that says I am in control of my insides and no one else. Please forgive me, and help me, to learn how to hang on to me and what goes on inside of me. Help me, to be the driver of my own I feelings, thinking, actions or reactions. Thank you, for this life lesson. Thank you, Lord, for being my guiding hand, amen.

Day One Hundred Forty-seven

> *Mark 4: 24 `Consider carefully what you hear, he continued. With the measure you use, it will be measured to you and even more.'*

Some of us have the belief that says I can do whatever I want to do, without any consequences or back firing happening. We think that there are no repercussions for our actions and the choices we make. We especially think that we can use a short measure and get a long measure in return. That is so far away from the truth. The truth is: what we sow into our lives and the lives of others is, what we reap back. If we sow in a small measure, we get a small measure back. If we sow in large measures we get large or lots back. It is called the law of the harvest. What is sown is what is reaped. If you sow corn in your field do not expect wheat at the end of the season. If you do not put anything into your field, all you will get back is weeds. When we sow little, the return for our sowing is little. When we sow in abundance. What we get back is the abundance of what was sown. For example: if you have lots of love in your heart and share that love with others, what you will get in return is love. However, if you keep your love locked in your heart then locked in it will stay and others will not be able to love you, for you will not let your love out or their love in. If you are generous and give to others of your time and talents, then you are in the need of help from others; it will be there for you. What we put out into the lives of others is what we end up getting back for ourselves. That is not the reason we do this. It is one of the blessings we get from God when we choose to live in God's economy. It is the blessings we get when we choose to live life according to God's design. The wonder of living life God's way and in God's economy brings so much to others and even more to us. Let us choose this day to sow full, abundant, plentiful measures into all we do and into every aspect of our lives, as we share life and live in the relationships God has given to us. Let me end with this question. How do you feel when you are short-changed or when you pay for one thing and get something else in its place? Chances are you feel not very good. There is a part of us that wants what we paid for and the right change in return. It is the way we are brought up. It is the innate expectation within all of our hearts. Have you ever heard yourself saying, "it's not fair"? We want life to be fair and just and equal and when it is not we get upset. If that is true for you, then why is it okay for you to use a half measure when living your life and giving to others. When you want life to be fair, equal and just? We have to do our part as we go about in dealing with others. Something to think about! Life is so very short. Let us embrace and enjoy everyday in everyway, not having to be concerned about what will come back upon us knowing we have chosen to use the full measure in all of our dealings in life. Choose daily to give life your best shot. When we live this way there is no shortchanging of others or ourselves. Therefore the measure used against us is the full measure.

Prayer: Holy God, I do want life to be fair, equal and just even though I know it can never fully be that way. Help me, to do my part in all of my dealings with others and myself. Help me, to live my life in such a way that at the end of the day, I can honesty say I have done the best I can with what I have and been the best I can be. Forgive me, for all the times I shortchanged others, you and myself. Forgive me, for the time I tried to take more than I have given. I am truly sorry, amen.

Day One Hundred Forty-eight

Mark 5: 19 'Jesus did not let him, but said, Go home to your family and tell them how much the Lord has done for you, and how he has had mercy on you.'

The man with the legion of demons had just been set free by the love and power of Jesus. Now he was asking Jesus if he might travel along side Jesus and be close to Jesus. Jesus turns to the man and says; 'go home to your family and tell them how much the Lord has done for you. Tell them how God has had mercy on you'. There are three events happening here. 1- wanting to stay with the Lord because of the healing Jesus brought upon him and the freedom he is now feeling. 2- Jesus is saying no I do not want you to stay in the safety and security of me. I want you to go back to your family and tell them all about me and what happened to you because of your trust in me. 3- The proclamation, the announcement of the mercy Jesus showed instead of the judgments he was feeling from the member of his town. When we have a life changing experience of Jesus in or upon our lives we want to hang on to Jesus and not let him go. We want to stay in the moment and in the high we are feeling, because of the touch we have experienced from God. That is the safe place to stay and live out your new found freedom. The problem with hanging onto Jesus is, it is not realistic. Life is not lived on the mountaintop or the high we feel after being touched by the Messiah. Most of life is lived in the valleys with all the struggles, strains and stresses. Reality says we need to go back to our families or communities and share the wonder and mercy of God's touch in and upon our lives. We need to go back so others can have the opportunity of experiencing God like we did and then we need to take hold of the responsibility of opening the doors for others to know the mercy of God for themselves. Life is so full of judgments and all that judgments do to us as people. When we have received the mercy of God we need to take that mercy and tell others about how it is available to them as well. Mercy, compassion and kindness of God are open and available to each and every one of us. Some of us do not know that truth, nor do we know how to embrace it for ourselves. When we take our experience of God back to our families along with God's mercy, we open the door for them to know God for themselves and to experience God's mercy and love first hand, a true gift for the ones we love. Yes, we all want to stay in the incredible moment when we are touched by God. Yes, we all want to not have to come back to reality and all that reality holds for us. The truth is we must. That is how life is. Life is to be lived in the moment. Life is not to be lived on the mountaintops. We are to embrace the fullness of life and all that life has to offer. We learn and grow in the valleys, having the mountaintop experiences in our memories and lives reminding us, that the mountaintops keep calling us onward to encourage us through the valleys. Both are necessary and needed for the good and bad times we all have and share.

Prayer: Thank you, Jesus, for loving us so much. Thank you, for looking beyond our outer package and looking right into the beautiful, lovely child you created us to be in the first place. Thank you, that I can have your mercy and healing instead of justice and judgment. I am truly grateful and I open my heart to your loving touch of mercy and grace. In Jesus' name I pray, amen.

Day One Hundred Forty-nine

Mark 5: 36 'Ignoring what they said, Jesus told the synagogue ruler. Don't be afraid just believe.'

"Don't be afraid just believe." I am always amazed at how many times we let fear rise up within our hearts and lives. The many times we let fear steal so much of us, which in turn leave us so empty, hollow and powerless with our selves and hearts. The many times we let fear tell us who are and what we will do or not do. Fear is such a powerful negative force in our lives that does not do anything good. Fear does a whole lot of bad. Fear steals everything that is good about us. Fear puts us in a place of not having enough personal power to move forward. Fear locks us in a prison and runs away with the key. Fear renders us powerless and in a place of having no hope or life forces within us. There are a couple of good acronyms for fear. 'False Evidence Appearing Real' and 'Face Everything And Recover'. When we live in fear we do not have the personal power or ability to face things confronting us. Nor do we have the power the break through to the other side of whatever it is we are afraid of. Jesus is telling the synagogue ruler (and us), to not give his(our) power away to fear. He was not to be afraid or let fear well up inside of him(us), because of the bad report he had just been given regarding his daughter. Instead, Jesus told him "just believe in what I have told you. Just believe in me and my power and the authority I have as the Son of God/Son of Man." Just believe in the evidence you have seen. Just believe in who and what I say I am. Then watch and see all that will happen. If you stay in your fear, then your fear wins. There is no chance of growth or victory over whatever it is you are afraid of. We too are faced with the same challenge in so many areas of our lives. Either we choose to give our power away to our fears (false evidence appearing real) and let our fears define who and what we are as people, or we decide what we think, say, feel, act, react not to mention telling us what we will do or not do. We hold on to our power and decide which direction we will take and what we will do. We can just believe and see the hand of God at work in our lives, or we give our power away to our fears and suffer the consequences, lose the blessing and maybe even get lost in our fears. The challenge is to just believe even when everything inside of us is telling to run and have no faith. We can give into our fears or we can face our fear and recover. We all have fears they are natural and normal. The challenge is to not give into our fears and let them define us. Instead we need to embrace whatever it is we are afraid so we can come up the other side, free and released from fear. Just believe and walk as people who choose to walk in faith and trust.

Prayer: I am sorry Father, for the number of times I let my fears win. For the number of times I give into my fears and ended up more afraid than ever. Help me, to trust you more and to hold on to all you are and all I am in you. Help my faith to grow and get stronger. Help me to 'just believe'. Father, I need your help and power within me. I pray for more of your in my heart and life, amen.

Day One Hundred Fifty

Genesis 50:1 'Joseph threw himself upon his father and wept over him and kissed him.'

Joseph is a great example of what it means to be honest in our feelings and emotions. Being honest with who and what we are as human beings. A freedom some of us do not have. Joseph saw his father after many, many years. His father thought Joseph was dead, when they saw each other they were both filled with so much emotion and strong feelings they could not hold them inside. The feelings welling up within them burst out in uncontrollable, agonizing tears and weeping. There was no shame or hiding back of the emotions and feelings that were happening and wanting to happen. There was an honesty and truth that sprung forth. Joseph threw himself into his father's arms and he wept like a child giving himself permission to feel and express those feelings, with freedom to be real with what was happening inside of him. What a gift they gave each other that day. A true gift of honesty and truth as they embraced each other in the sadness and joy they were feeling. Some of us have such a hard time with expressing our feelings and trusting the expression of them. Why? Perhaps of what we have been through or the way others have reacted to our tears and us in the past. We may also be afraid of the power behind our feelings, which have often been locked away for a long time. What will happen if I let them out? Can I survive the power they hold? Will my feelings destroy me if I feel them? Will I be considered weak if I cry or show any kinds of emotions? The list of fears and concerns go on and on. We see Jesus giving us another example of how it is okay to express our tears and emotions. When Jesus stood with Mary and Martha, He wept for His friend Lazarus. Jesus cried for His friend, who had gone into death, even though Jesus knew that Lazarus would be raised from that death. Tears and emotions are a very important part of life. They are a part of our design and makeup. Therefore when we deign our tears and run away from our emotions. We are deigning who and what we are as human beings, and the makeup of tears and emotions God has placed within us. For those of us who have had a hard time expressing our tears and feelings, who may have fear around expressing feelings and tears. Maybe it is time to take back our rights to them and their expression. Maybe it is time to reclaim who and what we are as a child of God, time to reclaim the natural and normal functioning of our bodies and emotions. Let us tell our loved ones, that we love them. Let us express our love for them in healthy and life giving ways. Let us take back our right to feel our feelings, and the expression of them, in whatever way is right at the time. Joseph threw himself on his father and wept over him and then kissed him with love and affection. It is okay to show others how we feel and why we feel that way. It is okay to own and express our feelings and to express them in healthy and life giving ways. It is okay to be real with who and what we are as people and the feelings and emotions we have been given. It is okay to own and express our tears and to let them flow. It is okay to be real with what is happening inside of us, even if what is happening is being sad. Today let us determine to let others and our selves have the permission to feel and express feelings, by expressing them in whatever way is appropriate and true to who and what we are as feeling human beings.

Prayer: Father, there are times when I am afraid of my tears and feelings. I find it hard to laugh when others are laughing. Times when I want to hide what I am feeling. To not give myself permission to express what is really happening within me. I regret deigning who and what you created me to me. I regret that I have given my God given right to cry or laugh away. Help me, to be honest with myself and my feelings and emotions. Help me, to be honest with others and you. Help me, to cry my tears or laugh my joy. Help me, to know that it is okay to cry or laugh and feel the feelings. In Jesus' name I pray, amen.

Day One Hundred Fifty-one

Mark 9: 23 'If you can?' said Jesus. Everything is possible for him who believes.'

Jesus, what a powerful name, the name that is above all names. There is no name in heaven or earth that is more powerful, than, the name of Jesus the Christ. Philippians 2:10-11 says; 'at the name of Jesus every knee should bow, in heaven and on earth and under the earth and every tongue confess that Jesus Christ is Lord, to the Glory of God the Father.' If this is true---and if the name of Jesus has this power, than everything does become possible, for those who choose to be in the power and the name of Jesus? If Jesus really is who He says He is, and if what He is saying is true. Then everything becomes possible for those who call upon His name and believes in that power. A wide door opens up for all who choose to walk through it. Think about this for a moment. If what this passage is saying is true, if the name of Jesus is the true power, the beginning and end, then would it not make sense to at least test it out and see for our selves? Would it not make sense to put what this verse is saying to the test, to test and see whether or not this is valid or just a bunch of empty words that have no meaning? Personally, I think the testing of it is the only way to go, as I usually need proof before I jump into anything. The possibility of asking for healing for others and our selves enters into the options. Asking for help in our times of need becomes more than just a request, it becomes a great possibility and even a reality, when we need comfort or peace during a great time of loss or grief. Asking can bring that comfort and peace for they are now available to us in and through the realms of Jesus' power and authority. There is no end of things we can ask for because the name of Jesus is above everything. Therefore everything has to fall under His power and authority. Whatever the need, whatever the situation, whatever the circumstance, calling on the name of Jesus and choosing to believe causes the presence and power of Jesus to be brought forth to help, heal, comfort or bring peace into whatever it is we are holding up to God. Everything becomes possible when we pray and act through the power of faith and belief. This brings such comfort and peace to my heart and spirit. Just knowing that I am not alone and having to face life alone, brings comfort and peace. Knowing that there is a real, alive and willing God, who is available to us when we call upon God. This reality brings a sense of being safe and secure in this very troubled world we live in. Knowing that no matter what, when I pray God listens and begins to answer my pray. That in it self helps, just knowing that if I ask and pray, all things are possible and even probable. I can rest in that knowing with peace and security. We are not alone! The Most High God of the all creation is with us, even when we do not know it. And because He is with us, we can rest in His promises and truth. We can rest knowing that He cannot tell a lie or harm us in any way. Let us today, risk and trust, that all things are possible for those of us who choose to believe. That all things are possible for us who ask for whatever it is we need in faith.

Prayer: Thank you, God, for being who and what you say you are. Thank you, for sending Jesus who does have the power and authority to make all things possible. Remind me, when I forget, and help me to always turn to you, no matter what is happening in my life or the lives of those around me. I am truly grateful for having you in my life and available to me whenever I call upon you. In Jesus' most holy and present name, amen.

Day One Hundred Fifty-two

Mark 11:24 `Therefore I tell you, that whatever you ask for in prayer, believe that you have received it, and it will be yours,'

Trust in what we are praying for. Trust in the one we are praying to. Trust in the expectation of our prayer request. This is what believing prayer is all about. We need both in order to pray with confidence. In order to wait in expectation for the answer to what we are praying for or about. Without trust, there is not the confidence, that the one we are praying to can answer our prayer request(s) in an active and real way. Trust says that I can allow myself to be vulnerable and open. I can be willing to be exposed in my faith and my ability to put my hope and trust in the one I am praying to. I can rest in that trust that my prayer will be answered. For us to pray there needs to be trust between God and us. The trust has to be there in order for us to pray with the power of faith and belief. Without trust there is not the belief inside of us that says, God can or will answer my pray. If I am not praying in and through a relationship of trust and trusting, then how can I have the confidence, that God will be able to answer my prayer requests? When I pray in an attitude of faith and choose to believe that God can and will answer my prayers, then when I pray I am praying in a place of confidence, believing that God is listening and is open and receptive to prayers and to what I am praying for and interested in. When we are praying with trust and confidence, we believe that God can work through our faith and the relationship we have with Him. We pray believing God will answer our prayer(s). Our trust and faith take an active role in both giving and receiving when we offer up our prayers. Believe that God wants to answer our prayers and wants what is best for us. Trusting and believing that God listens and responds to the things we are praying for. Praying in faith and belief truly opens the door for God to actively work in and through us. Therefore, let us pray with trust and belief as a child. Knowing that God can and will hear our prayers, and answer them as is best for us and for the things we are praying for. Let us pray in an attitude of faith and belief choosing to trust that the one whom we are praying to is capable of answering our pray requests. As pray let us choose to believe that our God and Father in heaven is listening and answering us. When children ask, they just believe. Let us be as trust as a child and just believe. Then watch and see everything that God can and will do.

Prayer: Holy Spirit, help my unbelief! Help me, to trust and believe more fully that my prayers are important to God, and that God wants to answer even my prayers. Help me to have the knowing inside of me that says, I am a child of the Most High God. The Most High God is my Father and my friend. The Most High God is my Saviour and Redeemer, my all in all. Thank you, Lord, and Holy Spirit, amen.

Day One Hundred Fifty-three

John 1:16 'From the fullness of his grace we have all received one blessing after another.'

This devotional is by Selwyn Hughes an excerpt from Light from the Path, Published by B&H
The Amplified Bible translates this verse: 'For out of His fullness (abundance) we all received---all had a share and we were all supplied with---one grace after another and spiritual blessing upon spiritual blessing, and even favor upon favor and gift (heaped) upon gift.' I love the phrase 'one grace after another.' The thought contained in the original text is of grace succeeding grace. Our capacity to receive grace at any level depends on our use of it at the lowest level. Refuse God's grace at one level of our life and you make it difficult to receive it at another level. We must use the present proffered grace to be granted the grace, which succeeds it. One preacher said: 'I remember when I sat for my first scholarship. I recall going to my professor

and saying: `What will I do when I have used the paper up?' He laughed, `you needn't worry about that, he said. When you have used all you have, just ask for more.' Much relieved I added, `Will he give me all I want?' `NO, replied the professor, but he will give you all you can use.' God is eager to give His grace to every one of us, and there is so much of it. Grace is flowing like a river. Millions there have been supplied..... But it mustn't be wasted. You can have all you are able to use, but to have more you must use what you have. How good are you at using God's grace?'

Such a good question and one we could all take some time reflecting on and about. Are we using the grace God has given us for today or are we wasting it? Are we asking for enough of God's grace to do all we are to do? Are we short-changing ourselves when it comes to God's grace, because we have a negative belief that says; "I don't deserve it or I can't ask"? God's grace is here for everyone bar none. It is here for all who ask and desire its presence in their lives. It is here, ask and it will be yours. God promises that. God's grace of unmerited loving favour is here for all of us to embrace and make our own. Let us today call upon our most merciful, loving God. Asking for His grace and love this very moment and throughout the rest of our lives. Let us ask for grace upon grace so that we never run out!

Prayer: Father, I am sorry for the times I wasted your grace and did not use the grace you have given to me. Please forgive me, and let us start afresh today. Help me, to see your grace given to me and then help me to use it to your glory and mine. I pray in the grace and mercy of the Most High God and giver of all sufficient grace, amen.

Day One Hundred Fifty-four

Mark 12: 17 `Then Jesus said to them, give to Caesar what is Caesar's and give to God what is God's.'

There is a separation between what belongs to God and what belongs to the state or the country we live in. There are things in our life that we must honour the state with, such as paying our taxes and not cheating the government of their due share of the tax bill. Like following the rules of the road and not speeding or parking the car in illegal parking spaces. Not breaking the law regardless of the reasons or rational in our minds or hearts, being good citizens and so on. There are things in our lives that we need to honour God with. Things like honouring God in our finances and giving back to God a portion of what He gives us. God gives us 100% all He asks of us is to give Him back 10%. We are to forgive each other and ourselves, when we have fallen short in our behaviours or attitudes. Giving to God is not holding on to grudges or anger or hatred or resentments. Another area God asks us to give back to Him is in our need to live according to His law of love. The law of love is putting love first, and loving each other first and foremost. When we live in the balance of giving to God what belongs to God, and giving to the state what belongs to the state, life is truly balanced. God then blesses us and fills in any missing pieces in our lives. When we do not honour God or the state, we find ourselves in a place of disharmony and upheaval at times. When we do not honour God, we block the grace and blessings God wants to pour down upon us. When we do not honour the state we find ourselves breaking the rules. The more rules we break the more likely it is we will get caught and have to pay the price. For example; cheating on our taxes, it may work for a couple of years until an audit is done. Then our cheating is exposed and will have to live with the consequences, which may not be very pleasant. We can get away with speeding at times, but sooner or later we will get caught, then not only do we have to pay the fine, but also may lose point off our license and have to pay higher insurance premiums. We can get away with not honouring God. We cannot give back to God what He asks of us. The reality is sooner or later that catches up with us as well. The blessings, mercy and grace are withdrawn or diminished greatly in our lives. We may fine ourselves living more and more in the darkness, without the presence of God's light. What I am discovering in life is that there is no free lunch. Everything in life has a price tag. The only constant thing is one day we will be called to pay the bill in full. There is an expression I use a lot. Pay me now or pay me later, but sooner or later we have to pay the bill. We can pretend or lie to ourselves by saying no one knows it does not matter. Who will find out anyway? The reality is God knows! God knows when we are cheating Him or cheating the state. Sooner or later whatever it is we are cheating in will one day find us out. Therefore let us be people who choose to live honest and upright lives. Let us live our lives in such a way that they will not one day come and bit us in the butt. Let us be honest in paying Caesar what belongs to Caesar and paying God what belongs to God. That way we never have to look over our shoulder wondering what is coming up behind us.

Prayer: Lord, help me to give to you what belongs to you and to give to the state what belongs to the state. Show me any areas of my life which are out of balance and which need adjusting. I want to be both honouring to you and to the state. I want my life to be pleasing to you in every area of my life. Thank you, Lord, for being my source of life, true life. I am grateful and do appreciate all you do for me both known and unknown. In the name of the Lord, amen.

Day One Hundred Fifty-five

Mark 13: 31 'Heaven and earth will pass away, but my words will never pass away.'

Heaven and earth will pass away. When we look at all that is happening in our world and with the natural disasters that are hitting our world, this statement seems to be holding more truth to it. It is beginning to look like a reality. Look at what the ice age did to the earth and how it changed everything. When we look at the number of animals who have become extinct, who are no longer on the face of the earth. When we see how much life changes with each passing year, someone from 100 years ago would not recognize the places he or she once walked. It is just like a flowing river, you can never put your foot into the same spot in the river twice, for the river is constantly changing. All we need do is look around and see how much the earth has changed over the past few years, and how it continues to change. There are more earthquakes now than ever in all of history. The force of our hurricanes and the number of tornados increase with every passing year. A fisherman I know once told me how much storms have changed since he began his career as a fisherman. Now-a-day, when a storm hits there is a much greater need to take cover and get off the water and to tie down the boats. For if not, then the chances of surviving the storm unscathed is not very high. The gale force winds are just too strong to survive in. Our planet earth is having a harder and harder time coping with all that is happening to it. I am speculating, but I would imagine that it is the same with the heavens. All of God's creation both the heavens and the earth are groaning under the weight of sin and the destroying of our planet home because of sin. There is only one sure thing in all of life, that sure thing is God will never change and God's word will always exist. No matter what happens or does not happen God's word will always be alive, real and available. There is nothing that can destroy the word of God, nothing. Let us take comfort in this truth. Things we know and hold true and valuable may change or even pass away like a person dying or a friendship ending. But God's word will never die and never be removed from God's creation. God's word is the one sure thing we can count on, no matter what. It is a promise of God and God cannot go back on a promise. Let us take comfort knowing God is the same yesterday, today and forever. Therefore His Word is the same yesterday, today and forever. Everything in life may change or disappear and on some level it will. Some things may all together disappear, but God's Word will not. God's Word is the one sure thing we can count on no matter is happening around or in us. God's Word is and will always be the same no matter what happens in creation or in our lives. This is the wonder of God and who and what He is as God. This is God's promise to us.

Prayer: I do take comfort in knowing your Word, your Truth, is sound and sure. No matter what happens in life, I know that I can put my hope, trust and faith in you. Your Word, for it will always remain the same and be available to me. I thank you God for giving us your Word and the power it holds in your creation and my life. I am truly grateful and humbled. I do put my trust and hope in your Word. In the precious and holy name of Jesus and His all sustaining Word of life and truth, amen.

Day One Hundred Fifty-six

Mark 14: 36 'Abba, Father, he said, everything is possible for you. Take this cup from me. Yet not what I will, but what you will.'

It is so comforting to me to know, that even Jesus had feelings of wanting God to step in and take away His humanness and struggle. Even Jesus wanted to be set free from what He was about to face and endure. Even Jesus wanted to run away from what life was asking of Him. Knowing that even Jesus cried out to God, asking God to remove the cup of suffering from Him gives me strength to face my struggles. There is such a sense of peace and comfort knowing that God was well able to be there with Jesus in His hour of need. God will certainly be with us as we face the cup of suffering we have to face. No matter what we are facing, God the Father, our Abba, Father, our Dad, is right here with us. Our Abba Father/Dad is facing the suffering with us. Our Abba Father, or Dad knows how we are feeling and knows the pain in our hearts and lives. Abba Father watched His Son go through His suffering. He is watching us too. He is walking the path with us, going the through the journey right by our side. Our Abba, Father/ Dad is supplying our needs just as He supplied Jesus' needs and gave Jesus what He needed in order to face the cross. I pray God will touch you in your suffering and if possible take it away, but if you are to face this one through to the end then I pray for God's courage, strength, mercy and grace to fill you to overflowing, just as He did with His Son. We do not always understand the will of the Father and His plan for us His children. We do not always understand the whys of life and the suffering that happens. We may never fully understand, but we do understand the truth and fact that God is our great Abba, Father and loves us and will always love us. God will always be here with us, no matter what is happening or not happening in our lives. God our Abba, Father/Dad will always be by our side. That is a promise God gives us. I will never abandon you, forsake you or leave you orphaned. I am your Father; you are my chosen, precious, beloved child. You are my own and I cannot abandon what is mine. I do not always understand the will of God! In some ways I will never understand the will of God. What I do understand is that God loves us and no matter what He will always love us. That truth is solid and real. God can turn whatever we are going through into something good, when we love Him and are His children. The challenge is to trust God when everything inside of us is screaming NO, I CAN'T DO THIS, just like Jesus did. When we do trust no matter what, the wonder of God is present in amazing in awe-inspiring ways. Job 13:15 says; 'Though He slay me, yet will I hope in him'. Let us have that kind of trust and faith in God, who says you are mine and I am yours no matter what and for all time.

Prayer: Abba, Father, I am so grateful that you are in my life and I can trust in you no matter what is happening in my life. Help my unbelief, so that I can love and trust you more. Dad, you are such a gift in my life and I value you so much. I am truly grateful for all you are and all I am in you. Thank you, for loving me so much and being my Father and Dad. Thank you, for your promises and the hope your promises give me. I am so very grateful my Father/Dad and will always be grateful, amen.

Day One Hundred Fifty-seven

> *Mark 16: 15 'He said to them, go into all the world and preach the good news to all creation.'*

The great commandment is, to go into the entire world and preach the good news to all of God's creation. The commandment is to tell others about what God is doing and has done in our lives and to share the good news of what it means to know God and be in a personal relationship with God. Having God in our lives and seeing all that God is, makes us want to tell others about how good God is. It compels us at times to want to tell others how much better life is with God in it. When we know the loving mercy and grace of God and His never-ending love and blessings upon our lives, we want to share the blessing with others. We find ourselves having a need, a desire inside our heart, to share that love and blessing with the people who come across our path or into our lives. Knowing God really is the best news we could ever have and it pushes us to share that news with others. It really is the good news of God and His unconditional love for us His creation and children.

For those of us who choose to have the good news of God's love, mercy and grace in our hearts and lives, we know the difference it makes. Therefore, we want others to have the same opportunity we have had. I see it all the time here at the treatment center residents give themselves permission to open their hearts and lives to God. God in His love touches them in ways that stir their very beings. When they are being touched by God's love for them, they in turn show others how to get touched by God and the love God has for them. They tell others and the message of God continues to move and touch in real and restoring ways. This is the wonder of God's presence in His creation and in those of us who choose to open our hearts and lives to the incredible love, mercy and grace God. The incredible love God has for us, no matter who we are or where we have come from. No matter what we have done or not done. The reality is God does not attach strings to His love for us. There are no strings to the good news of God's love, mercy and grace. God in His infinite mercy and compassion has decided to extend us grace and love, instead of the justice and wrath, which we all deserve on some level. God's love and mercy is available to all who humble themselves and simply ask for it, then when it comes into our lives and hearts we tell others about it, because it is the best thing that has ever happened to us and we know it. Our lives are touched in ways that often blow us out of the water and we want others to have the same opportunity we had.

Prayer: With an incredible sense of gratitude, I say thank you, God, for loving us the way you do, for loving me the way you do. Thank you, for showing us the path to that love. Help us, to not keep your love to ourselves, but share it with others, so that they too can know the amazing gift of your love. Thank you, for loving me so much, so very much I am truly grateful and I thank you from the bottom of my heart. I don't know why you would choose to love someone like me, but I am thankful you do. I receive your love, mercy and grace into my life and heart. Change me, from the inside out. I want more of you and your love in me and in my life, amen.

Wendy Bussell

Day One Hundred Fifty-eight

Exodus 14:14 'The Lord will fight for you; you need only to be still.'

I know first hand just how true this statement is. I have seen God fight the battle for me. I have seen God step in and defend me when I was wrongly accused. I have seen the hand of God working on my behalf and righting the wrongs that were done. I know our God can and will fight for us if we give ourselves permission to be still, and trust His provision and power. I can remember on one occasion, I was being wrongly accused and wanted to defend myself. I wanted to fight for my rights. I heard very clearly in my spirit, as I sat in the meeting, God saying to me, 'be quiet, say nothing'. It was so hard to just sit there and not open my mouth to defend myself. I wanted, needed, to justify my position and my rights, but I didn't. I let myself sit there and trust God and His presence in my life, and in this situation. It wasn't long before the truth came to the surface and I was cleared of the accusations. The truth had risen to the surface and I was cleared and vindicated, because of God's faithfulness. I was released from the power of the lie, because God fights for us, His children, when we are being wronged. Are you living a faithful and obedient life? Are you walking to the best of your ability by the Word of God? Are you living a life that is pleasing to God? If you are and you are being wrongly accused, trust in God. Trust God and His promise to fight for you. Be still and let God, not only speak to your heart and spirit, but to the situation as well. Reach out to God and invite Him into whatever it is you are struggling with. Then watch what God does. Let the Most High God into you more deeply, so that you can trust God more. The truth always comes up to the surface. I know that first hand. All we need do is put our hope, trust and faith in God, and keep doing what is right. Keep living and acting in a way, that is pleasing to God, and if we are living and acting that way God will fight for us. When we do our part, God does His part. That is the wonder and mystery of God evident in our lives, and the situations

266

we find ourselves in. The part of God that is absolutely trustworthy and safe becomes available to us, in real and almost touchable ways. We really are safe and secure in God no matter what is happening or not happening. God is our refuge and our strength, especially in times of trouble. We are so blessed to have such a real and alive God on our side. We have the Most High God, as our God. The God of the living and not the dead! The Most High God who is well able to meet all of our every need and even more. Put your hand in God's, and trust His love for you. Put your hand in God's hand, just like a small child, and watch how Dad works through whatever it is you are going through, at this point in time. The Lord will fight your battles for you. All you need do is keep your eyes, heart and total self in that trusting place of God's love. When God says He will fight, fight He will. We do our part God does the rest. What more can we ask for?

Prayer: Most High God and Father, I am so thankful that you are my God and you are here for me, even me. I do choose to trust you. I do choose to let you help me and be my ever-present help in my times of trouble, and when life is moving along smoothly. I put my hope, trust and faith in You, and choose to believe you are who our say you are. I choose to be your child, and you my Father and Dad. Thank you, for loving me and always being here with me and for me. Thank you for your promises, love and faithfulness, amen.

Day One Hundred Fifty-nine

Luke 1: 37 `For nothing is impossible with God.'

Nothing---no thing is impossible for God. There is nothing in all of creation that is beyond the power and authority of God. Everything is less than the power, ability, provision, capacity, and capability of our great and awesome God. Our

God has the power to conquer everything in His path and even more. Do you have what seems to be an impossible obstacle in your path or confronting you? Take it to God. Then watch what God can and will do. Are you facing what seem to be insurmountable odds? Do you think there is no way out of whatever it is you are facing? Take it to God and let God have His hand on it. Do you feel cornered and trapped in a relationship or situation? Open the door and let God move as only God can. In all of life and in every situation we can and will find God is bigger still. Nothing, absolutely nothing, is impossible for our great and awesome God. As children we often proclaim that our dad can do anything/everything better than anyone else's dad. Well, that statement and belief is even truer today than ever before, because we now do have a Dad who can do everything. God will make a way where there seems to be no way. God will open a window, when a door closes. God can put back the pieces of our lives that are lost, broken or eaten by the dog. There is no situation in life where God's hand and power is not well able to touch, heal, restore, fix, put back together, redeem, and make righteous and so very much more. Are you feeling alone? God can touch your heart so that you feel His presence and know His love. Are you trapped in an addiction, feeling there is no way out of its grip? Give the addiction to God, then ask for the help you need. Are your finances in a mess and there just isn't enough to go around? Pray and seek God's help and guidance; then watch and see what God does for you. There is not one thing in this world that can cause our God to be in a place of lack. Seek the presence and power and provision of God in whatever it is you are going through, and then wait and see what God does. For I know that God hears every prayer we give Him. Remember God's promise is to never leave us orphaned, abandoned or alone. God is always with us even when we may not feel His love or touch, or know His presence. God is still there helping us and meeting our needs. Nothing is impossible for our God. What makes things impossible is the fact that we hold on to them, and do not let God anywhere close to what we are going through or are facing. When we hold on really tightly, then God has no room to help. When we loosen our grip and ask for help and guidance, help and guidance comes our way. Invite God in and you may be amazed at the response and help you get. Invite God in. What do you have to lose? Open your grip on whatever it is you are facing and watch God work in it. Let God be God and you be the faithful child. Life works so much better that way. Trust me!

Prayer: God, help me to trust you more and to turn over to you all my cares, worries and needs. Help me to seek you and your face in every part of my life, especially those places where I have kept you at arm's length. I am sorry, please forgive me and help me, for I need you more today than ever before. I am really in need of you more and more with each passing day. In Jesus' Holy and Righteous name, amen.

Day One Hundred Sixty

Exodus 15:2 `The Lord is my strength and my song; he has become my salvation. He is my God, and I will praise him, my father's God and I will exult him.'

"The Lord is my strength and my song",-----what an interesting combination of words. My strength and my song! We know from Scripture that God is our strength, our refuge, and our strong tower. Now we are being told He is also our song. The Lord is the music of and in our heart. The Lord is the song that keeps us going when we are tired, disappointed, out of resources or just plum rundown. He is the song that lifts us up and puts a smile on our face, and the music back in our lives. What is the song God puts in our hearts? It is the song of love! The song that says we are valuable and worthwhile; so worthwhile that He became our salvation. We are so valuable to God that He gives us strength at all times, and fills our hearts with the music of His love. Then God takes it one step further and opens the way of salvation, so that we can spend eternity with Him, dancing on streets of gold. We will have His song of love throughout all time. The Israelites were right. God, is my God and I will praise Him, giving Him all the glory, exulting His Holy name, for all He has done and all He is to His creation and us. Here is the great blessing of God: the more we sing of His greatness and praise Him, the more He lights up our lives. The more we acknowledge God as God, giving Him all the glory, honour and praise, the more we see His strength, song and salvation. The more we let God in, the more He comes in, and the more whole our hearts become. The wonder of God! The wonder of all God is and all we are because of His great love for us His children! The wonder of God's plan for us His creation and children! We have the most awesome God and Father. Our God gives us everything we need, and fills our insides with such life, hope and music. We are so greatly blessed by all that God is. We are so greatly blessed by all we become by being His children and living in His arms of love. The blessing of God's mercy and grace is ours just because God chooses to love us, and be in a living relationship with us. I stand in awe of God! I stand in awe of all God is and how He loves us His children. There are no words to express this amazing feeling of awe, as we begin to take in just how much God loves us. We are so very precious and valuable to God. We are the children of the Most High God. The Creator of all things, the maker of the universe, is totally in love with us. The Creator of all things has chosen us to be His beloved children. This great and awesome God is our Father and Dad. The one who was, who is and who will always be, is madly in love with us and longs to have us love Him back. Our God truly is amazing and awesome, and we are blessed beyond measure. Even you and I are blessed beyond all measure! Go figure.

Prayer: Thank you, Father God, for being my strength in all times and the song in my heart, which causes my heart to sing. Thank you, for being my salvation and showing me the way to true life and living. I am learning that true life comes only from you and having your light within my heart. Thank you for the truth and life you are filling me with, and the music and song you are putting in my heart. My heart does sing in response to you. I stand in awe of you Father God, amen.

Day One Hundred Sixty-one

Genesis 50: 20 'You intended to harm me, but God intended it for good to accomplish what is now being done, the saving of many lives.'

When we look at our lives at times and all the stuff that has happened to us not to mention the harm that has been caused, we wonder why? We wonder "why me"? What did I ever do to have all this happen to me? Then we read about Joseph and all he went through by the hands of his brothers and the Egyptians. We begin to see that there are times when God allows bad things to happen, so that good can be wrought in the end. Joseph was put in a cistern, left standing in the mud, cold, hungry and afraid, not understanding why his brothers were doing this. Then he was sold as a slave, betrayed by his master's wife, put into prison, betrayed by the baker and cupbearer and left in the prison to waste away. It was only after many years; Joseph began to see God's hand at work, and the good that was being brought out of all the bad. Joseph was beginning to see that God's hand was at work redeeming him, his family and all of Israel through the hardships he suffered. Thousands of lives were saved, through the lessons Joseph had learned, and the skills he had acquired because of all he had lived through. I do not believe it is God's plan for any of our lives to suffer and live through the bad things we have lived through. What I do believe is God can use everything we have gone through to His glory and ours. Joseph, in all he went through, had the choice of being either a victim or victor---Joseph chose to be a victor! We have the same choice. But you don't know what I have been through, you don't understand-----I hear some of you saying. Yes I do! I know what God can do when we give Him our pasts and all that has happened in them. I know how God can turn them into something not only GOOD, but also very life giving. There is an expression: "what doesn't kill you makes you stronger". That is the bottom line truth. With God, not only does God make you stronger, He uses whatever we have gone through to make us better. Is it easy? No. Is it worth choosing to be a victor and not a victim? Oh yes! When we follow Joseph and his choice to not become a victim, choosing to trust God and God's plan, it is amazing what God can do with everything we have gone through. Yes, our past is or was awful, but that does not mean we have to stay there and give our power to it. We can choose to overcome it, and become the victor we were meant to be and live in the victory. What are you choosing to do with your past hardships, abuse, struggles, etc? Are you letting them turn you into a victim or are you allowing God to make you strong and a victor? We can either be bitter or better. We choose.

Prayer: I am so sorry for choosing to be a victim at times. I am sorry for choosing to sit in my pain and past, instead of looking to you and trusting you, God. Please forgive and help me, to let your light shine in my darkness, so that I can use my past to make me stronger. Thank you, for having the ability to turn something bad into something good. I give you permission to take my past and turn it into something good. In the name of the Most High all powerful God, amen.

Day One Hundred Sixty-two

Exodus 16: 3 `The Israelites said to them, if only we had died by the Lord's hand in Egypt! There we sat around pots of meat and ate all the food we wanted, but you have brought us out into this desert to starve this entire assembly to death.'

Feeling sorry for ourselves is such a deadly trap we can fall into. It not only prevents us from seeing the truth in the situation(s) we are in, it also prevents us from moving forward in and with our lives. It prevents us from moving on with our lives, and gaining all the blessings and the healing God wants us to have. When I am feeling sorry for myself I cannot see past the end of my nose, and, therefore cannot see the beginning from the end. Feeling sorry for ourselves is like drowning in a sea of self-pity with no way out. Self-pity does nothing but steal everything inside of us that is good and life giving. Not to mention it does not stop there. It goes on to destroy our hope, dreams, desires and everything that is valuable in our hearts, spirits and life. It moves on to the outside and begins to steal our family, friends and relationships. Self-pity is like an endless pit of nothingness with no way out or in. Self-pity is like a bottomless pit that can never be filled up. There is no end to the hunger of self-pity and its need for feeding and to be fed. Self-pity is not at all, in any way shape or form. Therefore, it is not of God. For God is life, and desires we all have life within us. Every single one of us has reasons to feel sorry for ourselves. We all have times in our lives where it seems hopeless and not worth struggling through any longer. We have all had bad things happen to us. That is the human condition. That is sin. That is how life works at times, but those times pass, if we let them, and brighter days do follow. Brighter days do come, if we take our eyes off the moment, and look ahead at what is coming down the pipe. How many times in my own life did I and, still do say to myself, "this too shall pass". This too shall pass; hold on----this too shall be a part of history before too long'. To my amazement at times, every single time the situation did pass and a new day dawned. Was it always easy. No. Did it take everything I had to just make it through another day? Yes. Did the brighter days come? Yes. How did they come? By me trusting God and His provision in and for my life. Feeling sorry for our selves is not the answer. It is not the answer at all, for it only leads to more death in our lives. Believing in the power and love of God in and for us, is the key to making it through. It is the power and love of God in our lives that give us the ability to come up on the other side. Feeling sorry for ourselves only makes whatever we are going through worse. For when we are in our pity pot, we do not have the resources to make different choices, which leaves us stuck in our mud puddle of self-pity. When we move away from our pity pot, it is amazing just how much courage and strength we find within ourselves. Let us move forward in our lives becoming all that we were created to be. Choosing to live in victorious lives with all the blessing and love we have as God's chosen Beloved Children.

Prayer: I repent Lord, for sitting in my pity party and feeling sorry for myself. Please forgive me, and help me to move forward with my life, trusting and believing in your power and provision in and for my life. Help me to believe that no matter what I am going through, it will pass, and a new day will happen. Thank you, for reminding me how important it is not to feel sorry for myself, and for reminding me how easy it is to get caught in a mud puddle of self-pity. Help me Lord, I can't do it without your help. In Jesus' name, amen.

Day One Hundred Sixty-three

Exodus 17: 9-12 Moses said to Joshua. "Choose some of our men and go out to fight the Amalekites. Tomorrow I will stand on top of the hill with the staff of God in my hands." So Joshua fought the Amalekites as Moses had ordered, and Moses, Aaron and Hur went to the top of the hill. As long as Moses held up his hands, the Israelites were winning, but whenever he lowered his hands, the Amalekites were winning. When Moses' hands grew tired, they took a stone and put it under him and he sat on it. Aaron and Hur held his hands up—one on one side, one on the other—so that his hands remained steady till sunset.'

Today in our scripture reading we have a great illustration of how much we need each other. The reality of how life is to be lived. How life is to be lived with the helping hands of those who are in our lives for a reason, season or a time. When Moses held his hands up for a long time, his arms and body began to grow tired, and in his tiredness, he let down his arms. When he let down his arms the enemy began to win the battle; when he raised his arms again the Israelites were winning. When Moses grew too tired to hold his arms up, Moses was given a stone to sit on and rest. Then Aaron and Hur came along side Moses and held his arms up for him, supporting him, and helping Moses carry the load. They came along side Moses, so that Moses did not have to be there alone doing it all himself. Aaron and Hur stepped in and helped where help was needed. Aaron and Hur gave Moses the extra strength he needed to keep his arms held high. We all have times in our lives when we need people to come along side of us and help us carry the load. We all need to be supported at times in our lives as we face those things we have to face. If we do not have people in our lives we can count on, we may find ourselves in a losing battle, because we are not strong enough to make it on our own. There is no shame in needing help; there are no negatives in it either. Needing help is called being human. Needing other people to see us through our hard and difficult times is the way we are designed to work. We are not designed to live as Islands all alone fending for ourselves, without the help and support of others. Remember my friend who lost her mom quite suddenly? As she faced the loss of her mom, I asked her what I could do? Her response was, just be there during the wake and funeral in case I need you. All I did was just be there for her. Her fighting the battle was made easier by my presence, and just being there for her. Remember how she would, every once in awhile; look over to see if I was still there? All I did was to hold up her arms as she faced her loss and grief. She did not need me to say anything or do great things. All she needed was 'the knowing' that she was not alone as she faced this really difficult time in her life. All she needed was me for was to stand along side her, helping her carry a really heavy load. Our greatest need is relationships and without relationships we die. Would she have made it through without me being there? Yes. Would she have won the war? Yes. Was my gift of friendship and presence making it more bearable? Yes. Did I do anything great or amazing? No. The relationship and trust gave her the added strength she needed, when her strength was low. Just like Aaron and Hur giving Moses strength when his was low. Walking the path together, helping each other journey our way through. That is what life is all about! Walking this life-path together with others standing with us, and along side us, helping us carry the load when our strength is not enough that is the way we were designed to live.

Prayer: I am sorry for all the times I needed help but was too afraid to ask, or did not trust enough to ask for the help I needed. I am learning that I need others around me, to help me journey through life. Forgive me, Lord, and help me to ask for the help I need, and to be there for others when they need my help. Thank you, Lord, for always being here with me and for me, helping me even when I do not realize you are there. I am truly grateful, amen.

Day One Hundred Sixty-four

Exodus 18: 10-11 `He said, "praise be to the Lord, who rescued you from the hand of the Egyptians and of Pharaoh, and who rescued the people from the hand of the Egyptians. Now I know that the Lord is greater than all other gods, for he did this to those who had treated Israel arrogantly".'

How big is your God? Is your God big enough to save and rescue you from the Egyptians in your life? Is your God big enough to help you when you need help? To make a way out of whatever it is you are in? Can your God open up a path or door when you are trapped and unable to find a way out yourself? I ask you to think about how big your God really is to you. Is He huge or small or somewhere in between? Is He strong or weak? Can He do anything and everything? Does He have limitations, or is He capable of doing whatever needs doing? I ask these questions because if your God is small, He will not be able to help you when you need help. If He has limitations or is incapable of doing some things, then you cannot rely on Him. If your God is huge and well able to do whatever needs doing, then you can turn to Him and He will be there with all His strength and might. Now I am asking you to think about how big you want your God to be. Here Israel is rejoicing because God has rescued them from the Egyptians and has saved them from the bondage they were in. The Most High God set them free to live again in a land flowing with good things, a land filled with great abundance and bounty. The God who set the Israelites free is the same God we have today. God never changes; God is the same yesterday, today and forever. God is God no matter what is happening in His creation or in our lives. God can rescue us just as He rescued the Israelites! God is the Almighty, the Great I am. God's mighty presence and power can be in our lives, if we will allow ourselves to be open to Him and His presence in our lives and situations. God will make a way where there seems to be no way. God can do it in the most amazing ways if we let Him and invite Him in. In the Hebrew, the connotation for I am is; I am everything you need me to be, and if you need me to make it, I will. That sure sounds like a God who is well able to help me/us when I need helping and rescuing. What do you think? The question stands: How big is your God? Is your God the kind of God you want in and for your life? If the answer is yes, great! If the answer is no. Then call upon the Great I Am. He will gladly come and be your God. Let us not settle for anything less than the Great I Am, in our lives. We all need a God who is well able to do all things. We all need a God who is well able to do all things and to make a way when a way is needed.

Prayer: Most High God, I do believe that you are well able to be God in my life and situations. I choose now to invite you in and let you help me. I need your help. I just cannot do it alone any longer. Thank you, for loving me the way you do and for being all I need you to be. Thank you, for always being the same and never changing. Thank you, for being all I need you to be, amen.

Day One Hundred Sixty-five

Exodus 18: 14 `When his father-in-law saw all that Moses was doing for the people, he said, "What is this you are doing for the people? Why do you alone sit as judge, while all these people stand around you from morning till evening?"'

Moses is such a great teacher for us. Moses teaches us all about being human and how hard it is to be human. Today the lesson Moses is teaching is, our need to be all things to all people and do everything ourselves. There are about a million Israelites under Moses' guidance and authority. A million people are far too many people for Moses to carry alone, and be the judge over. Yet Moses being Moses takes his call to leadership very seriously (as he should). Only the task is far too great for just one man to handle or cope with. When Moses' father-in-law comes for a visit, he sees all that Moses is doing. Jethro suggests that if Moses tries to keep up this pace, he will fail in his duties as leader of this great people and wear himself out. Jethro tells Moses that he needs to divide up the responsibilities amongst the people. The dividing happens by choosing responsible men, to sit as judges before the people, to help take the load off of Moses. Moses listens to Jethro and chooses some responsible men to help decide on the disputes of the people. If there were disputes too hard for them, then Moses would hear the dispute. What a great lesson for us, especially us women. We cannot do it all! Are you hearing me people? We, none of us, can do everything and be everything, to everyone. We need to share our workload so that everyone gets to do a little bit. Many hands make for light work. The lesson is: we need to share some of the responsibilities, and/or cut down on how much we are doing. Why? None of us are super women/men who can do everything. We need to have balance in our lives. For without balance we get burned out and over loaded, to the point of break down or burnout. The sharing of the load and responsibilities is the healthy way of handling everything that needs to be done in our lives, and the lives of those around us, with whom we share space and life. Living in a slower paced life helps us to have time to smell the flowers, enjoy the beauty of God's creation all around us and generally see and enjoy life as it passes by. When was the last time you stopped and looked up at the stars? Or stopped long enough to see the fresh fallen snow covering the ground and everything else? Have you ever taken a long drive just to see the leaves changing and the incredible beauty that is happening all around you? Have you stopped long enough lately to hear and remember what the silence sounds like? Maybe it is time to change your pace and let others help you carry the load. Maybe it is time to take Jethro's advice to Moses, by sharing some of what you are doing with the others in your life. In the end it will be one of the best things you can ever do for yourself and your well being. Not to mention the gift it will be for the ones you love. When we do everything, it does not give others the chance to learn and grow in who they are. Something to ponder about today, as you evaluate your schedule, and all you are doing.

Prayer: I am sorry for letting my life get so busy and out of control. I am sorry that I have not only lost my way in the business, but I have also lost a part of myself. I have not taken time to fill my need to enjoy the beauty that is all around me. Forgive me, for allowing myself to get so busy that I have nothing left for you and the beauty of your creation. Forgive me that I have nothing left for me. Help me, to slow down and smell the flowers and share the load. Thank you, Jesus for helping me and showing me a better path, amen.

Day One Hundred Sixty-six

Nehemiah 7: 17a 'Nehemiah said," go and enjoy choice food and sweet drinks, and send some to those who have nothing prepared."'

It's party time. Time to rejoice and be glad in everything God has provided, from the provision of His abundance, for us, His children: the children who choose to be a part of God, and God's great kingdom, grace and mercy, and who choose to enjoy the wonders of God's great love. God has blessed His creation/us in so many ways. The blessings we see and the blessings that are hidden to our eyes and sight. God's blessings are all around us, for us to behold and enjoy. It truly is time, to step back, and begin to enjoy and celebrate all that God has given to us. Then take the next step and share the abundance with others. So many times I see Christians with such long faces; faces who look like they have lost their best friend; faces that say they are carrying the whole world upon their shoulders. I know there are times when a long face is right and even appropriate. I am not talking about those times in our lives. What I am talking about are the regular everyday times, when there is absolutely no reason to have a long face. The times when we could so very easily support a smile and grin, instead of a long sad face, that say only negative things. Times when we forget to tell our faces that we are blessed beyond measure. We really do have so very many reasons to smile and enjoy life. We can smile even when life is hard, or in a state of upheaval, or any other reason for being sad or down cast. Life is far too short not to enjoy all that God has given to us His children! God has abundantly blessed us with food, drink, joy, peace, love, mercy, grace, compassion, patience-----the list goes on forever it seems. If God is blessing us with so much, then why is it that we carry a long face, and do not celebrate all that God is giving us? Why are we not taking it to the next step of sharing the amazing blessings with others we meet and greet along life's path? When was the last time you invited friends over for supper? Or had an impromptu gathering? Have you ever, on the spur of the moment, invited friends over for coffee and desert, without a reason to do so? Or bought a homeless person a lunch or supper, just because they are homeless? Let us enjoy the abundance God has given to us. Then take that abundance and share it with others. You will be amazed at how it begins to change your life. How it changes the way you look at God, and others, and the blessings that are all around us. You will be amazed at how much a simple smile can change another's day for the good; or a simple hello to someone who needs to be acknowledged and valued! We can share the blessings God has given us in so many creative ways. Let us take up the challenge and share God's love with someone today. Blessings can be very contagious! Let us start the blessings flowing.

Prayer: I do thank you, Father, for blessing me the way you do, and for all that you have given to me. I am blessed beyond measure! Remind me to be thankful for all that I have. Remind me to share my bounty with others. Forgive me Lord, for hiding your blessings away, and not showing others and myself how blessed I truly am. Thank you, for all that I have and for all that you have given to me. I am

281

grateful. I thank you for the great wonder, of being your chosen child. Thank you, Lord, amen.

Day One Hundred Sixty-seven

Exodus 20: 1-17 'And God spoke these words. "I am the Lord your God, who brought you out of Egypt, out of the land of slavery. You shall have no other gods before me. You shall not make for yourself an idol in the form of anything in the heaven or on the earth... You shall not misuse the name of the Lord your God. Remember the Sabbath day by keeping it holy. Honour your father and your mother, so that you may live long in the land the Lord your God is giving you. You shall not murder. You shall not commit adultery. You shall not steal. You shall not give false testimony. You shall not covet.'

The Ten Commandments, not the ten suggestions! Why did God give us these commandments? The commandments seem to be really heavy rules to follow. Let alone, even possible to live out in our lives. Why would God give us such impossible rules? I feel God was actually being gracious when He set these rules in front of us. When I sat down and really looked at the commandments, I found that God actually loved me/us, when He set them before us. The purpose of giving these commandments was to show us, how to stay free and clean on the inside, in our hearts. I have worked with lots of offenders in my time. Every single one, especially those who committed a murder would all say: "If I had the chance I would go back and change what I have done". The desire to go back and change the past is, not so much to right the wrong, as much as it is to get the memory out from inside of us. Once you break the commandment, the memory is inside of you. There is no getting rid of it. It is there forever. Therefore, if you did not murder in the first place, you would not have to deal with the memory, guilt, shame, remorse and so on, regarding the murder. If you are never unfaithful, you don't have to look at yourself everyday in the mirror, regretting what you have done. If you always pay for everything you have, you can hold your head up high, because the possessions you have are yours and no one can say differently. When we live according to God's ways and commandments, we have a clean heart and conscience. Therefore, there are no hindrances inside of us at all. We are free to live our lives without regret or other negative feeling inside. God was being gracious to us, when He gave us these commandments. For when we follow them, we are free, truly free, on the inside. We do not have the haunting knowledge of what we have done. Those memories and truths, we regret or wish, we had never done or ventured forth with. The freedom from those regrets and memories is the greatest gift anyone could ever possibly give someone. God knew what would happen to us, when we broke the commandments. God knew how breaking of them would affect our lives for the rest of our lives. That is why God gave us the commandments. That is why God said, 'don't go there'. The Ten Commandments are actually a gift from God, not a heavy hand trying to keep us under His power and control. The Ten Commandments are actually, when we follow them, preventive medicine to help us stay free. God's ways and commandments are a freeing hand that helps us truly live our lives in a state of truth and freedom.

Prayer: I see now, God, that you actually had my best interest in mind when you gave us the Ten Commandments. I am sorry for breaking the ones I have broken. Please forgive me, and help me to live my life in such a way, that I choose to not break anymore. It really is for my good. Thank you, Father, for loving us so much. Thank you for giving us what we need in order to have true life within us. Thank you, amen.

Day One Hundred Sixty-eight

Psalm 42: 2-3 `My soul thirsts for God, for the living God. When can I go and meet with God? My tears have been my food day and night, while men say to me all day long, "Where is your God."'

There is a God shaped hole in each of our hearts. God gives the God shaped hole to us, at our conception. A God shaped hole that only God can fill. We try to fill the hole with lots of things. The problem is, they are just not enough or the right shape for the hole. Some of the things we try to fill the hole with are: money, lust, relationships, thrill seeking, possessions, fame, power, food, etc.. Without the presence of God in our God shaped hole, we find ourselves searching for something, anything, to fill the emptiness we are feeling on the inside. We find ourselves chasing after anything, everything that will, might, fill us up and help fill the emptiness we are feeling inside. Our souls, spirits really do search for God. They search for the one thing that can take away the emptiness and void we feel in our heart and lives. Without God in our hearts, there seems to be no end to our tears or sorrows. No end to the emptiness we feel inside. Our tears and sorrows do become our food. They become all we can think about. They become the only thing left in our lives. Everything else is drowned out or buried within, because of the emptiness we know and feel. The hole is only fillable, through the One who has the power and ability to fill it. The One, who can fill the hole, is the one and only living God. The living God is the one who can fill our voids and emptiness. God is the only one who has the right shape, to fill us up and make us full. Where can we go to meet God? Where can we go to find God, so that God, can fill us up and make us whole? It is so very simple to find God. It is so very easy to step into God. For God is only a prayer away. To invite God into our God shaped hole, we pray a simple prayer like: God I am sorry for searching everywhere else, but to you, to fill this hole/void in my life.

I have made a royal mess of me, with the choices I have made, and by the people I have hurt including myself. I am sorry, please forgive me and come into my heart, so that this hole inside of me can be filled. I just can't keep going down this path I am on. Help me get on to a new path, with new choices for my life. Help me to fill this hole with what is good and life giving. Fill me up so that I can stop trying to fill my heart with the things that only steal and hurt me and others. Thank you for loving me. Thank you for forgiving me. Thank you for making me your very own. Thank you for filling my heart and life with your Spirit and truth. Thank you for making me your own.

Prayer: I am grateful, Jesus, for the gift of your Spirit that now fills my heart and life. I am grateful for your sacrifice on the cross that made my being forgiven possible. Thank you, for loving me so much that you gave your all, so that I could be free today. Help me become whole, for I cannot do it without you. In Jesus' name, amen.

Day One Hundred Sixty-nine

Luke 6:27 `But I tell you who hear me: Love your enemies, do good to those who hate you.'

Love your enemies; do good to those who hate you. For most of us, we yell inside of ourselves, when we hear these word and say something like: "NO WAY I'M NOT LOVING HIM OR HER!!!!!" How can God be asking us to love our enemies; they are our enemies! How do we love someone who is an enemy not to mention, why would we want to love them? They are our enemies? The answer is not how do I love. The answer is, will I choose to love them. Not why would I love, rather why would I not love them? What happens inside of us when we hate someone or are angry with him/her? Does not our inside become hard and dark, empty and void, filled with negative thoughts and maybe sleepless nights? We may feel powerless and hopeless; lost in our hate and anger. The sad things about hating our enemy and carrying all that anger, bitterness and resentments is that it does NOTHING, hear that NOTHING, to the one we are angry with or hating, but it destroys us, big time. When we allow our enemy to get inside of us, what we are doing is, giving them permission to define us; giving others permission to tell us how we will feel, think, act, react, what we will do and not do. When our enemy is inside of us., we give them power and control over our lives, feelings and thoughts. That is why God says; `love your enemy'. When we pray for our enemy and choose to do good to them, what we are actually doing is taking back our ability to live our lives without that person, situation or event defining us. When we love our enemy and do good to them, we are no longer giving them permission to live rent free inside of us. We are giving them an eviction notice, and commanding them to vacate the premises. We love our enemies not because of him or her. In fact loving our enemies has nothing to do with them at all. Did you hear that friends! Loving your enemy has nothing to do with them. It has everything to do with us. It has everything to with our lives and the affect it has upon us and not them. When we choose to let go of our hate, anger, bitterness, resentments, unforgiveness, what we are doing is heaping hot coal upon them as Isaiah says. Doing good to them, not only releases you from them driving your bus, it sets you free to go on with your life, feelings and thoughts, which is the blessing God wants for us. God wants us to love our enemy; yes, because it is the right thing to do. More importantly, it is the freeing thing to do, for us. When we love our enemies and do not hate them, we are actually setting ourselves free. We are releasing ourselves from the power and control our enemy might have over us. By releasing the hate, anger, bitterness, resentment, unforgiveness we take back our power and our lives as well. When we love our enemies we are releasing them from our insides. We are taking back our lives and hearts, to live a healthier, more balanced, life. Loving your enemy allows you to decide for yourself. It takes back your power so that someone or some things are not deciding for us.

Loving our enemies brings us freedom. It takes back our lives and the power to live them.

Prayer: I am realizing, Father, that when I hate someone it only hurts me and not them. I can't do that to myself anymore. I am choosing to start today to love those whom I hate, not because of them, but because it is time for me to get my life back. It is time for me to be the person I was created to be. Thank you, for showing me how important it is to love my enemies for my sake and not theirs. Holy Spirit, help me to accomplish this in my life, amen.

Day One Hundred Seventy

> *Luke 6: 37-38 'Do not judge, and you will not be judged. Do not condemn, and you will not be condemned. Forgive, and you will be forgiven. Give, and it will be given to you. A good measure, pressed down, shaken together and running over, will be poured into your lap. For with the measure you use, it will be measured to you.'*

The command to not judge, I feel is universal. No matter who we are or where we have come from, we all have the same need to be loved, accepted and valued. It is from that need of being valued, loved and accepted, the request comes to not judge or condemn. When we judge others, we set ourselves above them and they below us. We say that our way is better and that every one should live, do, or act our way. In reality, that is an impossible request. We are all different. We all come from different families, beliefs, customs, morays, values, and so on. We all have a different starting and ending point. Hence, one of the many reasons why judging others is not a good thing. Another reason is: when we judge, not only do we set ourselves apart from that which we are judging, but we also set ourselves up to being judged. For in the same measure you judge others, you yourself will be judged. The same way you condemn others, you too will be condemned. This is one of the spiritual laws that exists and we cannot get away from it. If you judge and condemn others, you too will be judged and condemned. Have you ever said to yourself, what goes around comes around? It is the same principle. What you put out there will be brought back to you. If you are putting out judgments and condemnation, then judgment and condemnation will be what you get in return. If you forgive and accept others for who and what they are, then what you get in return is forgiveness and acceptance. You get mercy and grace. The demand for justice is placed upon you every time you demand justice. When we give mercy, the cycle of demanding justice is broken. Let me give you an example. When I demand justice and get it, then the one I demanded justice from wants justice back from me. I then have to get my justice back from him/her and so on. If we are granting mercy instead of demanding justice, then we are set free from the cycles of justice and the fulfilling of the law. The law is very simple actually. It is attached to the law of the harvest. What you sow into your life is what you will get out of your life. If you are sowing seeds that produce a bad harvest, a bad harvest is what you will get in the end. If you are sowing good seeds, then you will not only reap a harvest from the good seeds, but God will add His blessing: 'a good measure, pressed down, shaken together and running over, will be poured into your lap'. (Luke 6:38). The amazing thing about God's gift of free will to us, is just that: free will. We decide what our harvest will look like. We decide what we will sow into our harvest field, and what will be reaped in the end. If you judge and condemn others, then judgment and condemnation will be your reward, according to the law that is before us today. Here we go with free will again-------the choice is ours! Judge and you will be judged. Condemn and you will be condemned. Forgive and you will be forgiven. What we sow in our lives is what we get back in our harvests. It is all up to us.

Prayer: I repent for sowing judgments and condemnation into my life by judging and condemning people, things, events or situations. I am sorry, Lord, please for give me and help me not to judge others. I am learning that it is more harmful to me than to them. I want to be free. I want to have all the blessings you have stored up for me in and for my life. Thank you, Jesus, for the lesson I have learned today, amen.

Day One Hundred Seventy-one

Psalm 46: 1 & 10 `God is our refuse and strength an ever-present help in trouble. Be still, and know that I am God; I will be exalted among the nations, I will be exalted in the earth.'

We all have storms in our lives that we need to deal with. From what I have learned as I have journeyed through life is that storms come in a wide variety of shapes and sizes. Some storms are raging storms that blow through, with such force and intensity, that they seem to have a huge power all their own. Others are gale force storms that seem to pick up everything in its path. Then there are the milder storms that seem to even refresh us, after they have passed us by. Almost strengthening us by their presence. There are also the storms that come and go, without much thought or concern. Storms are a part of life. For the most part, the only thing we can do with storms is, face them and make our way through them. If storms are a fact of life and a reality that faces us all at points in our lives, then the other reality is that God is a port in the storms. An ever-present help in our times of trouble, no matter what the trouble looks like or how strong it might be, God promises to be with us as we journey through the trouble. We know God cannot lie. Therefore God will be there no matter what. It is a promise God has made to us. How do we know God is with us? How do we know that we can trust God and His promises? We know God is there by asking God for what we need in order to make it through, whatever it is we are struggling with. If you are asking for peace and comfort, is the peace and comfort within you and your heart? Are you asking for strength and courage to face this storm? Do you find yourself with strength and the courage that comes from the presence of God in your heart and spirit? Is it knowledge and wisdom you need to see you through the storm? Ask, then take a step back and see if you are given the gift you have asked for. Be still, be still and listen to what the Holy Spirit is saying to you and your heart and spirit. Be still so that you will know that knowing that comes from God and God's presence in our hearts, mind, body and spirit. If we allow ourselves to be still, then we can hear and know the answer to our prayers and the calming of the storms within us. The storms may still rage, or batter or pound around us, but inside of us, it is calm and peaceful. The calm and peace is there so we can do whatever it is we need to do. Exalt God in the storms of your life, as the one who can calm the storm and bring you through it. God is the one who has the resource to fill us and meet our every need, if we will but let God in. If we ask for the fulfilling of the promises in and for us, the fulfilling will happen. God wants to help us and be here with us. All we need do is ask. Then watch and see how God works with us in whatever is happening around us. Be still and know that I am God! When we let God be God in our lives, God always comes through for us. That is His promise to us, and we know God can never tell us a lie. Therefore it is true. Life storms are a reality we cannot get away from. The other reality is we have the One within us, who has the power to calm the storm, calm us in the midst of the storm, or put us on dry ground.

Prayer: Thank you, Father God, for your promises and their fulfillment in my life. Thank you that I can put my hope, trust and faith in you, no matter what is happening in or around me. Thank you that you are a faithful God who loves me more then I will ever know or understand. Thank you for being here with me during the storms of my life. With a deep sense of gratitude, I say thank you, Holy Spirit, and Father, amen.

Day One Hundred Seventy-two

Luke 8: 50 'Hearing this, Jesus said to Jairus, Don't be afraid; just believe, and she will be healed.'

Here we go again with this much needed reminder to: Don't be afraid just believe! How simple the statement is; yet at times it takes everything we have inside of us not to be afraid. It takes everything we have to just believe in the presence and power of God. Fear seems to have a life of its own at times and we get caught up in that life. It is so easy for us to move into fear and away from the presence and peace of God. Remember: FEAR: False Evidence Appearing Real. GOD: Good Orderly Direction. Jairus was moving into that false evidence regarding his daughter. The false evidence was: your daughter is dead don't bother the master. Jesus, hearing, this false evidence, turns to Jarius and says with confidence: "Don't Be Afraid, Just Believe"! Don't give your power away to fear. Just believe in who I am and all the evidence you have regarding me and my promises and power. Just believe in who I am and what I say I am. Trust that my words and promises are true. Trust what has gone before you. Use that trust to make it through today. Jarius decides to trust Jesus. Jarius chooses to turn away from his fear and his daughter is restored to life. Would his daughter have been restored to life regardless of Jarius' choice to move towards Jesus and just believe? We don't know. What we know is Jarius did trust Jesus and His word of life to him, and his daughter's life was restored. That is what Jesus is asking of each and every one of us. Jesus is asking each and every day for us to trust Him and believe in who and what He is and says He is. Jesus is asking us, as He asked Jarius; will you move out or away from your fear and just believe that I am the One, who can and will restore all things. If you choose to just believe and not be afraid God will work in your life as well. The challenge is to trust and let go of our fear and whatever else is happening inside of us. We so many times lose our blessing, because we move into fear, which is away from God. Have you ever wonder why we do not get our miracle, healing, touch, experience, presence of God? Our fear is what drives our life and heart and not the power, presence and love of God. Do not be afraid; just believe, that Jesus is who He says He is. Then watch and see everything God can and will do in your life. Jesus promises to always be here with us no matter what. Jesus promises to help us in all of our needs. Just Believe! That is the difference between those of us who see the hand of God working in and through our lives and the lives of those we love. We see the hand of God working because we choose to believe. We choose to trust and not be afraid. We choose to walk in faith and not fear. We choose life. Therefore, life is what is given in return.

Prayer: Today, Father, I am choosing to just believe and trust you. I am choosing to trust you and your word and promises in and for my life. Thank you, for always telling me the truth and for never lying to me. I do love and trust you Lord, amen.

Day One Hundred Seventy-three

Isaiah 30: 9 `These are rebellious people, deceitful children, children unwilling to listen to the Lord's instruction.'

Have you ever heard yourself saying. "I don't have to listen to you! You don't have anything to say that I want to hear!" Shut up---I'm not listening-----or any other such saying coming off your tongue or in your mind? When we have this kind of attitude, belief or opinion towards life and authority, we usually find ourselves in a place where God's voice is not audible to us either. God's voice begins to fade, and it becomes harder and harder to listen to God as well.

A rebellious spirit may begin to settle in our hearts and minds. We get to the point where we are unable to listen to any kind of authoritative wisdom, not even God's. We close down our hearts and nothing gets in. The Israelites were a good example of what being rebellious does. How being in a place of resisting authority causes harm and hardship in our lives. When the Israelites were following God and living according to God's decrees, laws, percepts and commandments life went along a smooth path. When they turned away from God, and started following the paths of the surrounding peoples, life got miserable and hard. Their enemies attacked them, food supplies were harder to come by, individuals and communities got ill, and eventually God stopped talking with them. They were on their own, because of their rebellious or stubborn hearts. Is it time to check our lives and see if we too have areas in our lives that are shut off to God and God's ways? Have we stopped listening to God through His Word? Do we think God's Word and ways of living are too restrictive or confining at times? Do we have the attitude that says: everyone else is doing it, it must be okay? Or maybe we sense or know God is asking us to do something, or go somewhere, yet we find ourselves running from it or just saying no to God? We become like Jonah and run the other way. Are we hiding a sin in our lives and therefore do not want to be close to God? We know God will suggest we stop the sin and repent for our choices and behaviour. There are so many ways we can turn away from God and towards rebellion or resistance. They can be subtle or out in the open. There are so many pulls upon our lives and hearts that want to draw us into areas of rebellion and resistance. Am I following God and God's ways, or am I following the ways of the world and rebellion? Only we as individuals can answer that question. If we are living in an attitude or belief that says rebellion is just fine-thank you very much, then do not be surprised if life gets harder and harder, and more and more difficult to live in. A rebellious heart and spirit gives us a return of hardship, hurt and discomfort. That is the consequence of turning our backs away from what is right and true, and towards what is stealing and false.

293

Prayer: Father, I want to be an obedient child. I want to do what is pleasing to you. I repent for the areas in my life that are rebellious and resistant to you and your ways. I repent for the times I chose to walk away from you and into the arms of rebellion and disobedience. Forgive me, and help me to be the child you created me to be. Thank you, Father, amen.

Day One Hundred Seventy-four

Leviticus 19: 1-2 'The Lord said to Moses, "Speak to the entire assembly of Israel and say to them: Be holy because I, the Lord your God, am holy."'

Be holy for the Lord your God is holy. What does that mean? Be holy for God is holy. It actually means, be whole for the Lord your God is whole. Live as one who is complete, living in perfect goodness and righteousness. Be devoted to the One who is holy, having the Lord's divine qualities within you and without. Living your life in such a way, as to honour and uphold the holiness of God and all that God is. Living our lives with respect for others, ourselves and especially respect for God. Living in such a way, that we live in honesty and truth. Not short changing others, God or ourselves with half measures or less than our best effort. Being willing to live in integrity, where our words and actions meet they are the same. Where our lives are a reflection of honesty and truth. When we say we will do something, we do it. When we give our word, others know that they can count on our word. When we say something, people know we are talking from a place of integrity and truth. Therefore, it is okay to trust us and give their trust to us. Being holy is choosing to not steal or lie, or cheat, to not swear falsely or use the name of the Lord your God in profanity. Honouring the name of the Lord your God with your words, life and actions. Choosing not to defraud another, even though it would be the easiest thing to do. Living and working out our lives in such a way that we choose to not hold back something we owe someone. Refusing to give someone something, just because we want to be miserable and hard to get along with. Being holy is not putting stumbling blocks in the path of anyone, especially the weak, blind or lame. When we are holy we choose to live in justice, not showing favouritism or partiality to one at the expense of another. It is not treating people differently for whatever reason. Holiness is not talking about people behind their backs, gossiping, telling tales out of school. Choosing not to do anything that would endanger another person or put them in harms way. Holiness is having no hate in our hearts. It is choosing to be holy and living a holy (whole) life; allowing God to have the last word in our need for vengeance. When we are holy/whole, we live our lives in such a way that brings glory and honour to God and therefore to ourselves. Our lives become a reflection of the holiness/wholeness of God in us. Therefore that reflection shines outward. When I am holy my life is lived in such a way, as not to cause harm or shame to God, others or myself. Each day is lived so that our friends can defend us, but never are put in a place where the defense is necessary. No one has to lie to protect or defend us, for our lives do not need protecting or defending. We are choosing to do the right thing every chance we get. Be holy for the Lord your God is holy. Then watch how the holiness changes who you are and your view of life and living life.

Prayer: Father, I want to honour you in every part of my life. I want my life to be lived in such as way that it is a reflection of you and your presence in me. Holy Spirit, I need your help to be holy and live a holy life. Please help me this day and every day. In Jesus' name, amen.

Day One Hundred Seventy-five

> *Deuteronomy 1: 42-43`But the Lord said to me, "Tell them, `Do not go up and fight, because I will not be with you. You will be defeated by your enemies.'" So I told you, but you would not listen. You rebelled against the Lord's command and in your arrogance you marched up into that hill country.'*

The Israelites are such good examples for us to learn what not to do. The Israelites had just been disobedient. God had told them to go and take the land. God had just told them He was with them, and they would have success. They decided that there were giants in the land. Therefore they could not win against the giants. They were already defeated, because the people living in the Promised Land were much bigger than they were. Therefore, what was the use of going in to fight? They were going to lose anyway. They went into their fear, instead of trusting God and God's provision and promises. The Israelites have heard through Moses how disappointed God is with them. How they walked away from God and into their own needs and fears. The Israelites can now see what they have done the wrong choice they had made. God was grieved by their actions. The Israelites said to themselves. "We will make it right with God. We will go in and take the land." They were trying, in their own steam, to get back the blessing they had lost. They decided to go and do what God had asked them to do in the first place. The problem is, God is no longer with them, guarding and guiding their steps. Did the Israelites listen to God when God said, "do not go for I am not with you"? Did they humble themselves, repenting for wanting life on their terms and conditions? No, they decided to take matters into their own hands. The Israelites decided to do it their way, so that they could reclaim what they lost. What happened? The Israelites lost the battle, their dignity and pride, returning home with their tail between their legs, totally defeated. My friends, God has not changed. He is the same yesterday, today and forever. If God says do not go and we go, then His blessing is not upon us. If God says go for I am with you, and we do not go, God disciplines us in order to teach us the lessons we need to learn. When we demand God to do things our way and in our terms and conditions, do not be surprised to find God silent, or even absent from our lives and choices. God asks us to be obedient and to follow Him. When we do, God's blessings and provision are with us. When we choose to live life our way and on our terms and conditions, God pulls back, until we humble ourselves and repent for our disobedience. We have the same choices the Israelites had. We can either live life our way or God's way. Whichever path we take, there will be consequences; consequences that bring us life and closer to God or consequences that bring us death and away from God. We can either live in the blessings of God or we can live life on our terms and condition, which is outside of God great mercy and grace. Had the Israelites listened to God in the first place they would not have spent an extra forty years in the desert? Think about that for a while. It may change the way you deal with God and the choices you make.

Prayer: Holy and gracious God, slow to anger and abounding in love. I admit that there are times when I want my life to go, as I want it to go. I want it to look like I want it to look like, forgetting that my choices cause me either blessings or curses. Remind me and help me to live my life in such a way, that it is pleasing to you and to me. Forgive me, for being so stubborn at times, and demanding life as I see it unfolding and happening. Thank you Lord, for your love and forgiveness. I need it every day, in every way, amen

Day One Hundred Seventy-six

Psalm 77:7-9 ' Will the Lord reject forever? Will He never show His favor again? Has His unfailing love vanished forever? Has His promises failed for all time? Has God forgotten to be merciful? Has He in anger withheld His compassion?'

There have been times in my life and faith journey, when I have felt just like the Psalmist here. I have felt like God was nowhere to be found. God had forsaken me and set me up to fail. I felt like God had forgotten all about me. I was out there, all alone with no one to turn to. I felt like God's promises were just like everyone else's I had known, filled with lots of holes, for the promises to leak through. The feelings were mine. They were true feelings, but they were nowhere close to the facts. The facts were that God had not set me up to fail. God had a different plan for me. God was, yes, silent, but He was teaching me more about faith. More about what it truly means to live in faith. God had not forgotten me. God was right there with me holding me, and carrying me through the struggles and pain. God was not holding anything back from me. God was using this time to help me to grow, to take my place more and more. I know first hand how hard it is when our feelings are yelling and screaming at us. I know what it is like to think, God is not who God says He is. The reality and truth is God is exactly who He promises to be, and so very much more. Sometimes the only way to know this truth is to have the same experience the Psalmist is talking about today. The same experience I have personally experienced. For it is in those times of total lostness within ourselves, that we find out first hand just how trustworthy and faithful our God is. Without the valleys, there can be no mountaintops. Without the mountaintops, there can be no valleys. Am I thankful for the 'valleys-times' in my life? I am grateful for what they have taught me. Would I give them up or exchange them for something else? The answer is a loud and resounding no. Do I want to repeat them? Absolutely not! If you are going through a valley time in your life, or know someone who is, my best advice is to let go and let God love you through it. Give yourself permission to feeling, what they are feeling, in a loving and supportive way. Help yourself to know that these are just feelings, they too shall pass. Give yourself permission to be angry with God, and all that you are experiencing. Be honest with yourself and with God. God already knows. Believe it or not, God truly does understand. Remember God gave us these feelings in the first place. Just be real with what is happening to you. Then when you are ready, move out of this place and back up the mountain. Some people will tell you that you cannot be mad at God. That it is not okay to be this space or place. They are wrong. It is okay and it is the right thing to do at the time. As I said, God knows and understands. God has not brought us this far to drop us. God will never bring us anywhere to drop us. When we are in the valley. God is right here with us loving us through. God will see us to the other side. Remember our God is a faithful God, who cannot break a promise. The promise God makes us is to always be with us no matter what. We can truly trust God's promises, for they are always yes and amen.

Prayer: Thank you for knowing me, and understanding who I am, and what I am going through. Thank you for not being afraid of my feelings and what I am feeling. I am learning that I can be totally honest with you, Father God, no matter what is going on inside or outside of me. Help me to never stay down when I fall. Help me to not get stuck in whatever valley I am going through. I need you, Lord, in my life more and more and more. Come and fill me up, for I leak. I need you in me every single day. Fill my cup, Lord, fill it up, Lord. Thank you, Holy Spirit, for being my constant guide and everything else I need, amen.

Day One Hundred Seventy-seven

Joshua 22: 26-27 `That is why we said, Let us get ready and build an altar---but not for burnt offerings or sacrifices. On the contrary, it is to be a witness between us and you and the generations that follow, that we will worship the Lord at his sanctuary with our burnt offerings, sacrifices and fellowship offerings.'

How quick we are to jump to conclusions at times! We see something, and automatically think, this or that has to be the reason or the cause. The 2 ½ tribes had just finished their commitment of helping their fellow Israelites claim their land and help settle their families. They were now released from their promise, and sent home to build their farms and territory allotment Along the way they were thinking about all that had happened, and thought to themselves, what if we lose contact with our fellow Israelites because we are on the other side of the Jordan River? In order to prevent any future possible conflict or questioning, let us build an altar, as a reminder of our connectedness and oneness together with the 10 ½ tribes. The motive was pure and upright. When the Israelites found out the altar was being built. They jumped to all kinds of conclusions. They thought the 2 ½ tribes were, after all they had been through, now doing their own thing and building an altar to sacrifice on. They made ready for war. When they arrived at the sight, instead of rushing in and declaring war they asked a simple question. `Are you now turning away from the Lord?' (Joshua 22:18.) This is a good lesson for all of us to learn from. We can either jump to conclusions, which get ourselves in all sorts of trouble, not to mention a place of conflict. Or we can take a step back, evaluate what is really going on, and decide where we will go from here. Gathering information and data, really helps us see things as they really are, and not as they appear to be. Had the Israelites just taken the surface information, there would surely have been a senseless war, with lots of innocent people losing their lives on both sides. Instead the Israelites asked the right question, and found out that the altar was a reminder, and a symbol of the relationship. The altar was a reminder of all that was good and life giving about the community and its people. Harmony was restored and trust rebuilt. Let us today decide to not jump to conclusions. To not be too hasty in deciding what we will do with the events we see all around us, without having the proper facts and data at hand. Let us live as wise people, discerning what is true from what is false.

Prayer: Holy Spirit, I no longer desire to go through life jumping to conclusions. I am tired of coming up with the wrong way of dealing with whatever it is that life has put in my path. I am asking for you to fill me with knowledge, wisdom, discernment and understanding I need to become wise in my dealings with life. Thank you for filling me and showing me the new path for living my life. Holy Spirit, you are so life giving to me. I truly value you in my life, amen.

Day One Hundred Seventy-eight

Psalm 23: 4 'Even though I walk through the valley of the shadow of death I will fear no evil, for you are with me; your rod and your staff they comfort me.'

Even though I walk through the valley of the shadow of death, fear, sickness, loss, divorce, separation etc., I will fear no evil. I will not fear the valley I have to pass through, for my God is with me, and His rod and staff are well able to protect me and comfort me. Your promise, God, is to be there with me even though I do not realize it at the time. Just like the poem 'Footprints in the sand', I choose to believe you are with me, carrying me safely to the other side. Carrying me when I do not have the strength to carry myself. Being with me especially when my resources are at an end, and there is nothing left within me. You will still be there walking with me and seeing me through. Your promise says: no matter what life is putting on my plate, you are always there to help me see it through. The reality of life and living as human beings in a sinful world means, we all have or will have valleys in our lives. None of us are exempt from the struggle of going through the valleys life puts in our paths. The valleys will be there, that is called life! The promise of God is: I will be with you in the valley. I will walk the valley with you and you are never alone. My rod and my staff are at your side, no matter what life is giving you or throwing your way. There is no valley deep enough, long enough or wide enough that can ever separate us, or cause me not to be by your side. I promise to see you through to the other side and up back onto solid firm ground again. At the end of every valley there is a mountaintop, just as every mountaintop has a valley. The only choice we have is, either we embrace both experiences and learn from what they are trying to teach us, or to try and run from them, hiding away. If we stay and learn, we gain the skills and lessons the valley is teaching us. If we run, we delay our healing and recovery from the valley experience. If we stay and learn, we become much better people for having experienced the valley. We become more compassionate, loving and understanding of others. If we run, we spend our whole life running! Remember this old saying; pay me now or pay me later, but sooner or later you will have to pay the bill. That sums up the lesson for today. Either pay the price of going through the valley now with the help of our loving heavenly Father and His Holy Spirit, or avoid the valley, and pay not only the bill, but the interest as well, later on down the line. The valleys are a reality. We cannot escape the valleys. They are real times we all have to go through. The mountaintop experiences are what make the valley times bearable. What makes the valley times either or life-stealing, is what we do with them and how we allow them to affect our lives.

Prayer: Thank you, Father, and Holy Spirit that you are always with us, no matter what! There is never a time when your presence is not right here in the midst of us. Thank you that no matter what is happening in my life, you are faithful in your presence with me. Thank you that you are just who you say you are. I know my faith in you is not misplaced or wrong. Help me through my valleys, so that I can come to the other end as whole as possible, knowing that I have had your grace carrying me through. In Jesus' name, amen.

Day One Hundred Seventy-nine

Genesis 18: 2 'Abraham looked up and saw three men standing nearby. When he saw them, he hurried from the entrance of his tent to meet them and bowed low to the ground.'

Being humble and living in a state of humility is often most difficult for us. We think or feel at times that if I am humble, then others will have opportunity to walk all over me or use me. The reality is, that is the farthest thing from the truth. Just because we are humble, it does not mean, we are less than. Being humble does not mean that I put myself down, or allow others to put me down. To be humble is to not think less of yourself, it is to think of yourself less. To be willing to put others first and yourselves second. To be humble means, we can allow others to have first place without any negative thoughts, or actions on our part. Abraham, the leader of his clan, and the most respected man in his community, was willing to bow low to the ground at the sight of the three men standing nearby him. Abraham knew that these men were important. Abraham knew he needed to humble himself before them. Abraham allowed himself permission to lower himself and raise the men up. Does it mean that Abraham lost face or was considered less valuable, or important, than these men?

303

The answer is no. In fact, because Abraham lowed himself, he was raised up. It even elevated him in their eyes! Why? Because Abraham knew right from wrong, and was willing to choose what was right. Arrogance would say: I am not lowering myself to them. I am not putting myself in a place of being lower than they are. Arrogance would put us in a place of being right with our own thinking, but wrong in our dealings with others. When we live in arrogance what we are really doing is stealing our blessings, and not seeing life through life giving eyes and actions. Abraham could have not humbled himself. He could have done the right thing. He could have ignored his visitors, or treated them without honour or respect, but what would Abraham have gained? These men brought the promise of an heir from God, with the promise that Abraham would be the father of a nation. Through Abraham's seed the Saviour of the world would come. Would God have still used Abraham if Abraham did not humble himself? I do not have an answer to that, but it is an interesting thought to think about. Do we lose out on so much of what life is all about, because we are stuck in our need to be right, and to live in our arrogance? Or are we being willing to humble ourselves, which in turn opens the door, to so much more than we could ever have thought or imagined? We will never know the answer! Being humble is a true gift we give others and ourselves, as we go about our daily lives. Remember being humble does not mean you are less than, it simply means you can allow others to have the higher place, and you the lower one, without being less than they or less important than they are.

Prayer: Father, I need to repent for I am not very humble at times. I always thought that if I was humble, then others were better then I am. I am learning that when I am humble, I am just honouring the other person, and allowing them to be honoured for who they are. Please forgive me, and help me to be more real and honest with myself, and who and what I am as a person. Then I can allow others to be who and what they are as people. Thank you, Lord, amen.

Day One Hundred Eighty

Romans 15: 5 `May the God who gives endurance and encouragement give you a spirit of unity among yourselves as you follow Christ Jesus.'

Resentments are the biggest destroyer of relationships. There is nothing that can destroy a relationship faster, than holding resentments and allowing those resentments to grow into bitterness. Resentments do not allow us to see clearly. Nor do they let us see beyond the resentment. The next destroyer is disunity. If there is no unity in our relationships that means, we are going to be at odds with those we are in relationship with. The disunity divides, which in turn causes the falling away of all that is good, and the embracing of what is not good. We get to the point where we only see the negatives in the relationship. We only see the things that separate us or tear us apart. Disunity causes us to look at what is different, what is not the same. If we go through life living in disunity, guaranteed we will find lots and lots of things to be different about. Just look at your family. How many differences can you find just in your family unit? Not one of you is the same as the other. Not one of you looks at life in exactly the same way. What we learn from our family differences is, to over-look the differences and seek out the things we have in common. That same principle needs to be used in all of our relationships and life situations we find ourselves in. There is no shortage of differences. Therefore, we need to seek out the things that are the same, in order to build up, instead of tear down. United we stand, divided we fall. What a simple truth. United, we stand together strong and well able to face whatever life throws our way. Divided, we stand alone without support or resources around us. There is nothing stronger or harder to tear a part, than the unity of those who chose to stand together. Divided, a part, separated from, causes us to stand alone. Alone is just that alone---without help or others standing with you. A single thread is easily broken, but a bunch of threads together is strong and not easily broken. Try to break the bunch of threads. It hurts your fingers and the threads fight back not wanting to be broken. If the threads break, it takes a lot of energy and strength to do so. A single piece of paper easily rips, but a thick phone book takes more energy and ability to tear apart than I have or will ever have. United we stand strong, divided we stand alone and chances are we will fall. Search out unity. Search out the things that we all have in common. Then build on those resources and ability. When we work together building on what we have in common, it is amazing how soon we forget about the things we have that are different. Unity and harmony grows and division disappears.

Prayer: Father, help me to see through eyes that see the good in others. Help me, to look beyond the differences we all have, into the things we share in common. I want to be a part of life that truly is life and to me and to others. Teach me unity and how to live in unity. Teach me, how to see others as you see them through the eyes of love, amen.

Day One Hundred Eighty-one

1 Corinthians 10:23 `Everything is permissible—but not everything is beneficial. Everything is permissible ---but not everything is constructive.'

When we look at life, everything in life is permissible. As human beings, we have the ability to do whatever it is we want to do. We can choose from everything that this good earth offers and more. There is no limit to what we can choose. The limit is our imagination and desire. Just because I can choose whatever I desire to choose, does not mean that it is going to be good for me, or beneficial to who and what I am as a person. Food is a good example: we all need food to survive. Food is a very good thing and very necessary to our existence. Not to mention necessary for the maintaining of our body, mind and general well being.

But if we take in too much food, then our bodies suffer. We suffer by storing up too many reserves, called fat. The body becomes sluggish and heavy, and often gets sick, from too much food on a regular basis. We are learning that less is better than more. There is nothing stopping us from eating far too much and over indulging. Too much food is not beneficial to our bodies and consequently us as well. Everything is permissible, but not everything is constructive. I can have a very lazy and non-active life and lifestyle. I can sit around all the time and do nothing, but what is the end result? I get to the point where I can no longer get up and move. I get to the point where, my muscles are so weak they have a hard time holding up my body. I end up not being able to move or function, because my body to too weak. The reality is, we have the freedom to choose and do everything our heart desires. God has given us that freedom, and it is called free will. We have the ability to take our free will, and do whatever it is we want to do with it. God will not stop us! I see the gift of free will being exercised every day at work. I also see the consequences of what free will can do to us, if it is not kept in check. When my free will is allowed to go wild and do whatever it wants to do, the end result is always death in some form or another. With the offenders I work with, death is the loss of their ability to say no to drugs and alcohol. The drugs and booze drive their lives, and what they will or will not be able to do. A little wine is good for the stomach, a little brandy helps the heart, a little of anything is not bad. A lot of anything becomes harmful and destructive to our ability to function as well rounded human beings. As Paul says: yes, we can do whatever it is we want to do there is nothing stopping us. Only remember, not everything we do is beneficial, or constructive to who and what we are as human beings and people. Not everything that is at our disposal gives us life and well-being. Not everything adds to who and what we are as people. Not everything produces inside of us the end result we are looking for. That end result is being health, wealth and wisdom.

Prayer: Thank you, Father, for your gift of free will and all that free will gives my life and me. Help me, today, to use my gift of free will to my betterment and life, instead of using it to my death and destruction. Help me to choose everything that is , and to turn away from those things that are life stealing. Thank you, Holy Spirit, for helping me be strong and to make choices. I am truly grateful, amen.

Day One Hundred Eighty-two

The following is from hugs for Women, Andrews McMeel Publishing, Kansas City

My daughter (son) you are My workmanship, created in Christ Jesus to do good works. I've already prepared you in advance for everything I've planned especially for you to do.

Love,
Your God of purpose,

> *Ephesians 2:10 `For we are God's workmanship, created in Christ Jesus to do good works, which God prepared in advance for us to do.*

You look inside and see the unfinished project that is your life, but do you know what God sees? God sees the untapped potential that trickles deep within you, like a stream on the floor of an ice-bound river. When you see yourself as insecure, God doesn't. He sees a woman (man) with a rich capacity for empathy. When you stare into the mirror of imperfection, God sees the etching of His artistry---designs He drew so that you could be you. When you look around and see a roadblock in your path, God sees all the interesting side roads you could take to get around them. When you see all the people who never fail to depend on you, God sees all the lives that are blessed by you. When you see a thankless routine, God see the fruit of your faithful life. When you see lost relationships, God sees room for new friends. When you see tangled complications, God sees a place for a miracle. When you see loneliness and abandonment, God see the gaping hole in your heart and knows that only He can fill it. When you see a past-empty bank account, God sees the perfect chance for His cherished child to watch how He'll provide. When you see truckloads of stress begin to roll your way, God sees emerald-green pastures besides crystal-clear waters and makes His plans to take you there for refreshment. And when the jobs come that all you can see is darkness and gloom, God sees only the bright new hope shining on your horizon—and He smiles, for He knows the endless joys that a future with Him will bring to you. Depending upon him alone, I go forward---though my eyes are wet with tears, I must go forward. O Lord, fill me with the Holy Ghost. Give me power to move the people. Amen by Kiye Sato Yamamuro

Prayer: Father, help me to truly know who I am in you and who you created me to be, help me to see my creativity and use it to your glory and mine. I want to be the person you created me to be. I no longer desire to settle for less. Thank you, for making me unique and giving me everything you have. I am grateful, for your love and care of who you created me to me, amen.

Day One Hundred Eighty-three

John 8: 32 `Then you will know the truth, and the truth will set you free.'

There is no truth in lies! The one thing that hurts us the deepest, and cuts down to the very core of our being, is being lied to. We hate being lied to, yet we lie to our self so very often. We spend a good portion of our life lying to ourselves. Then we wonder why we get stuck in our mud puddles? Only the truth gets us out of our mud puddle. Only the truth sets us free. The problem with knowing the truth is once you know the truth you cannot go back and live in a lie comfortably. You can go back and live in the lie, but it's not comfortable any longer. It is not our safe and comfortable mud puddle. We cannot deceive ourselves any longer. We cannot hide in the lies, for the lies have been exposed. The reason the lie is not comfortable is, because the truth has shown the light, into the darkness of the lie. The truth has shone its light, exposing the lie, for who and what it really is. That is the power of truth. Truth is what is real. Lies are what is not real. Both cannot live side by side. Therefore, once you know the truth, living beside the lie is terribly uncomfortable. In fact, it is so uncomfortable we either have to remove the lie or find a way to deaden its power. We need to find a way of taking the power out of the lie. We need to take the power out of the lie, so that the lie does not scream at us any longer. We deaden the power of the lie, through the use of anything that will cover it up, such as alcohol, drugs, food, risk-taking activities, and so on. We deaden its power by putting something in its place. Something that is nosier or louder than the lie. The other choice is to kick the lie out, replacing it with the truth. We replace the lie with the truth therefore the lie has lost its power and cannot affect us any longer. When we choose to move out of the lies and into the truth, those lie voices that keep screaming at us, lose their ability to control our lives. They lose their ability to tell what we will do or not do. The truth then allows the real person inside of us to live, and have true life within us. There is true freedom to let go of what was. Freedom to come into all the possibilities of what could be. There is freedom in our inner house to live and let live. To truly run and be free! Thank you, Father God, for telling us the truth. Thank you, for wanting us to be free to be all you created us to be. We are so grateful.

Prayer: I want to be free. I want to live in freedom. Holy Spirit, show me the lies that are in my life. Then help me to get rid of them. Help me to set them free, so I can be free as well. I am so very tired of having the lies run my life. I want to be free of them. I want to be able to enjoy all that life has to offer me. Thank you, Holy Spirit, for revealing the truth in my life and setting me free to truly live, truly live, amen.

Day One Hundred Eighty-four

Romans 12:10 `Be devoted to one another in brotherly love. Honour one another above yourselves.'

What is brotherly love? Brotherly love is being related to another by common ties or interests, a fellow member of a church family or other organization that has strong emotional ties, people who are similar to each other and have similar interests and connections, and considering another human being as being part of your family. Brotherly love is choosing to love another human being. Of valuing and esteeming them as important and significant. What is it to honour someone? Honour is a showing of respect. A showing how one's worth brings respect or even fame; showing love, devotion or awe and giving great reverence for the person we choose to love. To honour each other is to regard them as valuable and worthy of love and being loved. To be devoted to one another in brotherly love is, to say to each other, we are connected like a family and are like siblings, within the family God is creating. As a sibling I will honour you and love you. I will be devoted to you and give you the respect you deserve. We are more than just two people walking through this journey called life, we are family, and as family I will love you and honour you. I will guard your dignity, and treat you as the valuable human being you are. I will not deliberately hurt or harm you, nor will I do anything that causes you deliberate hurt or harm. I will walk with you and be there for you in true brotherly love. As we journey through life together, we are committed in every way possible to love, honour and respect each other. This sounds like an awesome task, and on the one hand it is! For we often fall short of doing good, and doing what is best for the people in our lives. There are lots of people journeying with us along our path. Some we totally enjoy and others are not too sure about. There are so many times we think only of ourselves, forgetting about those we say we love. The saving truth is, once we start honouring each other and loving them, treating them respectfully and valuing who they are as a child of God, we find ourselves wanting to live and act this way with everyone we meet. This way of treating others becomes our norm, instead of a once off act when necessary. Honouring each other and loving people, really does become the comfortable way of being with others. To our amazement after awhile it becomes the only way of being with others. For we benefit equally from our honouring and love. It is not long before we see ourselves living in the spirit of love and loving. We move away from the selfish or self-centered ways of our past. It truly does become easy and even enjoyable. The end result is a heart-felt desire to bring love to everyone we meet, greet, know and love. We find ourselves wanting to live in love and in no other way. That truly is the amazing investment return of love. Once you start investing your love into others, your investment grows. As your investment grows you desire to love more. The more you love the more your love investment grows. The wonders of God's economy!

Prayer: Thank you, Lord, for this lesson today. I so needed to hear that there is a better, more way to be in relationships with those in my life, especially those I have love connections with. Thank you for teaching me to love first and to treat everyone with love and a sense of honour. To love others for who and what they are as a child of God's and as another human being. I am grateful. Guide me, Lord, as I live this lesson out in my life, amen.

Day One Hundred Eighty-five

Hebrews 13:5 `Keep your lives free from the love of money and be content with what you have, because God has said, "Never will I leave you; never will I forsake you."'

What a promise, `Never will I leave you; never will I forsake you.' For some of us that promise is a really hard thing to believe. So many different people have left us or cast us to the wayside. The promise of God is He will never, no never not be there. God promises to always be with us. No matter what is happening in or to our lives. God promises to always be the one constant we can trust, no matter what! And because God cannot tell a lie or deceive us in any way, shape or form, the promise is true and trustworthy. God promises to be with us, no matter what is going on within us or without. God will be with us in every, and all circumstances we may or may not find ourselves in. God will even carry us, when we are unable to carry ourselves. This is the promise God has given to you and to me. We can find our rest in God and all God is. Another key to having a life that is free from worry and stress is, to be free from the love of money. To be content with what you have. This truly is a key to joy and happiness. If we can stay away from the love of money, and the need to chase after money, we can find contentment in what we have. When we find ourselves chasing after money, then we cannot be content. For we have learned that we will never have enough money. We will always be trying to gain more or accumulate more money. The money pull is a really strong pull. The only way to break away from its grasp is, to be content with what we have. I have truly started to learn this lesson. At 36 I left my position as a purchasing manager with the salary that went along with the position and went back to school. I went from having a nice salary to having the bear minimum to live on. I had to learn how to refocus my what I thought were needs, to what were actually real needs, and not wants. When I let go of the false belief of I needed this or that, I learned to get by on what was truly needed. To my surprise, life became a whole lot easier. I was content. I could and did manage on what God gave me. There was always enough to go around. I was not searching after what other people had. I was able to receive what I did have and be content with it. It has made such a vast difference in and to my life. Now I can look at what others have and not find myself wanting it or needing to have it. I can choose what I buy and spend my money on, without chasing after what I thought I needed or wanted. God proved Himself more and more every time I trusted God, and let God have control of what I spent my money on. God's promise is true. God is always there and if I keep my eyes and heart on God, searching after God, I really do have everything I need. It is a bit of struggle in the beginning, but once you go through the withdrawals, you will look back and say something like why didn't I do this earlier?

Prayer: Thank you, Father, that you always tell me the truth. Thank you that I can put my hope, trust and faith in you and not be disappointed. Thank you that you are who you say you are. Help me to trust you more. Help me, to be content with life and what I have, so that I do not get caught up in the trap of searching and seeking after whatever everyone else has. Thank you for always being here and loving me just the way I am, but loving me too much to leave me here. I am so very grateful, amen.

Day One Hundred Eighty-six

> *2 Corinthians 10: 3-5 `For though we live in the world, we do not wage war as the world does. The weapons we fight with are not the weapons of the world. On the contrary, they have divine power to demolish strongholds. We demolish arguments and every pretension that sets itself up against the knowledge of God, and we take captive every thought to make it obedient to Christ.'*

We live in the world and have to function within the world, but for the most part our battles are not against the world. Our battles are not against the things we can see, feel and touch. Our battle is against the powers within the spiritual realms. Think about that for a moment. Think about the times in your life when you were fighting against someone. The person is attacking you, but you have not done anything wrong or anything to deserve the action or reaction you are getting. The energy coming against you just does not make sense. Then you take a step back and ask God to open your eyes to see what is really going on. God will answer your prayer. As God opens your spiritual eyes, you can begin to see the attack is actually not against you, but against what you believe. Or the light you are shining in your daily choices and witness of your faith. The attack is against what your spirit is giving out and the salt you are sharing around you. The attack is not against you personally. Although you have to deal with the attack, the attack is really against your faith and what your faith represents. The attack is against the light you are shining. The attack is against the difference your faith makes in your life; in the way you present yourself when dealing with people, situations or events. The darkness does not like the light you are shining. Therefore, it wants to put your light out. The darkness wants to make it hard for you to shine your light. Why? So that you will stop shining it and stop being a threat to the darkness. The battle you are fighting is not against you or the world. It is against the powers of darkness in the spiritual realm that does not like what you are doing and vibrating spiritually. When we are facing an attack or upheaval in one way or another, just know and understand that, not all the attacks or upheaval is coming from the earthly realm. Some attacks are coming at us because of what is happening in the spiritual realm. When being confronted take a step back. Pray, asking God to show you why the attack is happening and where the attack is coming from. If it is because of what you are doing and the confrontation is legitimate, because of your actions or choices; then you can do whatever adjusting needs to take place. If the attack is from a spiritual perspective, then the only recourse you have is to pray. Then allow God permission to work in the attack, helping you as only God can. Know the enemy and where the confrontation is coming from. Then you can use the right tool for the job. Then, and only then, will you have the right resources to deal with whatever it is you need to deal with. Wisdom is our best defense. Let us use the wisdom God is giving us, to stand firm and tall against any and all attacks that may come our way.

Prayer: Heavenly Father, I am realizing that I know very little of what really happens in the spiritual realm, and consequently in the natural realm. Help me to see with your eyes, so that I do not get caught off guard finding myself fighting a battle that is not mine to fight. Help me to seek after you at all times, because when I have you, I really do have everything I need. Thank you, Holy Spirit, for being my ever-present guide and help, amen.

Day One Hundred Eighty-seven

Deuteronomy 28: 1, 3-4 `If you fully obey the Lord your God and carefully follow all his commands I give you today, the Lord your God will set you high above all the nations of the earth. You will be blessed in the city and blessed in the country. The fruit of your womb will be blessed, and the crops of your land and the young of your livestock—the calves of your herds and the lambs of your flocks.'

If: what an amazing word! It has so much power for life or for death within and about us. If we choose life God's way, we get life in return. If we choose life our own way and on our terms and conditions, what we usually get in return is not always so life giving. At least in the long run. God promises that if we follow His ways and laws, we will know and receive God's blessings. All we put our hands to will be blessed by God. If we choose to walk the path God set out for His people, then God will shower down blessings upon us in every way. The blessings will fall upon our crops and fields, our herds and flocks and our offspring, the children we bring into this world. God's blessings will touch every part of our lives. God's blessings will be visible to all who see the fruit of our obedience to God's laws, and commands. Here Moses is challenging us to choose today to follow the Lord our God. To live according to His commands and laws. The amazing thing about living life God's way is, life is so much better and easier. Life is what we thought life should or would be if and when we got our act together. If we live life God's way the promise is: God will set us high above the nations of the earth and will bless us not only in the city, but also in the country. God will bless us no matter where we are or where we are living. God's blessings will be upon us, showering down upon our lives, no matter what is happening on the outside of us or where we are living. When we choose to live our lives according to the ways of God and God's commands, our lives will reap the return of God's blessings and the fulfillment of God's promises to His people. Everything we put our hand to will be under the grace and blessings of God, and His promise of provision for our lives. Living life according to God's commands means we set ourselves without hesitation towards pleasing God and doing what God requires of us. What does God require of us? God requires us, to live justly, love mercy and to walk humbly with our God. (Micah 6:8b) To love first and foremost, and treat everyone with honour, dignity and respect, in everything we do, say and think. To do the higher good for everyone bar none. To live our lives in such a way, that they are pleasing to God. When we do, life reflects our obedience, by the blessings we get. Will life always be smooth and easy? The answer is a resounding no! Life is not fair and will never be fair. That is called life. God's promise is: I will be with you in the valleys and on the mountaintops. I will journey with you, providing for your every need. God did not say He would always take away the storms of life. He does say He is with us in the storm, giving us His peace and comfort. Yes, there are times God stills the storm but there are just as many times when He leaves the storm and stills us.

Prayer: Father, God, I find it hard to trust you at times and your promises. I find it hard to live my life not totally relying on me, but on you. I need your help to learn how to trust you more. I need your help to live my life reaping the blessings you have stored up for me. I want to be obedient, but there are times when my head and my heart just cannot seem to meet and agree. I want to live in your blessings. Therefore help me to follow your ways, living according to your commands and laws. I surrender my will to you and ask for your never-ending love and help. In Jesus' name, amen.

Day One Hundred Eighty-eight

Romans 2: 6-8 `God will give to each person according to what he has done. To those who by persistence in doing good seek glory, honour and immortality, he will give eternal life. But for those who are self-seeking and who reject the truth and follow evil, there will be wrath and anger.'

This is the age-old life question. What I am choosing to do with my life? What am I choosing to do with this life I have been given? How am I using this life for good or for evil? It is said that our life is the gift God has given us. What we do with our life is the gift we give back to God, depending on the choices we make and the directions we choose. They will determine the outcome, which will decide our life and future destiny. This is so hard for us to hear and receive at times. We want to hear and think that we are the masters of our universe. The decider of what happens in and for our lives. The beginning and end of all happens in and for our lives. Deep down inside of us, we want to believe that in the end, no matter what I choose or decide with my life, I will end up in a better place. No matter what, at the last minute or just before, I can obtain the permission slip, which will allow me entrance into heaven, or at least somewhere other than hell. We even joke about our eternal destiny by saying things like: I'll be going to hell because all my friends will be there. Or, I know where I am going. I'm going to the party and the good times. I am going to where there are no rules. Where I can do whatever I desire and want. Others say I'm going to heaven, because it is my right to go to heaven. God cannot refuse me. Therefore, I know where I am going to end up. God has to let everyone into heaven. Therefore, when I die, that is where I will be heading. We truly do believe on some level that we are able to control our futures. We can control what our eternity will look like. That is what we think. The truth and reality is, I can do whatever I want and not have to pay the price at the end. The real truth is: God will give to each person according to what he or she has done. There is no free lunch. Everything has a price tag attached in some way, shape or form. There is a cost to pay in everything we choose or do not choose. Pay me now or pay me later, but sooner or later we all have to pay the bill. It catches up to all of us at some point in time. If we seek after good, glory, honour and immortality, you will reap the reward of eternal life. If we are self-seeking and living life, only to please our self, rejecting what is true and right, when we follow what is evil and dark, then what we will reap from our life choices is God's wrath and anger. The wonderful gift of free will says: we can choose whichever one we want to choose. The reality is both have a price tag attached. Both have a cost to the choice we make. One cost is eternal life and all that it brings, and the other is God's wrath and anger and all that will give us. For whom does the bell toll? It tolls for you. That sums up the lesson for today. One day the bell with our name on it will toll. At that point, what has been stored up in heaven by our life choices will be brought to account. The bill will have to be paid. The payment will either be the gift of eternal life or the wrath and anger of God. The end result will be totally based upon the choices we made here on earth.

Prayer: Father, today's lesson scares me. I am afraid of this truth. I want to run away from it and hide. For I do not want to know that in the end it is me, and only me, who decides my eternal fate. I am sorry for living my life to please only me. I am sorry for all the times I chose the selfish path to live on. I am sorry for all the times I put me first at the expense of others. Please forgive me and help me to make the necessary changes in and for my life. I want to live a better and more life here on earth. I want to have eternity with you. In Jesus' name, amen.

Day One Hundred Eighty-nine

Proverbs 25:11 'A word aptly spoken is like apples of gold in settings of silver.'

I am so amazed at times how true this saying is. A word spoken in due season or aptly spoken brings a soothing to the heart and a quieting of our spirit. A word spoken at the right time and in the right way calms a raging storm. The right words at tithe right time can bring a broken heart to a place where it can begin to heal. Words aptly spoken can draw someone out of their darkness and into the light. Using the right words at the right time and with a suitable voice can do the most amazing things. I see it here all the time, during my many dealing with the offenders and the staff. Often times the offender will come into my office all worked up and bent out of shape. They are ranting and raving about one thing or another. They are lost in whatever the issue is for them. After a bit, I begin to speak my words and before we know it the tension is going. The heightened emotions are beginning to calm down. Words spoken in the right way or at the right time, brings the pressure down on the inside of the person. The person can begin to see things more clearly. The right word for the situation truly helps to defuse whatever is going on. They are like water to the thirsty or food to the one who has nothing to eat. There is an incredible amount of positive or negative power in words and how the words get used. Think about times in your life when words have hurt. The negative affect they have had upon your thinking and how you were feeling. The way those negative words got inside of you, and changed the way you even saw yourself. Those damming, harmful and hurting power of words that changed the way you saw yourself and others. Often it takes years to get those words out of your heart and spirit. Now think of a time when a word came to you out of the blue, that shone light into your spirit they helped you to see yourself in a different light. Think of the power those words had upon you, and who you are today as a person. I remember my High School guidance councilor saying to me my last year of high school, whenever you have to make a decision ask yourself two questions: 1) Is this going to hurt me? 2) Is this going to hurt anyone else? If the answer to both questions is no, go ahead with whatever you are deciding. If the answer is yes to one or more of the questions, rethink whatever you are trying to decide about. That simple advice changed the course of my life. From that point on, every time I had to make a decision I asked myself those two questions. It has prevented me from making some pretty bad choices. He spoke the right words, in the right season of my life. Do not ever think that your words have no affect or power, for they do. Our words have much more power for good and for evil, than we ever think. With the offenders here, towards the end of their stay, they will often come up and say "thank you" for your teachings and your words. They have really helped me. We never know the impact our words are having on another person, hence the warning to use our words wisely, and to not use them lightly or in anger. A good word spoken at the right time can change the course of a person's life. It is the same with a negative word; it can cause a person to turn down the wrong path, or start believing things that are just not true about themselves. Be careful with the words you use and how you use them, for they can cause a ripple affect that you may not want to have happen.

Prayer: As I look back on the words I have used, I see there have been times when I used my words to hurt and cause harm and for that I am truly sorry. Please forgive me and help me to think before I speak, that I may use my words to bring life to those I am speaking with, instead of bringing hurt or harm. Again, dear Lord, put a guard around my mouth, so that my words are and used to build others up. Teach me to use my words wisely. Thank you, Holy Spirit, in advance for all your help to me, amen.

Day One Hundred Ninety

Proverbs 17:22 'A cheerful heart is good medicine, but a crushed spirit dries up the bones.'

Think back to a time when you had the most incredible belly laugh. The belly laugh that hurt your cheeks, and your sides felt like they were going to split open. You were laughing so hard you thought you were going burst open. You were hanging on to your sides, as you doubled over in your pain and laughter. Remember how you felt and how your body reacted to the laughter. How good you felt afterwards, even though your sides hurt and your cheeks ached. How you felt so filled with joy and wonder. Now think about the times when you have let yourself laugh, really laugh at yourself. A time when something truly struck your funny bone and you bust out into uncontrollable laughter. Now look at your face; I am sure you will see a smile on it. I am sure your heart is feeling light and hopeful. That is what laughter and joy does to us. It brings out the smile and allows us to feel good on the inside. Laughter releases natural endorphins, which not only brings the feeling of being full, but also promotes healing and a rebalancing of our inner beings. Laughter is God's way of helping us see the funny or humorous side of life and the benefits therein. Laughter sets our hearts on a lighter path, with the end result of having a smile and a sense of contentment within. Now think about a time when you felt really sad. Maybe you lost a loved one or something very special to you. A time when you felt totally defeated and down hearted. The tears were flowing and your spirit was filled with agony and grief. You felt like this was never going to end. The road you were on was too long and hard to be traveling on. Now look at your face. It is most likely downcast and sad looking. You might even be reliving the memory or feelings. Your heart is heavy and you feel weighed down. You are probably lacking energy and feel sluggish, just thinking about the loss and sad times. A cheerful heart is good medicine, but a crushed spirit dries up the bones. This illustrates the power of a cheerful heart. How a cheerful heart is good and it does good to our entire being. When we focus on the sad or soul crushing moments in our lives, what we produce is a truly crushed spirit. Even our bones hurt from the sadness. The other side of the coin is, when we focus on being happy and are content, our whole being reflects the joy within us. We have learned that when our heart is filled with laughter we have the resources to travel on. Let your heart sing. Let the joy of laughter fill your heart and spirit. Let the wonder of God's gift of laughter be a part of your life and daily living. You will be amazed at how you begin to feel.

Prayer: It is true, Father, I forget to laugh. I forget how good it feels to laugh and feel the joy of laughter within me. Remind me, to laugh and to see the humorous side of life. I am sorry for being so serious at times. Please, forgive me, and help me to enjoy this life I have been given. Help me, to laugh more and to see the funny side of life, amen.

Day One Hundred Ninety-one

Psalm 119: 105 'Your word is a lamp to my feet and light for my path.'

Have you had the experience of being in total darkness? Where there was absolutely no light at all? I remember being in the salt mines in Germany, where you go down a steep slide and land by a pool of water. You cross over the water on a boat/raft pulling on a rope. The pool is where they collect the salt from, and then we went up the elevator to the surface once again. It was an amazing experience. The experience gave far more, than just seeing the salt mines and the retrieving process. When in the mine there is no natural light. When the lights are turned off, it is pure darkness. It is so dark that you cannot see your hand outstretched. You cannot see your fingers moving, your brain knows they are moving, but your sight is removed from the sensation. Therefore it distorts the information coming to you. What is astonishing about this experience is--- you cannot feel your fingers move. The darkness impedes our ability to feel the movement of our very selves. It is hard to believe this to be true, but it is. Test it out for yourselves. You will see and feel the wonder, of what being in the absolute darkness, does to our perception of what is happening around us. Our word for today says God is the lamp to our feet and the light for our paths. God is the lamp that shines into our darkness, making our darkness light. The most incredible thing about light is, it does not take much light for the darkness to be pierced. A small match will light our way. A birthday candle can give us enough light to see clearly. A small flashlight can shine its light for a far distance. Light pierces the darkness! Jesus says He is the light of the world, in Him there is no darkness. "I am the light of the world. Whoever follows me will never walk in darkness, but will have the light of life." (John 8:12) Jesus is light and, as light, He can be the lamp we need to see clearly the lamp to keep our paths well lit, so that we do not stumble and fall. Jesus can be the light source we all need, in order to maneuver this life journey we are on. Having the Word of God in hand allows us, the opportunity to see our path clearly and to make the necessary adjustment; the adjustments that prevent us from getting lost in the darkness, or hurt by tripping over the rocks, stumps and logs along the path. Having God's Word in our hearts opens the door for the light to shine brightly, for the light to be our constant and faithful supply. Over my years I can remember several black outs, where we have been left in the dark for hours, and how that felt. With the Word of God in our hearts, no matter how dark it gets on the outside, it is never dark on our insides, even when we are facing the dark night of the soul. God's light still shines, bringing light to our darkness, and helping us to see clearly through the storms we may be navigating. With God's light in our lives, we need not fear the obstacles that may come our way. With your light, God, we will never be without enough light to see clearly. God's Word is the lamp for our feet and the light for our paths.

Prayer: Thank you, God that I do not have to live in the darkness anymore! Thank you that I now have your light shining within me and lighting my path. I feel so much safer in your light. I feel the power of the darkness has been taken away. I am truly grateful. Keep filling my life and shining your light. I am realizing more and more just how much I need you in every part of who and what I am. A grateful child, amen.

Day One Hundred Ninety-two

> *Acts 3:17 `Now, brothers and sisters, I know that you acted in ignorance, as did your leaders.'*

How many times in our lives do we act in ignorance? How many times are there in our lives when we find ourselves in a place, when we don't know, we don't know? I would venture to say lots of times. The older I get, the more I realize, just how much I don't know. The more education I have, the education I realize I need, the more knowledge and wisdom God fills me with, the more I realize how unwise I really am. Acting in ignorance, I think we have it down pat. Now the good news! God knows how ignorant we are. How much we need to learn. To our total amazement at times, God patiently fills us. Giving us what we need, so that we can live as wise, individuals. God is such an amazing and wonderful teacher. When we open ourselves up to God and God's presence in and for our lives, God really does take us seriously and begins to gently fill us with what we need in order to do the things we need to do. God, in His infinite mercy and grace, does not stop there. God continues on filling us so that we can become the people we were created to be. I watch when people first find God or God first reveals God to them. They start the often slow process of changing from the inside out. They start saying things that are so wise and often times so very brilliant. I watch as the words come out their mouth and the looks on their faces that say: "where did that come from". Or they give an example, which is spot on, to the situation we are talking about. I smile and give them the nod of approval or the high five. Yes, there are so many times when we are ignorant and do not know any better, but with God in our lives, we begin to let go of our ignorance and begin to walk a path of wisdom and knowledge. When we think about our relationship with God, and how much we have changed since we first met God, we see just how much the presence of God has affected us, and continues to affect us. I get a wonderful smile on my face that says, yes and a sigh flows forth from my inner most being. We are blessed! We have a God who truly does care about us. God cares about the tiniest details of our lives. God loves us just the way we are. But as we are learning, loves us too much to leave us here. A reminder: we cannot ever do anything that will make God love us more. We can never do anything that will cause God to love us any less. God loves us just the way we are. Patiently drawing us to the place He has set for us. I don't need to know all the answers. Thank you God. All I need to know is God, and God helps with the rest. I am called to do my best, and then give myself permission to trust God will do the rest. That is all that God asks of us. What more can we ask for? Talk about having it made in the shade!

Prayer: Father, God, I am sorry for my ignorance, and the messes my ignorance have caused and often times continue to cause. Thank you that I do not have to get stuck in those messes. Forgive me, for trying to do things on my own, when I can be relying on you, and your presence in and for my life. Teach and show me, more and more each day what it means to trust you. Father, to trust your presence in and for my life. I surrender my life, and will, to you. Help me in all I say and do. With a grateful heart, amen.

Day One Hundred Ninety-three

Deuteronomy 11: 14 `Then I will send rain on your land in its season, both autumn and spring rains, so that you may gather in your grain, new wine and oil.'

God is so very gracious and compassionate in His dealing with His creation and all therein. His grace abounds to everyone. No one is left out. We all get the general blessings of God: the rain that fall in due season, the sun that brings light and warmth, the stars that shine so brightly, expressing the wonder and majesty of the one who created them, the beauty all around us, the beauty of everything God has created. The blessings of God are available to each and every one of us. I do not know about you, but I am extremely grateful for the graciousness and wonder of God's love and provision for His creation, and all who inhabit it. Without the marvel of God's mercy, grace and love for His creation, I wonder how everything would hold up. Without God in the midst of His creation, sustaining and supporting it, I can see evil taking hold and making our world a horrible place to live. I see all that this world is. All this world can be, with the loving hand of God watching over us. Can you imagine what this world would be like if God took away His mercy and grace? I cannot. I do not even want to begin to think of what everything would be like. It goes beyond my ability to understand and comprehend. God chooses to be present in His world and in His creation, because that is who and what God is. His gift of mercy, love, compassion and grace abounds, if we will but open our eyes to see it all around us. I see it every day with the offenders I work with. On the one hand they can be the biggest, badest, meanest people you would ever want to meet. Then out of the blue, they do the most amazing act of kindness. They show such mercy and compassion. When normally that is the farthest thing from their minds. I feel we offer grace and compassion, because we see how God works. We see what God does for His creation and for us. Even though we are far away from God, or do not acknowledge God at all. Intuitively we know the grace in our hearts. Therefore, pass it on to others in their time of need, or as an act of kindness. God still sends what we need, in order to have what is needed to keep us alive. I know you are thinking yea but. What about all the natural disasters and draughts, etc? Yes, they happen. We live in a sinful world. A world that is so very selfish and self-centered. Natural disasters often happen because of the choices we make. For example, we cut back the forests, to the point where there is no longer a natural barrier to stop the water from just running off with the soil. The water carries the topsoil away, preventing usable soil from being there. Then we get angry with God for the flooding. We choose to live in a flood area or in places where natural disasters normally happen, then get angry with God, because we are caught in the middle of the flood. We at times blame God for so much, when, in fact, it is ourselves who are responsible for being caught in the whatever. All I can say is thank you God for being there. For being in your creation, no matter what we choose or how selfish we may be. Thank you, Father God, for always being willing to help us through whatever it is we are going through. For loving us and providing for us, even though we turn our backs on you, often running away from you. Thank you for giving us the blessings. We do not deserve the blessings we get. Yet you get them to us anyway. Thank you for your mercy, grace, love and compassion that passes all understanding.

Prayer: Father, you choose to bless us at all times and in so very many ways. You choose to love us, and always be here with us and for us, no matter what. You are truly the most amazing, loving, compassionate God who never changes. Thank you, for being available to me and for loving me the way you do. I am grateful, even if I do not show it at times, amen.

Day One Hundred Ninety-four

Philippians 3: 8 `What is more, I consider everything a loss compared to the surpassing greatness of knowing Christ Jesus my Lord, for whose sake I have lost all things. I consider them rubbish, that I may gain Christ.'

In our need to be selfish we think that the world evolves and revolves around us, around what we are as self-made, self-defined human beings. A quote like the one Paul is making, makes our insides turn and our human sides cringe! How could everything that I have worked for and everything I have accumulated in my life be a waste? Look at all I have and all I have accomplished in my and with my life. How can all of this, be a waste? I have a beautiful house, a car, a bank account; I can travel and go anywhere I want to go. How can all of this be a loss? When we look at this statement from a worldly perspective it cannot. From a worldly perspective, everything we have gained, and made of ourselves is, what the world says is important. Like the bumper sticker that says: he who has the most toys wins. In the reality of our spiritual existence, everything we have from an earthly perspective is loss. Yes, our earthly things are valuable and important. Yes, they give us pleasure and comfort. Yes, they show the world what we have done with our lives, but from a God reality in our lives. They cannot hold a candle to all we have gained in our hearts and spirits, when we have the surpassing knowledge of Christ Jesus in us. Having the knowledge and presence of Jesus the Christ in us, makes everything else seem less than. It is makes everything else, like having a plain cake with no icing or sprinkles or chocolate shaving. Having the knowledge and presence of Jesus within us, really does add the icing and all the trimmings. It is like, as Paul says, everything else is rubbish. Psalm 73: 25-26 says: `Whom have I in heaven but you? And earth has nothing I desire besides you. My flesh and my heart may fail, but God is the strength of my heart and my portion forever.' I agree that it is nice to live in a comfortable house, drive a reliable car and have enough money to basically do what we want to do. It really helps make life good, pleasing and comfortable. But when all is said and done, there is only one thing that makes life complete. That one thing is, knowing Jesus and who and what Jesus is, and all that Jesus has done for us. Knowing the wonder of the love of God. Knowing God's mercy and grace, makes everything else pale in its shadow. Having the forgiveness of God. The release God gives us, from all that was and all that kept us in bondage or in prison. The wonder of who we were created to be in its fullness would be enough. It does not stop there. For we can have all that and so much more, by knowing the one who created us and gave us all that we have. When we have the unsurpassing knowing of God and God's provision for His creation, we have a deep inner peace and a knowing that cannot be bought, or beheld any other way, than by knowing the one who is and was and is to come. The One who is the beginning and the end and source of all life and wonder.

Prayer: Thank you, Jesus, for giving me the open door to knowing you and your incredible gift of life. The incredible gift of God, the God knowing God gives of where life truly does come from. I am blessed beyond measure. I am so grateful and do thank you from the bottom of my heart. I am learning that when I have you, I really do have everything I need. In Jesus' name, amen.

Day One Hundred Ninety-five

Psalm 126: 3 `The Lord has done great things for us, and we are filled with joy.'

When I think about all the Lord has done for me and for us His children, I truly do stand in awe of God and all God is. The wonder of God and His love for us His children, His creation. God has done such amazing and wonderful things for us. So much has He done for us, that we do not even know it. We take everything for granted and miss the wonder and beauty. The expression; take time to smell the roses. Do we take the time to smell the roses and see beyond the obvious? Most of the time I think not. We are so busy running here and there and everywhere. I look at the wonder, the absolute wonder, of fall and the changing of the season. The beauty, the colours, the majesty and I see God smiling down, as we enjoy His gift of fall and the beauty of His design. I see God smiling down, as we take the time to enjoy the gift of fall, which that God has given us. Why does God give us so much? I feel He does all He does, just because God enjoys doing great and good things for us. Again when I look up and see the night sky, the stars in their place---how do they stay up here? Everything else falls to earth in the gravity pull, why not the stars? Their light shining, telling the passing of time, how magnificent God is. How much God cares for His creation and us, His children. I see the moon shining in such power and authority. The heavens are ablaze with such light and life, all reflecting the wonder of God and who God is. Reflecting God's desire to do great things for us. I have only had the privilege of seeing the Northern Lights a couple of time, but I just stand in awe. Gazing up at the red, pink, green flashes of lights, dancing across the sky; it takes my breath away. The sky was ablaze with the lights in streams of colour and wonder. The absolute majesty of God and all God is. Look at the great care God took in the making of the animals, the fish and even us. We are so perfectly made, yet so very different! I see the handiwork of God in so very many ways. To see it, all I had to do was open my eyes and my heart, and a whole new world of God's majesty opened up for me. Our God has done such great things for us and we do not know it most of the time. When I think of His gift of forgiveness, I stand in awe. How God gives us mercy and grace, instead of what we really deserve. I think of how God chooses to love us. Not for anything we do or say, but because He chooses to love us. How can that be? How can it be, that our God, would put into place a plan that would open the door for us to be returned to Him. When we were so far away and lost, in all we have done and not done? I see God's love for us and His creation, and how God just cannot allow it to go to waste. So God constantly calls us back into a love relationship with Him. God has done so much for us. He has done great things for us. And if we are honest with ourselves, we are filled with joy. A joy that surpasses all understanding! A joy that touches to the very depths of our being, and goes deeper still into everything God created us to be. I am so grateful for all that God is showing me. For all I am seeing as my eyes and heart are opened to the great things God does. My heart truly sings with such a joy that goes beyond words, because our God loves us so. Therefore, let us rejoice and be glad.

Prayer: Thank you, God, for doing such great things for us, especially when we do not even recognize you doing them. Thank you, for being you and creating me to be me. Fill me, with more of you, so that I can be more of who you created me to be. Fill me, Lord; fill me up, amen.

Day One Hundred Ninety-six

Leviticus 19: 35- 36 `Do not use dishonest standards when measuring length, weight or quantity. Use honest scales, and honest weights, an honest ephah and an honest hin. I am the Lord your God, who brought you of Egypt.'

Be honest! Be honest in all of our dealings with others, God and ourselves. Think for a moment what happens in our lives when we are dishonest? What happens to our insides, when we choose to live in dishonest ways? Does not our inside start feeling tense and worried? Are we not more afraid of meeting the wrong people, or being in the wrong place at the wrong time? Do we not feel valueless in ourselves, and in who and what we are as people, and especially as children of God? Do we not find ourselves hiding more and isolating ourselves more? So that others do not find out about what we are doing? We push away certain people and relationships, because what if something happens or something does not happen. If I am using my seat belt and not speeding, I do not care if the police show up. I do not care if they see me on the road, because I am not doing anything wrong. But if I do not have my seat belt on, and I am speeding, the police are the last people I want to see. It is the same with all of our dealings. If we are being honest and up front with and in everything, we have and do, there is no fear in our hearts and lives. But, if we are being dishonest, we have lots of fears about meeting the wrong people, etc. When God gave the laws and rules to the Israelites, He gave them to them because of His love for them and us. Not because God wanted to keep them under His thumb and in His control. God gives us the standards to live by, because when we live by His standards, we are free. Not only are we free, we are also the people He created us to be in the first place. Think about that for a moment. When you are living in an honest life and life-style, you have no fear, as I said. You have high self-esteem and value, on who and what you are as a person. You live and love more freely, because you are free to live and love. There is no fear within you. You see yourself as valuable and worthwhile. Therefore, you can see others as valuable and worthwhile. You can trust, for there is nothing to hide in your life or actions. Life can be lived on life's terms. Life can be lived as the full life it was meant to be. Life can be lived without fear, worry or anxiety. It can be lived with blessings and much joy. Joy can fill your life and relationships, because there is room in your life for freedom, life and much joy. When we choose to be honest in all our dealing, the end result is true freedom. Freedom from all the things dishonesty brings.

Prayer: I am sorry for the times in my life when I chose dishonesty and the lack of truth in my life and relationships. I can see now that honesty really is the best policy. Forgive me and help me to be more honest in my dealing with others, myself and with you, Father God. Thank you, for this life lesson today. I needed the reminder. Thank you, Lord, amen.

Day One Hundred Ninety-seven

John 6: 40 `For my Father's will it is that everyone who looks to the Son and believes in him shall have the eternal life, and I will raise him up at the last day.'

I am amazed at how many people fear death and dying. They fear that when death comes, that is the end of everything. There is nothing beyond this world. There is nothing but what we can see, feel, touch and taste. There is such a terror within some people it causes them to push away death at all cost, because death is the end. There is nothing after death. Therefore, avoid death at all costs and perils. Live as much as you can today, for today is all we have. When I leave this world I am going into nothingness. Therefore, do everything you can to get as much out of life as you can. For when you die that is the absolute and total end of everything. There is a belief that says: when I die, I die. According to today's reading that belief is false. There is no truth in the belief. God's will is that everyone who looks to His Son, and believes in Jesus, shall have eternal life. That means this is not the end! When we die our spirit moves on to the next phase of the journey. Death is a beginning and not the end. When we die it is not goodbye---it is `so long' until we meet again. If this is true, then we do not have to fear death. We do not have to run away from death. We can enjoy our lives here on earth. Then, when our time comes, we can enjoy the next phase of the journey. Our life here on earth is such a short amount of time, it is like a spit in the bucket. Life is designed to be just long enough to enjoy our relationships, have the human experience, and then move on into eternity. If we know who God is and His gift of salvation, then when our time comes to leave this human existence, we have a place to go. We will have others waiting for us to arrive. To welcome us home. We will be with all the others who have gone before us. We have others who are now on the other side, waiting for us, expecting our arrival. When we have God's gift of His Son in our lives, we need not have any fears or worries about what comes next. For we will know the assurance and the blessing of having the plans laid out for us. The wonder of God's love for each and every one of us, the wonder of God for His Creation. The absolute wonder of God's creative plan! We are so very blessed, if we choose the blessing. Death is now not something to be feared. Death is now the gateway to the next phase of the creative plan of our great and awesome God and Father. What a major difference this new truth can have on how we live our lives. Not to mention how we celebrate our deaths.

Prayer: Father, God, I do not want this to be the end. I do not want this to be the only page upon which my life is written. I accept and receive you gift of salvation into my life and heart. I accept the love you have for me. Forgive me, for taking so long to come to this understanding; I am here now. I love you, Lord, and value you in my life and heart, amen.

Day One Hundred Ninety-eight

Isaiah 43: 18-19 'Forget the former things; do not dwell on the past. See, I am doing a new thing! Now it springs up; do you not perceive it? I am making a way in the desert and streams in the wasteland.'

Forget the former things; do not dwell on the past. We are so good at keeping our pasts in our presents. We love to hang on to the past, so that we can keep going back there for whatever reason. Nostalgia is popular. We at times pay really big bucks for things that are old or have great memory value to us. The problem with holding on to the past and living in the past is, we do not get to have a today, or live in today. Yesterday is gone. We can't change it or alter it in any way, shape or form. Tomorrow is a mystery. Who knows what tomorrow is going to bring? Today is a gift, that is why it is called the present. If we keep living in the past and hanging on to the past, then we rob ourselves of all that today can bring us. If I am holding on to past hurts, pains and resentments, I find it hard to live and love in the present. To trust and open myself up to love and being loved. When I allow myself to be hateful, angry or bitter, because of the choice of another, than I am allowing that person to live rent-free inside of me today. Or as I say, I am allowing that person to drive my bus, which in turn usually causes it to crash and burn. When I live in resentments, anger, bitterness or hatred, I am taking poison, expecting the other person to die. The serenity prayer says accept the things we cannot change, change the things we can, and the wisdom to know the difference. If we stay in the past, in the former things, we get locked in and at times cannot get out. The other reality is if we always do, what we have always done, we will always get, what we have always gotten. For nothing changes, if nothing changes. That is why we are being told here to let go of what was. To let go so we can have and experience all that is and can be. Yes, God is the same yesterday, today and forever, but He is always doing new things to surprise us. New things to show us more and more of who and what He is. If I am stuck in the past and the old ways of living, then how can I be open and receptive to the new things that are coming my way? Therefore, I miss out on what God is doing today. I miss out on everything else new as well, for I cannot see it, or I choose to close my eyes to it. Letting go of the former things, truly does allow us to have the freedom to receive, and live, in the current and present happenings. God is making a way in the desert. The streams of the wastelands are being opened. Let us be receptive to what God is doing so that we do not get stuck in what was. Can we allow God to revitalize our desert and wastelands? Can we let go of the former things, so that we can enjoy and experience the new things our Great God is doing? Come out of what was. Come out to all that is available to you now and in the future.

Prayer: Father, God, I am so sorry for living my life in the past. For letting my past be my present. Please forgive me, so that I can let go of the former things. Help me, to come into the new and exciting things that you are doing and causing to happen all around me. I want to be free from my past and the hold it has over me. I do not want to be locked in it any longer. Set me free, Lord, amen.

Day One Hundred Ninety-nine

> *Isaiah 30: 15 `This is what the Sovereign Lord, the Holy One of Israel says. In repentance and rest is your salvation, in quietness and trust is your strength, but you would have none of it.'*

In repentance and rest is your salvation. In repentance: a turning from sin and then dedicating one's self and life to the amendment of one's life. To feel regret or contrition for one's actions and choices, to change one's mind about what was done or still being done. Then go in another direction. To feel sorrow for what we have done or not done with our lives, and the lives of others who we have influence or had power over. Salvation is found in our desire to be honest with who and what we are as people. To be honest with the choices we have made or not made. Then being willing to grow and change. Salvation being: the deliverance from the power and effects of sin upon our lives. Salvation is the preservation or reclaiming of our lives, from the destruction or failure that has been left in us, because of the impact of sin. When we repent and rest in the saving mercy and grace of God, we get quietness and trust in God, and who and what God really is. Being honest with ourselves, and the choices we have made or not made, and being willing to share those choices with God, brings us forgiveness and rest. Whenever we tell God what we have done or not done, brings us peace on the inside and freedom from the bondage the choices put us in. Honest repentance opens the door of our hearts and lives to the forgiving mercy and grace of God. Every time we repent with a humble and honest heart, God forgives us and restores us to a right relationship with Him. Every time we allow ourselves to speak the truth to God, God listens and allows forgiveness and rest to enter into our spirits and hearts. In return for our honesty, we get quietness in our spirits and heart, and a greater ability to trust God, and who and what God is. Our ability to trust is being restored, which means we can trust more. The more we trust, the more we can trust. The more we can trust the more willing we are to be open and honest with God and with ourselves, then with others. Life is restored and salvation from the past is now ours. When we choose to be honest with ourselves and who and what we are as people, then our ability to be honest with God grows. As our honesty grows so does our desire to live in honesty. The growth of honesty in us then brings the freedom we have all been searching for. The freedom to let go of the secrets or shame, the freedom to risk love and being loved, the freedom to be who we were created to be in the first place, without all the regrets, secrets and negatives in our lives. Getting down and honest with ourselves, and then with God. Telling only the truth and what has really happened brings true life into our beings. It is this true life we have all been searching for. It is this true life that enables us to be real and honest and truthful, both within and without.

Prayer: Father, thank you, for showing me the way to a deeper relationship with you, myself and then with others. I do repent, Father, for all the choices I have made that have separated us. Forgive me, Lord. Thank you Lord, for being my hope and my salvation. Thank you, for always telling me the truth, even when the truth hurts. I truly am grateful, Father, for your love for me, and your desire to see me whole and living in true life, amen.

Day Two Hundred

Exodus 31: 1-3 `Then the Lord said to Moses. See, I have chosen Bezalel son of Uri, the son of Hur, of the tribe of Judah, and I have filled him with the Spirit of God, with skill, ability and knowledge in all kinds of crafts.'

God gave Bezalel and Hur the Spirit of God. Which in turn gave them skill, ability and knowledge in all kinds of crafts. Our God is so amazing and awesome! Our God takes care of every detail and uses every opportunity He can to fulfill His promises to us. The Israelites were about to build the tent of meeting, the ark of the Testimony with the atonement cover on it, and all the other furnishings of the tent. God has given them the blue prints and now provided the skills, abilities and knowledge needed to carry out the design. That is how wonderful our God is! He calls us to whatever He calls us to and then gives us the skills, abilities and knowledge to carry out the call. I have certainly seen that to be the case in my life. God called me to full time ministry. To be a priest who stands in the gap for His children in my care. He called me to be front and center even though I was so dyslexic I could hardly read. Not only has God filled me with the ability to read, but has also filled me to overflowing with the skills, ability and knowledge I need in order to be the prison chaplain, I am today. God truly does fill us with all we need in order to do all that He is asking us to do. God never calls us to something without giving us what we need, in order to fulfill the call. Some of you reading this devotional today know God has gifted you and is asking you to step out. God will provide or has already provided what is needed for you, but you are afraid and do not feel qualified enough. Do you think when Bezalel and

Hur stepped out to the task at hand thought they could do it? If they were anything like the rest of us, it was a trial and error process, as they grew in their skills and abilities and knowledge. They trusted and walked in faith believing that if God said He had given them the skills and abilities to go forth, go forth they would. God loves us, He loves us so much, and He would never shame us or cause us to be shamed. If God is asking you to step out, then God has already decided on what skills, abilities and knowledge you will need to do the task. That is how God works. For some of you the skill may be in the crafts; all I can say is try-you may be totally surprised! For some of you the skills are in music or other such talents. The choice is to sit on what God has given you and possibly lose the gifts, or to step out and see what comes next. Some of you are gifted writers. What is God asking you to do with your writing skills? The list of gifts, talents and abilities is a long one. I could go on forever. The challenge is what is God asking of you? What is God calling you to? What is God asking of you and your gifts, talents and abilities? Is it scary to step out at times? You bet ya! Is it worth it in the end? Without a shadow of a doubt! The last place I saw myself was in prison ministry. Now I have a hard time seeing myself anywhere else. Step out, my friends, step out.

Prayer: God, I know you have gifted me and filled me with the skills, abilities and knowledge I need to do all that you are asking me to do. Help me, to trust your provision for my skill and to step out and risk. I am feeling afraid. Help my unbelief and my feeling insecure. I repent, and ask for your forgiveness. Help me, to trust you more, and your provision in and for my life. In Jesus' name, amen.

Day Two Hundred One

Psalm 55: 22 `Cast your cares on the Lord and he will sustain you; he will never let the righteous fall.'

Cast, spread, emit, direct, throw, release, discharge, give out your cares on the Lord and He will sustain you. What this means to me is, we are not to hang on to our cares in any way, shape or form. Our cares are to be given to the Lord. We are to let the Lord take them and in return the Lord will sustain us. What a deal! I give the Lord all my cares, He gives me the ability to be sustained, through whatever it is I have to deal with or live through. We are to let them go, put them off, cast them away onto the Lord. The Lord now has the ability or right, to take care of them, and not me having to carry them. This means to me that I am to take my hands off my cares and troubles, giving them to the Lord. Then the Lord can help me to carry my cares. Why, so that I am not loaded down with them. As human beings we are so good at holding onto our troubles and cares. We are often great at letting them grow and take on lives of their own at times. We let our cares and troubles pile up, until they are swamping us or drowning us. Then we wonder why life gets so hard and unmanageable? Here God is giving us great advice, and a resource that is beyond measure. God is saying to us: we can pile our cares and troubles upon Him, and He will do, whatever He can (and He can do lots) to help us and see us through. God wants us to let go and let God be, the God and Father He promises to be. In order for that to happen, we must do our part, by releasing our cares and troubles to the one, who has the ability and resources to handle them. We must trust God and His promises of always being there, and never taking us anywhere to drop us. We need to be willing to take our hands off, so that God can put His hands on our cares and troubles. Therefore, being able to work them through. Instead of holding on and hoping for the best, God is asking us to trust His love and provision for us. To be willing to let go and let God be God in our lives. That is a risk, but one worth taking. For the worst thing that happens is nothing changes. The best thing that happens is, God does take our cares and troubles and helps us through them. In my opinion we can't lose. What more can we ask for? This is a sure bet, if you are a betting type person. I give away the things that are too heavy or hard for me to carry. God gives me the courage and the strength to see me through whatever it is that I am asking God to help me with. I do my part, which is being willing to invite God in. God does His part by giving us what we need in order to do what we need to do.

Prayer: Lord, I confess, I am not very good at taking all of my cares and troubles and trusting you with them. I confess, my need at times to hold on to them, even when I can hardly carry them or survive under their load. I do repent. Forgive me, and help me, to trust you more this day and every day that follows. In the wonderful name of Jesus and His sustaining presence in our lives, amen.

Day Two Hundred Two

Luke 11: 9-10 'So I say to you: Ask and it will be given to you; seek and you will find; knock and the door with be opened to you. For everyone who asks receives and he who seeks finds; and to him, who knocks, the door will be opened.'

Working as a prison chaplain, I am always amazed when offenders and even staff say to me, "is it okay to pray for myself? Is it okay to ask God for what I need?" Or they will say, "I never pray for myself; it is not right to pray for myself". Those beliefs are incorrect and not scriptural. Scripture says very loud and clear, that we are to pray for ourselves. We are to ask for the things we need. We are to bring our requests before God. Inviting God into every need and request we have. If you have just lost a loved one, asking for peace and comfort to get through the loss, is what God wants us to do. That way God can fill us with His peace, love and comfort. If you are going for a job interview, praying for a sound mind and wisdom, to help you with the interview is the right prayer request. If you need courage and strength, then God wants you to have the courage and strength, you need to face whatever you are about to face. God wants us to pray for ourselves. God wants us to ask for the things we need, in order to be the people He created us to be in the first place. Remember God cannot go where He is not invited. Therefore we need to invite God into every area of our lives. Inviting God into the good things that happen. Remembering especially, to invite God into the not so good stuff. Inviting God into all of life's ups and downs. Prayer is such an amazing gift God has given us. In fact, it is the most powerful gift God has given us. Prayer opens up a channel between God and us. A channel between whatever we are praying for and God. Therefore, when we pray for ourselves, what we are doing, is inviting God into our needs and the areas of our lives that need the touch and care of a loving God. The Scripture before us today says, we are not only to ask and seek and knock, but we are to ask, seek and knock repeatedly and with intent. It is saying, not only are we to pray for ourselves, we are to ask and seek and knock, when doing so. In fact, it is it even stronger than just asking. We are to ask, ask, ask, seek, seek, seek and knock, knock, knock. In other words we are to keep asking, to keep seeking and to keep knocking, until we have our answers to the prayers we are praying. Knowing that there are times, when God says to keep praying, until He tells us to stop. We can also pray only once for the thing we are praying for and the answer comes right away. There are three answers to prayer, yes, no, wait. Yes, I will answer your prayer right away. No, that prayer is not good for you and who you are as my child. No, I will not answer that prayer in the way you are praying it. The last answer is wait. I want to answer your prayer, but you need to look at this area of your life first. For example: I want to heal your sore back, but first you must forgive this person, situation or event before the healing can take place. Your sore back is directly related to your unforgiveness. Therefore, I can heal your back, only when you release the bitterness and resentments, hatred or anger. Ask, seek and knock for that is what God asks of us His children. Putting our requests before our loving Heavenly Father.

Prayer: Holy Spirit, help me to pray at all times and in all seasons of my life. Help me, to ask and seek and knock, in every area of my life. Remind me, to pray for those I love, inviting you in and expecting you to answer me. Thank you, for your help and guidance, amen

Day Two Hundred Three

1 Corinthians 16:14 `Do everything in love.'

What does it mean to love? In my opinion to love someone is to do the higher good for the one we love. It is treating them with honour, dignity and respect. It is allowing them to be their own person, while you get to be who you were created to be. Love is the responsibility of everyone. No one is exempt from the call of love. We are to love others, even when we do not like them at the moment. To love them even though we do not value them very much at this moment in time. Love does not mean we allow others to mistreat us or us them. It does not mean, that we allow others to define us, or diminish us in any way, shape or form. Love means that we do whatever is best for the other person, and for ourselves. For example: if we have a child or mate or friend who is addicted to a substance or something, and refuses to get help; if they insist on staying in their addictions, we can put up a boundary and say----"I love you, but I cannot go down this road with you any longer. Stop your addiction and I will be there for you. Stay in your addiction and I have to push you away." Sometimes that is the best thing we can do, for the person we love. Working with addicts I see at times the addict only willing to get well when their parents die. When their safety net is no longer there for them. As long as the safety net is there, why change or do the hard choices? It is when the individual has to stand on their own two feet, because there is no longer anyone else to lean on, they begin to stand. Some choose to stay addicts, but surprisingly many choose a different path.

That is called tough love. Doing the higher good for the one we love. Doing what is best for them and for ourselves as well. If we do everything in love, we will always choose to do what love demands, regardless of the situation or circumstance we are in. Living in the spirit of love, brings love to everything. No matter what is happening or not happening. If we do not act in a spirit of love, we are acting in something other than love. If we are acting in something other that love, what is produced from our actions is not love. Loving, doing the high good for those we love, is not always the easy way to live or love. What I can say is, it is always the better way to live and be in relationships. When we choose to love first and foremost, the harvest we reap from our sowing is life giving and has a good return. When we choose to do the opposite of love, the harvest we reap is often small and not very life giving. Love is the answer to all of life. Without love there is no life, no real life. With love we have all we need to risk, love and be. True love gives us the ability to keep moving forward no matter what life throws our way. For we know that no matter what happens, we always have those special people in our lives, who are always there loving us and calling us onward.

Prayer: Holy Spirit, teach me to love. Teach me, to always do the higher good for the ones you have given me to love. To treat everyone I meet with honour, dignity and respect, choosing at all times to love first and foremost. I need your help, for on my own, I am not very good at loving, nor do I love well at times. Thank you, for helping me and filling me with the ability to love and be loved. In Jesus' name, amen.

Day Two Hundred Four

Psalm 59: 16 'But I will sing of your strength, in the morning I will sing of your love; for you are my fortress, my refuge in times of trouble.'

God is always our fortress and refuge, no matter what is happening in our lives. God is always there for us to run into for love, protection and care. God is our strong tower, which hides and protects us. We live in a world that can be very scary and frightening at times. It is so comforting to know that we have a fortress and refuge to run into. It is so comforting to know, no matter what happens in life, our fortress will stand. Our refuge will always be there. There will never be a time when our fortress and refuge are not open and available to us. It is so very reassuring to me, to know that God never changes. To know with certainty our place in God is safe and secure. If we look in the dictionary, fortress is defined as: a fortified place, a stronghold, and a large and permanent fortification, sometimes including a town. A refuge or a shelter or protection from danger or distress, a place that provides shelter or protection, something to which one has recourse in difficulty. Life can throw some pretty bad or hard curves at us at different times. Curves like illness, loss of job, broken relationships, lies, financial struggles and so on. No matter what life throws our way, we can know with certainty, God will always be there as our fortified place or safety and refuge. God will always be our recourse in times of difficulty. Our remedy of help with whatever it is we are having to face or go through. No matter what life does to us, we have a refuge and safe tower waiting, for us to run into. God understands He is always ready and willing to help and protect no matter what. In an illness we can trust our care to God and His peace will carry us through. God will give us what we need in order to walk through the time of struggle. God will always give us what we need, in order to do what we need to do. God truly is our refuge and fortress. God is our stronghold in times of struggle or hardship or even in times of peace and comfort. We are both now and always safe and secure in the love and care of our awesome, loving, caring and compassionate God. Nothing can ever separate us or stand between us and our God. NOTHING. This is a sure truth and foundation upon which we can stand. We can stand strong and secure on the truth of our Heavenly Father and God who loves us more than we will ever truly know. Our Heavenly Dad keeps His promises to the end for He can never tell us anything but what is true and real. Therefore, if God says He will do something, we can trust it to be done. If God says we can trust God, then my friends, what do we have to lose by trusting Him? In my opinion and experience of God in my life and in the lives of those with whom I have worked, we have nothing, absolutely nothing to lose and everything to gain.

Prayer: Thank you, God, for being my fortress and refuge. Thank you that you are always there for me to run into, no matter what is happening in my life. Thank you, for loving me the way you do. It truly helps me live and cope through life. Thank you, God, for being my Father, Dad and God. I really need you and your truth in my life, amen

Day Two Hundred Five

Luke 14: 11 'For everyone who exalts himself will be humbled, and he who humbles himself will be exalted.'

Have you ever known someone who thought they were God's gift to the world and everyone in it? Have you known someone who raised him/herself above everyone else? Who put him/herself on the top rung or a high pedestal above everyone? How they thought they were the best thing since sliced bread? Now can you remember how you felt when you were around them? How you thought they needed to come down a peg or two. The thought that went through your mind that said: What right do they have to think so highly of themselves; who do they think they are anyway? Remember how it feels to be around someone who exalts himself/herself, to such a high place, that everyone is to look up to him/her? I do, and it does not feel good to be around such people. The other side of the coin being, the person who was so humble, you marvel at them. You marvel at how they are. How they allow others to be themselves and to walk their own path and so on. Someone like a Mother Teresa, who was so humble and gentle, yet with an inner strength and power that drew you, almost demanded your attention. So meek and humble, yet there was so much more. It was the so much more that drew your attention and respect. Mother Teresa was so humble the world tried to exalt her. The world tried to raise her up to a higher position. She was even given the Noble Peace Prize for her work and treatment of individual life. For the way she helped to give dignity and honour to everyone, especially those in need. When we exalt ourselves, the chances are, someone will try to pull us down or maybe put someone else above us in stature or place or position. If we are humble, then the door is opened for others to raise you up and exalt you, because you are not exalting yourself. Again as Mother Teresa was raised up to the exalted place of honour. I can think of so many people in the news that have raised themselves to the high place of self imposed honour, only to be pulled down with their names all over the news. I can also think of the ones for who the world has raised up. The ones the world has exalted for their humble attitude, towards life and the people around them. When we are humble it does not mean that we do not claim who and what we are as people. What it means is, we do not think more highly of ourselves, than we ought. We see ourselves, as we really are, humans on a journey called life. Journeying together with different positions and places in the journey, having different jobs and positions to fill, yet all heading towards the same end, death. How we live our journey of life will determine what our end looks like. If we exalted ourselves, then chances are we will be humbled in some way shape or form, but if we humbled ourselves, chances are will be exalted.

Prayer: Father, I repent for all the times I put myself above others, to make me feel more important than I really am. Please forgive me, and help me to be humble. Not to think less of myself, but to think of myself less, so that I might be exalted in your eyes. Help me, to be real with who I am and who everyone else is. Thank you, Father, for loving me, even when I am not very loveable. I am very grateful. I do thank you for being the one who loves me without end and for all times, amen.

Day Two Hundred Six

Acts 17: 5 `But the Jews were jealous; so they rounded up some bad characters from the marketplace, formed a mob and started a riot in the city. They rushed to Jason's house in search for Paul and Silas in order to bring them out to the crowd.'

Jealousy what a wasted emotion to me! Jealousy does not bring life at all to the person who is living in jealousy. Jealousy does not give life to the one(s) we are being jealous of. Not to mention how relationships have been torn apart because of jealousy. Jealousy has destroyed relationships, stolen the blessing the relationship was, not to mention the blessing it could have been in the future. Jealousy when unchecked, takes away the life of the person who holds the jealousy. All they can think about is the person they are being jealous of. Their jealousy consumes their every thought. It even invades their sleep patterns and ability to sleep at times. The scary thing about jealousy is, it is sometimes in the person's heart, because of what they are doing. The jealousy is there because of what they have done. Then the jealousy fueled by our own choices and actions moves into our own ability to trust and be trusted. It projects itself into almost all of our relationships, taking hold where there in nothing to take hold of. It breaches trust on almost every level of our lives. Let's say the jealous person has been unfaithful. They think because they were unfaithful, everyone else is unfaithful. They think because they did what they did, others are doing the same things. Most of the time, their thoughts and insecurities are far from the truth or the reality of the relationship. How sad for the person who is jealous. How much sadder for those they love and are in relationship with. I have heard several people over the years say to me, 'my partner kept accusing me of being unfaithful. I finally went out and proved the accusations'. How true that reality is! We are so caught up in our thoughts, in what we think is happening. We cannot see what is really happening and the destruction we are causing. We let our minds run away with themselves, creating an unreal event to the destruction of all that is good in our lives today. Our Scripture reading for today, has a few Jews who were jealous of Paul and what Paul and Silas were teaching. They were so caught up in their jealousy, they chose to lie, cheat and even tried to commit murder, because someone was getting more than them or so they thought. They let their jealousy take such control of them, they were even willing to risk starting an illegal riot to appease their jealousy, now turned to anger. They allowed their jealousy to cloud their thinking and even their actions. The power of jealousy and the harm it can cause to others. Not to mention the harm it causes us. For those of you reading this devotional today, who suffer from jealousy, my suggestion is, you take the root of your jealousy, to the Lord in the form of confession. Talk to God openly and honestly about your need for being jealous and where that need comes from. Then repent and ask God to remove the root of why you are jealousy. Set yourself and others free from this deadly, so very deadly, sin in your heart and life. Set others free from the snare of your jealousy and the negative power it holds you and others in.

Prayer: Heavenly Father, I am so sorry for the times I let my jealousy get the better of me. Forgive me, for being jealous and help me to release any feelings of jealousy from my heart and life. I do not want to live or love as a jealous person. I want to be able to trust and be trusted. Thank you, Jesus, for loving me in spite of being jealous at times. Forgive me, for allowing my jealousy to get in the way of my loving you and others. In Jesus' forgiving and healing name, amen.

Day Two Hundred Seven

*Luke 16: 10 'Whoever can be trusted with very little can
also be trusted with much, and whoever is dishonest with
very little will also be dishonest with much.'*

Whoever can be trusted with a little, can be trusted with
a lot. Whoever cannot be trusted with a little, will not be
trustable with a lot. If you are dishonest with a little bit,
you will be dishonest with a whole lot. It does not matter
the amount you are being asked to take care of. What
matters is the state of your heart and your choice of how
you want to live your life. If you are choosing to live your life
from an honesty perspective, you will be honest no matter
what lies before you. Conversely, if you are choosing to be
dishonest and live your life from a dishonest perspective,
whether from a little or whether a lot, you will be dishonest.
The condition of the human heart is set with a little or
with lots. If your heart is bent on dishonesty, you will be
dishonest, no matter how much you have or don't have and
vice versa. If you are trustworthy with a little, you will be
trustworthy with a whole bunch. It does not matter which
side of the coin you sit on. The side you have chosen is the
side from, which you set your life premise and expectation
for yourself and your behaviours. It boils down to this
simple statement. The heart of the human problem is the
problem of the human heart. Where is your heart? What is
the condition of your heart? For the condition of your heart
will dictate your behaviour. That sounds pretty hopeless!
But thanks be to God who always leads us into triumphant
procession. God can change the condition of our hearts.
God can restore us to our innocence and trustworthiness.
God can do all things, when we invite Him into whatever is
happening inside of our hearts and lives. I have seen God
radically change the offenders I have worked with over the
years. I have seen God take a liar and thief, and turn him
or her into an honest person. The wonder of God's healing
love and power. God can do anything; there is nothing our
God cannot do. All things are possible with our God. All
we need do is ask and believe and then watch it begin to

take hold of our lives. God is a really big God---is your God really big? If He is, then ask Him to change your heart, so that it reflects God and God's light and life within you. If your God is still small and not big enough to do these great and wonderful changes in your life and heart, then ask my really big God, and He will hear you and help you grow and change. My God is, the "G" God for whom nothing is impossible.

Prayer: Holy Spirit, change my heart. Holy Spirit, give me a new heart for my heart is broken. I want to be an honest person. Honest with myself and with others. I want to be known as someone who is trustworthy. No matter how much I am responsible for or how little. Forgive me, for all the times I have not been honest. I am asking to be set on the path of honesty and truth. Thank you for teaching me this lesson today and showing me the condition of my heart. Holy Spirit, thank you for always being here with me and for me, amen.

Day Two Hundred Eight

Luke 18:17 'I tell you the truth, anyone who will not receive the kingdom of God like a little child will never enter it.'

Think back to when you were a child. Think about your children or other children you know. Remember how when you were young, you used to jump into your father's or mother's arms. You would jump even though there were times when they were not looking, yet you knew they would catch you. You just knew they were going to protect you and be there for you. Think about the children you know who used to jump in your arms or maybe still do. How, as children, the trust was just there! There was no debating or wondering if? The child just jumps knowing mom or dad would catch them. Even if mom or dad were not looking some how they were going to catch then no matter what. I remember my great niece was out on the balcony leaning over the railing. I told her to get down, because she might fall. Of course she went running to her mom crying and complaining bitterly about my request and how unreasonable I was being. When her mom backed me up, Kaylani was horrified. Her immediate response was; "mom you can catch me". Mom had to proceed to explain that catching her was not possible. They were nine stories up, mom could not get down in time to catch her. If she fell off the balcony, she would get hurt very badly. Simple child-like trust! Trust without hesitation or fear. That is what Jesus is asking of His child, all His children. We are being asked to trust Him no matter what. To believe in Him and trust Him just like a little child trusts her/his parents. Remember how safe you felt when your dad or mom held your hand when you were out together? How safe and secure your heart and being was, even though you did not know where you were going or what was going to happen. All was well with the world, because you were with your parent(s). You were safe and secure in dad or mom's hand. As adults we can have that same feeling of safety and security, when we put our hands in God's hand and never take it out. We can have that sense of being safe. No matter what is happening in or to our lives. Our childlike innocence needs to be restored. The childlike innocence, which says we can trust God no matter what. The innocence of childlike faith and trust in our heavenly Father, regardless of what life is throwing our way. The knowing that says yes, I can trust my God to be here with me, as I face this struggle, adventure, trial, loss or whatever. The letting go of our adult fears and lessons, and just trusting who and what God is and His promises to us His children. When we do that, the kingdom of God is upon us. We get to experience its blessings here on earth and throughout eternity. Put your hand in your Heavenly Father/Dad's hand. Know the wonder of being truly safe and secure in Him and His love and protection. Let yourself trust as you trusted as a child. The rewards go beyond our wildest dreams and hopes.

Prayer: Father God, I am so sorry for not trusting you. For taking me hand out of yours and trying to make it on my own. There have been so many times, when I have felt so afraid and alone. I am realizing now that I do not have to feel that way. Father, you can always be with me, keeping me safe and secure, if I keep my hand in yours and my eyes on you. Help me, to be innocent and trusting like a little child again. Help me to jump into your arms of love. Help me, to truly take my place as your chosen, beloved child, amen.

Day Two Hundred Nine

Luke 19: 10 `For the Son of Man came to seek and to save what was lost.'

Such words of comfort! The Son of Man came for one reason and one reason only. To seek and to save that, which was lost. God sent His only Son into the world to seek out you and me. To seek us out so that we could be given the option of staying lost, or putting our hand in God's hand and being saved. That still blows my mind, even today, after all these years of being in a relationship with God. That God would come into the world to give us the option of how we want to live our lives. To either live our lives hanging on to all that we have done and all that others have done to us. Or to repent and be forgiven from all that was, so that we can move into all that could be. We are so blessed! We are truly blessed beyond measure. We do not have to be lost any longer. We do not have to feel like we do not fit anymore. We do not have to go through life carrying all the baggage. The baggage we have created and the baggage others have given to us. We can be set free from all that was, and has been for a long time. We can come into the wonder of God's saving gift of life. This is hard for to me to get my head around at times. It is hard to think that God loves us, you and me, that much. That God's love goes beyond our wildest dreams, hopes and realities. God loves us so much that He gave His all just so that we might, if we decided to, enter into a relationship with Him. God knows not all of us will choose His gift of life and freedom from what was. God knew some of us will choose to stay in our mud puddles and die in our shame, pain, past, hate, anger and so on. Yet God was still willing to come to earth as a human being incarnate. So that the ones of us who choose to allow God's love, and gift of restoration and reconciliation could be a reality. A true act of love! A true act of love, that chooses to love first and foremost. Even though some of the love you have to offer your creation is turned away and rejected. I do not always understand that kind of love, but what I know is that I am truly and eternally grateful for it. I choose to receive the love. I choose to set my heart towards you and the love you have for me and for your creation. Help me to be totally open to the love that you want to pour into my heart and life. Then help me to embrace it and make it mine. I want to know unconditional love and the hope and freedom it gives me. I know my heart longs to be loved unconditionally. My heart longs to know what true love really is. I do find myself lost in many different ways. I want to be found by the one who loves me more than life itself.

Prayer: With a deep sense of gratitude, I say thank you, for loving me so unconditionally. For all the love you have for me, even me. I may not understand it, but I am grateful for it. Fill me, Lord, with all the love you have for me. Help me, to receive it and make it mine. In Jesus' loving and precious name, amen.

Day Two Hundred Ten

Luke 19: 16-17 `The first one came and said, "Sir your mina has earned ten more." "Well done, my good servant!" His master replied. "Because you have been trustworthy in a very small matter, take charge of ten cites."'

Building trust. The Lord said, 'Because you have been faithful, trustworthy in a very small matter'. I can trust you to be faithful in larger matters. Therefore take charge of ten cities. Trust-building process. We learn trust and trusting by testing and proving. We put tests or opportunities out there to see if they/the people, we are proving or testing, are trustworthy. If they are, we up the ante, until we reach the point where we know that knowing that says yes. I can trust this person or these people. I know they will not breach the trust I am putting in them. It is the same with God and us. God gives us gifts, talents and abilities, then watches to see what we do with them. If we bury them and never use them, God might take them away from us. God may give them to someone else who will use them and put them to good use. If we on the other hand, take the gifts, talents and abilities God has given us, put them to good use, not wasting them, God may give us more gifts, talents and abilities, because God knows that if He gives us more, we will use more. I remember when I was a new believer in the Lord. I was watching my relationship with God and evaluating what it all meant to me and about me. As I observed the relationship I saw the gifts, talents and abilities, I was being given. I saw that most other Christians I was meeting had a few gifts, but here I was discovering lots and lots of gifts. I did not know what to make of what was happening. Then I got the position in corrections as a Chaplain. Then it all came together. I was being gifted, because I needed all the gifts, talents and abilities to be the Chaplain God was calling me to. Without all the gifts, talents and abilities, I would not be the Chaplain I am today. I asked God one day why me? Why was I so gifted? His response was just like the reading today; `You proved yourself trustworthy in small matters, so I have given you more'. If I had not been trustworthy in the first gifts God gave me, I probably would not have all I have today. I would probably been called to chaplaincy, but with what gifts and doing what kind of job? I do not have an answer for that. What I do know is God chose to test me with His gifts and I chose to walk with them. Trust is earned! Trust is what we build, as we get deeper into relationships with the people in our lives and with God. The more you test and prove God, the more God will prove to you that He is trustworthy. God will show you time and again. The more you can put your trust, hope and faith in God and it will not be betrayed or misused. That is a fact! God is totally trustworthy. I know I have tested God lots myself. Every single time God has proven God to be trustworthy and exactly the person He says He is. Every single time!

Prayer: Father God, thank you, for my gifts, talents and abilities. I am grateful. Help me, to use them and embrace them. Help me, not to waste them. Thank you that you are a trustworthy God who never takes us anywhere to drop us or abandons us. I am grateful, for the trust you have in me, help me to not disappoint you. Thank you, Father, for being exactly who you say you are, amen.

Day Two Hundred Eleven

Numbers 13: 30-31 `Then Caleb silenced the people before Moses and said, "we should go up and take possession of the land, for we can certainly do it." But the men who had gone up with him said, "We can't attack those people; they are stronger than we are."'

There are giants in the land! We can't go there, there are giants in the land! The Israelites had forgotten all about what God had done for them. They forgot about how God had made a way, where there seemed to be no way.

They did not remember how God had saved them, from every opponent that tried to come against them, including Pharaoh. They were giving in to their fears and insecurities. Instead of trusting God and all that God had shown them God was. They were giving their power away. They were letting their fear of the unknown render them powerless. They had seen first hand what their God could do and all that their God had done. Yet because some of the Israelites were afraid, they all became afraid. Yes, there were giants in the land. Yes, there were obstacles that needed to be overcome. Yes, they had to fight to claim what God had promised them. Yes, but----God had proven Himself, was bigger, than everything they were ever going to face. All they needed to do was trust God. God would show them again and again, His might and power. He already had. Are there giants in your life that you are running away from? Are there giants in your promised land? If there are, then maybe it is time to trust God, and let God help you. Let God make a way through your giants, into the blessings He has for you. There are so many times we, like the Israelites, give in to our fears. We give in especially to the fears, regarding the giants in our land. The giant of fear is a good example. Instead of facing our fears and breaking through to the other side, we run and hide and lose our blessing and freedom. How about the giant of grief, stress, illness, or finding a new job? How about the fear of going through recovery, reclaiming our lives and our promised land? There are so many giants in the land at different times in our lives. We can either face our giants like Caleb and Joshua wanted to. Saying our God is greater than the giants. Our God is greater than any giant I may have to face. Or we can be like the ten other men, who were giving in to their fears, shaking in their boots and running away from the gift God had promised them. The God promised gift of a land flowing with milk and honey. Are we running into God and all that God is and promises God has given us. Or are we running into our fears and away from the giants in our life? If we are running away like the Israelites did, then we too may spend undo years in the desert, never reaching the Promised Land. There will be giants in our lives we have to face. That is called being human and living in a fallen world. That truth remains. The other truth is God is bigger, so very much bigger than our giants. God can make a way where there seems to be no way. God can help us fight our giants if we will but let God. God can help us to overcome whatever it is that needs overcoming. God can if we will but trust God and let God be God of our lives.

Prayer: Thank you, God, that you are bigger, so very much bigger than any giant I may face in my life. I repent, for not trusting you. I repent, for forgetting about who you are and who I am in you. Forgive me, and teach me, how to not run away from my giants, but to face them with you by my side. I want the Promised Land; I do not want to stay any longer than I have to in my desert. In Jesus' name, I pray, amen.

Day Two Hundred Twelve

Numbers 14:3 'Why is the Lord bringing us to this land only to let us fall by the sword? Our wives and children will be taken as plunder. Wouldn't it be better for us to go back to Egypt?'

How many times in our lives do we want to go back to Egypt? To go back to what was and what we remember. Egypt holds a feeling of familiarity of being safe and even secure. There is comfort in the memories for us back in Egypt, regardless of what the truth really is, about what Egypt was really like. Egypt is what was and not what is. Egypt is our desire to move out of what is going on in our lives at the moment, so we can go back to what we remember is good from the past. As we know Egypt for the Israelites was anything but good. They were slaves being very mistreated and abused. There was no freedom, and the work was hard and backbreaking. There was not enough provision for them to get by on. In reality Egypt was a terrible place for them to live. If Egypt was such a terrible, hard place to live, why were the Israelites crying out to God for help to get them out of Egypt? Why were the Israelites crying out, pleading with God, to get them back to where the Egyptians were making their life miserable and extremely difficult? Going back to Egypt was a way of not being in the desert with the hardships the desert was causing to happen in their lives. To get away from the feelings they had to feel. The reality of living in today is much harder at times than in the memories of yesterday. My friends, we can never go back to Egypt! Hear that, we can never, no never, go back to what was, all we can do is live in what life is giving us today. For today is all we really have. We can never go back to the past. For the past does not exist anymore. All we have is what exists today, the present. The past is gone and can never be reclaimed or relived. The past is like putting your foot in the river, when you take your foot out and put it in the river again the water is new water. The water you stuck your foot in originally has moved on down the river. We can never go back to what was. For what was, does not and cannot exist anymore. Once we move on, we move on and things change. Going back is never the same. People move on, friends change, buildings go up and are torn down, and even old familiar landmarks are no longer there. Once we leave Egypt, we leave Egypt and there is no going back. The Israelites were angry that life was not looking as they thought it would look like. They were feeling sorry for themselves and wanted the comfort of their past. Even though their past was not very comfortable. The challenge is to make the most of today. For today is all we have. If we make the best of today, then our tomorrow will be better as well. Yesterday is gone, tomorrow is a mystery, today is a gift, that is why it is called the present. Let us embrace the gift of today to the best of our ability.

Prayer: Father, I am sorry for wanting to go back to yesterday. I am realizing that yesterday is gone today is all I have. Help me make the most of today. Forgive me for not celebrating the life you have given me. Forgive me for wanting to go back to Egypt. I am realizing Egypt is not all I remember it to be. Thank you, amen.

Day Two Hundred Thirteen

Luke 22: 40 `On reaching the place, he said to them, "Pray that you will not fall into temptation.'

Good advice for all of us. Pray that we do not fall into temptation. Temptation is all around us. As humans we are so very often easily lead into places and situations where we are tempted, lead down paths by our own making or through the actions or advice of others. If I have a hard time with chocolate, then walking into the candy store or Laura Secords, is going to put me in a place of temptation and risk. If I choose to put chocolate in front of me and at arms reach, I do not have the strength within my own resources to say no. Therefore, I am lead down the path of eating chocolate and giving into my temptation. It is the same with all areas of our lives. If we put ourselves in the path of temptation, we know that sooner or later temptation is going to win. Sooner or later we will give into the temptation and all the consequences that will follow. That is the way temptation works most of the time. If we set ourselves up to be tempted, tempted we will be. The ability to resist the temptation diminishes and even fails us all together. In this passage Jesus is reminding us of our need to pray (for prayer is our most powerful tool and help so as not to fall into what tempts us). Prayer helps us to be wise. Prayer helps to not set ourselves up to fail and be led astray by the temptations that are all around us. Prayer is the fuel source and supply we all need in order to resist temptation. To stay strong in what we know is . Without prayer we tend to focus on what we cannot have instead of focusing on what is life giving to us, we focus on what is tempting us. Prayer keeps our focus on the gifts, blessings and grace in our lives. Without prayer we move away from what is good for us into those areas and temptations of our lives that steal everything we are working towards. We move away from what is honouring to ourselves and to God. We move away from God's plan for our lives and into the temptation, which may cause us to lose so much more than what we gain from giving into what is tempting us.

Prayer is asking God to help us be strong. With the Holy Spirit's help we will be less likely to fall into the temptation. We are less likely to be pulled back into the harm and death the temptation may cause. Without the power of prayer in our lives, the only resources we have are those naturally within us. When we pray, we have all the other resources the Holy Spirit places within our hearts and spirits, which enable us to resist and truly live. Prayer is the light shining in our darkness and weaknesses that give us courage and strength to go through life in a life giving way.

Prayer: Holy Spirit, help me to pray more and to trust your power within me. Help me to resist temptation by trusting in your presence in my life. I am sorry for not praying as much as I need to. Remind me, to pray. Thank you, Holy Spirit, for your power and presence in my heart and life, amen.

Day Two Hundred Fourteen

I John 1: 7 'But if we walk in the light, as he is in the light, we have fellowship with one another, and the blood of Jesus, his Son, purifies us from all sin.'

Jesus said 'I am the light of the world. Whoever follows me will not walk in darkness, but will have the light of life'. If we have the light of life within us, then we have the resources to be in fellowship with one another. We have the light of Christ shining in our hearts, and that light gives us the courage and the strength to reach out and love others. With the light of Christ in us we have the knowing that we are loved. Therefore we can risk and truly love others. We are standing on a firm foundation that cannot be moved, no matter what happens or might happen. The light of life is our light! The blessing continues. We also have the blood of Jesus, which washes us clean and purifies us from sin, all sin! We are clean. We are washed. We are no longer covered with the transgressions of our pasts and the wrong choices we have made. We are in a right relationship with God through the washing of our sins, through the sacrificial shedding of Jesus' blood. We are cleansed from all sin and guilt. Our sins are removed from us never to be listed again against us ever again. They are washed away like the footprints on the bleach when the waves roll in. Therefore, if I am clean, washed and no longer guilty, I can reach out and love others unconditionally because I am now loved unconditionally. There is a knowing of being safe and secure no matter what happens or befalls us. The unconditional love we know and feel from our Heavenly Father and God fills us to overflowing. Therefore when we fall or get hurt in some way, we know we can always run into the arms of our Father/Dad's love and be loved and comforted. Then restored. We can risk our love, because we know that no matter what happens. We are safe and secure in Jesus and His cleansing, healing power. We are free to be ourselves, without any fears of what may or may not happen. We are standing in the light of God, having been washed by Jesus' blood, no longer guilty of sin. Now we have the ability and desire to take that gift of forgiveness and love we have been given and share it with others in our life, either permanent or casual. We are free to love and live. Then when love hurts and it will, we can run into the waiting arms of love with the assurance of our place in the love being given.

Prayer: Thank you, Jesus, for being the light of the world and for washing me with your blood. Thank you, that I am now clean and forgiven. Thank you that I am no longer burdened by my wrong choices and mistakes. Help me, to love others as you have loved me. Help me, to show others the truth of what real love mean, without fear or worry. Thank you, for loving me the way you do. I am truly grateful, in Jesus' name, amen.

Day Two Hundred Fourteen

2 Peter 1:3 `His divine power has given us everything we need for life and godliness through our knowledge of him who called us by his own glory and goodness.'

Have you ever known someone who was living an ungodly life? Remember how selfish and self focused they were? How they often did things that were hurtful, or at the least very inconsiderate? Now remember them after they opened their heart and life to God. Did their attitude, beliefs and behaviours change? Were they more considerate or kind? Did they offer assistance or help out of the blue and without reason? Did they start living life differently? The answer is usually yes. When a person opens their heart and gives God permission to help them live their life, there is a change that happens. The person begins to do things out of character for the old person. They seem to be living life through a different set of perspectives or glasses. What was important to them before does not seem to be important now. What took a priority before does not even enter into the picture anymore. How many of us can see changes in our siblings after they accepted God into their hearts and lives? I have heard so many people say over the years "when my brother or sister accepted God, they changed for the better. They became so much easier to get along with. They stopped doing the hurtful things they did in the past." The reason for the changes is in the divine power that is now flowing through them, changing the person from the inside out. The divine power of the Holy Spirit living in the heart of the person alters the way the person sees life. The Holy Spirit alters their way of living life. Our spirit is brought to life by the presence of the Holy Spirit within us; but more importantly the Holy Spirit begins to put a desire for godliness in us. Therefore, we begin to choose godly choices. There is knowledge, a knowing within us, that produces godly choices and behaviours. The sibling who becomes nicer! The friend who is now easier to get along with and be around, the parent who stops their hurting or harmful behaviours to themselves or others. They now do nice things for us, or treated us in ways that shocks us at times. Why? Because they were not being mean or selfish or self-centred any longer? The presence of God in their hearts and spirits is now evident in their choices and behaviours. God's glory and goodness is now living inside the person changing their thinking, behaviours, ways and total selves. The mystery of God! The mystery of God's presence in our lives! The presence of God in our lives changes us from the inside out by filling the void in our hearts and giving us the glory and mystery of God Himself. The mystery of God whose love for us causes us to see life differently and through a different set of glasses. The wonder of the unconditional love God has for us! The life-changing and absolute power of God's amazing love in and for our lives truly does set us free to let go of what was and to come into all that is and could be.

Prayer: Holy Spirit, I want those changes in me. Father, I want your glory, goodness and mystery living in me. I want to know that knowing that comes only from you. I want to be different. Thank you, for coming into my heart and changing me from the inside out. I am totally grateful, amen.

Day Two Hundred Fifteen

2 Peter 1: 5-7 'For this very reason, make every effort to add to your faith goodness; and to goodness, knowledge; and to knowledge, self-control; and to self-control, perseverance; and to perseverance, godliness; and to godliness, brotherly kindness; and to brotherly kindness, love.'

Now that we have the Holy Spirit living in our hearts and working in us, the mystery of God's love for us, it is time to grow in God's love and goodness. Now we can start putting in the effort to help the changes that are happening inside of us. We can add to the faith God has given to us, when we asked The Holy Spirit to fill us up, to increase the gift of faith God has placed within our spirit. What can be added to our faith is goodness, choosing to do good, instead of evil, choosing goodness over any other behaviour you may have in the past. To our goodness we can add knowledge, smarts, wisdom, the knowing that comes from familiarity, which is gained through experience and association with the Holy Spirit; the knowledge the Holy Spirit gives to us, by the presence of God in our life. To our knowledge, we then need self-control, the self-control so that we do not live as impulsive or irrational individuals any longer. Self-control when exercised is the ability to have restraint over our impulses, emotions and desires. To our self-control, we then need to add perseverance, so that we can stay on track, moving forward towards the goal of living a godly life and life-style; to be steadfast in our desire to live a life worthy of being a child of the Most High God, with all the love and blessings we have. To our perseverance we add godliness, which is being like God and living as God would live; to live a life that is honouring to God. To our godliness we are to add brotherly kindness, loving each other as members of the family of God. Treating everyone of the family of God with love, honour, dignity and respect. Building each other up, instead of tearing them down. The need to be kind to one another, choosing to function as loving, responsible human beings, instead of selfish and self-centred ones. Finally to brotherly kindness, we add love, which is doing only the higher good for the person with whom we are in a relationship. When we choose to add to our character these qualities and characteristics, not only are we pleasing to God but we are also pleasing to ourselves and then to others. When I am growing in my godly character and the way I see and live, my life begins to bring more life to me. My life is enhanced by the way I interact with people. My relationship with God grows and deepens because I am much more able to be in God's presence, drinking in everything God wants to pour into my life and heart. My relationship with God changes and deepens because I am reflecting more of God in me. To not grow means we stay stuck in ourselves. We all know what it feels like to be stuck! Therefore, to grow and evolve and change not only gets us out of being stuck, it also moves us forward to a better life for ourselves and others.

Prayer: Lord, I want to grow. I want to be all you created me to be. I so much do not want to be stuck in what was any longer. I want to be on the move, learning and growing and truly taking my place as the person you created me to be in the first place. Help me, to let go of the things in my life that hold me locked in and stuck. I want to fly and be free. Thank you, Holy Spirit, and Father, amen

Day Two Hundred Sixteen

Jeremiah 1: 4-5 `The word of the Lord came to me, saying, "before I formed you in the womb I knew you, before you were born I set you apart; I appointed you as a profit to the nations".'

Before I knew you, I formed you in your mother's womb! Before any of us were given life on this earth God knew exactly who we were. Every single human being, before they are given life, has life with God and a relationship with God. I know this is hard to believe at times. Before you had life as the person you are today, your spirit was alive with God in the heavenly realms. You were born in this time frame for such a time as this, no matter what the circumstances were surrounding your conception or birth. God decided that you were to live, not your parents or any other act of conception. God wanted you born. Can you hear this truth? God wanted you born for such a time as this. God wanted you to be alive today, having all the gifts, talents and abilities you have. God has a purpose for your life, in this time frame. Please hear this truth. You are not a mistake, inconvenience, not good enough or any other lie you have been told. You are here in the here and now because God held you in the palm of His hand and gave you life. For those of you who think you were a mistake---wrong. If people have told you, you are junk, garbage, not good enough, a mistake, or any other negative impression. They are wrong. Are you hearing me? Are you hearing that you are already enough? You are exactly who you were created to be. How do we know they are wrong? We know because God does not make junk, mistakes or anything defective. God only makes things that are valuable and worthwhile. God only makes things that have value and worth. God makes everything for a reason. Everything God makes in all of His creation, is made, for a reason and has a purpose. You are here on this planet earth, for a reason, and for such a time as this. We are all set apart to be a blessing to God and to each other. We are all here on earth because this is our time to be here. Before you were formed in your mother's womb God knew you, and you knew God. You are the Beloved! You are the chosen, beloved child of God. Let that sink in deep within you. Regardless of what the world says about you, regardless of what your parents, others, or the world have said about you. God looks at you with amazing and incredible eyes of love, and calls you His beloved. You are so valuable to God. So very valuable that He gave His only Son to die on the cross, so that you and God could be restored. Brought back to the place of oneness you had before you were given birth. We are all regardless of who we are so loved by God that He gave His all, so that we could be in that love once again—safe and secure—loved, valued and cherished---His chosen beloved. God knows us and loves us no matter what!!! The reason we were created was to be loved by God, and that is the truth. We were created to be in a love relationship with God. We were given life because God wanted us to have life and for no other reason. Let us take our places as God's chosen beloved, knowing our value and worth in God.

Prayer: Thank you, thank you, thank you. I have forgotten how much you love me God. I have let the world and people's opinions of me steal the truth of your love for me. I am sorry. Please remind me, of how valuable I am to you and how much you love me. Help me, to take my place as your beloved child. I want to be back safe and secure in your arms of love. I want to be back in our love relationship. I have missed you and your love for me, amen.

Day Two Hundred Seventeen

1 Corinthians 2:5 'So that your faith might not rest on men's wisdom, but on God's power.'

What is God's power? God's power is truth, light, love, freedom, hope, salvation, mercy, grace to name but a few. God's power is being able to live in the power of God, which enables us to live free from what others think, say or do. To walk as individuals in the great family of God with all the wisdom and power that comes from the presence of God in our lives and hearts. God's power is being able to live according to God's path of life and by His Word, which is life. When we live in God's power, we live as the individuals we were meant to be. We let go of the things that prevent us from being all that we were created to be. God's power within us truly does give us the ability to live whole, productive lives in freedom and light. The way into God's power is through faith, through choosing to believe in what God says and putting that belief into action. Believing is great and good, but putting that belief into action brings life to our beliefs, making them real and visible in our lives. Resting on the world's or man's power is trusting in what man and the world says is true and real and valid. Trusting in the world says that I believe as human beings we have all the answers, plus the ability to get the answers. It says our wisdom is enough to get us through to the other side; our wisdom is equal to or greater than God, and who and what God is. Man's wisdom or the world's wisdom says we ourselves are the bottom line. We as the bottom line have the ability, authority and power, to do whatever we want and not have to suffer the consequences. If we are being honest with ourselves, when we trust and rely on man's power or the world's power, we fall short and end up with a whole lot of emptiness. When we trust solely in our own power, in the power of man, if we are being honest with ourselves, it usually comes up short. What happens when we reach the end of our resources, and there are still questions? What happens when we reach the top rung on the ladder to find there is nothing but emptiness, the feeling of being hollow on the inside? Where do we go when we have tapped out all possible avenues of life, only to find a dead end, and have nothing to show for all we have done or thought we have done? When we trust in man or the world we come up short of the mark. When we trust and have faith in the power of God and God's wisdom and truth, we find ourselves having more questions. Yes, sometimes having more questions than answers, or not having all the answers. However, what is left is a knowing and peace that makes the not knowing or not having all the answers, okay. Why? Because we know the one who does have the answers. We know God is well able to see us through whatever it is we are facing. The difference between trusting in God and trusting in man is God is the beginning and the end. Therefore God has the all-knowing power sitting outside of time. Human beings are finite and sit in linear time. Therefore we are limited to what we can see within linear time and its limits and limitations.

Prayer: Heavenly Father, I am so grateful that you are all knowing and have the truth of true life and living. Help me, to trust you more, and the power of you and your word and spirit in my life and for my life. I am beginning to realize that without you I sit in darkness. I fall short of knowing the answers, because you are the beginning and the end, having all the answer to life and living. Help me, to be that person you created me to be in the first place, with all the gifts, talents and abilities you placed within my heart and spirit. In Jesus' name, amen.

Day Two Hundred Eighteen

Romans 8:1 'Therefore, there is now no condemnation for those who are in Christ Jesus, because through Christ Jesus the law of the spirit of life set me free from the law of sin and death.'

There is no condemnation for any of us who choose to be in Christ Jesus. No condemnation for those of us who have opened our heart to the truth of God's gift of salvation, who walk in the way of righteousness. We stand free and forgiven before God through the gift of life and forgiveness given to all of creation. When Jesus the Christ chose to die on the cross to pay our sin debt, the penalty of sin was wiped away. What is given in return is the gift of eternal life through faith, hope and trust in Jesus' resurrected power and truth. Once you repent and ask for God's forgiveness, you are forgiven! Your sins are remembered no more. They are separated from you like the east is separated from the west. It is like what happens on the seashore when the waves come in, any foot prints that might have been there are no longer there. The waves have washed them away. There is no memory of the footprint in the sand. When you look all you see is fresh, smooth sand waiting to be walked on once again. That is what God says to each and every one of us, who enter into the free gift of God's mercy and grace. We are no longer condemned for what was. We are set free from the bondage, the prison that held us in. All those things are remembered no more. We may remember what we have done and try to remind God, but God does not remember. In fact, when we say something like "don't you remember when I did xxxx?" God says with all sincerity "no". You have to remember this one. God replies with 'sorry, I don't'. You have to remember when I----God says "No that one is gone as well". It is like the chalk on the black board. Once you wash the black board clean and let it dry, the evidence of what was on the black board is gone. There is no memory of it. A new set of writings is put on the board, which will be washed away that night. It is the very same with us. When we tell God how sorry we are every time we do something wrong or displeasing to God, God washes that sin away. Never to be remembered again. There is therefore, no condemnation for those who are in Christ Jesus. NO condemnation, NONE, NOT ANY. We are set free. We are truly free and can freely stand before God forgiven, loved and accepted, as one who has been washed, no longer guilty of sin. No longer caught in the power of sin and darkness. We are no longer on the path to permanent death and darkness. Hallelujah! What a gift God has given to all of us who want the gift. I say yes and amen to the mercy, grace and great compassion of our God and Father in the Heavenly realms.

Prayer: Thank you, Jesus, for paying my sin debt, for opening the way for me to be set free from my wrong choices, and the wrong choices of others. Thank you that I can stand free and forgiven before God because of your love for me. Thank you, for being my Saviour and Redeemer, for buying me back. In Jesus' more precious and holy name, amen.

Day Two Hundred Nineteen

Galatians 2:21 'I do not set aside the grace of God, for if righteousness could be gained through the law, Christ died for nothing!'

There is a belief in some of our minds that says "If I am good enough (perfect), if I follow all of the rules and not break them, if I can manage to do things right, then I will be acceptable before others. Then I will be acceptable before God. If I am above reproach, then I am okay and have reached the mark, whatever the mark is." The problem with this belief of being perfect and never making a mistake or messing up is an impossible reality. None of us can possible be perfect and not make mistakes or wrong choices. None of us have the ability to be perfect, to live without defects or shortcomings. We are designed to be perfectly imperfect.

We are designed to need other people. We are designed especially to need God. Hence the reason for not being able to gained righteousness by following the law, by living solely for the law. Don't get me wrong. I am not saying we ought to break the law or live against the law. What I am saying is. The law is not enough to save us and make us whole or complete, without defects or shortcomings. The law is there to keep us safe, to live in such a way as to respect the rules, living in harmony with the law. The law with all its benefits cannot give us or cause us to have righteousness. Righteousness comes from the grace of God! God chooses to make us righteous, to grant us forgiveness and mercy. Without God's grace, mercy and forgiveness, there would be no way out of all that we have done and others have done to us. For once an act has been done, it is forever out there. Just like words------once they are spoken they can never be taken back. God's grace, which is God's unmerited loving favour, is the only thing that can set us free from what was, into all that could be. Without God's grace and mercy we would be bound by the power of the law. God's grace, God's unmerited loving favour, releases us from the power of the law, and the justice the law demands. God's mercy overrides the demands of the law, which in turn sets us free to be righteous, and in a right relationship with God, regardless of our past and the choices made in it. God's grace grants us, gives us, enables us to walk out of our pasts and into the blessings of God's mercy, grace and forgiveness, which causes us to be righteous before God. My friends, freedom, true freedom, comes from God and His love for us, His creation. Freedom does not come from anything we do, say or think. It is all about God and what God does. It has nothing to do with us. It is not about us, and what we do, for we will always fall short of the righteousness of God. Our best efforts cannot save us from the demands of the law. The only thing that can save us from the law is the free gift of God's grace, mercy and forgiveness. God's mercy is the key to forgiveness, the key to true freedom and being forgiven set free from what was. God's mercy and grace releases us to live again, to truly live again, without the demands of the law.

Prayer: Most High Living God, I receive your gift of grace. I repent of my belief that I was powerful enough to free me from the demands of the law. Forgive me, and set me free to truly live in your mercy, grace and forgiveness, with all the blessings and mystery of your love for me your child. Thank you for loving me, the way you do, and for setting me free. I am truly grateful. I stand in awe of you and all you are, amen.

Day Two Hundred Twenty

Hebrews 11:1 'Now faith is being sure of what we hope for and certain of what we do not see.'

Let me start today with explaining the difference between faith and beliefs. A belief is something we hold to be true. A belief can be given to us from another person, system or organization. Belief is a state or habit of mind in which trust or confidence has been placed in someone or something. Faith is taking the belief and putting it into action. Faith is action. Here are some examples of how faith and beliefs work. I believe if I put the key into my ignition and turn the key my car will start. I really do believe that. Faith is turning the key and watching the car start. Although I do not know how electricity works, I do believe that if the bill has been paid and I turn on the light switch, the light will come on. Even though I do not know how electricity works, I believe that it does. Therefore, when I hit the switch, the light will result. Faith is hitting the switch and watching the light come on. I believe if both the employer and I agree to work together, there will be a pay cheque at the end of the pay period. Faith is going to work everyday trusting the payment of my wages. Belief is what we hold to be true; faith is taking that belief and putting it into action. We all have faith! There is not one person who does not have faith. Faith is an innate gift within each and every one of us. We believe the sun will shine every day. Even though it is hidden be hide the clouds, we have faith that it is still there. Therefore we do not even think about it. We just put our belief into action trusting the sun is still there, even though we cannot see it. Every time we go to the doctor when we are sick, and he/she gives a prescription, we believe that the prescription is going to work; therefore, we take the pills in faith and get better. Faith is a part of our daily lives. In fact, to live means we have to have faith. If we did not have faith, there would be only fear and anxiety, and we would have no ability to trust and move forward in our daily living. The challenge to us is taking the faith we already have, and applying it to our relationship with God and His presence in our lives, in His creation. The challenge is to choose to take our belief that there is a Higher Power beyond ourselves, moving our belief into action, accepting that Higher Power has the ability to help us and be there for us. To hit the 'light switch' of our belief in God, trusting that belief into action, which is what faith is all about. `Now faith is being sure of what we hope for and certain of what we do not see.' I do not see electricity work. I have faith that it does. I do not see how the car works. I trust that it does, every time I turn the key. I do not doubt that the sun is going to shine every day. Therefore when I go to bed I do not worry that the sun might not shine. It is the very same with our belief in God. Faith is just taking that belief and moving into an action.

Prayer: Thank you, Father, for my gift of faith. Help me now to take my faith and put it into a deeper trust in you. A deeper trust in who you are in this universe and creation. Thank you, for the lesson you have taught me today. I open my heart to living more by faith, than by sight. In Jesus' name, amen.

Day Two Hundred Twenty-one

Hebrews 12: 29 `for our God is a consuming fire.'

Fire is both and life-stealing. Fire, when used and controlled, gives light, heat and protection from the cold. It has so many purposes and blessings. When fire is not controlled, it can destroy vast amounts of forestland. A wildfire consumes everything in its path, destroying everything it touches. It has a life of its own, going and doing whatever it wants, regardless of what is in its path, or what it destroys in its wake. Fire is a very necessary part of life. Without fire we would be cold in the winter and hot in the summer. We would not be able to cook our food or warm our suppers. When I was in South Africa fire was used in one of two ways. One was a fast burn fire, which was started to burn up the thick under bush to help keep the parasites under control. The fast burn fire helps keep the under bush from getting so thick, it cuts off any possibility of new life from growing and spreading. The fast burn fire also left a white mineral on the ground, which the animals ate to keep them healthy. The second was a destructive burning fire, which was wild and destroyed everything in its path. A wild fire! Scripture says God is a consuming fire, a fire that wants to consume everything in our lives that is not . Destroying everything that prevents us from growing into the people we were created to be in the first place. That is the fire. The fire leaves life in its path, helping the natural creative process to continue. The other side of God's consuming fire is it has the ability to destroy. Matthew 10:28 says, `Do not be afraid of those who kill the body but cannot kill the soul. Rather, be afraid of the one who can destroy both soul and body in hell.' The consuming fire of God has the authority to kill both the body and soul (spirit) within all of us. We have two choices. We can choose to be on the fast fire burn side of God's consuming fire that burns off everything that prevents us from being all we were created to be so we can have the light of life shining within us.

Or, we can know the wildfire side of God's consuming fire that burns up everything in its path, not caring what it burns, just so long as it keeps burning. One side of God's consuming fire brings us life and life abundantly. The other side of God's consuming fire brings death and destruction. We know the destroying side of God's consuming fire when we choose to stay in our selfish and self-centred attitudes, beliefs and choices; when we continue to go through life with the "I want what I want when I want it" attitude; when we demand life on our terms and conditions, regardless of whom we hurt or who gets in our way. We know the life giving side of God's consuming fire, when we choose to live life God's way, following His laws, commandments, decrees and precepts. That is the amazing gift of God to us, the gift of free will to decide what will happen in and to our lives. Freedom to choose to live life God's way or our way, knowing that when we choose God's way, we will have abundant life in return. Free will says we can choose to live life our way, ending up with death and the consuming fire of God. What amazing love our great and awesome God has for us! Such amazing love which allows us to choose even when the choice can deal us death and destruction.

Prayer: Thank you, God, for being a Holy and Righteous God who honours us with free will. Who honours us with the ability to choose for ourselves the path we will take. The problem with this freedom is we sometimes choose paths that are destructive to ourselves and to others. Help us, to use our gift of free will in life giving ways, that honour you, others and ourselves. In Jesus' name, amen.

Day Two Hundred Twenty-two

Hebrews 12: 14-15 `Make every effort to live in peace with all men and to be holy; without holiness, no one will see the Lord. See to it that no one misses the grace of God, and that no bitter root grows up to cause trouble and defile many.'

As human beings we are so good at creating stress in our lives. Not to mention the lives of others at times. The reading today tells us to live at peace with everyone. Did you hear that? We are to live at peace with all people, not just the ones we like or the ones we can get along with. We are to live at peace with all, every, bar none people. Why would God ask us to live at peace with every person we know, greet or meet? The answer is quite simple. What happens to us, and our insides, when we are in conflict with someone, or when we have a hate on for an individual or group or organization? What does it do to us? Do we not get all bent out of shape? Do we not want to avoid the person or be caught anywhere close to the group we are struggling with? The person or organization is on our hit list of things to hate, get even with or cause harm to. When we have resentments or bitter roots as the reading says today, we do nothing to the person, group or organization we are being angry with hating, resenting or feeling bitter about. What those feelings, beliefs and attitudes are doing is destroying our ability to live in healthy whole relationships, not to mention destroying us. Resentment and bitterness do NOTHING, absolutely nothing to what we are resenting or feeling bitter about. What the resentment and bitterness is doing is destroying our ability to live in healthy growing ways. They are destroying everything good about us. Think about it. Think about a resentment or bitterness in your life that has caused you incredible trouble. Maybe even for some of you the resentment or bitterness has defiled your life, heart and ability to live. We miss out on the grace, mercy, love, compassion, freedom and so on, that God has for us, because we are so busy thinking, feeling and living in our anger, hatred, bitterness and resentments. We can't embrace the wonder of all God has for us. God wants to bring you freedom to live in His mercy, grace and forgiveness. In reality God can't, because there is no room left in our hearts for anything but the bitterness, resentments, anger and hatred. We miss out on the gift of life and everything God has for us. We miss out on everything God wants to give us because we are lost in our self-created prison or mud puddles. We find ourselves living a lonely and empty life, for who wants to be around someone who is angry, bitter, resentful and hateful all the time. We push everyone away, because how else do we survive the pain and suffering we are feeling? Hence the reason for living at peace with everyone at all times. When we live in peace and harmony, we are freed from the bondage of the bitter root, which in turn opens our hearts and lives in more harmony and love, not only from others but from God as well. Forgiveness is the key to pulling out the bitter roots and resentments in our lives. Remember forgiveness has nothing to do with the person we are forgiving. It has everything to do with us. Forgiveness sets us free, not the one we are forgiving. Forgiveness gets us off the hook, not the other person. Forgiving releasing us to live in freedom. That is why God gave us forgiveness.

Prayer: Father, I realize that I have let better roots grow inside of me. I am beginning to see how holding on to the resentments, bitterness, anger and hate is only hurting me. It does not hurt the ones I am holding this stuff against. I want to be free, to live and not have these defiling things in me. Forgive me, for hanging on to the past the way I have. Set me free, to forgive and live again. Help me, for I cannot do this alone. I need you with me helping me and guiding me. In Jesus' most holy and precious name, amen.

Day Two Hundred Twenty-three

1 Corinthians 7:15b `God has called us to live in peace.'

Today is story day. Picture your most favourite car. Mine is a British racing green Jaguar, with tan leather interior, with all the bells and whistles. Picture your car. Now see yourself going down to the dealership and ordering your car. You give the sales representative your down payments cheque. He tells you the car will take eight weeks to come in. If you are anything like me, the only thing you are thinking about over these next eight weeks is your new car. The phone finally goes. Your car is ready. You call a buddy. He/she drives you down to pick up your new car. After all the paper work is finished and the final cheque given, he walks you out to your new car. Your eyes light up. You examine the car, taking off any dust that may have settled on your new car. You push a button and unlock the door. You push another button to start the engine. It purrs like a kitten. You reach for the door handle and open the door. New car smell, there is nothing like a new car smell. You sit in your shiny new car, feeling the seat under you and smelling your new car. You adjust the seat, the mirrors. Turn on the air conditioning and push a CD into the CD player. You just sit there listening, smelling and enjoying your new car. The time comes for you to drive away. You wave goodbye to the dealer and pull out into traffic. Along comes a lady and smashes your new car!!!!! What do you want to do to her? Hurt, maime, kill, destroy greatly. Yea, okay, your insurance will pay for a new car. Over the next eight weeks while you have to wait for the replacement car, about whom are you thinking? The lady. What is it doing to her? In reality nothing! The car is ready you go and you pick it up. As you drive out of the dealership whom are you thinking about? The lady----what is it doing to her? You are right-zero, nothing. You are thinking about the lady so much, she is in your dreams. Aren't you lucky! What is it doing to her? Zip, zero, nothing. The car is old, you sell the car, every time you think about the car------who do you think about? The lady------what is it doing to her? Zilch, zip, zero, nothing, nada. What has it done to you over all these years? That is the negative power of resentments. They do nothing to the people we are resenting, they destroy us. Are you hearing me? Resentments destroy us. There are four categories of people we resent. 1- those who are dead, 2- those who do not even know they have dinged us, 3- those who could care less and finally 4- those who know they have dinged you, but who do not know how to correct the situation. Of the four categories you may collect from one. Try to collect from the ones who are dead! Try to collect from the ones who do not care! My friends, resentments do nothing to the people we are resenting. They only destroy us. Resentments are you taking poison and expecting the other person to die. Resentments are letting what you resent live rent free inside of you. Then you wonder why you do not have enough space for yourself. Resentments are letting the things you resent drive your inner bus. Now you know why you crash and burn all the time. It is time to take your bus back. It is time to forgive, so that you can get on with your life. It is time to start living in today.

Prayer: Father, I am beginning to see the negative power of resentments and the damage they can have upon our lives. I confess that I carry resentments. I confess that there are people and situations I hold resentments against. Help me, to forgive. Help me, to let go of those things and people I still resent. I want my life back. I want to live uncluttered in my own space, driving my own bus. With your help all things are possible. I claim that possibility for my life and me. Holy Spirit, work in my heart setting me free. Help me, to set others free, amen.

Day Two Hundred Twenty-four

Matthew 7:6 'Do not give dogs, what is sacred; do not throw your pearls to pigs. If you do, they may trample them under their feet, and then turn and tear you to pieces.'

On one hand humans can be so very selfish and self-centred, while on the other hand we so easily give ourselves away and let others, situations or events walk all over us. Telling us who and what we are and what we can be. Today we are being taught to keep a watchful eye on what we do with those things in our lives that are special and precious to us, with those things that make us, us and unique; to guard our personhood and the uniqueness of who and what we are as human beings. We are valuable and precious unique human beings created by God. We are His chosen beloved children and need to keep a watchful eye on what we do with the sacred things in our lives. Are we holding them dear and near to our hearts in and healthy ways, or are we throwing them to the dogs or pigs? For example are we allowing ourselves to be real, to be who God created us to be, with all of our gifts, talents and abilities? Or are we diminishing ourselves and letting others tell us who we are? Are we letting others define us in ways that are just not true to who God created us to be? My fellow sojourners, let us stop throwing what is sacred to us to the dogs, who stomp all over it and destroy it. Let us protect what is sacred in our lives. Let us honour it and hold it dear to us and our reason for being here for such a time as this. You may be asking what do I have that is sacred? How about your body? It is a sacred gift God has given you. We give away our sacredness when we sleep around or give ourselves sexually to lots of people. Giving ourselves away to multiple partners is the same as throwing our sacredness to the dogs. The ones we give ourselves to, do not honour us or value who and what we are as special, precious, beloved children of God. Throwing ourselves to food or not enough food is exactly the same. It prevents us from honouring ourselves and caring for the sacredness of who and what we are as chosen, beloved children of the Most High God. Throwing our pearls to pigs can be for example letting others have all your money or misuse or abuse your finances so that there is nothing left for you; not enough for you to live your life in a healthy way. I am not saying we should not be generous. What I am saying is we need to guard our money and finances, so that we can be wise with what God is giving us. How about those of us who are totally out of control with our finances and have debt beyond our means? That is another way we throw away the blessings and benefits God has given us. Living beyond our means has such negative affects upon ourselves and our lives. The creditors demanding payments, the bills mounting up, and the utilities being cut off steal our peace and dignity. This is against what God wants for our lives and us as His children. We are being asked to guard all that is sacred and precious in us and in our lives so that we can truly be the children, the precious, chosen, beloved children God wants us to be. Without consciously guarding our sacredness and those things which are precious to us and to God, we lose sight of what makes us human and the children we were created to be.

Prayer: Father, I am not sure where I am giving my sacred things to the dogs or where I am throwing my pearls to pigs. Please help me, to see and know where I am doing these things so that I can make the necessary adjustment in my life, heart and spirit. Forgive me, and restore me, to a right relationship with you, with others and with myself. Thank you. I am grateful for all the ways you love me and want to help me be all you created me to be. Thank you, for always being willing to teach me and help me, your precious, chosen child, amen.

Day Two Hundred Twenty-five

Matthew 7:12 'So in everything, do to others what you would have them do to you, for this sums up the Law and the Prophets.'

Do unto others, as you would like others to do unto you. In other words treat others as you like others to treat you. If you want to be treated with love, honour and respect, then treat others with love, honour and respect. Don't expect others to treat you respectfully if you disrespect them or if you do not give them the same respect they are offering you. Likewise do not expect others to honour you and value you when you are not honouring or valuing yourself or others. If you sow warm fuzzies you, for the most part, get warm fuzzies back. If you sow cold pricklies, you will get cold pricklies back. A warm fuzzy is anything that makes you feel warm on the inside. A cold prickly is any thing that does not make you feel warm on the inside. A hug, a smile, laughter, a hand up when needed are all warm fuzzies. A put down, a smack across the head, a door slammed in your face is a cold prickly because it does not make you feel warm on the inside. What you sow into your life will be what you get back from life. If you are treating others in a way that you do not want to be treated, do not expect them to give you back warm fuzzies. For chances are, they will give you back what you have given them. Conversely, if you treat others warmly and with kindness, honouring who and what they are as human beings, even if they are the kind of person who sows cold pricklies, chances are they will at least give less cold pricklies than if you sowed cold pricklies to them all the time. It is said people may forget what you say, they may forget what you did, but they will never forget how you made them feel. That is so true! When I think back over my life. The people I remember most are the ones who touched my heart and caused good or bad feelings within me. That goes right back to the lesson we are being taught today. Do unto others what you would have them do to you. Treat others as you would have them treat you. However you want to be treated by others is how we need to treat the people who are in our lives for whatever reason. Whether an instant, a moment, a time, or a very long time, we need to do to others as we want done to ourselves. When we live this way, life becomes what we thought it was going to be when we got important or made it. When we treat others as we want to be treated life takes on a completely different perspective and the value we place on life and ourselves changes drastically. If I am sowing only cold pricklies, then my perspective of life is going to reflect the cold pricklies. If however, I am sowing warm fuzzies, then chances are my life is going to reflect the warm fuzzies. My perspective will be one of wanting to do things that help others feel warm on the inside, wanting to stay away from attitudes or behaviours that cause everything but warm fuzzies to occur.

Prayer: As I look back over my life, I must confess that there are times when I treated others poorly or in unacceptable ways. Please forgive me and help me, to love everyone who is in my life for whatever reason. Help me, to treat everyone with honour, dignity and respect, doing the higher good for them all. Help me to not treat others, as I do not want to be treated. Help me, to be a sower of warm fuzzies and not cold pricklies. In Jesus' name, amen.

Day Two Hundred Twenty-six

Romans 8:15 `For you did not receive a spirit that makes you a slave again to fear, but you received the Spirit of Sonship. And by him we cry, "Abba Father".'

Fear is such a real and often devastating reality in most of our lives. Fear gets in deep and seems to have a life of its own at times. That is a reality most of us have to deal with at some times and points in our lives. That may be a reality, but the truth is fear does not come from God. When we have God in our lives, we are no longer bound by the negative power of fear, or the control it may want to have over our lives. Fear is not of God. Therefore when God is in us we have the power and authority to eliminate fear from our lives. We have the spiritual and emotional ability to take back our power from the fear. When we are in Christ, we get, receive, are given, already have, the Spirit of Sonship. We are given the power, rights and authority of Sonship. In fact, we are given the ability to cry out "Abba, Father". Abba being daddy, the one who comforts us and holds us when we are afraid. The Dad who sits us upon His knee talking with us, speaking the words we long to hear. The Dad who is always there no matter what is happening in or to our lives. The reliable Dad who helps us through everything life may throw our way. Then we have Father. Father is the one who is in authority, who can fix everything. The Father who blesses us and guides us along life's path, the Father who helps us to know who we are, and what we were created to be. The Father who helps us fight our battles, giving us the encouragement to go forth with the knowledge that we are never alone and are not going forth by our selves. We have our Heavenly Father who is always there with us, guiding us and giving us what we need in order to be all that we were created to be. We have everything we need in order to be the true son or daughter we were created to be by the Most High God. If all this is true, then in reality there is no need for fear. There is no need to be afraid of anything. We have our Father and Dad who promises to always be there no matter what, who promises to give us what we need in order to do what we need to do. We can rest in the arms of the love of our Heavenly Father and Dad with the firm assurance of that love and our place within it. When we are loved, there is no need to be afraid for true love casts out all fear. True love does not have fear in any part of it. True love is pure and clean, innocent and trustworthy. True love is in every aspect of its nature. That is the love we have in our Heavenly Father and Dad. I pray you find rest and the safety and security you need from the love

God has for each and every one of us. God loves us just the way we are, but too much to leave us here. Therefore, give God permission to transform your fears into love, trust and all the blessings we have because we are the child/children of the Most High God. The child/children of the One who loves us with a never ending pure, clean love.

Prayer: Father/Dad help me to trust your love for me more, to rest in your arms of love so that I can feel the feeling of being safe and secure in you. Help me, to let go of my fears and the power they have over me. So I can walk as a true child of yours. Set me free, to live again in your love and the safety of your love. I need you Father/Dad in every part of my life for I no longer want fear in me. I now want only your love. Thank you, Father, for loving me the way you do. Help me to love myself, amen.

Day Two Hundred Twenty-seven

John 6:41 'At this the Jews began to grumble about him because he said, "I am the bread that came down from heaven".'

Grumbling I think is one of our favourite pastimes. We grumble about everything. Everything is open to someone grumbling about it at one time or another. We grumble about the weather, we grumble about money, people, countries, religions, politicians, teachers and preachers. We grumble about everything that does not meet our standard or expectations. I love watching people. Watching how they walk through life. Have you ever stood on a busy street corner and just looked up? Have you watched as people walking by look up? How curious they are about what you are looking at? In my opinion, it is the funniest thing to watch their reactions and what they do. I am a people watcher.

Therefore as I watch people. I also see how they grumble and complain about everything and anything. The problem with grumbling is we can never be satisfied nor content because there will always be something or someone who does not meet our expectations or standards. Paul says be content. No matter what is happening in or around you, be content. Be at peace with yourself and others. Be at peace and live in contentment, not for any other reason, than it makes your life so much better and so much easier. Can you imagine what our families, cities, country, world would be like if everyone stopped grumbling? What life would be like if people would but choose to live in peace and harmony, having contentment at the base of their lives? I think this world be such a wonderful place. If we could be content with what we have and stop stressing over what we do not have, life would be less stressful. To stop looking at what others have. To stop wishing, hoping desiring, coveting their possessions or place in life would be so much easier. Everything in life comes with a cost, a price tag attached. There is no free lunch. When all is said and done, paying the cost of having what others have may be a price that is higher than you thought. Not being content with what life is giving us means I can never be truly happy. There will always be something more out there. Something more I think will make me happy. The reality is if I am not happy today with what I have, I probably won't be happy tomorrow either. There will always be something more when we are not in a place of contentment. I can have a new car, but then when I see something I like better, I will not be happy with the car I have. I can't be content with my house, because another house is better than mine. The Jews grumbled at Jesus because He said something they did not like. Jesus said things they did not want to hear. When they grumbled, they gave Jesus the keys to their inner bus, allowing Jesus to tell them what they would feel, think say and do. They gave Jesus permission to get inside of them. We do the same thing when we move into grumbling, and away from being content. Happiness is found not in what I have. Happiness is found in what I do with what I have. Friends of mine have just come back from being in a third world country. Their comment was the people are so happy, yet they have nothing. We have everything and are grumbling all the time. What does this say about happiness? Happiness comes from what is within us, not from what we have or possess. We can choose to be happy no matter what is happening in or to our lives. Happiness is a state of mind, not something we can possess or have from an external perspective.

Prayer: Father, I am sorry for all the grumbling I have done in the past. I am beginning to see the harm grumbling has upon me. How harmful grumbling is to my ability to be content and to live in contentment. I want to be more content. I want to live in contentment. I want to have that balance and peace in my life. I need your help in order to achieve this goal in and for my life. Please help me, Holy Spirit. I am giving you permission to teach me and guide me in this new way of living and seeing life. Thank you, this lesson and for your help and love, amen.

Day Two Hundred Twenty-eight

Galatians 5: 16-17 `So I say, live by the Spirit, and you will not gratify the desires of the sinful nature. For the sinful nature desires what is contrary to the Spirit, and the Spirit what is contrary to the sinful nature.

When we invite God into our hearts and lives, it is amazing how our perspective of life changes. The things we thought were important before do not seem to hold much value, or any value at times. The things we thought were crazy or beyond our reach, are now what we hold dear and close to our lives. For example, before inviting God into our lives and hearts, we used to hang on to resentments and unforgiveness. Now that we know forgiveness from God through our willingness to repent, telling God all about what we have done, and discovering how sorry we are for doing those things, we can much more readily let go and forgive others and, to our amazement at times, forgive ourselves. The need to hang on to old hurts and pain is lessened. There is a greater desire to let go and live in freedom. Our hearts taste the forgiveness of God and we want more. Therefore as we choose to let go, more space is opened inside of us for God's forgiveness to enter in. Another example is after we start living according to God's ways and plan for our lives. We see the benefits and blessings. We begin to walk a different path and have different desires for our lives and the lives of those we love. Going to the bars, drinking and living in that lifestyle becomes less and less attractive to us. We find ourselves choosing to do other things and staying away from the bar scene. The desires of the flesh are replaced with the desires of our spirit. Our flesh's desire is to cause us to make choices that lead to death and dying. Our spirit desires choices that bring us life and abundant living. Living by the spirit pushes us to follow our hearts and what our hearts want. We stop listening to what our heads and bodies want. My body may want to live the fast life with all the perks and benefits of the fast life, not to mention to hazards and pit falls. Our spirit wants to live a life that leads us to love, joy, peace, wholeness, forgiveness, mercy and so on. The more we allow God into our heart and spirit, the more we choose to live by the desires of our spirit. Our spirit is or real selves, our essence, the part of us that is unique and precious, the part of us that wants what's best for us, and who and what we are as a person. Living by the desires of our spirit is what true freedom is all about. Living by the desires of our mind and body is where the heavy loads are built up, where the bondage we feel from those loads finds its fuel. To help protect ourselves we build walls around the bondage which in turn builds a prison. Once we move into our prisons, there is no freedom or way out. We seem locked in and caught in our self-made walls. Our spirit on the other hand wants out. Our spirit wants the freedom to live and truly express itself. Our spirits want to fly and be free. Our spirits want to get beyond the clouds and soar like the eagle, fly high and totally free.

Prayer: Holy Spirit, teach my spirit how to become free. Teach me, how to get out of my self made prison, so that I cannot only fly in freedom, but also soar like the eagle. I desire to live in such a way that I know true life and real freedom. Show me, Lord, and set me free, amen.

Day Two Hundred Twenty-nine

Ephesians 1: 4 `For he chose us in him before the creation of the world to be holy and blameless in his sight. In love he predestined us to be adopted as his sons through Jesus Christ, in accordance with his pleasure and will.'

Are you feeling alone? Like you fall short of the mark? Like you are not good enough and never quite meet the standards and expectations of others? Then do I have good news for you! God the Creator of the universe and everything in it chose you in Himself. God chose you even before God even started to create all that has been created. Before anything was, God had you on His mind. Before God put His creative hand to work, He was thinking about you! And God did not stop there. When He was thinking about you He was fashioning a plan that was to be put in place at the right time so that you could be hear this. You could be holy and blameless in His eyes. Yes you! Before anything came to be God decided He was for you and that you were to be chosen to be holy and blameless. That means without fault and in a right relationship with God. God knew exactly what you were going to do. He knew exactly what was going to happen or not happen in your life. God still chose you, fashioning the plan for your life. God put it into effect so that you could be chosen for holiness and blamelessness in His eyes. God predestined you to be adopted into His family. God chose for you to have a place that is all your own. God chose you to be set apart as one of His children with value and worth and a place to call your own with your name on it. You are and have always been pre chosen. You know how you buy a ticket in advance for a concert or a play. How you reserve your seat, so that on show day or concert day, you know exactly where you will be sitting. That is how it is with God. He bought your ticket and reserved your place so that when you were ready you could cash in your ticket and redeem your spot. The ticket collector already knows you are coming. Therefore there is no argument or challenge regarding your place in God and His family. Why did God do this? Why did God set this into place and the plan into motion? It is quite simple really. Because God wanted to. It is God's good pleasure and will to be in a living and alive relationship with you and for you to be a part of His family. It brings God great joy and delight to have you in His family, a part of His clan. God just loves having you around and sharing time and space with you. I know that is hard for some of you to hear and believe, but it is true. God just loves your company and you so much. God just wants to have you hanging around in His family and a part of everything God is. We belong, if we choose, to the family of God. God predestined for us to be chosen and given a place. God knew He wanted us with Him even before He gave us life. Even before we were conceived in our mother's wombs, we were chosen by God to be apart of Him and He part of us. Those of you who think you are not good enough, or fall short of the mark, or any other negative perception you might have of yourself, the perception is not true. God says you are good enough. God says you are exactly the type and kind of person He wants in His family. You are just the right fit for God, no matter what anyone says or has said in the past. God made you just the way you are. God did it long before anyone knew about it. Is it time to join the family and fulfill God is predestined choosing of you as His son or daughter? Is it time to take your place in the family? Is it time to be the chosen, beloved, precious, special child of the Most High God who chooses to be your Father and Dad? I think it is. What about you?

Prayer: Yes, Lord, it is time. I do choose to join your family and take my place. I repent for believing the lies that said I was not good enough and did not reach the standard and mark. Please forgive me and set me free. I want to know the truth and the freedom that comes from living in the truth. I want to take my place and be the person you created me to me. Thank you, for loving me the way you do. Thank you, for choosing me before the foundation of the world to be holy and blameless in your sight. Thank you, amen.

Day Two Hundred Thirty

Ephesians 1: 7-8 `In him we have received redemption through his blood, the forgiveness of sins, in accordance with the riches of God's grace that he lavished on us with all wisdom and understanding.'

Remember back when you were in school and the teacher wrote the lessons on the blackboard? Remember how white the board would get after a day of writing on it? Now do you remember how clean and black it looked the next morning after it had been cleaned and washed? Or, how about those of you who have gone walking on a sandy beach and as you walked along the beach you left your footprints in the sand? Sometimes we would even look back to see our prints denting the sand, reminding us of where we had been and the marks we had left behind us. Then a wave came in, washing over both your feet and footprints. The footprints were no longer there. The marks in the sand were gone forever. The footprints have been completely washed away, never to be remembered by those who will come after us. These two examples are the illustrations of what God does with our past sins, mistakes, wrong choices, blunders, and all those other things we have done. The ones we wished had never happened. When we embrace the forgiveness of God and receive His forgiveness into our lives and hearts, our past sins, mistakes, wrong choices and blunders become like the washed blackboard or the footprints washed by the wave. They are remembered no more. Forgotten forever! We may remember them but God does not. He forgets them and washes them from His memory, never to be brought up again. We may try to bring them up but God will always say "Sorry I don't remember that one. No, that mistake is not in my memory banks either." This is the absolute gift of love, mercy, grace and forgiveness given to us by our God when we confess our sins, and get down and honest with ourselves and who we are. The gift becomes ours when we choose to embrace it and make it ours. There are no ifs, ands or buts. When we accept the gift of God's forgiveness by telling God how sorry we are for the mess we have made of our lives, God is faithful and just and promises to forgive our sins/mistakes/messes, never to be remembered any more. Then, if we ask the Holy Spirit to come in our hearts, we have all we need in order to continue to live in the freedom of forgiveness; we have a new beginning through repentance and forgiveness. What more can we ask for? The greatest gift ever given is now ours. We can walk with our heads held high. We can walk with our hearts free from what was. We can now come into the plan of prosperity God has for our lives. God's love begins to rise up within us. Our spirit, say, yes. I know that I am redeemed and set free to live again. A new beginning is mine!

Prayer: Thank you, God, for giving me such a great gift. Thank you for giving me the gift of forgiveness, the gift of being given a second chance to do something with my life and to let go of what was and to come into all that is and could be. I am so grateful and thankful for your love, for your forgiveness, and your love for me. How do I ever say thank you? How do I ever express all that I am feeling with this truth inside of me? Thank you, Father, for loving me the way you do and for giving up so much for me, amen.

Day Two Hundred Thirty-one

Ephesians 1:3 `Praise be to the God and Father of our Lord Jesus Christ, who has blessed us in the heavenly realms with every spiritual blessing in Christ.'

You are blessed! To be blessed means we are made hallow or consecrated in God's eyes. We are divinely cared for and loved by God. We are spoken well of by God to His angels and everyone else in heaven. We have prosperity given to us. We can live in happiness. We are protected and preserved by the Most High God. We live in God's favour and peace. We are held in reverence as a saint of God. We can enjoy the bliss of heaven and all the perks therein. Being blessed by the Most High God, means that we can live truly live. We can have pleasures and contentment and have good fortune bestowed upon us by God. All this is ours and has been ours, since the beginning of time. God has in the past tense already blessed us, in the heavenly realms with every spiritual blessing in Christ. Every blessing that God has stored up for us, has already been set into motion by Christ in the heavenly realms. The plan of our blessings was set into motion, when God set the foundation of the world. When God decided to create the world and everything in it, God decided to bless us. The blessings were given and set in the creative work of God. We are blessed and have been blessed for a very long time, only we didn't know it. Therefore, we did not embrace the blessings and missed out on so much of all that God wants us to have. All the prosperity, love, forgiveness, healing, joy, mercy, grace, honouring and so on that we were not told could be ours. We lived our lives as if we were not blessed. We lived like we did not deserve the blessings God built into His creation. That was then; this is now. Today the truth is out! We are already blessed. All we need do is enter into the blessings, receiving all that God has in store for us. All we do is say "Yes, God, I want the blessings you have for me. I am willing to say yes to you and the truth of your love for me. I say yes to the provision you have for me, as your chosen beloved child. I am sorry for not living my life believing I was already blessed, for not living my life in a way that was open to receive all that you have set in place for me. Help me to start today living my life in your blessing, in all that you want for me to have. Help me to start today to open my mind, heart and life to the truth of your promises and blessings in and for my life and for me your child. Teach me how to be your beloved daughter/son. Teach me how to live in the glory of your name and truth. I choose to be a part of your blessings and all that they mean to my life, and who you created me to be."

Prayer: Thank you, God, for blessing me even before I had life within me. Thank you, for setting my blessings into motion when you were forming your creation. I am blessed. Help me, to live as one who is already blessed both now and forever. Change my heart and my mind, so that I can receive all that you have stored up for me and desire me to have. In Jesus' name, amen.

Day Two Hundred Thirty-two

Colossians 3:13 'Bear with each other and forgive whatever grievances you may have against one another. Forgive as the Lord forgave you.'

I was asked the other day what I thought about our world and how it had changed. My response was from what I can see, we have lost our ability to have respect. Respect for whom and what we are as people, for others and for God. We live our lives thinking only about ourselves, what we want, and what would make us happy. We get so focused on our desires for our lives, focused on what we want or think we want, focused on ourselves, we forget about others and what they need, want or desire. Today the lesson is all about bearing with one another and forgiving each other, no matter what the grievance. Looking beyond ourselves, seeing what is happening outside of us in the lives of others.

To bear is to move while holding up or supporting another or something, to permit growth of something, to support the weight of someone or something. In other words, to bear with each other is to walk this life journey together. Being there for each other. Helping one another carry the load, or give a helping hand. To be willing to not think only of ourselves, but rather to think of others even before we think ourselves. To be willing to do whatever it takes to live in harmony and peace. To live as people who are willing to let go of grievances by forgiving. To let go by letting all of us be human beings, who make mistakes and wrong choices. To be willing to accept everyone at face value, without trying to make him/her into something they are not. Forgiving them for not being exactly what you want them to be. Letting them be who they were created to be even if they have a whole bunch of bumps and bruises, cracks and crevices. Forgiving them for being different or thinking differently. Being willing to walk this life journey with everyone, regardless of who and what they are or do. We live in such a diverse world with so many differences and styles. The challenge is to love and live in the diversity with harmony and peace, not holding any grievances against anyone or anything. The grievance, when we are honest with ourselves, only hurts us. It does not hurt the one we are holding the grievance against. I know first hand. There are several correctional officers at work who are not talking with me, because of the last couple of strikes we have gone through. When they see me it is as if I do not exist. They have to work with me and do their jobs, but that is as far as it goes. They are holding such grievances against me they cannot be in the same room with me. What is it doing to them? Eating them away on the inside. What is it doing to me? The truth, nothing! I would like to be liked by everyone and have everyone talk and be pleasant to me. That would be great, but that is not how it happens, especially in corrections. In reality not everyone gets along, so either I choose to let them drive my bus because of the way they feel about me, or I let it go. I have tried to make things right. I have tried to right the wrong, but they choose to reject it. Therefore there is nothing more I can do. I choose to let it go and forgive them. That way I can get on with living my life. My choice is to live in harmony with them. I choose to forgive them. I do my part and that is all God asks of us. I bear the load of their anger and hate but still choose to love them and treat them fairly even if it does not come back to me. Why? Because when I do I am a) living in God's call and command b) driving my own bus on the inside and not them c) free to be me without the other person telling me who I am or what I will do. I get to be free and that is what God is asking of each and every one of us. The call of love! Regardless of what they do or of their choices.

Prayer: Father, help me to forgive, no matter what others are doing or saying, help me to, live in peace and harmony with everyone, regardless of how they are living or what they are doing. Help me, to be a light in this world of darkness. Help me, to be willing to be the one who lets go of all grievances. Help me, to walk in the freedom you died to give me. I no longer desire to get caught up in what others are doing or not doing. In Jesus' name, amen.

Day Two Hundred Thirty-three

Romans 12:2 `Do not conform any longer to the patterns of this world, but be transformed by the renewing of your mind. Then you will be able to test and approve, what God's will it is---his good, pleasing and perfect will.'

I am always amazed at what the world says is important. How I need to have whatever it is they are selling in order to be truly happy and have the approval of the world. Here are some examples. The shampoo commercial where they advertise if I use the shampoo, you will have an orgasmic experience every single time, with incredible excitement and pleasure. Well I used it for three days because I got a sample in the mail. Yes, it made my hair smell nice, but I did not have an orgasmic experience, nor did anyone even notice I used it. How about this one for aftershave, the person uses this brand of aftershave and all the girls are falling all over him. Just going crazy over him and his aftershave. Or, the chewing gum commercial where the girl puts the gum in her mouth. Every person she passes sings 'don't leave me this way or don't do this to me' suggesting that chewing gum can cause such a reaction in other people. The negative power of the world wants us to live by the world's standards and expectations; being conformed to what the world says is right, good and . Living this way is not true, nor is it the way to truth life and happiness. The Scripture for today says, don't go there. Do not get caught up in what the world says is important and valuable. Rather, listen to what God says will give you life. Listen to what God says will help you to live your life with value, worth and purpose. Only God can tell us how to have true life and real freedom within us. Truth and freedom need to come from and be fostered by what is true, by what is actually , which is the Word of God. It comes by not conforming to what the world says is important and the way to true life, happiness and freedom. There needs to be a transforming of ideas, thoughts, and beliefs that we now have because of what we have been taught or told. One way to transform our old selves, patterns and beliefs is to put new data into the memory banks and pathways of our belief systems. One way is to change what we watch on TV or at the movies; to change or alter our choice of words and the words we use to describe our feelings, thoughts or opinions. For example if I use a lot of swearing or cursing words, the change is to use other words instead, words that bless or build up. The result is new patterns being formed within us. The natural or automatic choice of words becomes , instead of life-stealing. Change is beginning to be a reality and now manifest in your choice of words or expressions. Maybe it will mean changing some of the products we use that remind us of what we are trying to change or alter in our daily lives. By starting small we can begin to change the path we are on so that our destination becomes different and the outcomes more . Start small and watch as you grow and achieve your goals of choosing life. The transforming of your minds, old patterns and behaviours leads to new more ways of living our lives.

Prayer: Father, help me to transform my mind and ways. Help me, to see life through your eyes and what you have for me. Help me, to be the person you created me to be, and not the person the world says I need to be. Thank you, Father, for loving me just the way I am, for helping me to be more of who you desire me to be, amen.

Day Two Hundred Thirty-four

> *2 Samuel 22: 2-3 'He said: "the Lord is my rock, my fortress and my deliverer; my God is my rock, in whom I take refuge, my shield and the horn of my salvation. He is my stronghold, my refuge and my saviour----from violent men you save me".'*

God, if we will but let God, is our rock, fortress, deliverer, refuge, shield, stronghold and salvation. When we study these words, we discover that they are really strong words. Strong words showing strength and protection, strong words that help us see ourselves safe and secure, love and protected. Words that help us to look beyond ourselves and our weaknesses, and into the powerful truth of God's strength and provision in and for our lives if we but allow ourselves to trust and venture forth in God. Words that give us hope beyond today and what we are currently going through, and into all the possibilities that are ours because of all that God is today and always will be. Words that embrace our weakness with God's strength! When we reflect on these words, we begin to see a place that is safe and secure, no matter what. No matter what is happening in our lives or not happening. No matter what we can see or not see. A place that is constant and sure, always available to us at any time or any place we may be. When we have our shield and rock with us, we are always safe and secure in the shelter of that shield and rock. What is a rock? A rock is solid, hard and if large enough unmoveable. Even a small rock can cause tremendous damage if used in the wrong way. Rocks can harm and cause harm to property or a person. Yet a rock can be a true and solid foundation upon which you can build a house a solid house on a firm foundation that can withstand the storms that come our way. Rocks are used to build walls and houses. Rocks are solid and a dependable building supply. Rocks are used to build fortresses and places of refuge. They can also be used as a shield to protect and shelter. God says He is our rock. The solid foundation upon which we can stand, knowing the protection that is ours, because we have God, the rock, as our shield, fortress, refuge and stronghold. I do not know about you but as for me this information brings me an incredible amount of courage and strength, not only in the times of trouble in my life, but in all times, no matter what is going on. If I take God at His word, I can forever and always have a shield and fortress protecting me and guarding me through everything and anything. When I keep my eyes and heart on God, I find the safety and security I am seeking and searching for in my life, and that part of me that needs the safety and security of God is at peace. Therefore, I am at peace. I do not ever have to be afraid or in a powerless place, for God is with me. God is everything I need, no matter what is happening in my life. I can honestly say with all the faith in the world that it is true. God is my safe hiding place no matter what.

Prayer: Thank you, Father, for being my foundation, my solid rock and fortress in which I can find safety and refuge. Thank you, that you are the biggest Dad on the block and I am safe and secure in you at all times. Thank you, for always being here for me and loving me the way you do, no strings attached. Thank you, for being my Heavenly Father and my Dad, because I need a Heavenly Father. I especially need a Dad. I am truly grateful and I love you, amen.

Day Two Hundred Thirty-five

1 Corinthians 16:14 `Do everything in love.'

Can you imagine what this world would be like if we did everything in love? Can you imagine how your life the lives of those around you would be affected? Can you glimpse at how different your life would be if you loved yourself and did only what was life giving for you? And then carried that same love over to your other relationships? It is hard to imagine, but if we would smile, how so much better life would be. We would look at others and ourselves so differently. The other reality is, if we are not living our lives in love and loving others, we are doing things and making choices that are not . If I am not actively loving myself or others, then I am doing something else. Whatever the something else is. A reminder of what love is. To love is to do the higher good for the one we are giving our love to. Doing the higher good is just that. Choosing to do what is best for the person we love, which is not necessarily what is easier or the easiest thing to do. To choose to build up and not tear down, to be and not life-stealing. 1 Corinthians 13: 4-8 describes love this way. `Love is patient, love is kind. It does not envy, it does not boast, it is not proud. It is not rude, it is not self-seeking, it is not easily angered, it keeps no record of wrongs. Love does not delight in evil but rejoices with the truth. It always protects, always perseveres. Love never fails.' To love in everything we do is to be willing to walk and do in such a way that the outcomes are always , even when we have to do the hard choices or the tough love. To love is be kind and patient in our dealings with others and situations. There are so many times when we are not kind or lose patience. Why? Because whatever is happening does not look or feel like we want it to look or feel. When we put ourselves first, forgetting about the other person or the situation we are in, we are not necessarily doing the high good for either ourselves or the other person. When we love first, we put the higher good of the other person or situation first, so that life can be the outcome and result. When I seek or do only what I feel or think is right, then I am putting me first, and what I want, which is not loving the other person or situation. It is only caring for or thinking about myself, what I want or think I need and forgetting about the other person and what they want or need. To love in everything we do is to be willing to walk, talk, act and react in the higher good of everything we are in and everything we are doing. That allows love to be the primary fuel, which in turns opens the door and pathway for more love, opening the door for love to be the result for others and for us. In everything, not just some things, putting love first. Putting love first and foremost in all we do, say, think and live. When we live this way watch what love does.

Prayer: Holy Spirit, remind me to love at all times and in all situations. Remind me, when I am not putting love first. Teach me, how to love more and more freely. Show me how to put love first no matter how I am feeling or what my carnal self wants. I know love is the answer. Therefore, help me to be a part of the answers to life by loving first in all I am and all I do. In Jesus' name, amen.

Day Two Hundred Thirty-six

John 4: 27 'Just then his disciples returned and were surprised to find him talking with a woman. But no one asked, "What do you want?" or "Why they are you talking with her?"'

The disciples returned and were surprised to find Jesus talking with a woman. The rule was men and women were not to be in close proximity. They were to be apart unless they were from the same family or married. There was to be a distance between them and men and women were not talk together privately. This was especially the case if they did not previously know each other. When we take time to think about it, there are so many written and unwritten rules we are asked to follow regardless whether they are or life-stealing. Jesus in all His relationships, whether with men or women, made it very clear that everyone is equal. Everyone is the same in God's eyes. There is no distinction between men and women. There is no difference between the sexes, the races, the peoples, the cultures or any other division we may want to make. God's love is for everyone bar none! No one is exempt from the love God has for each and every one of us. No One. If that is true and it is----in God's eyes we are all the same whether yellow, black or white, we are all precious in God's sight. God loves us all the same and equally. I know that is hard to believe and even harder to do times. I know when there is societal pressure to not like someone and to treat him/her differently, it is hard to stand on your own and say "no, I will not treat them differently or badly, just because I am being told to. I will not separate myself from them, just because others are telling me to separate myself from them and who they are." That is why when the disciples came back and found Jesus talking to the woman, they did not ask why Jesus was talking to her. They did not ask what was going on, or why Jesus was alone with a female. It is hard to not bow to social pressure, to not brush everyone from whatever group with the same brush even though they are not all the same. Besides what does it do us, when we set ourselves apart? When we see ourselves as better than another person or group of people? Does it not feel wrong or bad on the inside? Do we not become tainted and pent up on our insides? Do we not start feeling negative and dark on our insides? Does it not have a negative affect upon the way we see not only them, but others as well? Does it not affect the way we see ourselves? Jesus here is not saying we have to like everyone, or what they do or who they are. Jesus is saying that we have to love them and treat everyone with honour, dignity and respect. When we do treat everyone with honour, dignity and respect, we allow ourselves to be free from prejudice and other such negatives in our lives. When we love everyone as being equal and loved we love ourselves. When we love everyone as a precious, special, chosen, beloved child of God, we are blessed. We are free on the inside to be who God created us to be. We allow everyone the same privilege as we have both in society's eyes but more importantly in God's eyes. In the end pleasing God is all that truly matters. Pleasing God brings us true life with abundant living.

Prayer: Holy Spirit, show me in my life the areas where I do not love everyone equally or where I treat some people differently. Help me, to love everyone equally the way you love us. Help me, to be an instrument of love and harmony in this world of such hate and prejudice. Forgive me and teach me, your way of love. In Jesus' name, amen.

Day Two Hundred Thirty-seven

Acts 3: 18-19 `But this is how God fulfilled what he had foretold through all the prophets, saying that this Christ would suffer. Repent, then, and turn to God, so that your sins may be wiped out, that times of refreshing may come from the Lord,'

In order to be set free from a sin or wrong choice there needs to be a sacrifice, a shedding of blood. In order for us to be set free from all the wrong choices we have made, plus the ones others have made on our behalf, there needs to be a shedding of blood for the atonement of the sin/ wrong choice/mistake. God set into motion the ultimate sacrifice, which was His Son, Jesus the Christ, to be the atoning sacrifice for sin, all sin, throughout all of time. This means no one in any time frame is left out of the saving, atoning grace given to all of humanity, through the gift of God's Son's death on the cross. Our sin (our need for self and having life on our terms and conditions) can be released from our lives, wiped away, no longer a ball and chain around our necks, holding us back and preventing us from being the person we were really meant to be and not the person we have become. We can be set totally free from all that was, set free from the bondage it holds us in, set on a new path, which enables us to truly love and be loved as we are meant to. When we repent of all that we have done wrong, and the wrong choices we have made in ourselves and towards others, a time of refreshing comes into our hearts and spirits. A time of cleansing and washing that brings a freedom like no other, which in turn allows us to walk a new path of light, hope and freedom. A time where we can see with a new set of eyes, seeing as we have not seen for a long time or ever in our lives. When we give ourselves permission to really get down and honest with who and what we are as a person, honest with all the choices we have made and telling God all about it. God chooses in His infinite love and mercy to free us and forgive us, so that we can live in the light and not the darkness of what was. When we tell God all about the secrets and shame in our lives and the things we have done to hurt ourselves, God takes it one step further and sets us free from them. When we tell God about all the things others have done to us, we know a freedom, a releasing take place in our hearts and spirits. We know forgiveness and acceptance. We get to know what it means to have God's gift of grace (His unmerited loving favour) being poured into our hearts and lives setting us free to love again. Think about a time when you went on a vacation, or away to a retreat for a time out, or just took some time just for yourself. Remember how you felt afterwards and how your body, mind, spirit and feelings were back in a place of balance. You felt refreshed, almost clean again. That is how it is when we give ourselves permission to get down and get honest with God and with ourselves. When we take a time out to say it like it is, not holding anything back, the benefit or blessing that comes is a refreshing in our spirit that feels like no other. A refreshing, a cleansing of who and what we are as a person. The door is open for this to happen in and to our lives. God made sure of that when God allowed His Son, Jesus to die on the cross for us and our sins/wrong choices. All we need do is walk through the door with an open, receptive and repentant heart. Then watch everything God does as we risk and move through.

Prayer: Thank you, Father God, for setting into place a plan that would enable me to be free from what was, free to enter into all that could be. I am willing to risk and walk through the door of your gift of mercy, love and grace. I am sorry, for all that I have done in the past that has separated me from you and you from me. I am sorry for all the wrong choices and mistakes I have made, and the way they have affected others and myself. I am sorry, for holding onto all those things that just kept me locked in my self made prison. I want to be free and forgiven. Please set me free and forgive me, so that I can have a time of refreshing and freedom in my life. In Jesus' holy and precious name I pray, amen.

Day Two Hundred Thirty-eight

> *Luke 6: 20 & 24 `Looking at his disciples, he said: "Blessed are you who are poor for yours is the kingdom of God. But woe to you who are rich, for you have already received your comfort."'*

How can it be a blessing to be poor in spirit? How is it that when we are at the point in our lives where there is nothing left of our own reserves or power, we find the kingdom of God? Why can't we have the Kingdom of God and ourselves as well? Let us think about that for a moment. When we are at the end of the rope and have nothing left inside of us, all our resources are gone, the natural thing for us to do is to reach up to heaven and ask God to help us. While we still have resources within ourselves available to us, chances are we will use them and not turn to God. It is not until I am hopeless in my self that I even want to reach out to God for help, let alone admit that I do not have enough on my own to make it. It is not until we let go of everything we are, and everything that is happening around or inside of us, humbling who we are as people and say HELP, that help can arrive. When we do finally let go of self, and all self is, when we have reached our bottom and are totally open to receiving God, God's presence and provision comes into our lives. Until we take our hands off and let God have the reigns of our life. We are still using whatever resources we may or may not have to solve our problems or get out of the situation we are in. We are still driving our own life, depending on ourselves. When we take our hands off and let go, God now has control and starts driving our life. At our point of totally poverty and bankruptcy, the presence of God takes over. The Holy Spirit begins to fill us with what we need in order to do what we need to do. The Kingdom of God becomes present in and to us. We are blessed. It is not until we get to the point of poverty, bankruptcy in our lives and resources, letting go of our need for self and self-sufficiency, we can see and know the Kingdom of God present and active in our lives. If we are relying on our bank accounts or possessions, or intelligence or our ability to make it no matter what, there is no room for God's grace and provision. When I have nothing left but God, it is then and only then that I begin to see that God is all I really need. I do not need the other stuff to make it through. I just need the mercy and grace of God and God's love and provision for my life. Then the Kingdom of God is present, real and available to us. Then the poverty is lifted and the Kingdom becomes real and alive within us. Woe to the rich who rely only on their own wealth and ability to provide for themselves for they never develop a relationship with God or the ability to rest in God and His presence in our lives.

Prayer: I am learning that in order to be truly rich, I must be poor in my spirit and my need for God. I surrender! I surrender my need for self and for having life my way and on my terms and conditions. I surrender everything I have and everything I am and put my trust in you. I surrender me, and I take on you, Father God. I know when I do, I will be richer and more fulfilled and complete in you. I know I will have everything I need. Thank you, amen.

Wendy Bussell

Day Two Hundred Thirty-nine

1 Corinthians 2:5 'So that your faith might not rest on men's wisdom, but on God's power.'

What is God's power? God's power is truth, light, love, freedom, hope, salvation, mercy, grace to name but a few. God's power is being able to live in the power of God, which enables us to live free from what others think, say or do. To walk as individuals in the great family of God with all wisdom and power, that comes from the presence of God in our lives and hearts. God's power enables us to live according to God's path of life and by His Word, which is life. When we live in God's power, we live as the individuals we were meant to be. We let go of the things that prevent us from being all that we were created to be. God's power within us truly does give us the ability to live whole, productive lives, in freedom and light. The way into God's power is through faith, through choosing to believe in what God says and putting that belief into action. Believing is great and good, but putting that belief into action brings life to our beliefs, and this makes our beliefs real and visible in our lives. Resting on the world's or man's power is trusting in what man and the world says is true and real and valid. Trusting in the world says I believe that as human beings we have all the answers, plus the ability to get the answers; that our wisdom is enough to get us through to the other side; that our wisdom is equal to or greater than God's and who and what God is. Man's wisdom or the world's wisdom says we ourselves are the bottom line. As the bottom line we have the ability, authority and power to do whatever we want, without suffering the consequences. If we are being honest with ourselves, when we trust and rely on man's power or the world's power, we fall short and end up with a whole lot of emptiness. When we trust solely in our own power and the power of man, if we are being honest with ourselves, it comes up short. What happens when we reach the end of our resources, and there are still questions? What happens

410

when we reach the top rung on the ladder, only to find there is nothing put emptiness there, the feeling of being hollow on the inside with nothing to take away the hollowness? Where do we go when we have tapped out all possible avenues of life, only to find a dead end and with nothing to show for all we have done or thought we have done? When we trust in man or the world, we come up short of the mark. That is the way it works. When we trust and have faith in the power of God and God's wisdom and truth, we find ourselves yes, having more questions and sometimes not having all the answers, but we have a knowing and peace that makes the not knowing or not having all the answers, okay. It is okay because we know the one who does have the answers. We know that God is well able to see us through, whatever it is we are facing. The difference between trusting in God and trusting in man is God is the beginning and the end. Therefore, God has the all-knowing power, sitting outside of time. Human beings are finite and sit in linear time. Therefore, we are limited to what we can see within linear time and its limits and limitations.

Prayer: Heavenly Father, I am so grateful that you are all knowing and have the truth of true life and living. Help me, to trust you more. To trust the power of you and your Word and Spirit working in my life and for my life. I am beginning to realize that without you I sit in darkness because I fall short. I fall short because you are the beginning and the end. You have all the answers to life and living. Help me, to be that person you created me to be in the first place with all the gifts, talents and abilities you placed within my heart and spirit. Thank you, Father, that you are enough, for whatever life is, has and will be, in all circumstances, amen.

Day Two Hundred Forty

Luke 6: 21a & 25a

'Blessed are you who are hungry now, for you will be satisfied. Woe to you who are well fed now for you will go hungry.'

I have often wondered to myself how this verse in Scripture could be valid? How can we be blessed if we are hungry? How can we know the blessing of God in the place of hunger? The answer is not as hard or complex as I first thought it would be. When I am hungry my focus is yes, on food and the filling of my stomach, but once the hunger goes, I settle into the calm of emptiness. I feel an incredible satisfaction in the hunger that can only be the presence of God, the reality and truth of God within us, and especially when we are hungry and longing to be filled. I know this is hard to grasp and even understand, but there is an incredible presence that comes from God in our hunger and our need to fill that hunger. When I am in the place of need, not only from a physical perspective, but also from a spiritual perspective, there is a true searching after God and God's ability and desire to fill His children, His creation. God provides a satisfaction, a deep infilling, an infilling from God that can only happen inside of us when there is room for the filling to take place. When I am full, when my belly is satisfied. When I am not calling out for food or when my spirit is being filled with lots of things that are not of God. There is no room for God and no place for God to fill us. When I am full, I am not looking for anything, for I do not need anything! My hunger is satisfied and not calling out for more. When I am in that place of being full, I do not have need for food nor am I looking to food. BUT, when I am hungry, I am always on the outlook for something that will fill the emptiness and the longing in my belly or spirit. It is exactly the same with our relationship with God. When I am hungry for more of God and God within me, I am constantly searching for God, seeking God out wherever He may be found. My relationship with God deepens. I find

God everywhere I look. The result is a sense of being well fed and satisfied. A sense of being fed up with God. I am satisfied! If I am well fed by all kinds of things other than God, then when I need God. I will find myself very hungry. I will be empty spiritually with a longing for spiritual food. I will be longing to be filled with a sense of God and who and what God is. I will have discovered my need for God, but the cupboard is empty with nothing in it to help with my hunger or longing. Just like the nursery rhyme `Old Mother Hubert went to the cupboard to find her poor dog a bone, when she got there the cupboards was bare.' In order to fill our hunger for God we need first to know we are hungry. Then we can begin to chase after God. We can begin to chase after God who can and will fill us. Therefore causing us to be not only full but satisfied as well. It is not until I am truly hungry do I realize my need for food. It is the same with our relationship with God. It is not until I am truly hungry spiritually that I seek after spiritual food.

Prayer: Father, I am beginning to know that hunger in my spirit, in my heart. I do have a deep need of you in and for my life. I am learning that within me and in my heart, there is an emptiness that cannot be filled by anything else. I want you to fill me with your presence and your Spirit. I want my heart and spirit to be filled both now and always. Thank you, for showing me my need of you, and my need to be hungry for you in my life and heart. I am so grateful, for the way you chase after me and never give up on me. Please do not ever give up, amen.

Day Two Hundred Forty-one

Luke 6: 21b & 25b

`Blessed are you who weep now, for you will laugh. Woe to you who laugh now, for you will mourn and weep.'

One of the things life has taught me as a human being and as a Chaplain is if we stuff our feelings and emotions, bottling them up and hiding them away, pretending they are not there and not a part of us, we lose a part of ourselves. This hiding or pretending causes us to lose aart of ourselves. It blocks life from touching us or even being a part of our lives. When we shut our feelings and emotions away, locking them up and not dealing with them nor processing them, not only do we block or lock away the bad feelings, but the good ones as well. We lose our ability to feel and have a variety of feeling in our lives. There is such an incredible need to work through our feelings both good and bad, so that we can put them in a place of balance, so that we can have all our feelings and emotions available to us at all times. When we need to grieve over the loss of a loved one, we need to grieve. We need to let ourselves cry and weep and mourn, for it is in the crying and weeping and mourning that we find peace and the joy that comes in the morning. The ability to laugh is restored to us. We become whole again with all the feelings and emotions God has given to us to use and enjoy, even the tears and wailing. The reality is if you do not process the feelings; they will come back to haunt us when we least expect them. There is an expression that goes like this pay me now or pay me later. The reality is you will one day have to pay the bill. If you have stuffed away all the hard, difficult or bad feelings and emotions, when you finally do pay the bill, it will be a huge one that will cost you lots. But if you pay as you go, then when the final accounting is done, the unpaid parts will be small and easy to handle, not to mention you will have lived your life to the full, with a full range of feelings and emotions. You will not have been afraid of them or have had the need to hide them away. We are truly blessed when we weep when we need to weep, for we can also laugh when the laughter is there. When we laugh without weeping, the tears will eventually come and demand their fair share. They will come like the floodgates that have burst their way out. The water is running wild, maybe even uncontrollable, in its power and force. The wonder of living life God's way is to weep when we need to weep, and laugh when joy fills your heart. There is a time for everything. A time for weeping and a time for laughing! Let us enjoy both, for both are very much a part of us.

Prayer: Father, I am afraid of my tears and the power behind them. I have locked them away for so long. Help me to open up and let my true feelings and emotions out. Help me so that I can live in the joys and freedom you have for me. Father, I have cried my fair share of tears, now help me to laugh and let myself feel the joys of laughter once again. I need balance in my feelings and emotions. Help me, to have that balance. Thank you for loving me just the way I am, but too much to just leave me here. In Jesus' most precious name, amen.

Day Two Hundred Forty-two

Luke 6: 22 & 26

> *'Blessed are you when men hate you, when they exclude you and insult you and reject your name as evil, because of the Son of Man. Woe to you when all men speak well of you, for that is how their fathers treated the false prophets.'*

None of us like to be persecuted or set apart as different. None of us like the feeling of being excluded or insulted or rejected. We hate being hated; it hurts. In today's day and age, there is a lot of hating and hurting going on. If someone is different, they are often persecuted or excluded from the main stream. If you have a different faith or faith tradition, and that tradition has done something that in is evil the eyes of other people, everyone from that faith tradition is painted with the same brush. It is hard to face such hardships and find peace in the midst of all the insults and hatred. Jesus says when that happens because of your relationship with Jesus; do not consider it a bad thing, or a burden too hard to bear. Rather consider it all joy, for you are company with all those who have gone before you, who have suffered the same persecution and hardships. It is the way generations before you have dealt with those of us who choose to be a part of God and God's kingdom. When we are choosing to live our lives from a spirit of love, honour and respect, when we guard the dignity of all we meet, there are always going to be those who will hate us for loving and treating all people with love, honour, dignity and respect. There will always be those around us who want to put our lights out, for our light makes their darkness seem so much darker. Part of the cost of being a child of God is there will always be people and groups of people who want to hate, hurt, harm, insult and any other number of hardships upon you. They have always been a part of God's creation and will always be a part of it until God says enough. Know that God has not forgotten you!!!!!! You are actually blessed in the hardships, for God knows and sees all that is happening. You are company with the saints and prophets who have gone before us and who will come after us. Let your light shine. Do not put it out or let others put it out. When we let our God light shine, others can see there is another path. There is hope for them. When we let our God light shine, we pierce the darkness, exposing it for what it truly is, darkness. Yes, there is a responsibility in being a part of God and God being a part of us. At times it is hard to go against the flow and be different in this world, but the blessings so out weigh the hardships and insults. We have God on our side, and if God is for us, who can be against us? If God is on our side, who can stand against us? Are you being excluded today or insulted or persecuted? Then count it all joy for your God light is shining brightly. Others are seeing God within you. Rejoice. Count it all joy. For your Father in heaven is standing with you through it all as you face these hardships with Him by your side. Count it all joy my brothers and sisters, for you are not alone. You are a part of the great family of God. It is not easy to withstand the insults and persecution of others. It is not easy when people hate and want to harm you because of your faith and relationship with God. In my mind that tells me that I am on the right track. The darkness does not care if you are not a threat to the darkness. The darkness only cares when we know the truth and are standing in the light of the one and only true living God. Rejoice my friends, rejoice.

Prayer: Father, it is so hard to stand up when we are being treated badly and with such hate at times. It is so hard to not put our light out, to not try to stop the persecution and hatred from coming our way and the harm it brings to us. Without your help, I do not have the strength to keep standing. Help me, to let my light shine no matter what is happening around me and by whom. Help me, as you have helped so many before me. Thank you, for being my constant source of all life and light. I am truly grateful and will stand as light in this very dark world if you will stand with me, amen.

Day Two Hundred Forty-three

Romans 8:18 'Those controlled by the sinful nature cannot please God.'

'Those controlled by the sinful nature cannot please God.' That makes sense to even me. If I am living according to my sinful nature, I am not doing things that are pleasing to God. I am not living my life in such a way that brings honour to God. When I live according to my sinful nature, I am sowing seeds that will reap a harvest of sin (self).

What does it look like to live according to our sinful self or nature? When we are living for self, we want, or even demand, life to go our way. We demand and do what we want our life to do. I want what I want, when I want it, and that is now, thank you very much. I do not care whom I hurt, or who gets in the way of my getting life on my terms and conditions. I live life doing what I want, when I want to do it. What does this look like? I am attracted to another person and I want to be in a relationship with that other person, but they are married and so am I. I chase after them anyway, not counting the cost, or being concerned about who I hurt along the way, not caring about how my choices are going to affect others or myself. I see only my need for the relationship. I drink too much. I know I drink too much. I know the money I am wasting on the booze is costing my family and causing them to suffer unnecessary hardships, but I drink anyway. I drink because it takes away the pain, hurt, emptiness, etc. inside of me. I matter; therefore, I do not care about what I am doing to those I say I love. I want to move ahead in my career and advance in my work place. I know I am absent from my spouse and family. I know I am missing out on so much of what is happening in my family and their lives. I know all this but I still keep working and avoid the price tag being placed on the ones I say I love. Only to wake up one morning to find my family is no longer there, waiting for me to come home. Think of your own life now and what you are doing that fosters your sinful nature. What are you doing that is stealing not only your relationship with God, but with those you love. Think about how you are living your life for your sinful self and not for God. When I live to the sinful nature, I cannot be pleasing to God. When I am living for me and me alone I cannot live in healthy relationships. When I am sowing seeds into me and me alone, I am not sowing seeds into my relationship with God, not to mention what I am doing to those people God has placed in my life. I am living to me and not to others or God. Living that way is not pleasing to God, not to mention harmful to our family. Harmful to the ones we say we care about. To live our lives in a way that is pleasing to God we need to sow seeds that are and pleasing to God. We need to build healthy and positive relationships living our lives in a way that pleases God, also enables us to live our lives in a way that brings life to those whom we love and to ourselves. When we let go of our sinful nature and live life according to God's plan and ways, what we get in return is true life and living.

Prayer: Father God, I am so sorry for living my life according to me, and what I want when I want it. Please forgive me, and help me to live my life in a way that is pleasing to you, my family and other relationships. I want my life to be pleasing to you, Father, and to those you have given me to love. I need your help to be the person you created me to be, and not the person I think I should be. Help me, to be not so selfish, demanding my life my way. In Jesus' name, I pray, amen.

Day Two Hundred Forty-four

2 Corinthians 5:17 'Therefore, if anyone is in Christ, he is a new creation; the old has gone, the new as come!'

Think about that for a moment. If anyone is in Christ they are a new creation. They get a second chance to start over. There is a new beginning. A new starting point in and for their life. The old is gone and the new has arrived. Our spiritual selves are made clean. We get to begin again, making different and better choices this go around. Getting a second chance to truly start over. The past and all it holds is washed clean, with a clean slate before us. Yes, we still need to look at our feelings and thinking. Yes, we still need to process what happened to us in the past and how it has affected us and maybe still does affect us, but we are no longer stuck there in the past. We are no longer caught in what was. We can move on to all that can be and is with God in our lives. There are now endless possibilities and avenues we can take. There is a cleansing that is taking place. There is a cleaning of our emotional, spiritual, thinking and behavioural patterns and behaviours. We can move into being the person we were created to be instead of being the one we were told we had to be or thought we were created to be. Now that is exciting! That is the best news we could ever be given. A second chance to embrace and hold our gifts, talents, abilities and everything else we have going on inside of us without the hindrances of and from our pasts. The new is now available to us. We can move and walk in it if we choose to. We can let go of what was, truly let go, drop it and move on with our lives. We get to see life through a different set of glasses, and it is amazing what our eyes can see now. You might be saying to yourself, this is impossible. It cannot be, it is like a miracle. Yes, you are right. It is a miracle. Only a miracle could change us from the inside out. Only the presence and power of God can cause us to have the opportunity of having our slates washed clean. Only God could free us from what was. Only God can allow us to come into all that God has in store for us. Are you ready to let God in? Are you ready to let God give you this second chance? Are you ready to ask God in through repentance (I'm sorry God for all I have done or not done)? Please forgive me and wash me anew. God, please set my spirit free so that I may live again and have a second chance. I want the cleansing power of the Holy Spirit working in me.

Prayer: Father, I am sorry for all I have done and not done. I am sorry for living the life I have been living, holding on to the past and not giving myself permission to forgive and let go. I am asking you to forgive me and to give me a second chance at living my life. Please wash me from the inside out so that I can be clean once again. Cleanse me so that I do not feel dirty on the inside any longer. I need you in my life to help me be the person you created me to be. I need you helping me live in today and to let go of yesterday. Thank you for all your help and forgiveness. Thank you for giving me a second chance at life and for being my constant helper. Thank you, Lord, for loving me and being all that you are to me, amen.

Day Two Hundred Forty-five

Numbers 20: 4-5 'Why did you bring to the Lord's community into this desert, that we and our livestock should die here? Why did you bring us up out of Egypt to this terrible place? It has no grain or figs, grapevines or pomegranates. And there is no water to drink!'

There are times in our faith journey when we feel like the Israelites did, wondering why the Lord has allowed us to be in the place we are, that does not have enough provisions to keep us going. We feel like we too are sitting in a desert. Spiritually we feel almost dead. Emotionally played out, hanging on by a thread. The ceiling is like cement or brass. Our prayers seem to be falling down all around us. The presence of God is absent from our lives. We feel like we are all alone with God nowhere to be found. This is called the dark night of the soul or a desert experience. Most people of faith who are on a spiritual journey will at one time or another feel this way; it is part of the growing process. When life is easy and going along smoothly and God is right here with you, you can feel His presence, your faith is strong, your prayers are being answered and all is well spiritually. These are wonderful times and such great blessings. These times sustain us and help us to know the assurance of God's love and presence. As much as these are incredible times in our lives and much needed, they are not necessarily the growing times or the deepening of our faith times. It is in the desert or the dark night of the soul times, when we find ourselves having to trust. Our faith and relationship with God and His promises is all we have left. Everything else is inaccessible or at least that is what it feels like. It is in these desert times in our lives, when we grow on a much deeper level in our trust and faith relationship with God. It is during these times of barrenness we find out just how faithful our God really is. It is during these times as the 'Footprints in the Sand' poem says; 'God carried me'. We are in a place of having to risk, just believing that God is still there. Hang on to this-----this too shall pass. It is in the desert times when our faith is truly tested and refined. Will I still trust God even when I cannot feel God? Can I still believe in God and God's promises even though I am not sure He is there/here? Will I still walk with God regardless of my feelings, trusting in the faithfulness of God and who God says He is? Can I stay in my faith journey for the long haul, regardless of what life is throwing my way? When we come out the other side of our dark night of the soul or desert experience, we realize on a deep, deep level just how faithful our God is. We have an assurance that says, I know my God is real and His promises are real and true. Do we like these times in our lives? The answer is a resounding NO! Are they worth the journey? The answer is OH YES. Do we want to repeat them? NO! We would exchange or deprive ourselves of the experience, or miss out all they have taught us? NO. None of us enjoy our desert or dark night of the soul times. We would rather the lessons be taught in different ways. But with those who have paved the road before us we will all say we wouldn't have missed the adventure, for it taught us more than we could have ever imagined.

Prayer: Holy Spirit, help me to trust you no matter what is happening in or to my life. Help me to walk by faith and not by sight. Help me to know the knowing that comes only from you and your truth and presence in my life. You are so very important to me. I cannot imagine life without you in it, always stay closer than close with me. Thank you, for your love and faithfulness. Thank you, for always being here with me, whether I can feel you or not. In Jesus' name, amen.

Day Two Hundred Forty-six

John 3:17 'For God did not send his Son into the world to condemn the world, but to save the world through him.'

There are so many times in our lives when we feel condemned or just not good enough. Times when the world yells at us saying you did not meet the mark or measure up, you are less than everyone else. Times when we have tried our very best, have given it our best shot, only to have someone point the finger at us, indicating our failure or lack of skills. We are beaten down. The image we have of ourselves begins to become distorted or blurred. We have a hard time seeing ourselves as valuable and worthwhile. It seems to be a fight each day just to keep going at times. Why bother? We aren't good enough anyway. We are damaged goods. Now here is the good news. Should dare to say the great news! God did not send His Son into this world, or down to us, to condemn the world or us. God sent His Son, Jesus the Christ, into the world for one reason and one reason only. So that we could be saved, set free, redeemed, accepted, given a second chance to do better. Jesus came into the world, so that we could be given a chance to hear the truth about who God created us to be. A chance to hear first hand, about the options God has put into place. So we would know how precious and valuable we really are. God is not looking down at us writing a list, chalking up all our bad choices and mistakes. God is not making a list of all the ways He can condemn us or point His finger at us. God is in no way, shape or form using anything we do, to exclude us from God. In fact, God is always calling out to us. Calling us back into a right relationship with ourselves, others and with God. God wants us to know true freedom, joy, love acceptance and forgiveness that are ours through His shed blood. God wants each and every one of us set free from the lies that say we are less than and not good enough. God wants us to know the truth. God wants us to know the freedom that comes from knowing the truth, the truth about who we are. The truth about why we were created. Others may want us lost in condemnation and lies; God does not. God wants us free to be all we were created to be. God sent His one and only Son into the world so that we might be saved from everything the world throws at us and tells us on a regular basis. God wants us to know how precious, special, valuable, worthwhile and chosen we are. God wants us to know that we are His Beloved. God wants us to know that we are already enough and definitely good enough. God wants us to know we are not junk because God does not make junk. God made you just the way He wanted you made. The challenge to each and every one of us is to take our place and be that person. The challenge is to let go of the lies and hear the truth about who we really are and why we were created. The challenge is to walk tall and be proud of who we are and whose we are. The challenge is to take our rightful place as the beloved son or daughter of God. Are we up to the challenge?

Prayer: Lord, I need to tell you how I have believed the lies that I have been told. The lies about how I am not as valuable as others, and definitely not good enough in some places of my life. I am sorry for believing the lies and not the truth of who you created me to be. I want to be saved from all the lies and truly set free in you. Save me and help me to not only know the truth, but to receive it deep within my spirit and self. Thank you, for creating me to be already enough I am grateful. In Jesus' most holy name, amen.

Day Two Hundred Forty-seven

John 6: 35 'Then Jesus declared, "I am the bread of life. He who comes to me, will never go hungry, and he who believes in me will never thirst.'

As human beings we are all created with a God shaped hole in our hearts. A God shaped hole that only God can fill. A hole designed to be filled with the love and presence of God, with the gift of God and His Holy Spirit. Lots of us try to fill the hole with all kinds of others things that are not God and then wonder why we are still feeling empty and hallow, wondering why we are not being satisfied or filled. Some of the things we try to put in the hole to fill us up are earning lots of money and having lots of things. I'll be at peace and in a place of harmony when I have all the money I need, when there is nothing I am lacking from a material perspective. How about filling the emptiness with drinking too much or taking all kinds of different drugs? The drugs or booze will fill me up, and if it doesn't, then at least I can forget about the hole for a while and get lost in the alcohol or drugs, only to discover the drugs and booze brings their own set of problems and struggles. We think being famous and having the attention of others will make us feel full, or having lots of people around will help with the loneliness on the inside. When I am famous, I will be a somebody, a person of great value and worth. People will know who I am. I will be noticed and that will make life just fine and dandy. How about eating too much? How many of us try to fill our emptiness with food, which in turn causes all sorts of other struggles in our lives? We turn to all sorts of things thinking they will stop the emptiness inside of us. The reality is only God can fill the hole. Only God can take away that empty nagging feeling. Only God can make us not thirsty or hungry anymore. Only God! That is why Jesus said to us 'I am the bread of life. I am what satisfies. I am what fills the hole', the emptiness inside of you, so that you feel full, so you no longer go searching everywhere for the one thing that will stop the nagging hunger and thirst. When you fill your God shaped hole with God, with the Holy Spirit of God, then you are truly full and no longer need to go searching for that one thing that will solve your emptiness. When God is in our God shaped hole, there is a sense of fullness, a true sense of having enough, of not lacking anything on our inside. In essence we do not thirst any longer, nor do we feel hungry all the time. Our hole or emptiness is now full and we thirst no more.

Prayer: Holy Spirit, I am asking you to fill my God shaped hole inside of me so that I do not feel hungry or thirsty any more. I am sorry, for looking everywhere else but to you to fill my emptiness. Please forgive and set me, free from searching for the one thing that will fill my insides. I want to be filled with you. Thank you, for loving me so much and for filling me up. Thank you, for being my all in all, amen.

Day Two Hundred Forty-eight

> John 21:15 `When they had finished eating, Jesus said to Simon Peter, "Simon son of John, do you truly love me more than these"?'

Jesus asks Peter three times do you love me more than these? By the end Peter was feeling almost heart broken. How many times is Jesus going ask about my love for Him? How many times do I need to repeat the words, 'Yes Lord, you know I love you'? Three times Peter had denied knowing Jesus, three times Jesus asks Peter do you love me. Jesus knew how much Peter loved him. Jesus knew exactly where Peter stood in his love for Jesus. I feel Jesus needed to fully reinstate Peter to the position of the rock. Peter had to know in the very depths of his being that he was forgiven by Jesus, and was now ready to take his place as the leader of the new church being formed. I feel Jesus too asks us "do you love me? Do you love me more than these?" Working with drug and alcohol addicts I know at times their first love is the drug or the bottle. They love the drug or bottle more than anything else. They would say that the drug or the bottle is their first love. Jesus was asking Peter, "Am I your first love? Do you love me more than anything?" Peter in all honesty could say, 'Yes Lord you are my first love. There is nothing else in my life that I love more than you'. Can we say the same thing? Do I love God/Jesus more than anything else? Is God/Jesus my first love or is there something else that has first place? The something else may be: money, substances, sex, gambling, food, attention, resentments, self-pity, anger, bitterness, hatred and so on. There are so many things that we put before our relationship with God/Jesus. Just as Jesus challenged Peter, so is He challenging us. Who or what is our first love? Is God first? Or does something else have first place in your life? Truly food for thought! When you let go of everything in your life what or who has the first place? Be honest with yourself! What or who has the first rung on your ladder of importance. Whatever is first is what you are worshiping. Whatever has first place is your god. Now ask yourself the question. "Is what I have on the top rung what I really want there?" If the answer is yes--- then great you are living your life in such a way that there will not be regrets or disappointments in the end. If the answer is no---then who or what do you want on the top rung and what are you willing to do or change to make it happen?

Prayer: As I reflect on this challenge today, I feel there are things that I put first before you, Father. Therefore, I repent! I repent of the areas of my life that are more important than you, God. Please forgive me and help me, to put you first in all areas of my life. I want my life to be in a place of balance with my priorities in the right place. Thank you, Jesus, for loving me the way you do and for helping me to see the truth in my life, amen.

Day Two Hundred Forty-nine

John 1:16 'From the fullness of his grace we have all received one blessing after another.'

This devotional is by Selwyn Hughes an excerpt from Light from the Path, Published by B&H The Amplified Bible translates this verse: 'For out of His fullness (abundance) we all received---all had a share and we were all supplied with---one grace after another and spiritual blessing upon spiritual blessing, and even favor upon favor and gift (heaped) upon gift.' I love the phrase 'one grace after another.' The thought contained in the original text is of grace succeeding grace. Our capacity to receive grace at any level depends on our use of it at the lowest level. Refuse God's grace at one level of our life and you make it difficult to receive it at another level. We must use the present proffered grace to be granted the grace which succeeds it. One preacher said: 'I remember when I sat for my first scholarship. I recall going to my professor and saying: 'What will I do when I have used the paper up?' He laughed, 'You needn't worry about that, he said. When you have used all you have, just ask for more.' Much relieved I added, 'Will he give me all I want?' 'NO, replied the professor, but he will give you all you can use.' God is eager to give His grace to every one of us, and there is so much of it. Grace is flowing like a river. Millions there have been supplied..... But it mustn't be wasted. You can have all you are able to use, but to have more you must use what you have. How good are you at using God's grace?'

Such a good question and one we could all take some time reflecting on and about. Are we using the grace has given us for today or are we wasting it? Are we taking advantage of the grace God wants to pure down upon us or are we refusing it? If we are refusing God's grace then do not expect God to keep pouring it down upon you. God wants to give you as much as you need and use. God wants you to have all the blessings, mercy and grace He has stored up for you. But if you refuse it then God cannot force you to take it or use it. That is how God works. It is there if we want it. If we do not want it, God does not force His grace upon us nor does God demand we take it. The question is asked again------how good are you at using God's grace?

Prayer: Father, I am sorry for the times I wasted your grace and did not use the grace you have given to me. Please forgive me, and let start afresh today. Help me, to see your grace given to me and then help me, to use it to your glory and mine. I do not want to shortchange myself any longer when it comes to your grace. Show me, where I am lacking. Show me, where I am not using your grace. Teach me, how to use your grace more. In Jesus' name, amen.

Day Two Hundred Fifty

> *Galatians 2: 16 'Know that a man is not justified by observing the law, but by faith in Jesus Christ that we may be justified by faith in Christ and not by observing the law.'*

The Jewish book of the Law holds all of the laws within the Jewish tradition. To truly follow the Jewish tradition you must obey the law. The Jewish tradition has a foundation that is based upon following and observing of the law. The law is a focal point to their relationship with God and being justified before God. Atonement is found in following and observing of the law and all that the law requires. Without the observance of the law, one cannot be justified before God and the community. The struggle with this form of justification is one can never be justified by following the law, for none of us are perfect and without error in our lives. The only true way of receiving atonement (at one with) with God is through the sacrificial shedding of Jesus' blood, which is a once and for all time sacrifice. We are justified in God's eyes by having faith in Jesus Christ, who is the fulfillment of the law. We are justified before God not because we observe and follow the law, but because we have Jesus in our lives who has paid the penalty for our sin and sin debt; hence the releasing from the power of the law upon our lives. We in ourselves can never do enough to make up for all that we have done in error or through wrong choices. We can never make the past right in our own steam or resources. The only way we can be justified before God is through the sacrificial blood of Jesus the Christ on the cross at Calvary. For atonement to happen in the Old Testament there had to be the shedding of blood. An animal's life was given for the atonement of sin, both known sin and unknown sin. Without the sacrifice there was no forgiveness. Jesus is the atoning, once and for all time sacrifice that sets us free from the past. The atoning power of Jesus through His shed blood sets us on the new path of being restored and made right with God and the demands of God's law. The sacrifice of Jesus on the cross at Calvary is the greatest gift of mercy ever given. It is through Jesus' death on the cross that we can be set free to truly live. Jesus' sacrifice wipes clean the penalty of sin we all owe, the sin we all inherited because of Adam and Eve's choice to eat the forbidden fruit. By Jesus taking our sin debt we are allowed to stand justified before God. There is no other way for us to be free and forgiven, except through the mercy and grace of God's forgiveness. God's mercy, grace and forgiveness are given to all who accept the gift of mercy. We are made right or righteous before God when we accept the forgiveness that is offered to us. God's grace paid our debt when Jesus died on the cross. Jesus, when He chose to go into death, conquered sin and death, thus releasing us and setting us free to have true life within us. We now have a ticket into the Kingdom of God. We now have an open door for us to walk through. Without the atoning blood of Jesus washing us clean, there is no opportunity for us to enter into the Kingdom of God, because God cannot look upon sin. Therefore, if we still have sin in our lives, God cannot look at us. There is no sin in God's Kingdom. If we are stuck in our sin (our need for self and all self demands) we cannot enter into a sinless place. Our sins have to be washed clean in order for us to receive the gift of God's eternal Kingdom.

Prayer: Thank you, Jesus, for dying in my place. Thank you, for paying my debt, which you did not owe. For releasing me from the bondage of sin, I am truly grateful. Thank you, for loving me that much. I am so grateful that you have washed me clean so that I can stand before God free and forgiven from all that was. In Jesus' most holy and righteous name, amen.

Day Two Hundred Fifty-one

Matthew 7:1-2 `Do not judge, or you too will be judged. For in the same way you judge others, you will be judged, and with the measure you use, it will be measured to you.`

What does it mean to judge? To judge is to form an opinion about someone, something, or some event. A good judgment comes when we have evaluated all the data and material and come to a healthy, good, honest opinion or conclusion. Good judging is . Good judging keeps us well able to make good honest conclusions about the world around us. Bad judging is when we form a negative opinion or evaluation about someone, something or an event without proper data and material and when it is based upon a prejudice, narrow-mindedness, bigotry, discrimination or other negative attitudes or beliefs. To judge from a negative perspective sets us up to be judged back in the same measure we have judged others. It sets us up to have others judge us in the same way we judge others. This also holds true for positive judging. When we judge in ways, people see our honesty, integrity and good intentions and respond in like manner. When we judge in healthy and ways, that health and life is measured back to us. The positive good judging or evaluating continues and grows. We all need to look at the way we judge and evaluate life to see if we are using the freedom God has given us to judge from healthy ways or from negative life-stealing ways. Life means we take the data and decide what we will do with what is being presented to us. Is the person telling me the truth? Am I safe around this person because they are honourable and have my best interest at heart? Do I need to stay away from this person, situation or event, because the data coming my way says if I go there, it will prove harmful to others or myself? Good judging keeps us safe and able to live in healthy, growing ways. Bad judging keeps us in a place where the measure used to judge us is low and similar to the measure we are using towards others. Bad judging says all racial groups act and react the same way, or all people living in a certain country or from the same religion are cut from the same cloth. Bad judging clumps people, races, countries, events, situations in the same category regardless of the evidence presented. When we judge from a negative perspective, we leave no room for growth, life or change, not to mention that not all people, races, situation or events are exactly the same. There is a need to see everyone and everything on its or their own merit, taking every person, situation or event as a separate item, and seeing each one as it is presented and not as history or prejudice says it is. The measure we use to judge or evaluate others will be used to judge or evaluate us. We all need to process and evaluate the information and things that come our way every day. That is necessary to healthy life and living. How we process and evaluate will determine how we are judged and evaluated. The measure you use will be the measure used back to you. When we are prejudiced and prejudge people, races, situation and events. We really do reap a harvest that reflects what we have sown into the life of others. Let us follow the law of love by honouring, respecting and guarding everyone's dignity. When we live according to the law of love, it is amazing how God blesses us.

Prayer: Father, I repent of the bad judgments I have against any one, thing, situation or event. Please forgive me and release me, from their effect upon my life. Help me, to judge in healthy ways. I am sorry, Heavenly Father, for all the judgments I have made in my life that have set myself and others apart. Thank you for loving me, for forgiving me. Thanks for setting me free to live and love again. I am truly grateful and value your love for me, Father, especially when I am not perfect or and not doing things right, amen.

Day Two Hundred Fifty-two

Psalm 51:10 'Create in me a pure heart, O God, and renew a steadfast spirit within me.'

Have you ever found yourself in a position where you were crying out? Crying out to the heavens, the universe, God, whoever was out there that might be listening? Give me a new heart because this one is broken. Please give me a new heart, because this old heart of mine has been through so much that it is chipped, bruised and broken. The feeling is our hearts have been hurt and been through so much, they are just not repairable any longer. Somehow I think we have all, at different points in our lives, heard ourselves crying out the plea for a release from the hopelessness we feel at times. The hopelessness we feel regarding the condition of our hearts and lives. A way out of the pressure and stress of living with people and all people do to each other and us. A way out from under the load of hopelessness and despair that we feel when we have been dumped on again. We put ourselves out there, only to be dumped on. The result is we feel lost and confused in our hearts and lives. Well friends, here is the good news! No matter how badly hurt or damaged your heart is, we have a Heavenly Father and Dad who can help us put the pieces back together. We have our Heavenly Father and Dad who is well able to refashion us, making us better than new. There is no quick fix or magic wand. What there is, is a loving Heavenly Dad who loves us back together. Who patiently journeys with us as He tells us the truth of who and whose we really are. Who patiently reminds us of the truth of our existence and why we were created in the first place. Who teaches us to trust, love and live again! The good news is my friends; we do not have to get caught up in all that we have lost. We can move forward. Learning the lessons we need to learn from the experiences that have broken or damaged our hearts. We can continue to grow becoming more of who we were created to be. We can take all we are learning and have learned in order to help others see that there is a way out of our brokenness into a more fulfilling life and all that life has to offer us. Here is the hope for today and hope for tomorrow. We never need be stuck in what was. We never need to get lost in our hopelessness and despair. There is a way out. The way out is through the tender loving care of the one who loves us most and has the ability to see us through. There is joy in the sorrow and hope for the despair. All we need do is allow our Heavenly Father and Dad to show us, not only the way through, but also how to navigate the way. Put your hand in the one who has all the answers. Put your heart in the one who can put back the pieces and make you whole again. Put your hand in the one who loves you; yes you, more than life itself. Put your hand in the hand of the one who is the beginning and the end, the Alpha and Omega, the one who created you in the first place and has the blueprint to rebuild you better than ever. Trust the one who loves you the most. Then watch and see all that can and will happen in and to your life. Life says we will get hurt. Life says we will have our hearts broken at different points in our lives. Life also says that God our Heavenly Father and Dad has the power and ability to see us through the hurts, pain and brokenness. Then he takes our hurt and damaged hearts and loves them so that they can be whole again.

Prayer: Father/Dad, I am crying out to you. Please give me a new heart. This one is broken. I need your healing love and balm to make me whole again. I need you to put back the pieces of my heart. I give you my heart. Please put it back together for me. I need your healing love in my life and definitely in my heart. Thank you, Father/Dad. I am truly grateful, amen.

Day Two Hundred Fifty-three

1 Corinthians 2:9 'However, as it is written: No eye has seen, no ear has heard, no mind has conceived what God has prepared for those who love him.'

This verse in Scripture is so very true. We can hardly imagine what God has in store for those who choose to be a part of God and His Kingdom. It is beyond all we can even begin to imagine what an infinite, all majestic, all powerful God can do. God in the beginning created all things. God has created everything that has been created. Nothing in all of creation was created outside of God. There is nothing that exists or has ever existed that was not created by God. If this is true, then there is unlimited creative power to God and all God is. If God is all powerful and has the ability to create all things, then it is true 'no eye has seen, no ear has heard, no mind has conceived what God has prepared' for those of us who choose to love God and be in a relationship with God. Let your mind play for a bit. Let your mind wander and try to imagine some of the things God can do. My mind imagines God moving immoveable mountains. Mountains that are real and visible to the human eye, as well as the mountains that have built up in our lives and heart. My mind then wanders off to God's ability to protect us and open pathways that under normal conditions were holding us blocked or locked in. I see God making a way and opening the door allowing us free passage. This illustration is factual. I friend of mine was driving in the pounding rain when her windshield wipers stopped working. After she panicked, she prayed and asked God to help her as she was on a deserted road and could not stop. Right before her eyes, the wipers began to work and worked the whole way until she reached a gas station. She asked the mechanic there to look at her wipers. His response was something like "Madame your wiper motor is burned out; the wipers will not work." All my friend could think of was the amazing mercy and grace God had just shown her by allowing her wipers to work even though the motor was burned out. 'No eye has seen, no ear has heard, no mind can conceive.' Personally I know of a time when my gas tank was on E and the E did not mean enough. I knew I would not have enough gas to get me to the next gas station and I prayed. Boy, did I pray. To my great delight God answered my prayer and I did not run out of gas. I have heard other testimonies to the same effect, where God has also granted them grace and mercy, so they did not run out of gas. I was at Toronto Airport Christian Fellowship for a conference a few years ago where I saw with my own eyes how God was turning filling in people's mouths into gold. God also turned caps or crowns into gold. There was gold dust on some people's hands. I know this sound impossible, but I saw it happen. I know it is true. What I am saying here, my friends, is there is no limit to who and what God is. There is no limit to what God can and cannot do. There is no mountain too big, no valley too deep and no obstacle too large for our great and awesome God. There is truly nothing that is impossible for our God. 'No eye has seen, no ear has heard, no mind has conceived', what our God can do or what our God has prepared for those of us who choose to love God. Our minds cannot even begin to get around everything God has in store for those of us who choose to be in a real, alive and active relationship with God. Our God is the one and only true living God and HE LOVES YOU AND ME. How blessed we are, how so very blessed we are.

Prayer: Creator God, there are times when I make you so small in my mind and view. Please forgive me and help me, to take you out of any box I may have put you in. I want to be able to have the knowing that says nothing, absolutely nothing, is beyond you and your creative power. Thank you, for being my God and for loving me the way you do. Help me, to love you back with more love than I have today, and even more love than I will have tomorrow, amen.

Day Two Hundred Fifty-four

2 Corinthians 3:17 'Now the Lord is the Spirit, and where the Spirit of the Lord is, there is freedom.'

Here is another illustration of how we at times get caught in the traps people will often set for us. Traps that snare us because we are not living in the freedom God has for us. Traps that so easily ensnare us and hold us, causing us to lose our freedom to be the person God created us to be. Picture a bridge. The bridge is the type of bridge with no openings on the sides. The sides are approximately three feet high and solid. There are two men on the bridge. Each man is walking towards the center of the bridge from the opposite direction. They meet in the middle. One man is carrying a very long rope. As they meet in the middle the man with the rope gives the end of the rope to the other man. Then the man with the rope proceeds to jump off the bridge. The man holding the rope's end is standing on the bridge kind of stunned; he looks at the rope, and then looks at the man dangling beneath him. He looks at the dangling man and says, "Help me to get you back onto this bridge". The dangling man says. "My life is in your hands." The first man "I do not want to be responsible for your life, get back up here". The rope is just long enough and the man dangling is just heavy enough, that the man cannot pull him up. The man on the bridge does not know what to do, so he just stands there. After a while he begins to get tired. He looks down at the dangling man and says "I am getting tired, help me to get you back up onto this bridge." The dangling man says, "My life is in your hands. Tie the rope around your waist; it will help you to not be so tired." Like a fool the man on the bridge ties the rope around his waist. He stands for looking off into space, wondering what his next move should be. After a while his body decides that it needs to go to the washroom. He calls down to the dangling man "I need to go, I really need to go. Help me to get you onto this bridge." The dangling man calls back "My life is in your hands, you cannot leave and drop me into the water. You have to stay." Not knowing what else to do, he stays. Finally, the man on the bridge comes to his senses. He takes the rope off from around his waist, and holds it over the dangling man. He says, "Either you help me to get you onto this bridge or I am going to drop you." The dangling man is yelling and screaming, "You can't, and you can't. My life is in your hands". Second time, "Either you help me to get you back onto this bridge or I am going to drop you". The dangling man screams all the louder, "you can', you can't. My life is in your hands". Last time "Either you help me to get you back onto this bridge or I am going to drop you"! As the dangling man is yelling and screaming, the man drops the end of the rope and proceeds to walk off the bridge. The man now in the water, swims to shore, gathers the rope, and gets back onto the bridge waiting for his next victim. The moral of this story is who are you giving ropes to and who is giving you ropes. Who are you giving ropes to----who is giving you ropes? Who is saying to you "my life is in your hands"? Who are you saying to, "my life is in your hands"? Is it time to take your rope back? Is it time to give back a rope you have been hanging onto because no one told you, that you could give it back? Either way is it time to live rope-free?

Prayer: Father, what an eye opener. I did not realize that there are people who give me ropes and people for whom I give ropes to. I do repent both for taking the ropes and for giving ropes. Help me to live in the freedom you bought for me. Help me to not take ropes or give ropes to others. I want to live the life you have given me in the freedom that is mine because of you and your sacrifice for me. Thank you, for your love and patience. Thank you, for teaching me more and more about how to take my place as your child, your chosen, beloved child, amen.

Day Two Hundred Fifty-five

1 Corinthians 12:27 'Now you are the body of Christ, and each one of you is a part of it.'

Today, I want to remind you that we all belong. We all have a place with our name on it. We all have our part to play in life, in our churches, in our families, communities, even the world. We are all here with our own set of gifts, talents and abilities. We were designed to fill a slot, a hole, a position that only we can fill. In the institution where I work there are mentally challenged individuals who keep the institution clean. Their job is to ensure that the institution is clean and sanitary. Personally, I am extremely grateful for those men who come to work everyday making sure the garbage is picked up, the floors washed and clean, the carpets vacuumed and so on. Without their dedication and conscientious service, my workspace would not be cleaned. For example, in the worship space I work in, either I would have to clean the worship space myself, which would take away from my assigned work, or I would have to organize the offenders to come down to help clean. Either way, I would not have the available time needed to do all that needs doing during my day. We can look down at those cleaners and say "They have such a menial job, and they are less than the person who runs the institution". To say that would be terribly wrong. Terribly wrong indeed. The Superintendent, as much as he/she has a more responsible position, is just one of the many positions needed to run the institution. We all have our parts to play. None of us are any more valuable than the other. Each of us is important to the smooth running of our work places, homes, families, communities and yes, even the world. My Superintendent found this truth to be real when the union was on strike. The Superintendent took it upon himself to clean the washrooms. It was not long before he realized just how valuable our cleaners are. My friends, we all belong! It does not matter where you fit in or even how you fit in. You are needed, valuable and have a place just where you are. I am not saying, we should not strive for more or a higher position. What I am saying is "no matter who we are or what skills we possess, we are all here for a reason. We are all here in this time frame for such a time as this with our skills, talents and abilities". Yes, I am the Chaplain. Yes, I bring to the position who and what I am as a person, with all the gifts, talents and abilities I have. Yes, I am unique. Yes, the job is done the way it is done because of everything I am and bring to the job. The truth is when I leave the institution someone else will take my place and fill my position. Will they do the job as I did? No. Neither are they supposed to. Will they be me? No. They are not supposed to be me. They are supposed to be who God created them to be. Will the institution have to adjust to the new person? Yes. We are all unique! We are all individuals with our own set of gifts, talents and abilities! We are all designed to fill a place. We all have a place to fill. We know God does not make junk or anyone who is not good enough. Therefore, whatever it is you are called to do, do it to the best of your ability. Do it to the glory of God. Be the best person you can be in the position you are in, because without you doing what you do this world, your family, your community, even you as a person would be missing out. We all belong. We all have value and worth. We all have a place to fill. We are all unique and valuable just the way we are.

Prayer: Father/Dad, I am so grateful that when you created me with all that you created me with, you had a plan in mind for my life. I am not junk! I am realizing. I am your chosen, beloved child and I have value and worth. I matter, don't I, Dad! Help me, to accept who and what you created me to be and then to truly take my place, being the best person I can be, I am realizing it is time to take my place and to stop running or pretending or even lying about who I am. Bless me, Father, so I can be a blessing to others, amen.

Day Two Hundred Fifty-six

Ephesians 1:7 'In him we have redemption through his blood, the forgiveness of sins, in accordance with the riches of God's grace that he lavished on us with all wisdom and understanding.'

God knew exactly what He was doing when God created you. God knew exactly what He was doing when God redeemed you. That is when God decided to put into place the plan that would open the door for you to come back to God in a right state. You are bought back from all the wrong choices and mistakes you have made and others have made on your behalf. God knew exactly what He was doing when God decided to forgive you and wipe your slate clean. When God decided to forgive your debt and release you from the demands of the law, God knew He would have to step into your debt to pay it for you. God stepped in willingly and without reservation. When God decided to grant you mercy instead of demanding justice, He knew who you were and all that you had done or not done. Yet God chose to grant mercy anyway. God knew exactly what He was doing when God chose to set us free to truly live again, debt free without having to pay the penalty of the law and all the law demands. That is an amazing truth for me. God knew. I do not know about you, but as I write these truths, I am humbled. I am so very humbled that the Almighty God would choose to do all of this for you and me. God had the foreknowledge about us even before He set His plan into action. God knows what we really are as people. I stand in awe of God. How could God love us so much? How could God ever want to offer such a gift to people who are so ungrateful? What would ever prompt God to give so much to so many? The answer lies in the truth that God loves us. God loves us so much that He feels a void within Himself when we are not in a loving relationship with Him. Does God need us? No. Is God incomplete without us? No. God is our Father and as a Father He loves to have His children near and around Him. As a Father, God wants us to be an active member of His great family. As our Father,

God, wants us to be all that He created us to be and not lost in our sins or past choices and mistakes. God wants us restored to a right relationship with Him. That is why God set into motion the way back for us. That is why God lavished His mercy and grace upon us. To lavish something onto another means you pour so much onto them that it is like being submersed in a swimming pool filled with water. The water is all around you. When you are in the pool, unless you choose to get out of the water, you cannot get away from the water all around you. That is how it is with God's gift of His great mercy and grace. God pours His mercy, love and grace in such great, abundant, plentiful, copious, profuse, generous amounts that it is all around us. We are surrounded by God's great love, mercy and grace. All we need do is jump into it. Let us be open to the pouring God is doing. Let us give ourselves permission to take it in. God is even now doing the pour down to us, over us, in us and all we need do is receive it. Open up my friend, and let the love, mercy and grace flow. Open up, and take your place. Open up and let God speak His amazing words of love to you, telling you who you are and why you were born for such a time as this. This is the hour. The time in now. Let the river flow.

Prayer: Father, I say yes to you and all you want to pour into me. I say yes to your redemption, forgiveness and lavished love. I say yes to you, Father. Fill me up, Dad. Fill me up to overflowing. I want everything you have stored up for me, your chosen special, precious, beloved, valuable and worthwhile child. I want to take my place in your family, sitting upon your knee, hearing your words of love to me. I am an open vessel to you, Dad, amen.

Day Two Hundred Fifty-seven

Ephesians 4: 32 ' Be kind and compassionate to one another, forgiving each other, just as in Christ God forgave you.'

There are times when we want to desperately hang on to our anger, bitterness, resentments and hatred. It is my right to hate. It is my right to be angry and bitter. You do not know what has happened to me. You do not understand all that I had to go through and endure. If you only knew, then you would understand why I feel the way I feel. If you had of been there, then you would understand and know. You are right, I do not know what you have been through. I do not know what life has put onto your plate and into your life. What I do know, is when we live in the past and all the past has done for us, not only do we suffer because of the choices others have made for our lives, but we also suffer because we at times become our worst self-abusers; worse than the original abuse we suffered through. What am I saying? I am saying that if we stay in all that yesterday did to us, and all we suffered through, there is no way out and no freedom for us. We can never escape our past and all our past has done to us and given us. We stay stuck in what was and never give ourselves permission to move into all that could be. The key to truly living our lives in today is letting go of the hurts, pain and struggles of our past and learning how to be kind to ourselves and then kind to others. We Take all our past has taught and given us and then turn it into compassion and love. It is not always easy, but it is always worthwhile. When we stay stuck in what was, we set ourselves to stay stuck in our mud puddle. Here is what life is like in your mud puddle. Your mud puddle may be dirty and smelly, but it is your mud puddle. People may not want to be around you much, but you are safe and secure in your comfortable mud. You do not have to get out and for the most part people do not want to come in. The only struggle we have is, it is kind of lonely here at times. When we are stuck in our mud puddles we find ourselves living, for the most part, without too many people around. This life of solitude may be good for some of us, but for most of us, it just does not work. We need relationships. We need people in our lives. That is where the second half of this Scripture lesson comes in. When we choose to forgive and let our past hurts and pain go, what we get in return is the forgiveness God has for us. When we let go, there is room in our hearts for the forgiveness God has for us to come in. When we move out of our mud puddles, we are not nearly as dirty and smelly as before; therefore, more healthy life-giving people come into our lives. The more we live in forgiveness and letting go of what was, the more we can live in today and all that today has for us. The amazing reality that follows is, we are kinder and more compassionate towards others. For the simple reason we understand their plight because we have been there, done that. Kindness and compassion begin to flow out from us because we truly do know and understand. Therefore, we can give others the encouragement they need to move forward with their lives, helping them to see a way out of their mud puddle. Be kind and compassionate to one another. It brings us such life within, and incredible life to others.

Prayer: Father, I am so very grateful that you are showing me how to truly live my life. You are showing me how to live my life so that I truly do have life within me, and can show others how to have life within them. Help me, to be kinder and more compassionate to myself and then to others. I am learning it really is the only way to live and have life within us. Thank you, for forgiving me. Help me, to forgive others with the same level of forgiveness, amen.

Day Two Hundred Fifty-eight

Ephesians 6:13-14 'Therefore put on the full armor of God, so that when the day of evil comes, you may be able to stand your ground, and after you have done everything to stand. Stand firm....'

There are times in our lives when we need to fight. We need to muster everything we have inside of us, giving the battle everything that is within us. We need to give whatever the challenge is our full attention and resources. We need to fight the good fight, and do everything in our power to fight against the foe we are battling. There is no backing down on this one. This is my fight, and I am going to see it through to the bitter end, if I have to. Then there are times when after we have done everything that we possibly can do, we stop the fighting and just stand there. Standing there knowing that we have given it our best shot, and the rest is up to God and all that God is. Another way of looking at this is picking our battles. There are some battles that we have to just stand there and let God handle. Some battles are not ours to fight. We are to do everything we can do, but the rest is left up to God. From personal experience, just standing there can be the hardest thing you will ever do. I can remember one day sitting in my boss' office and being accused of something I did not do. I wanted to fight back. I wanted to defend myself with all the gusto I could muster. I wanted to justify myself, telling her she was wrong, with great force and determination. As I was sitting in her office, I heard God say to me in my spirit "Keep your mouth shut, do not say anything". Sitting there with my mouth shut, biting down on my tongue until it hurt, was most difficult. But I did it. I was being asked by God to just stand there. The institution knew me. It knew what I would and would not do. We had built up a trust between us. I had to trust God, and my relationship with the institution, and the truth. I had to just stand there. A couple of weeks later, the boss called me into her office and told me the accusations were incorrect. I was cleared of all suspicion. I had been vindicated. Keeping my mouth shut, just standing there, was the best thing I could have done. Had I fought back, there would have been another situation to deal with. There are times when we need to fight the good fight, and there are times when we need to do everything we are asked or called to do, and then just stand there. When we have the armor of God on, and are standing in the light of God, we will know when we are to fight, and when we are to just stand there, letting God do the fighting for us. Just standing, when the battle is raging all around, is not the easiest thing to do. In fact, it may be the most difficult thing you will ever do. When we ponder on just standing there-----what does it really mean? What does just standing in the battle really look like? I do not have a good answer to these questions. What I do know is God is faithful and if God is asking us to stand, God will also tell us how to stand there. We can trust God's provision at all times and in all places within our lives and life situations. Of this I have no doubt.

Prayer: Father, help me to know when I am to fight and when I am to just stand firm in all I am in you. Help me, to know when I need to fight the good fight, and when I need to stand back and let you fight the fight for me. Father, I choose to put my hope and trust in you. I choose to trust who you are and who I am in you. Thank you, for being a truly faithful God in whom I can totally trust, and be safe and secure within, amen.

Day Two Hundred Fifty-nine

James 1:2 'Consider it pure joy, my brothers, whenever you face trials of many kinds.'

Part of us does not want to hear this verse. We do not want to hear that we will have to face trials. We do not want to hear that life may be filled with trials and hardships. We do not want to face the realization that life is not always going to be easy and a cake walk. We want life to be smooth with no bumps or twists along the way. We want life to be without mountains to climb and valleys to cross. We want life to be easy. We definitely want life without anything in our path that may cause our ship to veer off course. That is the way we would like life! That is not the way life is lived. Life is lived both with the good times and the bad. Life is filled with struggles and hardships, and joys and true pleasures. Life has its ups and its downs. That is the way life works. Anything short of that is a fantasy, an illusion or delusion. James is telling us to count it all joy when we face trials and hardships. To count it all joy when life gets a little bumpy and the waves start increasing in size and intensity. To count it all joy when we, without choice, have to face the twists and turns of life. Why on earth would we want to count it all joy? Why on earth would we ever consider it pure joy to have trials in our lives? I feel for several reasons. Hardships and struggles certainly do ask us to evaluate all we are and have. Struggles and hardships hopefully, help us to appreciate all the good things in our lives. Bad times cause us to be thankful for the good times in our lives. When we face those times in our lives that are hard, and definitely not easy to deal with, we have one to two choices. 1- we can get angry and frustrated that life is not going our way. We can throw our temper tantrums, yelling and screaming at the world, for all that is happening to us. We can grumble and complain about how bad life is, giving our power away to the hardships and rough times in our lives. Or 2- we face the hardship, struggle, bad time or difficulty with a positive attitude, working our way through it. We can either look at the difficulty and say, "Poor me, life is so hard. It is just not fair. This should not be happening to me". Or, we can make the best of a bad or difficult time in our lives. If we evaluate the situation through the eyes of a victim, we will probably get stuck in the hardship or struggle. If we allow ourselves permission to face the struggle or state with a positive attitude and approach, we may find ourselves with joy in our hearts. We are much more likely to come to the other end a better person, having learned the life lessons the struggles have taught us and become more equipped to face life. Count it pure joy, when life throws us a curve ball. The pure joy will enable us to see, learn and grow as we deal with all that life is throwing our way. If we have a positive attitude, we are much more likely to come out of the curve ball, whole and intact. If we go into our pity party and feel sorry for ourselves that is what we will reproduce with in us. Bad things happen to good people; that is called life. The challenge is to take the bad things that happen and allow God to turn them into something good. The challenge is to allow the presence of God to be in the situation, working His healing, mercy, grace and compassion, instead of trying to struggle through it alone. When we allow the presence of God into all of life, it is amazing how God touches not only the situation, but us as well. We can struggle through life alone. We all have that choice. Or, we can struggle through life with God by our sides, doing all that God does best, which is to love us and help us through. As James is teaching us today, let us count it all joy when life throws us a curve ball. The curve ball is just another time and situation when God's love, mercy, grace and compassion have a place to shine.

Prayer: Father, I am sorry for the times I threw my temper tantrums, because life was not going my way or doing what I thought life should do. Please forgive me and help me, to see that my attitude towards any given situation is the difference between it turning out positive or causing me to stay in my mud puddle. I do not want to face life as a victim any longer. I want to be a victor in all of my life dealings. Help me, to count it all joy when trials and hardships come my way, amen.

Day Two Hundred Sixty

Ephesians 1:16 ' I have not stopped giving thanks for you, remembering you in my prayers.'

It is so very important that we give thanks. There is such a need within our being to be thankful people. When we are thankful it raises our spirits, it help us to appreciate what we have, it brightens our hearts and attitudes and generally makes us healthier people. Giving thanks only does good things for us. Giving thanks is a request God has given us. God reminds us in lots of places within Scripture about the need for us to be a thankful people, the need for us to be grateful for what we have and for what is happening in our lives. God knows how important and life-giving it is for us to give thanks. Therefore God reminds us regularly to give thanks and to be a grateful people. More than being a request of God to give thanks is the fact that giving thanks is good for us. Being a thankful person is more life-giving than almost anything else we can do. Giving thanks keeps us real with who we are as people, plus all that is going around us. It also keeps of in a place where we can be real with life, others and ourselves. When we are grateful for what we have, we do not have to go looking elsewhere to satisfy our longings or cravings. We can be content with what life is and has given us. We can enjoy the people, things and place we are in. We are not searching or longing for joy and happiness in other places, through other avenues. The other day I watched the 'Pollyanna' movie. I have seen the movie at least a couple of times, but it is such a good reminder of how important it is to make the best out of every situation. Pollyanna was taught by her father to find something in every situation that she could be glad about. No matter how bad the situation was or seemed, there was always something to be glad about. There is always something good in everything and everyone. Pollyanna changed the attitude of her town by her positive attitude and perspective of life. That is so true; if we are looking for something to be glad about, we will find it. If we are not looking for the something to be glad about, then we will for sure, not find it. The glass is half full or half empty philosophy. Pollyanna learned to always see the glass half full and never half empty. What a great reminder for us. When we decide that we are going to give thanks in all things, we will find lots of thing to be thankful for. If we want to see the things around that give us joy and cause a sense of gratitude to well up within us, we will see them. The other side of the coin is if we want to be grumpy and only see the bad side of life, there certainly will be lots to grumble about. In fact, there is always something to take our joy and gratitude away. Let us take this one step further. Paul is telling us he never stopped being thankful for the Ephesians. Paul never allowed whatever was happening or not happening in life to stop him from giving thanks for the people he loved. Then Paul took his gratitude, one step further. He remembered them in his prayers. What an amazing lesson for us today. Be thankful or glad in all situations and circumstances. Be thankful and glad for the people God has placed in your life. Then take it one step further by praying for them always. Always remembering them in your prayers. What an awesome gift we could be giving to everyone we know. The gift of remembering to bring the ones we love before God on a regular basis. The gift of bringing the ones we love into God's presence, so God can have permission to affect their lives. If we choose to live this way, we could change our world, and the world around us.

Prayer: Thank you, Lord, for reminding to be grateful and thankful for all I have, and all your hand has given to me. I must confess there are more times in life when I grumble, than when I am thankful. Please forgive me, and help me to have an attitude of gratitude. It really does make life a whole lot easier to be happy and filled with joy than to walk around filled with the grumps about everyone and everything, amen.

Day Two Hundred Sixty-one

Philippians 2:14 'Do everything without complaining or arguing.'

I feel we need to spend another day looking at the benefits and blessings of being thankful and having an attitude of gratitude. Here we go again. The amazing reality about all of life is we can either look at life through positive lenses or through negative ones. We can wear rose coloured glasses, or we can wear clear glasses and see clearly. The choice is always ours to make. Today the challenge is to do everything, that is all things, without complaining or arguing. Picture with me if you will. I am sure we can all identify with this example. Today is the day the family decided they were going to clean out the garage, go to the beach, have a family day, visit grandma, whatever the agreement is, it does not matter. You wake up not feeling exactly 100%. You would rather watch the ball game on the T.V. or do anything else, other than what was agreed to. The problem is you promised to clean out the garage, etc. Here is the kicker. You can either give in to your feeling of wanting life your way and on your terms and condition and make everybody's life miserable, or you can have an attitude adjustment. You can clean out the garage with a really bad attitude and make the task a horrific one for everyone, complaining and grumbling and fighting over the least little things, or you can bring joy and laughter to the job, and have a great family day together. Do everything without complaining or arguing, deciding to go through life with a positive attitude and not a negative one. In reality it is just as easy to be grumpy as it is to be glad/happy. It is just as easy to give our power away, being miserable and making everyone else's life miserable, as it is to keep our power and have positive and enjoyable results. Not to mention happier people around us. We can leave a wake of misery or a wake of joy and blessings. That is the wonder of being able to choose what we will do with all that life is giving us. We can grump and complain, argue with everyone we meet and greet, or we can put on a positive attitude and a happy face. I am told it takes more muscles to frown than to does to smile. We can either have a life filled with misery and all misery puts onto our paths, or we can have a life filled with gladness, just because we can be glad. We can make life better for those around us, or we can make it bitter. We get to choose. As I have mentioned before we can sow cold pricklies and get lots of cold pricklies in return, or we can sow warm fuzzies and get warm fuzzies in return. If we sow cold pricklies, we need not expect to get too many warm fuzzies coming our way. 'Do everything without complaining or arguing'. What great advice! Let us heed that advice today and change the way we react and interact with the world around us. You might be pleasantly surprised. It just may change your whole modus operandi, that is, the way you choose to go through life and deal with life on a daily basis.

Prayer: Heavenly Father, I am beginning to see my attitude affects the way I deal with life and the way life deals with me. There have been times when I have allowed my grumpy side to rule and reign. I am truly sorry. Help me, to follow my joyful, glad side. I know, I will be much happier, not to mention the people around me. Please forgive me, and remind me, when I am forgetting. Thank you, Father, for your love and patience with me. Thank you, for teaching me how to truly live my life to the full. I am truly grateful, amen.

Day Two Hundred Sixty-two

2 Corinthians 4:7 'But we have this treasure in jars of clay to show that this all-surpassing power is from God and not from us.'

I do not know if you have ever noticed this before, but we as human beings leak. We go to an amazing church service or conference, and are filled to overflowing with the presence of God. Our spirits are flying high with the joy and wonder of having been in God's presence. Then after a few days or a couple of weeks the glow starts to wear off. The presence we felt is not as strong, and life seems to be getting heavy all around us once again. We feel this way for two reasons 1- Life is lived in the valleys. Life in the valley is not easy. It can drain us of our light. Living in the valley can get so hectic; the presence of God can be missed in the business. 2- We leak! Our spirits leak out the presence of God. Our earthly bodies are not leak proof. As the Scripture verse tells us today, we are made of jars of clay. As jars of clay, we do not always hold onto everything that is being placed within our spirits and selves. I guess that is why God only gives us enough for one day. God knows we will need filling up again tomorrow. We will need to go back to God for more of God on a daily basis. The wonder of who and what God created us to be. God loves to be in our presence and have us in His. God loves spending time with us, loving us and just hanging around with us. I feel God created us with leaks, so that we would need to come to Him everyday, to have our spiritual selves filled up. I feel God knew that if He gave us enough for a whole week, we would only visit with Him once a week. Therefore, God only gives us enough for each day. With each passing day, we need to go back to God for an infilling of His Holy presence. We need to be filled or refilled with all God is, so that we have everything we need to meet the challenges we will be facing. What an amazing God we love and serve. A God who loves us so very much and cares even more about our well being and ability to live as whole, complete human beings than we do at times. I also feel as human beings. We can be arrogant at times and take the credit. When the credit is not ours to take, we let our arrogance puff us up. It can puff us up to the point where we become conceited and prideful. When we live and act this way, we have the tendency to take all the credit for who and what we are, and what we have done. This attitude makes life all about us. The problem is, life is not all about us. Life is about God. It is all about God and who and what God is in His creation. It is without a shadow of a doubt, not about us. Here is a suggestion for getting a healthy spiritual balance within our lives. Picture if you will a medium sized vase. Picture also a bunch of walnuts and some sunflower seeds. The walnuts represent our relationship with God and the spiritual things that keep us healthy, like going to worship on a regular basis, fellowshipping with other believers, reading Scripture, praying and meditation. The sunflower seeds are our daily lives, laundry, cleaning, dishes, rushing around, work and so on. What happens if I put the sunflower seed in the vase and then try to put the walnuts in? Is there going to be enough room for both? The answer is no. What happens if I do it the other way around with the walnuts in first and the sunflower seeds on top? That is right, the sunflower seeds fill in all the holes and everything fits nicely. That is the way it is with our lives. If we put spiritual enhancers first, and all that life demands of us second, there is lots of room for both. If we put life first and then try to squeeze in spiritual things, there just does not seem to be enough time in the day. Life is so much better when we have our spiritual selves balanced. The rest of life just seems to fall into place. A little something to think about and ponder as you go through your day today.

Prayer: Father, I am sorry if I have made life about me. I am sorry if I have put me first and foremost forgetting that you are the great I Am. Life is really all about you and not about me. Life is about all you are. All I am is only because of all you are. Please forgive me and help me, to live my life in humility and grace. Help me, to put spiritual things first so that I can always have my spiritual self filled up, amen.

Day Two Hundred Sixty-three

Numbers 30:2 ' When a man makes a vow to the Lord or takes an oath to obligate himself by a pledge, he must not break his word but must do everything he said.'

Today I would like to talk about the importance of making vows and taking oaths, both from a positive and negative perspective. We forget at times the power that making vows and taking an oath have in our lives and within our spirits. That is why professionals, when they are given their credentials, make a vow or take an oath to uphold the profession they are entering. A doctor makes their Hippocratic oath, a lawyer takes his/her bar exams, a priest or nun takes his/her ordination vows. An engineer makes his/her oath and then is given a silver ring for their little finger as a sign and reminder of hid/her professional standards. When we get married, we take our wedding vows. Positive vows and oaths are part of our lives in many different ways. They help keep us on the right track and conscious of the commitment we have made. Negative vows and oaths are just as powerful. Every time in anger we exclaim or proclaim, "I will never", we are making a negative spiritual vow. We are setting ourselves up to the negative vow we have stated in anger. Vows like, "I will never get married". Either we never marry or we marry and find ourselves divorced. "I will never be like my parents". One day we look at ourselves seeing ourselves just like our parents were. "I will never be an addict like......", to find yourself addicted to drugs instead of booze. Any time we say, "I will never" or any other phrase similar to that, we set ourselves up to fail. A positive vow or oath enhances our ability to be obedient to the vow or oath we are taking. For those of you who were married and have gone through or are going through a divorce, how hard is it to break your wedding vows? How hard it is to let go of the vows you made before God and each other, even though today you cannot stand each other? Whether you like each other or not does not ultimately matter. What matters is you are breaking the vow you made and that is what tears us apart. In order to be set free from the vow or oath we have made, we need to repent. We need to say I am sorry to God for breaking our vows and oaths. The principle is one of honour. When we are not living honourable lives, the spiritual consequences come back to bits us every time. To be cleansed, there is a need to be restored before God. For ultimately God is the one before whom we made the vow, or took the oath in the first place; even if we made the vow or took the oath in anger, and did not realize what we were doing, or the vow or oath we had just uttered from our lips was under our breath. Repentance is the key that opens the door for forgiveness to come in. Repentance is the key that releases us from the power of the vow or oath. Repentance is the act of humbling ourselves and allowing ourselves to openly and honestly stand before God in integrity and truth. Without repentance, restoration cannot become a reality for us. We made the vow or took the oath. We need to repent for breaking it. Then and only then can we be released from its power. Then and only then can we be set free to get on with our lives, without the spiritual bondage of the broken or negative vows or oath. We made the vow or took the oath. We are the ones who are responsible for making things right before God. We are the ones who are responsible for our lives. When we humble ourselves. We can have the restoration and balance we need. This allows us to move forward with who we are as the beloved children of God.

Prayer: Holy God, I am sorry for breaking the vows and oaths I have made. I am sorry for making negative vows and oaths in my anger or pain. I am asking for your forgiveness so that I can start moving forward with my life. I am asking you, Holy God, to release me from the vows and oaths I have taken or made that I can no longer honour or desire to honour. Please forgive me and help me, to move forward with who and what you created me to be. I want to have and live in integrity. With your help, I know I can achieve it, amen.

Day Two Hundred Sixty-four

Micah 6:8 'He has shown you, O man, what is good. And what does the Lord require of you? To act justly and to love mercy and to walk humbly with your God.'

God has shown us what we need to do in order to live healthy well-balanced lives. As we have journeyed through these past few months together. We have come to realize that life is a whole lot easier and better if we will but live life God's way. When we live life God's way, we live in the blessings and provision God has for our lives. When we live life our way, we move outside God's umbrella of mercy and grace, which inhibits God's commanded blessings from showering down upon us. When we live life our way we step outside of God's rules for living and our lives become much more difficult and burdensome. The Israelites have shown us this truth time and time again. Every time they chose to live life on their terms and conditions following other gods, life became unbearable. Nations invaded them, conquered their land. Their corps failed or their crops were not plentiful and the rains did not fall in season. God removed His hand of blessing. I feel it is the same with us today. When we live according to God's laws life is blessed by God, even though hard times will come our way. The hard times come, but they will not overcome us or steal our joy and the grace God has for us. The challenge we all face is to live justly, to love mercy and to walk humbly with our God. 1-To live justly is to live honest upright lives. Living in integrity and truth. Being people who are trustworthy and honest in all of our dealing with life, to live as people who reflect the light of God no matter what we are doing, where we are living, what we are speaking or where we earn an income. All of our lives are to reflect honour and integrity. 2-To love mercy. As children of God we have been shown such incredible mercy. We do not get what we deserve. We do not have to fulfill the full measure of the law. We are granted mercy and forgiveness for all that was and happened. We are to do the same for others. Instead of demanding our pound of flesh, we are to extend the hand of mercy. We are to allow others to be human, just as God allows us to be human and imperfect. When we choose to live in mercy, the mercy of God is showered down upon us. When we choose to live in justice, justice has the legal right to demand justice from us. When we are merciful, mercy is what we receive in return. Let us choose to offer mercy instead of demanding justice. 3-To walk humbly with our God. When we have a real, alive and active relationship with God, we can be humble, for we know whose we are and the love God has for us. We are able to be ourselves and let others be who they were created to be. We lose our need to be right and have life on our terms and conditions, for we know who we are and are learning how much we are loved. This gives us the freedom to let others be who God created them to be and to be humble in our dealing with others and life in general. When we are walking with God there is an assurance that God is with us and no matter what happens God will see us through. That assurance brings a joy and understanding about life like no other. We know that we know that we know that God loves us, and somehow all will be right in the end. This truth enables us to just be the children we were created to be and not try to be something or someone else. This reality of God within us gives us the freedom to live our lives, while letting others live theirs. Let us in humility and integrity commit to living our lives according to God's ways. That is to live justly, to love mercy and to walk humbly with our God.

Prayer: Father God, Dad, I am so very grateful for your love and presence in my life. I am so grateful for all you have taught me over these past few months. I do want to live my life according to your ways, laws and commandments. Yes, because you are asking me to, but also because I am learning, when I live life your way, I truly have life within me. I want that life and I want to truly live my life to the full. Thank you, Father, Jesus and Holy Spirit for showing me the way and helping me to live it, amen.

Day Two Hundred Sixty-five

2 Corinthians 2:2-4 'Out of the most severe trial, their overflowing joy and their extreme poverty welled up in rich generosity. For I testify that they gave as much as they were able, and even beyond their ability. Entirely on their own, they urgently pleaded with us for the privilege of sharing in this service to the saints.'

Our God is so very generous and giving. God gives us so much. God gives us more than we can even begin to know or even try to understand. Because God is so generous with us and gives so freely to us, we too need to be generous with others. We too need to share what we have with others on a variety of levels. Yes, we need to share our finances, especially when we have been blessed with enough to supply our needs with some left over. There is a need for us to help those who need our finances to run their ministries or social programmes. There is an inner need to share and give freely of what we have. The other side of the coin is if we do not give, then those ministries would not be there for those who need them. For example, there are a few prison ministries who continue to be there for the offenders and chaplains. Bridges Over Canada supplies testimony books and All Occasion and Christmas cards. New Life Prison Ministry, supplies Bible Studies and meaningful films for the offenders to watch and learn from. Gospel Echoes Team gives Bibles studies which enable offenders to get a Bible with their name engraved on the front. Kenneth Copeland Ministries gives us Bibles, reading material and films. The ones I have mentioned are but a sample of ministries who are there for offenders and chaplains. These ministries need our help in order for them to keep offering the blessings they do to offenders and chaplains. Our generosity can be in the area of volunteering when volunteers are needed. The list of organizations that need volunteers to keep their organizations running is staggering at times. Social groups like sports groups, Girl Guides, Boy Scouts, 4H clubs, all need people that are willing to give of themselves and their gifts, talents and abilities. A good example of offering a hand when an emergency arises is the Mennonites when they join together to rebuild a house or barn after a fire or natural disaster has destroyed them. The Mennonites are often one of the first ones on the scene after a natural disaster to help rebuild communities and peoples lives. There are so many ways we can be generous with our time, finances, abilities, gifts and talents. The question is where can I give? Where can I share what God has so generously given to me? That is an individual question that needs to be answered individually by each one of us. The AA Recovery Program tells its members they have to find ways of giving away what they are being given. If they do not give it away, they risk the possibility of losing what they have gained. We cannot out give God! We cannot ever be in a place where God owes us. My friends, let us find ways of sharing the bounty God is giving us. Let us find ways of sharing the blessings God is pouring down upon us. The Abraham blessings says 'God blessed Abraham so that Abraham could be a blessing to others.' May that be our prayer "God bless us so that we can be a blessing to others. Bless us so that we have the resources to generously give to, share with and bless others. Make us a channel of your generosity, Father. Make us a vessel through which you give to others."

Prayer: Father, I repent for the times when I am stingy, when I hold back my gifts, talents, abilities and finances. I am sorry for the times I could share but choose to be selfish with what you have given to me. Please forgive me and help me, to be more generous with all that you have given to me. I am grateful for your generosity towards me and all I am blessed with. Help me to be more like you, Father, amen.

Day Two Hundred Sixty-six

Isaiah 40:31 'But those who hope in the Lord will renew their strength. They will soar on wings like eagles; they will run and not grow weary, they will walk and not be faint.'

Today I want to talk about eagles and how God wants us to be like the eagles. Here are some facts about the eagle. Eagles mate for life. They are loyal to their mates. Eagles are not afraid of storms. In fact eagles will fly into storms, and if need be, will fly above the storm. Most other birds run and hide from a coming storm. They will find a safe place to ride out the storm. Eagles have a double set of eyes lid, which allows them to fly into the sun. When an enemy is chasing the eagle, the eagle will fly into the sun until their pursuer stops its chase. Eagles soar. They only fly long enough to enable them to catch the prevailing winds. Once they have the prevailing winds, they allow the wind to carry them, which enables them to soar upon the air. Eagles have great vision. They can see a rodent or snake from miles away. The eagle then swoops down and catches their next meal in their talons. Eagles in the wild only eat fresh meat. If however an eagle happens to eat something that is poisonous or hazardous to their system and being, they lay out on the rocks in the sun until the poison is sweat out of their system. This is where the expression spread comes from. When a pair of eagles decides to mate, they build a nest high above the ground away from danger. The eagles soften their nest with padding like feathers, animal fur, wool etc. making it safe and comfortable for the eggs and eaglets. Once the eaglets are old enough and ready to learn how to fly, the mother eagle ruffles the nest making the nest very uncomfortable and not nice to live in any longer. Then the mother pushes the eaglet out of the nest and lets it fall to the ground. The mother swoops down and catches the eaglet before it hits the ground. Mother eagle keeps pushing the eaglet out of the nest, until the eaglet eventually learns how to fly on its own, thus realizing the majesty and wonder of flight. The illustration of the eagle is the illustration God uses for us. God wants us to soar like the eagles. God does not want us to be earth bound like the chicken or ostrich. As people who believe in and trust in God, God wants us to know the freedom He has for us. God wants us to not run away from the storms of life; instead He wants us to run into them. God wants us to run into the Son whenever we are being chased by the enemy. God wants us to soar on the wings of His power and love for us His chosen beloved children. When we have eaten something that has the potential of poisoning us, God wants us to spread eagle before Him, so that He can purge us of the poison, poison like false gods, immorality, foul or coarse language, bad thoughts, sexual immorality and so on. He wants us to give ourselves permission to spread ourselves out before the one who can cleanse us from all unrighteousness. When we get too comfortable in our safe pews, God just might ruffle our nests, and push us out so that we can learn the freedom of soaring and not staying earth bound. We too are to have one life long mate, settling down with one person for the whole of our lives. We are to have great spiritual vision, which we get by spending time with God and in His Word. God truly does want us to be free to soar, soaring on His winds, being carried into all that life has for us. We are to live in freedom and truth. We are to be wise and knowing. We are to not settle for being earth bound. There is far too much for us to see and experience as the chosen, special, precious, beloved children of the Most High God.

Prayer: Father, I do want to soar. I do want to be free to soar above the winds, seeing life from the skies. I am so sorry that I have settled for being earth bound and comfortable in my safe pew. I am giving you permission to push me out of the nest so that I can be all you created me to be. Father/Dad, I really do want to soar knowing the freedom that soaring brings. Thank you, for not wanting me to settle for less than all you have for me as your chosen, beloved child. I am truly grateful. Thank you, amen.

Day Two Hundred Sixty-seven

Today I want to remind you of some of the promises God has given to us about who we are and whose we are.

Esther 4:14b 'And who knows but that you have come to royal position for such a time as this.'

Jeremiah 29:11-14 For I know the plans I have for you, declares the Lord, 'plans to prosper you and not to harm you, plans to give you hope and a future. Then you will call upon me, and I will listen to you. You will seek me and find me when you seek me with all your heart. I will be found by you, declares the Lord, and will bring you back from captivity.'

Jeremiah 33:3 'Call to me and I will answer you and tell you great and unsearchable things you do not know.'

Ephesians 1:4 'For he chose us in him before the creation of the world to be holy and blameless in his sight. In love he predestined us to be adopted as his sons (daughters).'

Psalm 139: 13-16 'For you created my inmost being; you knit me together in my mother's womb. I praise you because I am fearfully and wonderfully made; your works are wonderful; I know that full well. My frame was not hidden from you when I was made in the secret place. When I was woven together in the depths of the earth, your eyes saw my unformed body.'

Zephaniah 3:17 'The Lord your God is with you, he is mighty to save. He will take great delight in you, he will quiet you with his love, he will rejoice over you with singing.'

Joel 2:25a, 26-27 'I will repay you for the years the locusts have eaten......You will have plenty to eat, until you are

463

full, and you will praise the name of the Lord your God, who has worked wonders for you; never again will my people be shamed. Then you will know that I am in Israel, that I am the Lord your God, and that there is no other; never again will my people be shamed.'

Isaiah 41:10 'Do not fear, for I am with you; do not be dismayed, for I am your God. I will strengthen you and help you; I will uphold you with my righteous right hand.'

Isaiah 40:31 'But those who hope in the Lord will renew their strength. They will soar on wings like eagles; they will run and not grow weary, they will walk and not be faint.'

My friends, I truly do pray that these promises God has given to each and every one of us are beginning to hit home with you. We are not mistakes. We are not less than. We were created with a plan and a purpose. Each one of us was created for such a time as this. We are valuable, precious, special, chosen, beloved children of God and we matter more than we will ever know or truly understand. We have a place that has our name on it. A place to call our own! Most importantly we have a heavenly Father and Dad who loves us with an unconditional love that has no beginning and definitely no end. We can never do anything that will make God loves us more and we can never do anything that will cause God to love us less. We are the chosen, beloved children of God. And God rejoices over us with singing. God rejoices over us with singing regardless of the mistakes we have made or the wrong choices. God's love for us is not based on performance------it is based on God's desire to love us and be in a love relationship with us. Let us take our places as the beloved children we are, relishing in all God has for us His chosen, beloved and precious child. Rejoice and be glad, my friend; you belong to and have a Heavenly Father/Dad who loves you more than you will ever truly know or even begin to understand. And that is the way it is supposed to be.

Prayer: Thank you, Thank you, Thank you, Father/Dad. I belong! I really do belong! I have a place to call my own and a family that will always be here for me. I have the best Dad and Father one could ever have and I am a chosen, beloved and precious child. Today, yes today, I choose to take my place and be that child. I choose to let go of the lies and take on your truth. I choose to be yours and you to be mine. Jesus, I am your child and you are my Saviour, Lord, Master and Friend. I do love you Lord, amen.

About the Author

I am a prison Chaplain working at the Algoma Treatment and Remand Centre, which is a correctional treatment facility for substance abuse offenders, who desire to make real and true-life changes. I have been a prison Chaplain for the past ten years, working in the cognitive treatment model. I have also struggled with my own spiritual self and God, which has given me personal insight into what I say and teach. I have been gifted to see through to the core of issues and the ability to then see beyond the issue into the light and life that exists for all of us. I work in the healing ministry and have seen God's mercy and awesome grace first hand. I know first hand that God wants to bring each and everyone of us to completeness. Being the person we were created to be in the first place. I believe God is real, personal and available to each and every one of us, if we will but open ourselves up to who and what we are in ourselves and in God. I have been gifted with being able to apply Scripture to life and life to Scripture in unique and understandable ways. I bring life to what I teach and write, in ways that are easy to understand and apply to life and living. One of the complements I continually get is, "Wendy you make what you teach so easy to understand and apply to life". That is why I have chosen to write this devotional book.

Printed in the United States
32063LVS00004B/34-168